In the first section of essays, "The Self Displayed," Heilman reveals how he developed from a small-town boy into a distinguished critic and teacher, touching upon his participation in baseball and love of football along the way. "Writers Portrayed" and "Literary Types and Problems Inspected," the following sections, offer his opinions on the past and on the current state of American literary criticism, including personal portraits of such renowned friends as Eric Voegelin, Robert Penn Warren, Theodore Roethke, and Malcolm Cowley. The final section, "Education Examined," is an enlightening inquiry into the development of American universities in the twentieth century.

A fascinating chronicle of a significant academic life, *The Professor and the Profession* will appeal to a broad array of scholars, from young academics wanting to know where they came from to those of Heilman's generation who can appreciate this personal reminiscence into the world of letters.

the professor and
the profession

Books by Robert Bechtold Heilman

America in English Fiction, 1760–1800 (1937)

This Great Stage: Image and Structure in King Lear (1948)

Magic in the Web: Action and Language in Othello (1956)
   (The Explicator Prize)

Tragedy and Melodrama: Versions of Experience (1968)

*The Iceman, the Arsonist, and the Troubled Agent: Tragedy and
   Melodrama on the Modern Stage* (1973)

The Ghost on the Ramparts and Other Essays in the Humanities (1974)

The Ways of the World: Comedy and Society (1978)
   (The Christian Gauss Prize of Phi Beta Kappa)

The Southern Connection: Essays (1991)

The Workings of Fiction (1991)

The Professor and the Profession (1999)

the professor and the profession

Robert Bechtold Heilman

University of Missouri Press
Columbia and London

Copyright © 1999 by the Curators of the University of Missouri

University of Missouri Press, Columbia, Missouri 65201

Printed and bound in the United States of America

All rights reserved

5   4   3   2   1   03   02   01   00   99

Library of Congress Cataloging-in-Publication Data

Heilman, Robert Bechtold, 1906–

    The professor and the profession / Robert Bechtold Heilman.

      p.   cm.

    Includes index.

    ISBN 0-8262-1232-8 (hc.)

    1. English philology—Study and teaching (Higher)—United States.

  2. American literature—20th century—History and criticism

  3. English literature—History and criticism.   I. Title.

PE68.U5H45   1999

420.71'173—dc21   99-25129

                                      CIP

∞ This paper meets the requirements of the

American National Standard for Permanence of Paper

for Printed Library Materials, Z39.48, 1984.

Designer: Stephanie Foley

Typesetter: Bookcomp, Inc.

Printer and binder: Edwards Brothers, Inc.

Typefaces: Cancione, Garamond, and Nuptual Script

contents

V .   E d u c a t i o n   E x a m i n e d

preface

In putting together this collection of essays I have made one major change from my previous collections: whereas my earlier collections were devoted exclusively to educational and literary issues, I have in this collection admitted one section (the first, of four essays) that serves to reveal, at least in part, the writer of the essays. It seems that the essayist, purporting to have answers on various subjects, some quite large, should risk revealing what manner of man he is—that is, insofar as he exists, as in some way he must, outside the realm of problem-tackling in educational and literary matters, especially when he is aware of elements in himself that might not be expected in a person of his professional interests and attitudes. Who, for instance, would expect such an observer of "highbrow" problems to have ideas about baseball, be devoted to football, and prefer trains to planes? To acknowledge, however, such aspects of the unexpected is in no way to play for surprise and shock, with their presumptive aids to remuneration, but to suggest a wider range of human responses and relevance than might be expected. This runs the risk, of course, of limiting the range and pointedness of pure academic concerns. It is a real risk, but it seems worth taking.

The sketches of several distinguished colleagues are, then, a sort of transition from the purely personal to the basically professional. The portraits, of course, are more descriptive than analytic, since it has seemed to me fitting that great writers and thinkers should also be seen as passersby in the academic hallways, appearing thus and so to their colleagues, in ways more routine than distinguished. The portrait of Malcolm Cowley, of course, is less a portrait of a man than a record of historical events in which he was a major figure.

On, then, to the more purely academic—that is, critical ideas emerging from my experiences as a college teacher. First, in Parts III and IV, I deal with works that I had to think about for teaching or writing—the contents here arranged in an order roughly reflecting the chronological status of the writers. Obviously one includes essays that deal with issues that seem worth talking about. Then the final two essays in Part IV lead us toward general educational issues, the subject of Part V. The final essay in the book is the only one that retains its original lecture form, generally not considered suitable in a printed volume, but here admitted, if riskily, because of the difficulty of separating out the critical issues and the only too apparent references to a present audience.

The essentially literary essays make no issue of the critical approaches used. One hopes that what is said will seem apposite and hence useful and self-justifying.

the professor and
the profession

I

the self
displayed

1

From Parsonage to Podium

Some years ago I proposed to the editor of a literary journal that he base an issue on various contributors' reflections on how their fathers' professional activities influenced their own careers—whether by imitation, by resistance and opposition, or by other modes of interaction, perhaps more complex. The editor did not act upon my suggestion, however strong my conviction that the subject would make a good issue. You will have guessed that my suggestion came out of a sense—indeed a new one—of a development of my own that I am embarking on here.

My father was a Christian minister, and I became a teacher of English ("English" being everything from basic grammar and composition to all the literatures written in English, including British and, later, American; the basic term *Department of English* is still standard, even where most of the material taught may be American literature or English translations of various other literatures—European, Asian, and now of course African too). My new idea about the relation between my father's work and my own turned on my having a fresh and more accurate sense of a key word than I had had before. The key word was *Bible,* which I need hardly define. But what is important is the literal meaning of the key word *Bible.* It is an Anglicized form of a Greek plural, *biblia,* which means, of course "books." The work that has been called "the good book" is actually a plural, "the books." It suddenly struck me that I had taken *Bible,* or *biblia,* "the books," to be the standard components of English literature, which was still the main area of literary study during both my undergraduate and graduate years (the 1920s and 1930s). English was what you did if you weren't doing classics, the Romance languages ("Romance" originally meant Roman, that is, the languages derived from Latin—French, Italian, and Spanish were the main ones), Russian, or Asiatic languages, which came into curricular prominence more recently. (And of course American literature was later to come into

3

great curricular prominence, since no one found a good popular argument against the widespread nativist view, "We are Americans; we should study American literature.") However, those matters belong to a larger field of what a "liberal education" should be. My concern is the much more limited one of the secularization of *the Bible* as "the books"—that is, the whole literary field as distinguished from math, the sciences, the social sciences, and so forth.

This basic perception led me to reflect on the various personal styles I had seen among members of the class to which I belonged—the class of ministers' sons, or, in more popular terms, "preachers' kids" or sometimes just "pk's." It seemed to me that I had seen three types of development in this class of people: one, those who followed in the parental religious paths (or secularized them, as I did); those who formally revolted against the hereditary ecclesiastical beliefs, styles, and rules, that is, became more profane than the born secularists, and liked to behave badly with respect, let us say, to sex and drinking; and, third, those who simply fell into a sort of indifference to the ecclesiastical backgrounds of their bringing up. I don't think that I have ever had a thorough perception or analysis of this third category, which, in my personal experience, later appeared conspicuously among Catholics, of whom I knew little before adult life. (There were none in the Pennsylvania town where I lived from age three to age twelve, and few in the Presbyterian world of Lafayette College, where I spent my four undergraduate years, and where it was considered great indoor sport to look up topics in the then *Catholic Encyclopedia,* which described Martin Luther as a "sex-mad monk," and so on. I find it interesting that our sense of superiority to Catholic thought, or what we took to be Catholic thought, as it appeared in what we took to be revelatory articles in the *Catholic Encyclopedia,* seems rarely to have developed into anti-Christian or anti-religious attitudes.) In time I would get to know Catholics, to have good Catholic friends, and to find plenty of common ground. At one time in my life—I suppose mostly during World War II and the years following it—my observation of several cases of ex-Catholics who became warm Communists led me to generalize that this was a natural mode of secularization for Catholics—from authoritative ecclesiastical belief to an authoritative political school. In fact, I remember expressing this theory to a Catholic friend, who said I was wrong. His view was that a Catholic who lost his faith became indifferent to the whole realm of faith, ecclesiastic or political. I based my judgment on a case of a passionately Communist poet who was a fallen Catholic. I see him, in retrospect, as undergoing a secularization of the ecclesiastical heritage rather different from the one I have perceived in myself. Clearly my ex-Catholic friend who denied the general applicability of my idea of transmutation of a hereditary faith felt more at ease with what he believed to be the plain loss of it. But I suspect that he was like me in translating the original *biblia* into the books, that is, the books that we dealt with in departments of English.

So much for this special case. I now want to go back to my original idea of the three classes of ministers' sons—those who directly maintain the paternal tradition, as well as those who translate it into other terms; and those who formally revolt against it. First, the true believers: the class to which I originally belonged and from which I slid away, on the whole painlessly, into an alternative biblical life. The class of true believers really falls into two divisions: the first includes the truly devout practitioners of the churchly life, exemplified in Chaucer's "poor parson of a town" and, I think, in my own father's life (but who knows about his father, really? I have wondered at times whether my father had in some way lost his faith but went on in practices that had become second nature and for which there was no available alternative); the others are those who carry on church life in a style to which an American economic historian, Thorstein Veblen, gave the wonderful enduring term *conspicuous consumption*. Obviously I am thinking of those who, in the ancient term, "pray on street corners," or lead prayer there (in our day, of course, street corners tend to be some place like the White House, an irresistible pulpit to those whom we usually call "evangelists"; in this role the attractions of the parental life are apparently too magnetic to be resisted by a son of the original performer).

Then there are the ministers' sons who early on start rebelling against the paternal style of life. As I observed them in my day, they seemed to show independence of spirit by going in for conspicuous—that is, highly visible— bad behavior, from swearing to sex. I have never been able to follow one of these types from the teens to adult life, but I doubt they tended toward anything like criminality. What I would expect would be an outcome of standard conventionality, since self-conscious unconventionality—or anti-conventionality—is easily translated into its opposite.

From such histories, seen or imagined, I go back to my early parsonage life, at the ages of three to twelve, in Elizabethville (jokingly known as "E'ville"), Pennsylvania, a rural town some thirty miles north, and a little east, of the state capital, Harrisburg (indeed, several people with state government jobs commuted from Elizabethville—a fact that, I suppose, may have given the rest of us some feeling of significance). The population of Elizabethville was about one thousand. It had four churches, representing the denominations of Lutheran (my father's church), Reformed (described by the more knowing as "Calvinist"), Evangelical, and United Brethren (generally known as the "UBs"). It interests me, as I look back from more than seventy years later, to see that we turned these four churches from simply different styles of Christian practice into four different styles of society to which we attributed certain characteristics and status—characterizations I have no doubt derived from the atmosphere of the Lutheran parsonage in which I lived and which I automatically took to be a center of truth and valid judgments. We certainly thought of my father's Lutheran church as some sort of top dog in the community; it seemed to have cornered the top dogs in the actual community and thus to have symbolized its own priority status. (I can remember the head of a shoe company and his wife, an amiable and humorous couple, becoming intimates of my parents, who did not have a natural social ease—they both came from rural farming families—and who seemed greatly to enjoy this novel association.) Aside from the status of the church itself, my father had, before he took his divinity degree, been a professor of Greek and Latin in a state normal school (today known as a state university, where I suppose it would be impossible to study Greek and difficult to find a class in Latin), and knowledge of this fact no doubt permitted us to think of our church as representing some sort of intellectual as well as social leadership.

Next in line was the Reformed church, right next to our parsonage, so that we could hear, sometimes, the fulminations of the pastor, who was given to strong sermons that seemed to us to betoken a less sound approach to salvation. His name was Calvin B. Wehr—pronounced *Ware,* unlike my Seattle friend, the artist and paleobotanist Wesley Wehr, pronounced *Weer*—a great friend of many visiting artists and intellectuals at the University of Washington. I can't get over the contrast between Calvin Wehr and Wesley Wehr—the one a vigorous condemner of human weaknesses, and the latter a tolerant friend likely to make people think they had no weaknesses. Besides, Calvin Wehr reminds me of my late UW colleague Sophus Winther, a student of Victorian literature and a novelist. Sophus was violently anti-church in all forms because in the Midwest, where he grew up, the Scandinavian Lutheran pulpits were all, apparently, in the hands of violent denouncers of sin who from the pulpit would identify, by name, individuals who were headed, the preachers said, straight to hell. If Elizabethville's Calvin Wehr dished out such personal threats to his congregations, I never heard of it. He was simply known as an angry, shouting man of God. Indeed, the only point I want to make is that the Reformed operation seemed decidedly inferior to the Lutheran one which my quiet and fairly learned father conducted.

As to the Evangelicals and the United Brethren (the UBs), they were thought of—at least in our area—as emotional, noncontent Christians given to rather simpleminded paths to salvation. Their ministers were thought to be relatively untrained members of the laity, say carpenters or butchers who had somehow got the "call" and thus suddenly, with great faith but little training, if any, had ascended into pulpits and delivered the word. This view of the men would obviously have been influenced by my father's own experience as a teacher of Greek and Latin before he took his B.D., which of course meant also learning Hebrew. So within the very large community of Christianity there could be a good deal of familiar class feeling; no doubt we all looked down on the various sects known as Dunkards, i.e., those who believed in "dunking," or "total immersion," as a necessary route to salvation.

In such a small town there was a good deal of jesting about "preachers' kids" (the special designation, "pk's," was of later vintage, I believe). We ranged from those who were conspicuously pious to those who used profanity and other bad language as evidence that they were true members of a larger secular world. In spirit at least, I suppose, I belonged to the pious set. But my problems were otherwise in the single building where all twelve grades attended school, two grades to a room. Here the story sinks to earthy matters quite below the theological: I am thinking of the "need to go," a constant problem of mine. We had only outdoor johns, one for boys of all ages, the other for girls of all ages, and I suppose that "going" got so popular that the teachers needed to have some means of controlling it. So anyone who wanted "to go" had to get permission by a public, recognized process: raising a hand, with one finger stretched out to indicate "number 1," that is, urination, and two fingers raised conspicuously to indicate other needs. I seem to have been afflicted with an abnormal need for "number-one" departures (I have the impression that my parents had to make representations that would permit me to have more frequent number-one departures than were normally taken to be adequate, and that this did not help me win any popularity prizes, these put nearly beyond my reach in the first place by my being that rare bird, a boy who found it easy to do lessons and therefore tended to get good grades). But that skips away from the ecclesiastical background, which does get into this story too. The teacher in the room for third and fourth grades was Miss Florence Wehr, the daughter of the Reformed church evil-blaster next door. She had gone south for a college education at some school with a Calvinistic discipline and was now back in Elizabethville as a teacher. Florence Wehr was probably too gentle a soul for a job in a school where things could still be rather hurly-burly. (My father told me of a scene in a country school in which he had taught as a young man. Perplexed by a disciplinary problem with a talkative boy, he had brought in his own father, once a country teacher as well as a farmer, to help with the situation. When the bad boy burst into ill-timed speech, my grandfather went to his seat, put his hands around the boy's neck, and inquired, "Did I hear you say something?" Florence Wehr would not have been up to this.) I recall an occasion on which she chose to punish a lad by switching him (physical punishment was not yet considered spiritually damaging). She got him by one hand and aimed her weapon, no doubt an innocuous one, at his rear. But, held by her arm, he ran, and may thus have evaded all blows of punitive intent. He literally ran circles around her, and we all laughed, a tribute that no doubt lent vigor to his method of escape. What kept it going was that Miss Wehr, as we called her, did not let go of his arm. I still wonder whether the Reformed kids laughed as heartily as we Lutherans certainly did.

I want to go back, for a moment, to the subject of language and its users, who of course ranged from the decent and reverent to the risqué, and the pleasure of using conventionally offensive terms—clearly bad conduct to us who were deep in conventional practice. There were those who wanted to offend, and those who could offend with ease, without even trying. What my parents called "dirty talk" was of course rather widespread, and we who were supposed to be above it could run into social difficulties. I remember specifically an occasion on which the kids from some other ministerial family came to play with us—Evangelical or UB, I'm not sure which. The oldest in the group, a boy of maybe eleven or twelve, astonished me by asking, "Did you ever see your sister's pecker?" *Pecker* was a word in wide use and had different meanings: everything from a substantial nasal emission to male or even female genitalia. This was a shocking question; I remember thinking that it seemed to justify my father's view that the Christianity practiced by the UBs was an inferior, untrained, unscholarly kind of thing. The story ends there, I suppose, since I can recall no further developments. I can't remember reporting the linguistic experience to my parents; I may have feared that they would think they ought to take it up with the parents of the boy who asked the question, and that would only mean further uncomfortable reactions to me. I would be a "tattletale" as well as a moral "sissy." Maybe, too, I thought that the boy had shown a great deal of confidence in me by asking me the question.

Living next to, and seeming to have a special connection with, the church that seemed to be the most significant in town may have nourished an egoism that made me an intolerable brat. I can remember one occasion on which I was showing off by walking along the top of a fence in front of the church—thus exhibiting a rather unecclesiastical skill for people coming to Sunday morning services. Of course I fell off, and one of the spikes atop the fence made a deep puncture wound in my thigh (I may or may not have thought that I was having an experience of divine punishment for egoism). I can't remember any other experiences relevant to this point. Yet this is only one point to be made—and by no means an exclusive one. Quite aside from the social aspects of the case—that is, how one came to think of oneself as a local figure—the church connection provided valuable, significant experiences. I have a very clear recollection of the daybreak services at both Christmas and Easter, and the week of special services on both occasions; they had values which I came to understand— primarily a sense of great events of profound and mysterious significance— a sense which I think useful to humanity generally and indeed essential to the study and teaching of literature. Our "books"—from the *biblia* to their lay successors—were felt as rooted in great and significant mysteries, not always susceptible to rational dissection and diminution. One secularized the Bible—the *biblia*—into great literature generally, then the Greek and Roman classics, then the European tradition generally, and finally the works that created British culture. American literature was still something one did pretty much on one's own, though it has now achieved an academic status that makes it primary in American education. In this treatment it seems to illustrate what we believe we already know rather than to be the bearer of enlarging mysteries.

But as long as I am intent upon noting some resemblances between past and the long present of professional life, or the usefulness of one to the other, I must go on to other aspects of Elizabethville life than the ecclesiastical, basic as that was in introducing one to the vast experiences of meaning and mystery. In this town of a thousand we were close to nature, and of course in all seasons, and I value this closeness as making significant contributions to a fitting awareness of the world of literature. Although our house and church fronted on Main Street—which was indeed the main street of the town, running a mile or so from west to east, continuing an interurban that ran from the Susquehanna River valley (made famous by Coleridge) to the mountains in the east, a sort of minor alpine area to which we loved to go on picnics and from which we enjoyed long views of the country below—still Main Street was not an organizing center of a grid of streets, as it might be in a more urban conformation, but it was *the* street that made the town. Just off it, to the north, lay a considerable extent of open country, finally bordered, eight or ten miles away, by the long Mahantango Mountain range (the town's immediate southern border was the Berry Mountain, up which it was great fun to hike, especially during the chestnut and horse-chestnut seasons, and in the fall to gather leaves of wondrous color). So we were close to nature in its scenic aspects—they were various—and from it we derived a set of experiences different from those in the world of the church. In the summertime all storms—sometimes daily it seemed, and always at least once a week—seemed to come from the north. We would see dark masses of clouds slowly form above the top of the Mahantango Mountain, reach a threatening volume, as if about to explode (and we were always scared by them), and then rise slowly (leaving a lighter line of sky beneath), and move toward us gradually, bringing a storm and we knew not what damage, harm, and danger; but it took time for the storm to move over the intervening eight or ten miles, and we could manage to imagine the worst that might happen (being struck by lightning, of course). (I once saw what was called an isoceraunic map of the United States, showing the incidence of thunderstorms throughout the different regions; I remember that in our world here in the Northwest— and indeed all down the Pacific coast to Mexico—thunder could be heard about five times a year, whereas in the Midwest and the East the total could be from fifty to a hundred times a year.) The approaching storms brought volleys of thunder and numerous flashes of lightning; we seemed to be at the center of, if indeed not the object of, threatening and harmful events, perhaps meant to chastise us; indeed, if a storm came late in the day and the dark of evening came on, we could occasionally look out to the north and see a fire—one which we always supposed was caused by a bolt of lightning. What we developed, without putting it into such words, was a sense of nature at once beautiful, frightening, and potentially destructive— a good background for the diverse treatments of nature in literature, from the storm in *King Lear* to the Wordsworth pictures of nature as in some way nourishing.

But summer offered other experiences than the wonder and terror of electrical storms. Between our church and the parsonage was a row of splendid maples of which our awareness somehow produced pleasure. Around one of these there had been a pile of sand that our parents had had delivered to help make a special play site for my brother, my sister, and me. This tree had become known as "the sand-pile tree," and for some reason climbing it became a special summertime pleasure. I can remember climbing way up and sitting in the top branches, swaying in a breeze that was not too sharp to seem dangerous. What a pleasure that was: to feel the breeze making the top center of the tree sway gently was to experience another kind of at-home-ness in the natural world. It seems reasonable to see this as a physical experience that could be transmuted, years later, into a strong sense of the beneficent powers of nature as felt by the Romantic poets.

Or, enjoying a different kind of motion, one could walk—and later on, ride a bike—along the winding country roads, perhaps relishing the pleasant sensations of being ankle deep in the red dust—a soil we later learned was called "red shale." Once, I remember, some others and I—my sister and brother perhaps—threw handfuls of the red-shale dust in the air and enjoyed catching it on our heads. My mother was furious, for just before this, she had given us head-washes, not yet known as shampoos. Obviously I was preparing for the English literature of country life.

Then there were the wintertime effects, which in that countryside were of course different, but equally wonderful. After a snow the rolling country was very handsome, though we would never have thought of using a word like *beautiful*. We thought easily of sledding on snowy hills (the summertime grain fields or grass fields), and we gladly pulled sleds from one hill or hillock to another. But I also remember a great undefined thrill gained in simply walking—or perhaps pulling a sled behind me and, where there were declines, enjoying brief rides on it—and feeling some sort of undefined, indeed mysterious, thrill in just hiking, or occasionally sledding or sliding through the snow fields and occasional small hills. It was a free world; one had no sense of trespassing on other people's property. There was no risk; all was free and easy. Interpreting retrospectively, and using tools of definition not available to a boy of nine to twelve, I can say that the countryside—warm and blooming in spring and summer, and chill and snowy in winter—evoked kinds of aesthetic awareness that made one sensitive to delights for which he could have no name. These would include even the thunderstorm fears.

I have recalled some of the most striking experiences remembered from the heights of summer and winter to suggest a responsiveness to nature, as we would later learn to call it, that went along with the responses to the supernatural as intimated by the various experiences of church life. And such experiences of nature were also active when I later on made the reorientation from *biblia* (or the Bible) to the general world of *books,* be it the storms experienced by the exiled King Lear or the evocations of significant nature in Romantic poetry. This wide variety of responses would not have been possible, I think, if my father's parish during my early formative years had not been an essentially rural one. I really would not trade anything for those early years—ages three to twelve in my life—for that small-town, indeed essentially rural, environment. Recently I have come to identify, also, another kind of utility—a linguistic one; Elizabethville was in "Pennsylvania Dutch" country, that is, the population was almost exclusively of Dutch, or Deutsche or more properly German, origin. The patois known as "Pennsylvania Dutch," a folk variety of German, was still a common medium of exchange. But my parents, both of Pennsylvania German origin—never let us three children—learn Pennsylvania Dutch; I'm sure this was a bit of linguistic snobbery on their part (my mother had been the prize student in a Greek class taught by my father at the normal school where they met). At any rate, this ignorance of Pennsylvania Dutch meant that I was cut off from communication when we visited, often for meals, members of the three rural churches that belonged to my father's four-church parish, for at these places the children of our age often knew no English. It was an early lesson in the fact that English was not the natural, automatic, universal language that we naturally took it to be. This early lesson in linguistic problems and barriers had another form at home, where various texts in German and Greek were lying around and attracted a good deal of interest from me (and, I suppose, from my sister and younger brother, though there my memory is faulty). I soon learned that being able to translate the older German letters into the familiar English ones did not take me very far into German. But I am still surprised at my innocence with regard to Greek: I learned the alphabet and then found that still I was a long way from being able to read Greek. But at least, early on, one was introduced to the problems of learning a foreign language; one developed a sort of linguistic sense that was useful to have; at least one was saved from the linguistic ignorance of later generations who would come to think of American English as an automatic world tongue. Incidentally, Pennsylvania Dutch has some resemblance to Yiddish. Both are offsprings of German, but whereas Yiddish became an international tongue that in time produced a literature (various Jewish scholars are quite proud of it), Pennsylvania Dutch remained a subliterary patois of no use, so far as I know, outside the region that gave it birth. My father did most of his preaching in English, but on occasion he had also to preach in Pennsylvania Dutch and in what we then called "high German," that is, standard German. The resemblance between the two is not always automatic. Two of my aunts who grew up speaking, or at least able to speak, Pennsylvania Dutch found, when they traveled to Germany, that they had quite a few linguistic difficulties.

It is obvious that I think that in many ways that early life in essentially rural Pennsylvania was a good thing, with advantages for a later life in which I became a college teacher of English. Now I want to record another kind of response to the world about me when, at my age of twelve (in 1918), my father accepted a pastorate in Easton, a city with a population of thirty-three thousand. Family legend has it—a legend never actually confirmed by either parent—that father took this pastorate because Easton was the site of Lafayette College and hence he could afford to send his two sons to college (it did work out that way: we lived at home and walked daily to Lafayette; while I did this for four years I have the impression that my brother, who was more worldly than I—he later became a very successful lawyer in the

New York firm of Dewey Ballantyne—may have managed to live on campus for his last year or two). This story assumes that father, a Lutheran who went to Lutheran Muhlenberg College, would have tolerated the Presbyterian Christianity of Lafayette (which at that time had a required daily chapel service—about fifteen minutes—and required Sunday services—the usual hour—for students living on campus; and required nine hours, or three three-hour courses, of Bible for all students—courses which, among other things, provided some good materials for the study of literature). I have no evidence on father's attitude to the Presbyterianism of Lafayette. But back from these later days to our move to Easton at my age of twelve. Although not all members of the family were enthusiastic about the move, I was—so much so that I lost all sense of the charms and utility of country life, which I have been writing about here. The population of Elizabethville was one thousand; that of Easton was thirty-three thousand, and I blush to think that I must have supposed that that meant that Easton offered thirty-three times as many opportunities for significance and pleasure. I cannot discover the origins of the idea of bigness in itself as a source of advantages, significance, and pleasure. Certainly in literary studies we do not value large books as more significant than smaller ones. Elizabethville was on a minor branch of the Pennsylvania Railroad, whereas Easton was served by the main lines of the famous Lehigh Valley and the Jersey Central, an apparent continuation of the Philadelphia and Reading into larger worlds (the Lehigh Valley and the Jersey Central both went east to New York City, only seventy-five miles away), and besides, there was a major line of the great Pennsylvania coming north from Philadelphia and through Phillipsburg just across the Delaware in New Jersey. So I felt vaguely promoted in the secular world—a feeling for which I can find no source or analogy in biblical experience. And this sense of vague promotion meant my not recognizing, at least initially, that we had moved from the main church in a village to one of a dozen Lutheran churches in Easton, and, besides, one located in a lower-middle-class section of a city that in time would seem quite ordinary—a preparation, perhaps, for reading English novels that grew out of undistinguished urban life. Still, the comparatively large population, the railroads, the college, and the presence of perhaps a score of school buildings, as against the single school building which in Elizabethville housed all twelve grades—all this seemed to offer at least quantitative grounds for a sense of having been mysteriously promoted in the world. I am not debunking when I record that it took a long time to recognize that Easton was not heaven on earth and that Lafayette was only one of sixty-six colleges within the borders of Pennsylvania. That did not happen for a long time after arrival.

I do not know when I began to have some vague sense that the Eliza-bethville feeling—the feeling of being a part of a significant ecclesiastical and civic largeness—was being overtaken by a sense of parsonage life as limited (I was never consciously rebelling as some pk's are; I was never stirred by the spirit of revolt, or, for that matter, by an opposite spirit of acceptance and continuity that keeps an order of life on the track). But in retrospect I can recognize certain actions, however defined or undefined then, as signifying a kind of move into a larger world, or what I then took to be, without ever formally defining it, a larger world. One was the first connection with baseball, which I write about in the next essay. (Of course, in one aspect it did have a nominal ecclesiastical connection, but still it must have seemed secular enough to let me think I was experiencing a kind of enlargement. This was a small part of a general sense of being promoted from an unimportant small town—however well established, through ecclesiastical eminence, one's stature was in that town.) The other experience of a move into a larger, or supposedly larger, world had to do with a variety of jobs. In those days one could legally get a job at fourteen, and the state of parsonage income meant that at fourteen one naturally looked for a job. At the time I was a sophomore in high school. One of the first of my jobs was at the *Free Press,* one of two daily papers published in Easton (another promotion over Elizabethville, which had only a weekly, the *Echo,* which the freer spirits in town seemed to diminish by calling it the *Eeko*). This job meant delivering certain batches of papers to various downtown stands and hotels; I was, so to speak, the wholesaler making deliveries to the retailers. At least one of these stacks of papers went to a streetcar that would take them out of town to some suburban or village retailer. This meant standing at the streetcar entrance where one could see the passengers getting on. This had an advantage when the mounting passengers were female: they frequently provided a fascinating glimpse of stockinged leg and even, on a lucky day, of skin. This was a quite real pleasure, if not one that one could speak about at home. I did not know what this pleasure signified, since we were kept in massive ignorance of the facts of life. But it was for real, even though undefined and connected, one guessed, with something impermissible. That was almost eighty years ago.

Then I moved into a still more exciting job as usher at a movie theater—indeed the Third Street Theater, which was *the* movie palace in Easton. This job came to me because one of the most faithful of the women workers in father's church was the wife of an Easton police officer who moonlighted, as most cops did; his outside job was being the guardian of law and order at the Third Street Theater. The management of the theater had decided to institute a new system of uniformed ushers, and somehow our cop got called upon as a headhunter for four ushers. He got me into the act; I was accepted and was empowered, as a prospective head usher, to recruit three underlings. Then we were measured for new uniforms—these distinguished by an ornamental three rows of brass buttons on the fronts of our jackets, these rows rather close together at the waist and flaring out toward the shoulders. The other guys got flat buttons, but, as head usher, I was distinguished by having round buttons on my jacket (I suppose I had to point this out to high-school classmates, so that they would understand the distinguishing symbolism). The uniforms were in a sort of gray-blue military cloth, with plenty of gold-braid ornament, and we must have felt as distinguished as if we were military officers. At times we certainly acted as if we were, in controlling the crowds at the more popular of the five two-hour shows that constituted the daily offerings (the most popular was that at 7 P.M., closely followed by those at 3 P.M. and 9 P.M.).

What an experience this was for a parsonage boy who at this time— 1921—had seen very few movies and was not at all into movie lore and gossip. Here I was thrust into another world—the larger world of movies in general, and the smaller immediate world of a movie theater, with a working population different from any I had ever known. This theater had a live orchestra for the 3 and 7 o'clock shows, and I think part of the 9 P.M. show. It gave me my first experience of professional musicians, who ranged from relatively serious older players—family men, I suppose—to younger ones with a worldliness new to me. Once one of the younger men described something—maybe a new snow?—with the phrase "pretty as hell." I was shocked by this simile, since, from everything I had heard, hell was not a very pretty place. But I suppose I admired his aesthetic sense and in time spotted his quest for an emphatic comparative. The orchestra provided drama in another way. The leader of the orchestra was a pianist who was evidently good at running the musical show, the nature of which was determined by the movie people from whom the films were rented. What tunes the orchestra played was determined by signals in the film itself; they were called "cues," as I remember it, and I recall hearing one musician complaining about the multiplicity of cues in a show that was supposed to be an especially grand affair. The pianist-leader, of course, had primary responsibility for catching the cues and taking the orchestra along with him into every change of musical text as required. But the leader got time off from at least one show a day, and when he was resting up, the piano was in the hands of a young woman pianist who ordinarily played alone in the shows when the orchestra was not on duty. She was apparently a good pianist, but, according to theater gossip, not very good at holding the orchestra together. Once one of the instrumentalists—I think there were six or seven besides the pianists (some strings, including a bass, traps, and a woodwind or brass or two)—made some comment on the lady's leadership, and she responded by spitting in his face—a new kind of drama in the home of the silver screen. A new kind of drama for this innocent, at least. There were other kinds. For the first time I was hearing a good deal of what my parents called "dirty talk," this from people who looked like good citizens, especially the three or four in the office staff. I heard a good deal about "dingleberries," a new word for me; in time I discovered that it meant fecal particles clinging to anal hairs—apparently a matter of great import to the theater staff. I suppose that, learning about this, I felt much wiser than I had before. One of my staff of ushers—I had recruited him—enlightened me with stories of homosexual experiences (mostly with an oral expert), about which I was as ignorant as could be. One guy on the ushering squad, one whom I had especially thought of as a "nice boy"—my father had confirmed him after the usual sessions of a catechetical class—surprised me by reporting that he had said to the sister of a friend (both members of my father's church), "When are you going to let me run my machine into your garage?" Later I learned he had married a pregnant girl—he was not the begetter—simply to save her from threatening disaster. Many years later I learned that the attractive young married woman in the ticket box had planned to give me a lesson in sex sometime when her husband was away on one of his numerous business trips; she evidently had thought it would be a great game to take a virginal high-school boy to bed. It did not happen. She was very fond of her husband and perhaps decided in time that taking a high-school boy to bed was not a suitable course of action. Then there were the two brothers who ran the projection machines—from a small booth upstairs, to be entered only by a ladder against the rear wall of the auditorium. One brother was a mild smiling fellow who rarely talked about anything. He was evidently in awe of big brother, who had a strong, dominating face, and who was thought to be a "great reader" by other members of the staff, who seemed to be in some awe of him. He read Rabelais; and in talking about Rabelais, he gave me my first contact with a writer whom I was later to like and admire a good deal. He summarized or read me a naughty passage, and then he commented, triumphantly, "And they call him a classic." He seemed to me to be engaging in some sort of triumph over the book, as if a passage that was "dirty" could not possibly also be "classic." The operator was said to have all of the "classics"; it may be that he felt that a classic wasn't a classic unless it was boring. I don't know. And from him I learned that you could be well read without ever having set foot in a college—and no less knowing than if you had.

So the job offered all sorts of eye-opening experiences. And it seemed to open horizons everywhere. The most ample horizons, I suppose, were those on the screen—and, as I can see in retrospect, they were a step toward the literature that would eventually become my main academic study, from my undergraduate major at Lafayette College to the pursuit of a Ph.D. at Harvard. But all that was unforeseen in 1921, when I was just moving with various currents that were not formally defined. Unconsciously, I am sure, I felt myself to be moving from personage life, which for the first time may have seemed sort of limited, to a broader current of life. Whatever the new life was in itself, it had advantages that one was very conscious of: as a viewer of *all* the films at *the* moving-picture house of the city, one could, or at least one did, speak with authority on the major popular art form of the time: for the first time one *knew,* or at least *seemed to know,* all about what the current world was willing to, or even eager to, know about. It was clear to me, if I did not put it into words, that the knowledge I possessed as a minister's son was not widely pursued in the world generally. What a promotion, then, to become a voice of authority in the truly popular world of the movies. It was not that I gave up my other life. I continued to live at home and to go to four full services in my father's church every Sunday—even later, during my four years at college, where, had I lived on campus, I would have gone only to a one-hour Sunday service.

So for the three latter years of high-school attendance I was really living in two worlds—the domestic and Lutheran one, and the work-and-movies world. I cannot remember feeling any kind of division or split; it must have seemed easy to go two ways, and perhaps to claim, unconsciously, two kinds of knowledge that would lead, assuredly, to one kind of salvation or another. It was great to become a voice of movie knowledge. I think now that this was less a move away from the Lutheran church as such than it was, or unconsciously seemed to me, a kind of class triumph within the city. My father's church, as I have said, was lower middle class; few members, if any, went to college, and there was little of the worldliness that leads to conspicuous consumption. We were, so to speak, in contrast with the two sections of the city—the College Hill and the "downtown" residential sections—from which everyone of status and significance seemed to come. Being a movie expert—or managing to be accepted as one, because one saw all the movies and could advise all the laity about going or staying away—made possible a sort of contact with, if not actual transfer to, the more desirable parts of the city. So here I was moving into an apparently larger world or, translating ecclesiastical into lay terms—as I did in translating *biblia* ("books," that is, the Bible) into "the books," that is, the general classics of literature—making a kind of social move, a broadening out, as it seemed.

So, in a sort of acknowledged dictatorship over the world of local aesthetic judgments, I was laicizing a voice of authority that may have had distant origins in holy writ and church practice, but now functioned otherwise. But I say this in analytic retrospect; I had no such awareness of the experience then. But what a joy to have an authoritative voice in this lay world—to lay down the law about movies to people who otherwise had greater claims to worldly position. Aside from seeing all the movies, I listened often to the theater manager, who had a taste for movie bigwigs and was constantly dashing over to New York and coming back with tales of actors, directors, casting, and other such matters. So I could pass on to others his expertise as well as what I took to be my own gained simply from seeing a couple of movies a week. Glorious, glorious authority— and authority in a world much larger than that of our own Lutheran congregation. (I have no recollection of any responses of my parents to this new life—or warnings or censoriousness. They must have been immensely tolerant or self-disciplined.) As head usher at the Third Street Theater, I was prematurely a kind of professor dealing out knowledge to listeners who were far more devoted to my wisdom than were most of my later college classes. I felt that I knew more than most people, and I dealt out what I knew with a sense of authority that was accepted, it seemed. So I held forth magisterially about the famous case of rape or alleged rape that ended the career of Fatty Arbuckle, or about the sad drug addiction of Wally Reid, an actor who grew popular in various roles as racecar driver. I was not only a knowing insider about movies and actors in general: I spoke with the wisdom gathered at the Third Street Theater, which in that local world was like having a higher degree from Oxbridge. And I would try not to be condescending to a friend who was a sort of assistant manager at a rival theater, the Strand, which we took to be a lesser one. He and I could compare notes about goodies at our respective cinema palaces, and I can remember George's alerting me to a delightful Strand show in which there were splendid views of female cleavage. And I magisterially explained to him the case of an actress who always had to wear long dresses as she was a bit ample in the legs. Surely not the chief lady on our circuit, by name Agnes Ayres!

Despite its charms, I gave up the theater job at the end of my high-school career, after three years. By now I had become the high-school reporter on the *Free Press,* and there is nothing, or was nothing, like a journalistic job to minister to one's ego by giving one a sense of great knowing insidership. I suppose it was even better than being an insider, hot-shot commentator on the film world. But how deglamorizing it was during the summer, simply to be sent out to "West Ward" and told to walk the streets, make inquiries, and thus create some news. It was a good experience in the standard dullness of actuality. I often thought of that when, as a university department chair, I would be interviewed by young journalism students expecting quick fame from revelations, which they were sure they would make, of evil conduct in high places.

2

Baseball

Random Connections

In the spring of 1923, a high-school senior, I became "manager" of the school baseball team in Easton, Pennsylvania. I am vague about how I got this job. Was I elected? And if so, by whom? Appointed? Or did I, unlikely as this would be, come out ahead in some sort of competition? The job could not have been a springtime Christmas surprise; I must have applied for it. In retrospect I can surmise the motive: feeling the singular, and indeed irrational, attraction of a sports connection. This irrational attraction will be a recurrent theme in these reminiscences of several baseball connections, mostly rather peripheral, over many decades.

"Irrational attraction." It was not that I made a belated leap out of inactivity, or had taken no other steps toward approved semipublic "activities" through which one might hope to triumph briefly over expectable ordinariness (a human fate that bothers fortunate people not at all). I had worked on school publications—the weekly paper called the *Junto* (*pace* Ben Franklin), and the yearbook called the *Rechauffé*—and in various clubs. Besides, I was the high-school reporter for the *Easton Free Press,* a role that no doubt added greatly to my sense of being a worthwhile fellow, a somebody in the immediate world. Even in minor peripheral jobs reporters quickly gain a sense of being one-up on other people. So I had good reasons for being content with school life as it was and for not taking a last-minute plunge into a totally different style of activity. Hence I must have had a vague sense of something lacking in all that had gone before.

Back to writing for the *Rechauffé,* then in gestation. In the typed copy I had seen myself described as "a Latin shark and a French shark too" ("shark" was the going metaphor for one who got good grades). The words were neutral: they had none of the unfriendliness that good grades sometimes elicit. Yet in some way they may have suggested only a sideline achievement in the school society. My best friend, who in later years would become a distinguished medical writer, was described as "a prince of good fellows," and these words connoted a superior order of achievement. Maybe I yearned for a more mainline kind of accomplishment, and baseball may have seemed to open a magic door, or psychologically to provide a magic growth hormone for my sense of with-it-ness in the school. Of course I would have known that sports managers got letters, and the vision of that *E* on a sweater perhaps seemed to guarantee a nobler record than grades could ever create.

Motives aside, the baseball experience had its uses. The job was totally unglamorous, and one learned to live with that. If the title *manager* suggested either eminence or glory or seemed to ally one with John McCraw or Connie Mack, the managerial heroes of the day (who never fell into the brattishness that has distinguished some of their successors), the fact is that one didn't "manage" anything. One was only a menial who did routine sideline jobs that would be beneath the dignity of real athletes: one was a busboy on the fringe of a coterie of gourmet chefs. The team played on an only partly graded field on an open lot many blocks distant from the high-school building but near a junior-high-school building. Baseball supplies were stored there, and it was the manager's job to get them from building to field at the start of practices and games. Supplies: principally bases and baseballs. The bases were rigid canvas-covered bags, square in shape and maybe two inches thick; one lugged them out and fastened them, I suppose by clasps, to metal anchorages in concrete at each base position. (In retrospect I wonder how the players managed sliding: these massive aboveground bags must have held the threat of severe contusions or even fractures.) The baseballs, which were used until worn out, were few in number—maybe four or five; they were kept in a net bag that I lugged to the field along with the three bases. Probably the coach had an unacknowledged cache of balls from which he could now and then produce a new one (but nothing, I think, so rash as a new ball for every game). During practices and games one of my jobs was to chase and retrieve foul balls (and possibly home-run balls) and get them back as fast as possible for reentry into the game. Sometimes they disappeared, as long-hit balls are likely to do, the supply got low, and I felt the strain. In one such situation someone hit a long foul pop over the backstop (a limited setup of chicken wire); it got rolling on a street, for miles it seemed, and I chased it, in near despair. It was our last ball, the game was held up, and my chase seemed interminable and probably futile; already marked by a lack of brilliance that fell below even a decent competence, I would now be publicly and terminally disgraced. Did I get the ball? I don't remember. I do remember hurrying back—if slinking can be hurried—anticipating a dreadful public fate. Surprise! The game was going on! Another ball had appeared from somewhere. From the coach's pocket? Or a handout from a spectator?

There were no stands, and the spectators—probably no more than a hundred at even a big game—stood along the first-base line, which ran parallel to Twelfth Street and was close to it, and the third-base line. One of my jobs was to walk along these lines and try to sell tickets. Buying them was purely voluntary. The tickets may have cost twenty-five cents, and I probably lost sales through being unable to make change. Maybe on a big day I would have as much as fifteen dollars weighing down my pockets, and if the day was Friday or Saturday, I had a nervous weekend of guarding the treasure at home, the Lutheran parsonage.

The coach—the sole coach—was Mr. Richards, a recent college graduate who, it seemed, had not been a star college player. (We had not yet achieved the wisdom of big-league watchers who could see that great players rarely make good coaches and that poor players might make great coaches.) He was the son of some local bigwig (postmaster? city councilman?), and this fact was thought to have influenced his appointment. But, as far as I could tell, he seemed a perfectly satisfactory coach to those who knew something about baseball. To me he looked quite in charge, if rather irritably so. One day he gave me an order that seemed very strange: to tell the pitcher Lefty Takacs (pronounced "tack-us") that he was fired from the squad. I had a dual reaction to this strange command. On the one hand I felt faintly promoted, from errand boy as it were to official administrative status, say assistant coach; the other, and much stronger, feeling was that the coach was unsuitably unloading a tough job on an underling. I did not know what the case against Takacs was; I have no recollection of insubordination, quarrelsomeness, or other punishable conduct. Takacs may have had a touch of self-defensive pepperiness. He was the son of immigrants, and he had a slight accent. Although I doubtless shared the common feeling that we natives, as we took ourselves to be, were superior people, and though I had little of what we now call social conscience, I had some vague feeling that Takacs was being judged harshly because he was a little different from the rest of us. Anyway I did not carry out the order, not from principle I am sure, but from sheer inability to face so unpleasant an interview. Takacs stayed on the squad, I assumed as a result of a clarifying conference between player and coach.

Probably Coach Richards cooled down from whatever had heated him up, and saw that it would not do to dismiss his only left-handed pitcher and indeed one-third of his pitching staff. The two right-handers were another sophomore, as Takacs was, and a senior who was the star of the team, Francis Sigafoos (once, maybe a generation or two back, Ziegenfuss), a great halfback in football and in baseball so talented that when he was not pitching he played shortstop or center field. This local hero came from a very hard-up family, and we understood that the coach was giving financial help to the star player. There was nothing scandalous about this; at that time there were no rules that it violated. It simply meant that the coach was being generous, even if selfishly, instead of just throwing up his hands and lamenting about fate. Sigafoos was so good that he was soon taken on as an infield prospect by the Philadelphia Athletics, the team that excited hero-worship throughout eastern Pennsylvania. Sig did not make it; he told my father that he thought his not being a Catholic was a disadvantage. This intelligence obliged us to have some unpleasant thoughts about our hero Connie Mack (we felt very successfully insiderish when we could tell any available ignoramus that Mack's real name was Cornelius McGillicuddy). But perhaps we also reflected, if unwillingly, that a rookie just out of high school, even if devoutly Catholic, might have a tough time cracking an infield made up of Foxx, Bishop, Boley, and Dykes.

Sigafoos made this report on suspected prejudice to my father, who was pastor of the Lutheran church with which Sigafoos had some faint connection. Nominal church memberships by athletes were on the rise for a year or two when Protestant churches organized a summer baseball league. I recall our church's having another pitcher who had been in the Pittsburgh system but had returned to Easton under a vague cloud of a Black-Sox-ish hue. He lived in our neighborhood, and I thought it would be fine to play catch with him. I was wearing a catcher's glove, and the pitcher threw accordingly. I had never seen a really fast pitch or a curveball before, and I stopped the ball—or at least deflected it—with my bare right hand. Painful education, whether by the pitcher's intending to put me in my place or by his simple failure to grasp my inexperience. (The catcher's glove I was wearing was one of two gloves possessed by our family. The other was a fielder's glove. I played a lot of catch with my sister and brother, both a little younger than I, and we always made it pitching practice. The sibling with the fielder's glove was pitcher, and the other one was the catcher. The catcher was also umpire, and he, or she, was a stern judge of the pitcher's effort to get the imaginary batter out. We tried to throw every kind of pitch, even knuckleballs; the curveballs were then called "drop," "inshoot," and "outshoot"; it was quite a while before such terms were replaced by fastball, forkball, slider, sinker, screwball, and the like. This game was great fun in Fairmount Park when we visited our Philadelphia grandmother, whose house was on a street bordering the park.)

What I might call "churchball" has become vague in memory, except for an opening game in which there was conspicuous disorganization among our players. Some slightly older person, evidently trying to pull it together, shocked me by saying, "Well, you're the high-school manager. Take charge. Make up a lineup." I was too amazed to protest, and, knowing too little about our players to have any idea of batting relationships, I took the dullest and least skillful way out—infield, outfield, battery. Happily my memory of the season stops at this recollection of ineptitude; otherwise I have only an indistinct image of a record vaguely successful. I have more definite pictures of biking around Northampton County to watch, and perhaps cover as a reporter, amateur or semipro teams that then flourished and some of which had enough success to achieve regional fame. Here my sharpest memory is of a retired big leaguer who was much in demand and signed on with various teams by the game. He was Socks Seibold, once a Phillies pitcher, and now an exciting presence in any game in which he played. He was quite an eyeful—short, red-faced, and plump; he was choleric; and his pitches all looked ninety miles per hour to local eyes. Like many a hero returned to a local scene, he excited a dual response: on the one hand hero worship, and on the other that reductive jeering by nonheroes who need to see heroes cut down to common-man dimensions.

So much for the medley of spinoff and fallout from the high-school "experience," as it would be called now, and back for a quick summation of the educational 1923 season. Our team won a regional championship, which some people liked to call a state championship. It could not have been that, because the teams in the final playoff game represented only the third of the state lying east of the Susquehanna—not even the important Philadelphia area. In the championship game we were to play Lebanon High at Lebanon, and it would be a very exciting trip, about seventy-five miles by train. I loved trains (and write more about this in a following essay). Then the trip to Lebanon had special appeal: my mother's family were from that area, we had often visited there. I doubtless felt like a Napoleon dropping in on Corsica and letting the stay-at-homes gaze at a native son—well, grandson—coming in triumph from the larger world. So a week before game day I came down with what we would now call flu, and then called grippe, and was terrified that I would miss the spectacular trip. I came around just in time, and the day was glorious, even though my presence in the ancestral town was noted by no one at all. Easton won, 6–2, and the train rides were a total delight—the gentle sway of the local through the pretty undulating countryside moderating the pregame tensions and enhancing the postgame exultation. The local made many stops, and at every hamlet we could look out and feel superior to the unprivileged people who had to live there.

ii

Finally I got my *E,* and my mother or sister attached it to my sweater. I suppose I wore it occasionally, but maybe I was a little dubious about it, as if I had not quite earned it by athletic labors. Perhaps, as a symbol of that jockhood widely felt as the ultimate student achievement, it seemed a little tainted. But, if public display seemed open to question, private satisfaction was permissible. Maybe the letter felt something like a nonacademic honorary degree. At one time I actually thought of it as a sort of public penance for the attributed sharkhood in Latin and French, but that came to seem inaccurate, for good grades, though they might be jested about, were not hard-core misdemeanors in the school community. But what they did tend to do, I came to see, was set one apart in semisolitary confinement. Hence the baseball connection was a mode, or at least a sign, of belonging to a larger world of humanity where grades didn't matter, of being certified in an inclusive order of basic social life. The best word for my feeling may be *enlarged,* with its double sense: of being released, and of being made bigger. It was both a coming-out party and an entering in. If such experiences had taken place sixty years later, one might have thought of oneself as a budding Giamatti, a bona-fide member of two worlds. But then of course there would have been the danger of thinking oneself a "Renaissance man" (that cliché that journalists, rarely strong on historical exactitude, now routinely apply to anyone who has both read a book and been to a ball game).

The idea of belonging may be more convoluted, or at least less self-defining, than it sounds. I have applied it to achieving a new at-home-ness in a world apparently larger than that of the good-grades minority and than that of the parsonage from which I had made no major exits in my first sixteen years. (Not that I was in urgent flight from the parsonage, but I was aware of some vague outer realm that was only partly known and was inviting; baseball was at least one manifestation of this secular world.) But there is really a nice problem here: the impulse to belong may be less simple than it sounds; one may feel either a vague yearning toward something, or a rejective spirit. And, if one is rejective, he may repudiate either of two domains: the inclusive or the limited and special. One may think to grow by widening out or narrowing down, by belonging to the many or to the few, to the bourgeois or the bohemian, the general or the elite (there are different orders of the elite, of course, from art connoisseurs to the owners of big-league ball clubs). The sense of belonging did lead me, clearly, from certain limited particulars (as they seemed) to a larger world (as it then seemed). It was the opposite move from that of some individuals who, intolerant of all belonging, may become saints, geniuses, professional angry men, criminals, weirdos, or conspicuous consumers of solitariness.

Psychological issues aside, the baseball connection had benefits, some more substantial than others. A certain imagined benefit is amusing in retrospect: one felt much more knowing about baseball in general, including the big leagues. One could pontificate on what was happening, or ought to happen. One could interpret scores as if one were a genuine insider. And, oh, how we learned big-league scores in the 1920s! They were posted daily, in one's neighborhood, between 5 and 8 P.M., since all games were outside afternoon events, and the games in "the West" (that is, the Midwest) were played only an hour later than those in the East. In Easton, as no doubt elsewhere before radio became the standard medium, the eight scores (there were four games in each league if all the teams were playing) were received by Morse code and printed by some downtown entrepreneur on colored cards of about six by nine inches. The cards were delivered, no doubt by bike or motorbike, to subscribing neighborhood outlets all around town—drugstores, lunch counters, soda fountains. Advertising on the cards paid for them, and the subscribers made up their costs, presumably, by selling things to customers who visited the shops to get the scores. Score-seekers might hang around for hours, or make repeated trips, if the scores were delayed—agonizingly if one had passions about the fate of teams. And of course when the scores came, the manager of the championship high-school team could announce, "See, I told you so"—or else seek a quick inconspicuousness.

But the experiences with the team did have definite uses. In retrospect I can see that having an administrative title but only errand-boy status was a moral discipline (no doubt it helped prepare me for being the chairman of a university department twenty-five years later). It was good to learn that I could at least get by in a totally new kind of job, even though I never got very good at it. I learned something about how baseball works, and that has always been handy; what goes on out there is a bit more pleasurable if one can spot technical elements that make it more than spectacle. I learned to keep a formal scorecard, and keeping a play-by-play record has been a lifelong pleasure, however infrequently enjoyed. I do it routinely at big-league games, even though a modern electronic scoreboard flashes out a never-ending series of the facts that one has before him on the scorecard. I'm not sure when I learned scorekeeping; certainly not during the games, when I was into full-time legwork. Probably after the games, relying on the detailed memories of the coach and players, who no doubt collaborated in a record they would like to have. Anyway, formal scorekeeping was an indispensable part of baseball reporting, in itself a new phase of worldly life. I was already, as I have noted, the high-school reporter for the *Easton Free Press;* and now I got into the heady life of writing about baseball—an experience that would last through my first three years at Lafayette College (the paper then went broke). New as I was at the game, I began to register knowingness by slipping into occasional wisecracks. I remember two. Of Syl Seibert, the first baseman: "He didn't work hard trying for that low throw from short." Of Boob Caflin, the right fielder (Boob was his nickname, and Caflin seemed not to resent it): "Once again, he saw the easy fly bounce off his glove." Such cracks were evidently accepted with good nature, perhaps unconsciously interpreted as symbols of envy by a nonplayer who couldn't have done half as well as even the less competent players. But I evidently felt it best to be strictly factual in my references to Lou Ostroff, the second baseman and captain. The players were friendly enough, and for my part I greatly admired athletic skills that I lacked.

Baseball reporting at college: here the gratifying sense of belonging came from membership in the journalistic fraternity. While the brothers may habitually feel superior to the world they write *for,* in-house status may depend on what they write *about.* The ultimate insidership was that of the football writers, who surveyed sporting life and the attendant public from a very exalted viewpoint. Hence old-time writers owned the football beat unless, in condescension, they elected to turn a surefire one-sided game over to a youngster like myself. Still baseball was not negligible: one was a real journalist, an insider in a caste of worldly knowingness not really available to the average English major such as I was becoming. If one's basic home territory was an ivory tower, as a reporter one also had a foot in an exclusive worldly order. But one articulates this only in retrospect; at the time one's journalistic activities simply offered a vague undefined satisfaction.

One's journalistic status was publicly visible as one sat, perhaps with a dangling cigarette, in the baseball "press box," that is, several seats with writing surfaces in front of them, in the first row of the small baseball stand. One could saunter out and ask the coach, "How does it look, Bill?" (Bill Coughlin, a retired Detroit Tigers third baseman who was the longtime coach at Lafayette), or similarly exhibit at-homeness with the players. And the sense of being a knowing insider could impinge upon what one wrote about the game. One could slip into witty, as one thought, criticism. Example: "Catcher Grube again proved the famous strength of his arm. Trying to cut off a steal, he threw magnificently into deep center field." Or one might try hard for originality of style. I remember seeking a lively verb to picture an extraordinary catch of an apparently sure hit, a high hot liner, by the shortstop, Koch, who seemed to keep propelling himself up into the air, like a basketball player driving a long distance through the air toward the basket. I wrote *gyrated*. The copyeditor changed it to *jumped*.

I wish I could remember how I handled a ninth-inning play in a game that Lafayette won with the aid of an umpire (in those days a single umpire handled the plate and all the bases). In a close decision at the plate he either called safe a Lafayette player with the winning run, or called out a visiting player to shut off a rally that seemed likely to produce a victory. The umpire played the "homer" role too unsubtly, the visitors raised a dreadful outcry, and in a day or two Lafayette appropriately forfeited the game. The umpire confessed that he could not bear to see the home team lose. He was an Easton cop whom I knew (knowing cops was another psychological profit of being a reporter). My guess is that, writing about the game, I simply referred to the crucial call at the plate as a close play. And that may be really all that I saw. I hope so.

iii

There are two codicils to this tale of a coming out (and an entering in) in which the central theme has been the strange appeal of participation, even in peripheral ways, in a game that theoretically should have been of little interest to a bookish boy whose passionate devotions were to Latin and French and who tended to get good grades generally (of course, family tradition and practice made homework an automatic activity, in no way the cruel imposition upon innocent youth that it seemed to become in the 1980s). The codicils have to do with two later occasions of adult life in which I see something of the same irrationality that I have attributed to the more central baseball experiences of my teens. For the first of the later episodes we jump ahead from the mid-1920s to about 1940 when, having finished my Ph.D. at Harvard, I had a beginning job at Louisiana State University in Baton Rouge and was working hard at teaching and trying to write publishable literary criticism. Sometime in this prewar period the New York Giants picked Baton Rouge for their spring training and actually used one of the LSU fields. Somehow their presence seemed to add an almost metaphysical significance to the local scene: Baton Rouge took on a new dimension, and one began to feel a part, however small, of something larger than had been available previously. It was delightful to go down to the ball field of an afternoon and watch the practice, especially if it took the form of a game. One felt almost a personal connection with the stars of the day, and it was not difficult to manage a word with one or another of them now and then; they may have been under orders to be kind to local efforts at fraternizing. (Did I substitute this watching for tennis, which I was still playing passionately, maybe two or three times a week?) At any rate Baton Rouge seemed to have acquired an amplified status, in which one participated, however peripherally, with a satisfaction hardly to be expected of an academic whose fidelities are supposed to be of another order. Then the Giants moved elsewhere for spring training, and we all felt—well, all who noticed the exodus—reduced in size, deprived of a presence that, however illogically, had given the area a vague increment of symbolic status.

My first codicil required a leap of fifteen hundred miles and fifteen or more years. My second codicil requires a leap of twenty-five hundred miles and forty or so years: it takes us from Baton Rouge around 1940 to Seattle in the 1980s. Ah, yes, the famous case of the Mariners in the early 1990s involved in an ownership brouhaha that became virtually a national cause célèbre. The history of the Mariners has two aspects, the aesthetic and the economic, and of course each impinges on the other. Aesthetically the team has achieved a new record of persisting perennial second-rateness, at once a result of economic lusts and a cause of further economic ill-being. There is only one cure for such a situation, and that is knowledge: it should be utterly understood that a professional sports team is an owner's expensive toy of which the central, and for the most part, sole profit is high visibility in toydom, with shoulder-rubbing privileges among a set of highly conspicuous big-money bigwigs (and incidentally some tax-write-off schemes as a sideline toy).

Two disasters may impinge upon this marvelously satisfying form of public play. Sometimes an owner stupidly forgets that he is into toydom with a costly hobby that can be nothing more than a source of prestige among journalists and a general gawking world and thinks the team should be a big-time moneymaker like real estate, foreign cars, or market-juggling. The other disaster is the team's falling into the hands of some purchaser whose love of big showy toys surpasses his ability to pay for them. In both cases the owner promptly blames a local populace for not coming up with the wherewithal either (1) to keep him rolling in dough because he finds he likes to roll in dough rather than in toy owners' national visibility, or (2) to enable him to maintain his big-shot status among big-shot toy-owners when he can't pay for the glory himself. I describe, in order, the second owner of the Mariners (the get-richer-or-else type) and the third owner (who could hardly bear to give up the style of the big-bucks tycoon because he had succumbed to a form of chronic conspicuous consumption). "Pay up," these holdup artists (lusting after bigger bucks or simply needing big bucks to pay for a habit) threaten us, "or I won't play, and I'll take my baseball away. So there." Rational people respond, "All right, run. You are repulsive, and we'll do better without you." And there are large numbers of rational people around.

So it's a little embarrassing to find myself, though no more than an inconspicuous observer of these goings-on, at least feeling somewhat like the people who call for, and even take definite actions toward, keeping the team here. It's another instance of an irrationality that first appeared in my connection with high-school baseball and then showed up again in small later manifestations. Despite all rational considerations, the presence of professional baseball in Seattle somehow manages to invest the city with an air of achievement to which one vaguely assents, though without much faith in it and certainly without reaching for justifications for one's attitude. It is just there, even though one has not an iota of an economic stake in the scene, and though one may even have doubts about the validity of the batch of arguments served up to justify the ultimately successful efforts to prevent the departure of the team. No, one simply accedes, aware of his irrationality, to the feelings out of which all the rationalizations emerge, however much one may detest the owners and their styles of crisis, which extend from crass bullying to nauseous whining.

So one finds oneself on a side that, without an actual head count, appears to be the more popular one. This is a little surprising, and for two quite different reasons. One is that I do not go to many games, maybe four or five a year. And when one is in the stadium, one's awareness of the true delights of the game is woefully disturbed by the enforced horrors of the occasion: the endless ghastly noise, not the crowd noise, which is a part of the fun, but the official enforced noise: the ceaseless loudspeaker music, loudspeaker ads, loudspeaker video games of an infantile sort; the ghastly versions of the national anthem warbled, tickled, and vomited out by nightclub wanna-bes seeking originality with the most revolting sound effects; the sideline monsters, tedious and repulsive, evidently taken to be comedians; and the exhausting endlessness of a game that in the twenties was played in 80 to 100 minutes and now takes an excruciating 180 to 240 minutes even without extra innings.

The second reason for my surprise at finding myself among a multitude is that I was never one to be drawn to activities because they are popular, whether in the civic world or in the academic world in which I have spent a lifetime; in fact at times I have to forget about being on the "popular" side. Although most of my critical writing was in a mode that was "popular"—in academe, that is—for several decades in midcentury, I was not adjusting to a fashion. I was simply writing in a mode that was virtually instinctive: it was congenial without my thinking of it as being this or that. Hence I continued in it long after its popularity declined and academe, rather given to fashions, latched on to a new mode that I find uncongenial (a medley of novelties extending from "theory" and the "new history" to multiculturalism and political correctness). On the other hand I am in no way given to feeling independent by a perverse pursuit of the unpopular; indeed I tend to feel uncomfortable if I seem to be, even inadvertently, a camp-follower in a popular movement. Some years ago, in fact, I voted for a project that the area in general was strongly for, and academics in general were very dubious about—the construction of the big indoor sports stadium, now the Kingdome, that would make major-league professional sports possible in Seattle. I sort of slunk around looking inconspicuous, guilty of siding (and again only directed by some vague instinct rather than rational case-making) with a popular majority rather than with the much smaller, but bound to be right-thinking, intellectual minority. Then it helped a little when a distinguished geneticist (the kind of scientist who is likely to be a member of a string quartet rather than a sports fan of any kind) told me that he had voted for the structure. I almost fainted. Then he explained: "Not until we have professional sports in this town will we have decent places to eat." Here at least was a rational justification for an action that for me was only vaguely instinctual. The project gave me no chance for or sense of any personal gain or growth. I was only an unidentified figure in the multitude of the anonymous who would apparently feel better about the world if we built a stadium that could make local big-league teams possible and, more recently, if the baseball team stayed here rather than left. I was participating in a kind of community feeling that it was impossible to rationalize or to crown with a laudable motive.

iv

I have meant to record, without either justifying or crying *peccavi,* a series of connections with baseball hardly susceptible of rational placement, connections that range from the minor conspicuousness of being a high-school team manager to the absolute anonymity of sharing in nonrational community attitudes in later life. I only describe, without a major effort to place it, a mode of conduct and attitude that I suspect is not unique. One makes small tentative efforts, of course, toward rationalizing the non-rational. So I have spoken of the sense of belonging. Yet that sense is not a universal possession; some people so despise belonging that they practice conspicuous withdrawal (sometimes, of course, into limited communities of antibelongers). Baseball, I suppose, is one symbol of a generally successful secular world especially attractive in an age in which secularity itself has achieved almost religious status. Belonging to "the world" may have a subcutaneous attraction to one who grew up in a parsonage and was led by truly fascinating high-school studies into pre-Phi-Beta-Kappa-hood. Doing well in these studies, themselves, of course, might have given one a very significant sense of belonging. I have always felt sorry for subsequent generations of high-school students who, deprived of the requirements that blessed our early education, cannot know that marvelous sense of important insidership that came from knowing Latin, French, algebra, and English classics. And in the early decades of this century it was still possible to think of parsonage life as making one an insider in the most significant of all larger worlds. I am sure I had a sense of belonging in these ways, but I apparently felt some urge toward other memberships. There was, for instance, the kind of membership conferred by being able to dance, and I took what must have been the large and difficult step of getting myself from parsonage to dancing school (and just in the year before the baseball connection). This step meant not a revolt against, or a resignation from, the traditional family membership in the church world; it was just doing something that it seemed gratifying to do, though no prior generation of the family had ever done it. It took me a long time to feel easy in it. Later it became spontaneous, and one felt delight in doing it well. I still recall a dancehall event that took place when I was into my forties. A friend of ours, a sister of the dance-band leader (a star in the older jazz), told me that her brother had said to her, "Who's the big guy from the U? He surely knows what he's doing out there." It was a kind of honorary degree in worldliness, and an increment to whatever status one may have supposed one had by hereditary membership in the realm of otherworldliness.

I have spoken of belonging. But maybe it was not so much belonging in itself as it was a satisfaction from different kinds of belonging. The quantitative principle? Of course one hopes not. Or enlargement, to return to another term I used earlier? Possible, if the new gives one some individual status. But hardly applicable when one is just another anonymous member of an equally anonymous mass of people who irrationally want a third-rate baseball team, the stepchild of various sad owners who don't know about toys, not to move to another city. In sum, I irrationally assented to a world that I did not rationally consent to. Here I end a bemused set of glimpses of myself in a series of baseball connections, mostly peripheral, over the years. *Bemused* is the right word. In that condition one escapes truisms about the great national sport, a magniloquent phrase that signifies nothing. And I note with relief that I have said nothing about fathers playing catch with sons, and nothing about village greens. Or even a field of dreams. Bemusement is a good hedge against the going sentimentalities.

3

Football

An Addict's Recollections and Observations

"The real character of a man is to
be found out by his amusements."
—*Joshua Reynolds to Samuel Johnson*

Although, long ago and in a minor way, I had some formal
connection with baseball, it was never a primary object of
such interest as I felt in sports. In later years, I was fortunate
enough to have a friend who had season tickets for the home games of the
Seattle Mariners and who would occasionally take me to the games, and I
would have a good time there with him. But it was football that for many
years was my true love, and that persists even in years supposed to make
one sadder and wiser.

I saw my first football game in the autumn of 1918, and I have been
hooked ever since. That game was played by the eighth-grade team of the
Cottingham School in Easton, Pennsylvania, then a city of some thirty thousand. A few months before, we had moved to Easton from Elizabethville, a
town of one thousand, where the only sport, basketball, had just been
introduced. The adventurous new principal (fresh out of some normal
school, and now in charge of our single-building, twelve-grade school)
had put up a couple of basket standards, doubtless appropriately distant,
on the more even part of a sloping and lumpy playground outside the
school. The most agile boy in the upper grades, Art Hoffner by name, was
our hero: he made the school team, otherwise composed of high-school
students. Our interscholastic season began and ended with one game in
the spring of 1918. It was against Lykens, a larger school a half dozen miles
to the east. Lykens won, something like 28–4. It was a sobering occasion.
Some sage commentator doubtless said, in whatever was the going jargon,
"We must reconsider our priorities."

In Easton, the team-sport operation seemed, in contrast, very knowing and sophisticated, for a number of eighth-grade teams played some sort of schedule. (I can still remember hearing the school principal and the boys' eighth-grade teacher, C. S. Felmlee—who always frighteningly aimed his beady black eyes and bushy eyebrows over the rim of his glasses—using the classroom wall-phone to call another building about a game.) I suppose that some schools had a kind of faculty supervision, but at Cottingham, as I remember it, the boys put it together themselves. Hiram Shook, the quarterback, a genial cross-eyed boy with sturdy bowlegs, was one of the leaders, along with George Lutz, a tall backfield man. They were always trying to draft "big" boys for the team; even then, size was a basic value. A boy named Shaneberger (which is a Pennsylvania Dutch form of Schönberg, so I always think of him and Arnold together) already wore long pants, so he may have looked bigger than he was. He was teased into playing somewhere in the line, but he didn't have the sort of recklessness that often made classmates like Jim Sandt and Ster Watt good players. Each man provided his own equipment, if any. I remember seeing some cleated shoes and some pads. No headgear. Officiating? Probably by an informal committee of nonplaying squad members. The gridiron? I suppose an agreed-upon segment of public playing field at Twelfth and Northampton Streets, in those days a weedy and uneven area without a shred of the equipment that today seems needed to make any kind of play possible and bearable by boys and girls. The game-action that comes to the mind's eye is like that of touch football now, but the ballcarriers had to be tackled. Blocking was called "interference." I can still hear some heroic back snapping, "All right, you guys, where the hell was the interference?" That was tough talk then.

Cottingham played three schools that aroused different kinds of emotions. The South Side school was in a working-class area, and the boys from there were expected to be hardy combatants. But Francis March—named after the first American philologist, who taught at Lafayette College from 1857 to 1906—was on College Hill, a more well-to-do residential area, where relative affluence was supposed to render the youth milder than we more moderately circumstanced lads—a view infrequently sustained by the realities of combat. But then there was Taylor: it was in a part of downtown where there were several foreign neighborhoods and which today we would call "inner city" or "ghetto," though neither would have been applicable then. Anyway, to those of us in the "West Ward"—the Cottingham area, a middling sort of section without great heights or depths—the Taylor team seemed like a hatchet squad of Goths, Vandals, Turks, etc. They had a ballcarrier named Leon Burton, a black who really was what no man is—an island in a sea of whites; he was very fast, was said to be very tough, and became a great psychological threat to the opposition. "I'm not afraid to tackle him," quoth Les Eschenbach. But the one ballcarrier that I can still see making a long run is Leon Burton, followed by a train of ineffective pursuers of whom I thought (not censoriously, for I knew that if playing I would be among them) that they preferred chasing the guy to getting in front of him. Leon then disappears totally. Did he go to work instead of high school? Or move elsewhere? Or peak that early? Sad thought. Besides Burton, I remember one other player who had an instinct for the game, or at least for achievement through the game. He was Dinny Sullivan (baptized, I think, "Justin," which was not yet the rather faddish handle it would become), a gentle-faced, red-curly-haired boy marked primarily by a deformed leg and foot (polio?) that made him limp badly. He was a ballcarrier, and he ran with a passion that wonderfully compensated for the defect; I can still see that mild face tensed up in a sort of fighting twist that told the opposition, "Get out of my way or I'll wreck you." To me he was the soul of enviable fearlessness.

I can't remember who won the games we played. What I do remember, and with undiminished clarity, was the singular immediate charm of a game I had probably not heard of six months before. No need to go into analytic guesswork sixty years later. True, we kids all liked wrestling and running; in football they came together, and in a good cause, and heroes emerged. But theories are futile. The fascination was simply a fact.

During my years there, 1919–1923, Easton High football was coached by James B. "Pat" Reilly, a lesser local businessman who was forced out some years later when, in one of our characteristic surges of puritanism, coaching was restricted to teachers of academic subjects (a bit of theoretical virtue that did not always improve either coaching or teaching). Pat was a local hero who must have been some kind of football genius; he took the innocents who came to him—no recruiting then—few of whom ever made it in college, and turned them into teams that were steadily successful, winning say six to nine games a year. Now the informality of the eighth-grade games was superseded by organized scenes, not much changed in fifty years. The players had uniforms, which now look strange in old photos: heavy pants and shirts, less bulging pads than now, high shoes and full-length stockings, and soft leather helmets (without face masks) that fitted close to the head and seemed to peak up in a strange way (some heroes still disdained helmets, which became mandatory only some years later). I can't remember injuries; it seemed like an act-of-God disaster when Win Brunstetter, a neighbor of ours, got a broken leg when acting as a dummy in a tackling practice. There was organized cheering under cheerleaders who presided over special student assemblies to teach us new cheers for the upcoming games. The school band was outfitted simply in long pants and sweaters in school colors, only later to give way to ugly-ornate monstrosities that seem to get more hideous over the years. The marching band mostly marched, the music was mostly marches, and these were mostly by Sousa (whom I occasionally heard direct his band at Willow Grove Park outside Philadelphia); I never heard "The Stars and Stripes Forever" without also hearing, as if it were part of the music, the *plump* of foot on ball in punting practice and seeing the arc of the ball on its way. We had big games against Bethlehem and Allentown, who could always be suspected of evil machinations, especially in the days when Allentown had an irresistible back named Andy Leh (rhymes with "day"). A game with Mt. Carmel, a coal-mining town, was a terror. Carmelites would obviously be blackface demons, probably "foreigners," charging furiously out of the mines, hard as the rocks they drilled, intent on pounding our nice boys into coal dust. When they ran onto the field they held up their arms in a Popeye muscular display, and several shook their fists threateningly at us who stood by the entrance gate. What a ploy! Clearly the game was to take on the larger form of Good versus Evil, that paradigm which hovers over football more than any other sport. (The game was a sturdy affair; either we won 6–0, or it was a 6–6 tie.)

But the titanic event of the high-school football year was the Thanksgiving Day finale against P'burg (Phillipsburg), just across the Delaware River in New Jersey. An invading force from alien New Jersey was exotic by definition, and therefore ominous. All the regional bootleggers operated in or out of P'burg, and that implied a team of criminal dimensions which would be the ultimate test for the Easton Galahads. Besides, a fertile P'burg family named Bianchi kept producing halfbacks of notable wiliness and untrustworthiness on the field; so the very name *Bianchi* come to connote unscrupulousness and mysterious danger. (It was very charming to learn, many years later, that the author of the *Inferno* belonged to the Bianchi who as Ghibellines were exiled.) As many P'burgers as Eastonians came to the game, and they made a terrible noise that was in itself a terrible threat to the Pennsylvania good and true. Finally, when the P'burg band opened up with its fight song, the very sound of it had sinister implications. Only some years later did I recognize the tune as that of the Notre Dame fight song. No wonder the music voiced invincibility.

In view of the manifest heroism of the Easton High team, it was incredible that a local reporter should crassly accuse Alan Chidsey of a "bonehead play." Alan was the quarterback in the days when the quarterback played safety on defense; Alan had caught a punt on his own three-yard line or something like that. Later he played at Union College, which, in Schenectady, N.Y., seemed an inexplicably distant site for an education when a much better one seemed clearly available at Lafayette up on "the Hill." Alan's successor at quarterback, Fred Veile, did not, I believe, go to college. Fred was a jolly, curly-haired boy, a personal charmer alleged to have problems on the scholastic side. Maybe so, but he once made a crack which, of modest graffito intent, was a grammatical triumph. We had just been introduced to dangling participles (are they still introduced in good academic society, I wonder?), and Fred gleefully coined a wonderful example, better then he knew: "Dangling between his legs, Archie Brotzman bawled out the class." (Brotzman, baptized Floyd, was a brazen-voiced geometry teacher much given to drill-instructor tirades aimed at both classes and study halls.)

ii

Lafayette had a good four years (1923–1927) too (first under Doc Sutherland, who then went on to his alma mater, Pitt, and then under Herb McCracken), occasionally in competition for, and at least once claiming, a regional championship (in 1926 the team was undefeated and scored 328 points to 37). A few big names contributed glory. The famous Doc Elliott, who would have quite a career in pro football, was a rampaging fullback for a year; unfortunately he did not limit his rampages to the field, and my recollection is that his premature departure had to do with some grievous injury he inflicted upon a trolley car. Charlie Berry '25 was twice an All-American end in the Walter Camp days; his future improbably combined two kinds of dual role—player in both pro football and pro baseball, and then baseball umpire and football referee in the big leagues (no longer possible, I presume). Rabe Marsh, quarterback in our senior year, had a different career: he would become a federal judge. In 1924 the Lafayette halfbacks were Frank Kirkleski and Frank Chicknoski, who gained a breath of immortality in some verse in a Philadelphia paper (the *Bulletin,* I think):

> The longest forward pass e'er thrown
> Toward any mortal goal
> Kirkleski threw, Chicknoski caught:
> It sailed from Pole to Pole.

We would break in with, or get a rest with, Muhlenberg, Moravian, or Franklin and Marshall. The giant foes were Pitt, W. & J., Colgate, and Rutgers. Pittsburgh, about three hundred miles to the west, meant a pretty good trip in those days; if we were to bum (thumb) our way there, we had to start on Thursday. Two nights on the road could be costly; some of us licked the problem by stopping at small-town lockups and asking to share a cell for the night. I can't recall being turned down. In fact, my only clear recollection is of a not very soothing night on a bare metal bunk, my slicker (the current argot for raincoat) folded up to make a pillow, and the air rent by the snores of a drunk we were locked in with. If we did not go to out-of-town games, we spent game-time in front of a newspaper office, watching a long narrow board on which a small moving sphere, like a counter on an abacus, denoted visually the location of the ball while the plays were announced in bunches by a voicy man with a megaphone. He read from slips typed by the newspaper Morse operator translating the incoming spurts of dot-dash reports from the field. There was a lot of room for mistakes, and we street people didn't quite trust good news until it was confirmed by a run of subsequent plays, and we could always hope that bad news would be killed by a follow-up correction.

At home games I often had some sort of errand-boy job around the press box. In high school I had broken in as a reporter on the *Easton Free Press* and was now the Lafayette College reporter for that paper, in time covering various sports but in football only the unmistakable breathers. I was a natural hanger-on in news circles. The March Field press box was part of the top row in the not-very-high wooden stands: maybe room for twelve or fifteen people under a leaky board covering. Sometimes I had the job of play-calling: the p.a. system of the day was no more than a megaphone through which, standing in the aisle at the end of the press bench, I bawled down along the row, as loud as I could, the name of the ballcarrier and maybe the tackler. I was probably my own spotter; I am not sure. Spotting had problems; numbers were only on the backs of uniforms, they did not yet denote positions, and they were provided only for the top echelon of players (about fifteen to eighteen, I'd guess), so that if things got relaxed enough to let second-string troops into the fray, you'd have a number of numberless to identify. That was really not difficult if you covered practices more or less regularly, memorized the depth chart, knew precisely who had to be coming in at a certain position, and had studied the players enough to gain a sense of physical build and movement that would help in spotting the anarithmetics. Such sophistication I simply had not mastered, though I must have had the usual journalistic sense of knowing more than other people. Besides, I tended to err because of excitement over the plays that I was supposed to decipher with icy detachment.

Images: despite the conventional picture of single-wing play as power-oriented, both halfbacks throwing passes, and even passing to the quarter-back (who was then a blocking back, and as a pass receiver, I suppose, was like the fullback today). The occasional sixty-minute player. The pre-Goliath days: in my senior year the center (and hence defensive linebacker) on an undefeated team weighed 165. A Muhlenberg player, after a lopsided Lafayette win, throwing his helmet on the ground and jumping on it in frustration (a dangerous catharsis with today's crash-proof helmets). Pregame "pep smokers," where the air was so laden with nicotined school spirit that today it would be expected to produce instant mass lung cancer, though then it still permitted the bellowing of heartening predictions, notably by old local-boy faculty members, of a horrible fate for the opponent we were smoking against. I remember one old Pennsylvania-Dutch-accented vessel of "college spirit" stumping out, "Ve vill push them" (pause and cheers), "Ve vill run through them" (pause and cheers), "Ve vill pass over them" (pause and cheers), "Ve vill slaughter them" (prolonged thunderous cheers), etc. etc. etc. Monday-night bonfires to celebrate exceptional victories (perhaps one a year): wood and cardboard collected from stores and private donors, stacked twenty feet high, kerosened and sent roaring, the crowd emotions shaped and drawn out by orators, cheerleaders, and the band (Sousa and "Way Down in Easton There's a College), and then doubtless the Alma Mater at the almost whispering ember-end of the gladiatorial vespers. In four years, the most manic source of a pyrolatrous jubilee was the W. & J. game of 1926: down 10–9, a first down on its own twelve, and two minutes to play in the fourth quarter, Lafayette somehow made it—two long passes by McGarvey, a chunky '27 classmate who was a second-string halfback (for many years a doctor in Buffalo, N.Y.), to inside the W. & J. five, and then a series of offsides by W. & J. and two-foot plunges by Tuffy Guest, the sophomore fullback from Chicago, who finally got over as time ran out. Monday morning Tuffy was quietly helping stack wood for the celebratory blaze. We were both on the Student Council, which in those days had not graduated from the fulfillment of ceremonial to the evisceration of curriculum.

The climactic season-closer was invariably the Lehigh game (Lafayette-Lehigh games outnumber those of any other traditional college pairing)—an event joyfully preceded by mutual solemn accusations of effeminacy, crudity, sogginess, brutality, simplemindedness, wily treacherousness, and other failings to be shown up, and vices to be scourged, in combat. Unlike now, Lafayette was generally winning then. But 1924 was ominous. In the week before the Lehigh game, an apparently thriving Lafayette team has undergone some mysterious psychic cave-in—in itself one of the fascinations of football—against Rutgers and got murdered by something like 50 to 6 (I think the Rutgers hero was Homer Hazel, whom it seemed suitable to deride because he was oversized, overage, and, worse than that, married). The outcome was so improbable that it was virtually a laugher for us incredulous sideliners. Well, surely this would be Lehigh's year. But the team was taken off to a prayerful retreat somewhere in the mountains, underwent spiritual recuperation, and came back to wade and mush through a barnyard field still being flooded by a two-or-three-day deluge, and ooze home 6–0. Probably no fire Monday.

I said I was hooked on football. These somewhat detailed, though still selective, recollections should make that point in a concrete way that all the best abstractions in the world, even generously laced with hyperboles, could not do. One is not hooked because one remembers; one remembers because one is hooked. Like a stereotyped fiction, however, the story has a reversal or peripeteia, and then another: this might create a double-twist effect if everything were not so straightforward. For a few years after 1927, I fell short of being the madman in the stands, or being in the stands at all. Lafayette's undefeated season in 1926 had made most other teams seem hardly worthy of attention (a flawed addiction, clearly, though the flaw was conquered in time). As a teaching assistant at Tufts in 1927–1928, and an instructor at Ohio University in 1928–1930, I have little recollection of seeing games at either Medford or Athens. In retrospect I see that the rapid flow of undergraduate excitements was giving way to the slow grind of professional apprenticeship; a zest for many things, naturally cut back by the longer-term pace of adult work, may even have seemed out of place in a stadium, especially if the teams inhabiting it appeared little endowed with significance in the world (such as we felt at Lafayette, and as Wylie Sypher, a fellow teaching assistant at Tufts, had felt at Amherst). At Tufts, playing bridge of a Saturday afternoon probably seemed a better way of evidencing Mind. At Harvard in 1930–1931 and 1933–1934 I simply had no money. Tiny Bolich, a Lafayette classmate then in Harvard Business School, took me to a Harvard-Indiana game, but I can't even remember who won. During Harvard years, my football was mostly playing touch, especially during many weekends with the generous Wylie Sypher in Auburndale. But at the University of Maine, 1931–1933, and more sharply in 1934–1935, the second peripeteia took place, and I began getting to games again. Perhaps, even with the Ph.D. still hanging over me, the road ahead was clearer, the uncertainties of adjustment were fewer, and one unconsciously felt freer to yield again to an addiction even though it was shared by none, and regarded as infra dig by some, of one's peers. Probably a class in English for forestry students, who included a number of players, sent me back to the stadium (after all, Maine played only about seven games, maybe only three at home, and the season ended the first week in November). I remember one gorgeous Saturday afternoon when a sleet storm depopulated the stands, which were never well populated anyway, and I could move along with the team and see—and hear—every play from the head linesman's position. However, the true lifelong surrender to the drug was a post-Ph.D. affair—season tickets for 1935–1947 at Louisiana State, and ever since then at the University of Washington (where one vital privilege, faculty-rate tickets, is not canceled by emeritization).

iii

At LSU there was little of that comfortless discouragement of addiction—a succession of losing seasons. Outright championships were rare, but the Tigers were pretty regularly in the running, and in my day they made several bowls, Orange and Sugar. In 1935 the tailback—a BMOC and well-balanced survivor of hero worship by the late Huey Long (assassinated a few weeks before the start of the season)—was the brilliant Abe Mickal, later a distinguished professor of medicine. A succession of tailbacks became big-name professionals—Steve Van Buren and Yelverton Abraham Tittle in pro football, and Alvin Dark in pro baseball; likewise such ends as Ken Kavanaugh and Gaynell Tinsley. LSU games were virtually all played at night; true fans took in the afternoon Tulane game in New Orleans and then filled a half-dozen small trains that got them to Baton Rouge in time for the night game, the trains coming to rest on sidings near the LSU stadium. The train was evidently a running cocktail party, so that by game time the traveling fans were in as good spirits as the Baton Rouge tribe, who between 7 and 8 came pouring out of parties that prepared them for the evening. (Tony Thomason, an instructor in English, once declared that game-day parties went on as if the party were the only thing in the world, until some bottoms-up type would suddenly awake to true reality and yell "Jesus Christ, we'll miss the kickoff," and everybody would practically tear the doors off rushing for the cars.) Such rituals meant a wearing Saturday, and by game's end the departing crowd would always leave behind quite a few bodies whose souls had wilted under the strain. "Poor people," our young son once said, "they are too tired to go home."

Football was a Louisiana passion; following the LSU team through the season was for many Louisianans like following an army at war against Evil Hosts. Now and then, after a major victory, the students might "declare" Monday a holiday and try to close the campus down (an effort at disruption with no tinge of the sinister that marked such efforts in the late sixties troubles). An instructor might welcome the day as extra time for work of his own, or resist being pushed around. My friend Alec Daspit, an alumnus of LSU and a Rhodes Scholar recently returned to teach political science, was in no way going to take anything from hooligans charging into a class already in progress: he raised a chair above his head and assured them he'd bring it down on all their heads if they didn't beat it. He was convincing: they did, and he didn't have to. In contrast with "Monday off" victories was that sad Saturday in 1937 or 1938 when LSU went to Nashville highly favored and possibly bowl-bound and was swindled, 6–0, by an artful dodger Vanderbilt team long given to untrustworthy practices of the "hidden ball" type: a fraudulent student-body right suckered in the whole LSU defense, and then found a lone interior lineman, made eligible by a shift, rose from the ground, where he had seemed to be flattened, picked up the ball slyly concealed beneath his rear, and loped to the left, going some thirty yards to score. The radio announcer to whom we were listening didn't get a picture of the play until after the game. I did not see that play again for forty years: in a pro game in 1979 some team used it twice against the Seattle Seahawks. It's always our decent boys who are patsies for such unscrupulous goings-on. Why can't we be clever crooks too?

My football habit was gaining on me. The first added intake was freshman games. (I remember once inveigling Cleanth Brooks and Red Warren to go along to an LSU-Tulane freshman game, all blanketed up against one of those arctic air masses that, from November on, occasionally slide out of the Canadian plains and down the Mississippi valley to the Gulf.) But I had to take the next step alone, like a solitary drinker: high-school games on Friday nights. In the South, these games were played by sturdy well-drilled youngsters who were fiercely competitive in a sport that was the best, and all but the sole, route to community honor, heroic status, and so forth. Night games on not very well lighted fields combined the gladiatorial and the mysterious, especially when the T came in. High-school teams pioneered it in that area, and observers as well as defenders needed quite a bit of time to distinguish quarterback fakes from actual handoffs (as even TV cameramen, after long experience, still do not always do). Trying to diagnose plays, and then imagine defenses against them, was an absorbing business. Slick Morton once said to me that against a rightly executed T there was no defense. Of course this might be said of any rightly executed offensive maneuver (what a terrible cliché "execution" has become!): in this case it alluded to a T not yet really digested by defensive coaches. They digested, as we know.

I got to know Slick, an LSU assistant coach, when the Mortons lived across the street from us. He was amiable to a curious "prof," and through him I managed a little more insight into coaching style, coaching life, evaluative methods and habits, scouting practices, and such matters, though only in the rather superficial way that a rank outsider, however willing, is up to. We got to one or two coaches' parties, wonderfully raucous affairs where native zest, intake capacity, boyishness, naïveté, realistic knowingness in a special world, immense technical sophistication, and a vast irony about the way things go in games and in the sport ("Jeez, the pulling guards didn't knock each other out once"; "Yeh, Bubba's gonna know right from left, any day now") mingled to produce a verbal clatter that combined platitude and insight, ordinary language, pungent image, and esoteric argot that might have come from a Delphic master of ambiguity. Now and then I would go to high-school games with Slick, and learned to sit behind the goalposts to get that lateral spread that gives you a view of holes and of defensive moves, of quickness or hesitancies, that you can never get on the sidelines. (Of course you can't tell whether the play loses three or makes thirteen, except for the crowd noise, and so you don't really get the end-zone habit, whatever may be said for it.) Once I went to New Orleans with Slick when he was to scout a Tulane game against some team LSU was due to play; he didn't say much, but made rapid jottings in a shorthand or symbolic system of notation that, as I gazed at it from the side, told me little of what he was observing.

Quotes from Slick will stay with me. Of Bobby Clegg, a very fast, light back at Catholic High, due at LSU the next year: "He'll be faster next year when we get him running right. We'll get him up on his toes." Of Ray Coates, a laconic tailback whom I had in class and who, I was relieved to find, could write at least passably: "Out there he's thinking all the time. When he's running the team, he's really trying to figure out what the best play is every time. Most of these guys are just trying to think of some play, any play at all." Of some wartime players (not the predraft sixteen year olds that we used many of, but the 4-F's): "I tell you, when you try to explain something to some of these guys, and you see the expression on their faces, you can tell why they are 4-F's." Of Steve Van Buren, when he got loose on a long run and then fell down short of the goal: "Oh, he got a bear on his back. They do that sometimes."

As tailback, Van Buren ran the team. (Slick: "Inside the ten, he was told to carry on every play.") The coaches had the signal-calling done by different backs—and sometimes, as I remember it, by a lineman—depending on the wits or "leadership" of the personnel, or in part on the theory that the play-caller would give his all to make the play work, especially if he had a blocking job that would be seen only by the bench, and not the stands. One rationale for having the tailback call plays was that, as a key man in virtually every play, he especially needed to get a quick grip on the play. Probably only people of my age can remember when he had to be a triple-threat man—run, pass, punt. Partly this was sheer convenience, given the substitution problems under the old tight rules. But it had tactical utility too: a triple-threater could run or pass off a kick formation, and above all he could do the quick kick, that great play which has virtually disappeared in our era of specialists. (On one occasion it must have seemed that only a first-string tailback *could* punt: Alvin Dark was out with a knee injury, limping badly on the sidelines; but they sent him back in to kick, and all he managed was about a twenty-yard-er, which would have seemed within the range of almost anybody on the squad.) Triple-threating went out with the long grinding historical putsch toward unlimited substitution and specialization, and passing and running got split between quarterback and tailback. But once the quarterback is specialized as a passer, there can be profit in one turn toward the older system: the running quarterback poses a new offensive threat. And the past is a little bit restored with the halfback pass, which has the ambiguity inherent in the multiple roles of the old-time tailback.

Coaches always talk about "fundamentals," but in terminology they are anti-Thomists, forsaking eternal realities for novelties of nomenclature that seem to have charm in themselves. Only the quarterback has remained a quarterback. The right half became the wingback, and then the flanker (also used of split ends), and then the wide receiver (but all three terms still have some currency). The left half became a tailback (still used) and then a running back, and the fullback a running back; and of course "running back" may be generic for a ballcarrier as opposed to passer and receiver, or a specific for the speed man as opposed to the power man. Then there are the "set backs" and the "up back." For a while at LSU the coaches were denoting the positions only by numbers ("No. 1 back," "No. 2 back," and so on), and when I went to the Wisconsin–Michigan State game in Madison in October 1979 I found the printed program formally listing various types of Wisconsin backs as "x," "y," and "z." Clarity? Novelty? Convenience? Democracy? These innovations without radical novelty are fascinating. They parallel exactly the professors' fondness for renaming old ideas and thus creating a series of avant-garde "in" vocabularies in which one must operate if he is to feel with it.

I can't remember when the huddle came in. For a long time it seemed to me to give up spectacle and game-flow for a presumptive gain in efficiency. It had been an inherently pleasing part of the game to see, and hear, the quarterback, cupping his hands around his mouth, yell "Formation right" and then follow up with numerical and verbal symbols meant to define the play for the offense but tell the defense nothing. But one got used, as one does, to new ways; one could even learn to sense the huddle as a tension-producing factor in a continuous movement. For a long time, many years ago, Vanderbilt imaginatively used the huddle itself for spectacle by coming out of it in an organized single file, unwinding the original circle, gracefully S-curving toward the ball area, and then sliding into play formation, everyone in from one side, linemen first, and then backs, thus:

Pity such a suave movement did not last; it might have had the tactical utility of half-hypnotizing the defense forced to observe the double ominousness of an uncurling snake and an Indian war dance. With the cycles often found in football history, the ancient signal-calling style is now partially restored, through the "checking off" and "audibilizing" at the line—pro quarterbacks expected to do it, and college quarterbacks more and more free to. It may merge the best of two systems.

Brought up on the excitement of seeing the center pass the ball to different backs, I found it hard to get used to seeing the quarterback lean into the center and get the ball by an unseen short lift. The charm of the single wing, and of its lesser sibling the double wing, had held for decades, and one almost felt able to shed a ceremonial tear at the last fatal gasp of the system at Princeton not too long ago (fifteen years?). In spite of certain advantages in the T (the quick openers, the fakes, the concealment), it often seems cumbersome, especially in pass plays other than the quickies from a step back. One wonders whether it will have run its course, since now there is some evidence that, as with signal-calling, there are reversions to the earlier system. The obvious one is the Dallas third-down "shotgun," which Dallas manages with some variety (using it on second, not using it on third, not throwing off it); I'm surprised that there has not been more experimenting with this kind of thing. Oddly enough, this is the only variation in the position of the quarterback in many years, whereas there has been an unending stream of variations in the placing of the other backs (the T, from "full house" to "split T" and "wing T"; the "i," as "power i" or "split i"; the "y," the "wishbone," and the "veer," all of these capable of being suddenly produced, or deceitfully deformed, by multiple shifts, including back-in-motion in different varieties). One gets used to all of them and to what they make probable in both offense and defense. But any faith in one system as such is limited by the awareness that in the end all depends on the players' general talents, their specific skills, and above all their state of mind on game day—that ultimate intangible but conspicuous determinant of how things go.

iv

In my thirty-two years at the University of Washington, Washington has won 173 games, lost 151, and tied 10. In one season we won only one game, in three seasons only two games, and in six seasons only three games; in other words, in ten seasons we didn't even get up to the fifty-fifty mark, which I often told myself, and others, a rational person ought to be content with. Overall we were just about fifty-fifty; seventeen seasons with more wins than losses, twelve with more losses than wins, and three even-up. Being a fan here was not like being a fan at Notre Dame, Alabama, and other such places—oh those spoiled unworthy people, enviable to the last drop by which the quarterback would run out the clock. It was a comedown from LSU. There was another difference: at LSU "everybody" took in football; in the Pacific Northwest there were so many other things to do that football was just one of many Saturday activities. In the UW English Department, which once numbered ninety full-time people, football fans hardly numbered more than five or six (even after we had managed to appoint a former college end and a college quarterback who had gone on to get their Ph.D.'s in English). I don't think I ever felt really defensive about football, but it is possible that being in so small a minority, which one could hardly construe as an elite, contributed to an unconscious defensiveness. I remember telling some colleague—a nice person who like many professors equated indifference to football with a more civilized spirit but was civilized enough not to say so—that the pleasure of watching football was like the pleasure of watching ballet. Was I promoting myself spiritually? It could be. Aside from motive, however, the comparison still interests me; it is a half-truth, and the problem is to spot the other half. Music aside, the synchronized group movements, which one can see most clearly in a sweep, a fanning out of receivers, or even in flea-flicker patterns, afford the pleasure evidently inherent in an organized flow and design in which skilled and disciplined bodies work together. In ballet, of course, the interdependent movements are an aesthetic end in themselves, whereas in football they are instruments of battle; but the better the movements are carried out as military maneuvers, the greater their aesthetic quality (when one man's bad timing disrupts a pattern, the failure produces aesthetic incoherence as well as offensive breakdown). The ballet pattern, of course, evolves continuously, whereas that in football is brief, and it often ends in individual ad libs foreign to ballet. But in football the major addition to the balletic quality is of course the physical contact. Ballet is, or should be, utterly without contact beyond that of dancers as dancers in the traditional movements such as lifts, supports, and so on; in actions of the characters represented by the dancers, contact has to be mimed or ritually represented; nothing works against the ballet spirit as much as actual blows would, or as actual embraces and kisses do (not to mention the contortions in joint routines more like wrestling than dance). But in football, contact—from a brush block to a gang tackle, and from the strenuous effort to make it to the straining effort to evade it—is of the essence. I suspect that some of the charm of football lies in this paradoxical combination of relentless physicality with inherently pleasing movements that for identification we call balletic, of brute strength with acquired grace, either of which may dominate any moment of the game, but neither of which is long found without the other. We need to seek out such paradoxes if we are to escape from the simplistic clichés of media and of bystanders summoned to depose.

Twenty years ago, while trying to deflate the clichés mainly relied on by both defenders and attackers of football, I wrote that any discussion must begin with knowing how football works emotionally or psychologically. I made a proposal: that for both participants and spectators, football means "a kind of working off of latent savagery," or "in Aristotelian terms . . . a catharsis of savagery." This will not do for people who believe that we have left savage instincts far behind us as human nature has experienced more and more "progress." Since I regard this view as a delusion, I stick to my original theory. However, I add modifications. One of these appears above: the theory that football provides some aesthetic satisfactions as well as caters to the human love of combat, that is, the warlike spirit. Now let me combine aesthetic experience and the war-making spirit in a different metaphorical account of football: football becomes a melodrama, and thus it affords the satisfactions of stage melodrama. Here I shift from the psychic or emotional experience to the dramatic form that incorporates it in certain definable ways. Melodrama has special attractions not present in other dramatic forms: tragedy involves self-inflicted disaster, which may be profound and ultimately exalting, but imposes on us a sense of worldly failure that we would rather avoid; and comedy means a certain tolerance of discordant actuality where satisfactions are possible, but where there are also imperfections not treated as remediable. Thus tragedy and comedy both demand of us a rather complex adult response. But melodrama is the form in which we have a straight out-and-out struggle with an opponent; no self-blame here (as in tragedy), and no putting up with a mixed world where much that cannot be changed must be lived with (comedy). A football game is always an unmixed, straightforward fight, and it always simplifies itself into a battle of good against evil. In melodrama we always identify with the good, and the opponents are rarely felt as morally neutral fencers in a test of skill; they are, or quickly become, the bad guys to our good guys. Ferocious violence by an opponent is vicious; by one of our own, it is the heroic application of the principles of the game. The enemy's "enforcer" or "assassin" is a criminal type who should be banned; our own is a sterling cop who is keeping his beat clean despite the nasty acts of hoodlums, ruffians, muggers, and others. When one of our guys is hurt, it is an injustice that cries for revenge; when one of their guys is hurt, it shows a rare sense of decency in the gods, and serves him right. (Of course, if he is hurt badly enough to be taken out, perhaps for the rest of the game, we convert our sense of relief into applause that assures the wounded that now we can admire him, enemy though he is.)

The enjoyment of this kind of melodrama, gratifying the old primitive beastie surviving relentlessly within the civilized soul, provides an agreeable three-hour holiday from the actualities of life that can rarely be given so pleasingly simple a theatrical form. Of course the same psychological structure is sought in professional wrestling, but there it is grossly obvious, and there is none of the sheer pleasurableness of ordered movement by multiple bodies that I have proposed is like that of ballet. And now, having seen how much the melodrama of football involves the little old id that will not down, and how that id steals from the superego an alien moral stance with its separate gratifications, we are ready to appreciate more fully the paradoxical union of pleasures revealed by the balletic component in football: ballet charms us by separating us wholly from brute reality (it may be mimed, but the grace of the miming denies what is mimed), whereas the heart of football is letting the brute rip. Football, then, simultaneously takes the lid off the id and turns energy into form. It is the light fantastic plus the mighty fist, the graceful gestures plus the cruel blitz—in a word, (classical) art plus (unromantic) nature.

Besides giving neighborhood form to the eternal battle of good and evil, the melodrama of football offers another archetypal kind of pleasure: Jack kills the giant, David brains Goliath, the underdog plays the turning worm, and the low man on the totem pole bites the top dog. Thus we get the upset which we love as much as we love the form chart when we are among the top-ten types. When other loyalties do not rule, we are against the favorite. There is a whole colony of motives prodding us into this melodrama of the king killed, the dictator deposed, the system shaken. For one thing, we take pleasure in our own awareness of the intangibles, of a strange psychic flaccidity that may make Goliath freakishly vulnerable "on a given day" (the G-boys were "down after a hard game," they had "read the papers," and so on). The attractiveness of this pleasure is rather likely to make us think, after it has happened, that we have foreseen the upset. Stronger, however, is the moral ingredient in Davidism: victims, actual or destined, are always good by definition (any moral actuary knows that the Greeks had more no-goods than the Trojans), and so to be for the underdog is to pick the right side of the melodrama of good and evil when these combatants have not already been defined for us by some preexistent partisanship (of geography, personality, prejudice, or whatever). We enjoy a bouleversement of the bullies without general disorder, a revolution without a guillotine. Finally, and doubtless most of all, there is the sheer pleasure of the unexpected, especially when we have expected it; of course, the expectation of the unexpected has to be constantly defeated, so that the unexpected may remain itself and retain its ability to delight and thrill. The pleasure of the unexpected (provided we do not belong to that immoral gang, Goliath's cheering section) is manifest: it is symbolically the reversal of fate, the refutation of the ordinary actuality in which most of us spend most of our lives, honnêtes hommes more voting than voted for. But let Tulane upset Notre Dame, and we are on the road to becoming presidents, Knights of the Garter, or Nobel laureates.

Such satisfactions may be attributed to other sports by those who love them. There is one irreducible difference, though: football is the only one that brings into play so much skill and so much power, the chorus and the piledriver, aesthetic sense and id, Terpsichore and Mars. But my business is description, not glorification. Our subterranean pleasures cannot be translated into sales talk. Indeed, it is foolish to expand campaign oratory on a "substance" to which one is addicted; the addict out to make converts shows only that he hasn't much faith in the pleasures he attributes to his vice. That is one reason he is unconvincing. I find nothing more tedious than devotees of soccer or track or fishing holding forth on the modes of satisfaction that are supposed to render these activities irresistible to others. One should not suppose that his rational formulation of the obscure pleasures of addiction will so impress another's reason that it will direct his emotions until he comes to share the addiction.

Likewise with rational objections to a game that one is not addicted to. There are always rational answers to these, but they do not work. Why? Because each rational position is a would-be communicational form of an essentially nontransferable emotive state. Take the usual complaints about football by devotees of soccer, rugby, and hockey: that football is too stop-and-start, that it lacks movement, that it is "slow." This is almost invariably the accusation made by Europeans, brought up on constant-visible-flow games. My friend Rudolf Heberle, who came from Kiel to LSU, was a sociologist, and in his professional role he spotted football as a sociological phenomenon that should be inspected. So, unlike many Europeans, who tend to sample one game and then give it up forever (remembering only enough to keep reiterating those tedious jocosities—an especial vice of the English—about the fiendishly grotesque football uniforms, always assuming that one must share in their civilized amusement of these tasteless, pointless applications of the masquerade spirit), Rudolf really worked at it. But in time he confessed to me, more in sadness than in superiority, that he couldn't get with it; football just seemed boring. The main trouble, of course, was the quick ending of a play, followed by a moratorium of uncertain duration until the next play. Now I understand this objection completely, I know the rational answer to it, and even more I know that the answer cannot work for someone who is taking the game in only with his mind and who, however receptive he may wish to be, has not already felt it in his bones. The football fan's answer is that football is not discontinuous at all, that the interim between plays is not a cessation of movement but a shift to a different kind of movement, and indeed a very vivid kind. Between plays the spectator is not just sitting there and waiting, as any outsider to the game may be doing. Instead he is so busy that the interim may not seem long enough. He is doing at least three things: (1) completing the emotional response to the previous play; (2) evaluating the previous play critically ("It was a good call, but they loused it up"; "Do they have to come up with something as obvious as that?"); and (3), most strenuously, deciding what the next play ought to be—the most fascinating exercise of the interplay pause, a canvassing of options and possibilities, of ambiguities available for exploration, a guessing at an unexpected that will be better than an expectable unexpected—all in all, an imaginative effort that may not be complete by the time the team is trotting from huddle to line of scrimmage. This kind of interplay "movement" affords an extraordinary pleasure simply not available in the continuous-flow game. In this pleasure, one plays mastermind without responsibility, Napoleon without Waterloo; if everything goes wrong, it is the fault of some wretch not doing his physical job or mental duty. (My favorite short-yardage call is the quick fake buck into the middle, done with such sincere fury as to suck in all the defenders, followed by a two-man sweep, a naked reverse, or a quick flip off a bootleg, any one of these, of course, good for thirty yards. I can also see the problem: some eccentric defender, probably a cornerback, instead of being drawn in as a reasonable man would be, "stays home" and thus is there to ambush the surprise sortie.) But the finest statement of the pleasures of running the team safely in the stands is not an argument that can make converts. For the pleasure is simply not available to a watcher without considerable experience; one has to see hundreds of plays in scores of games to get that instinctive feel of things that makes the between-play interval a rich field for spectator mental movements. I have known only one exception to this rule. A young Englishman, Bill Dunlop, came to UW from Cambridge some years ago, and in a remarkably short time acquired a keen sense of what goes on in football, including even interior line play. On the other hand, even with a good deal of watching some years ago, I never got beyond seeing basketball as an exciting medley of individual skills and speed; I never learned to see the basketball equivalents of the T, the reverse, the draw, the screen, and so on, and without this sense of the forms of the game, I lost interest.

The lovers of the continuous-flow sports also claim for soccer, rugby, and so on, the pleasure afforded the spectator by the personal initiative of the individual player; he is not just a cog in a machine, a computer-programmed robot, but a living, thinking individual constantly faced with rapidly changing situations to which he must respond with a maximum of skill and genius. True enough. But that is simply one kind of pleasure, and I should argue that it is no greater than the pleasure afforded by the exact carrying-out of preassigned tasks by all the members of the team. Besides, football offers plenty of opportunities for unmechanized initiative, that is, for private enterprise. Think of them: the broken play, the intercepted pass, the fumble rolling wildly, the ballcarrier reversing his field (never mind the blocker), the unscheduled lateral, the unscheduled sneak. The pleasure afforded by what happens on such occasions is not a pure pleasure, however; what pleases is not the ad hoc or ad lib action itself, but its success. Its failure leads to groans, disgust, and the wish that such exercises of personal initiative did not come into it at all.

V

Up to a point one can enjoy the "form," the "art," the theater (the melo-dramatic experience), the rhythms almost objectively. But aesthete and partisan are not wholly separable. It is painful to see the graces regularly conjoined to unfriendly power. In the lean years at UW, as I have said, one was hard put to it to remain the equable, uncomplaining devotee, or to live up to my own rule of good sense, that a fifty-fifty season ought to satisfy a reasonable adult. (It was partial solace, in the years after the Wisconsin-Washington Rose Bowl game, when both UW's were in a decline that looked like a lingering incurable illness, to visit Madison and share lachrymosities with the addicts there. It was especially satisfying to weep with the Habermans—Fred was for many years the faculty athletics man at Wisconsin—for they, with Michigan and Ohio State looming up sinisterly as the Scylla and Charybdis of recruiting odysseys in their league, knew what it was to be in the same league as USC and UCLA. Over Fred's massive tutti-frutti old-fashioneds, erstwhile rivals could harmonize in a new funereal joy.) In theory one is a faithful admirer of Miss Right, and composes odes to her, but one tends to drift off and shack up with Miss Might. Sometimes it seems that she has brought Miss Right along with her, and thus created a lovely ménage à trois. Not all observers find it easy to reconcile this arrangement, and its implications of loose living, with certain utilities that football sometimes appears to have. A former president of the University of Chicago is reported to have said, "We have to get football back, or we'll have all the kooks in the country here." Whether he said it or not, the words are not without point: football apparently helps produce a widely representative student population that at the undergraduate level makes a better institutional society than does a highly specialized student clientele. Again, as the then President Boyd of the University of Oregon said at a College Board regional meeting at Portland, Oregon, in February 1980, football is one of the last emotional bonds among students, an almost solitary focus of general feeling, of sense of community, in a day when the university, and not only the outsized one, tends to be regarded as little more than an academic department store for course and degree shoppers. If these points have some validity, as I believe they do, they make a partial case for the maintenance of college and university football as long as the costs are bearable.

Now to return to Miss Might and the lusts that she inspires in many breasts: the severe problem arises when the values served by the presence of football are complicated by the values that accumulate around triumph. The joy of conquering, rather than being conquered (a common enough emotion), tends to translate itself into the idea that a "winning tradition" raises the general status of the institution. Somehow gridiron glory sunflowers out into a kind of halo over the place and all its doings. A university used to winning nine to eleven games a year, and to habitual "bowling," seems to have been diminished, if not actually disgraced, if it loses three or four games. The consequent rejoicing at other places that are regularly trampled on by the "top-twenty" giants only strengthens the conviction of the giant-worshipers that something has gone terribly wrong, that there has been a cosmic violation of truth, justice, and beauty. And among those not naive enough to suppose that gridiron mediocrity betrays some substantive university defect, a bad season, or certainly a series of bad seasons, may be felt as at least a PR misfortune. (Public responses being what they are, I was not surprised when I was told by a university president, who must be nameless, that in the year in which his school had advanced from so-so football to a major bowl game, the unrestricted gifts to the university were greater than in any other year. He felt it was no coincidence.)

Such extraordinary by-products of the simple-souled melodramatic love of triumph (which I admit I share) are responsible for a horde of clichés, problems, troubles, condemnations, reform proposals, and so on. Whether or not some past idol did literally say that "winning is everything," virtually every coach in the country feels compelled to repeat it or say something like it. The irony of it is that many coaches are pretty good ironists who know better than to attract the attention of the gods in such conspicuous ways. But when their sense of actuality surrenders to their sense of the expected, they not only sink in thought but sink into clichés (notably the ones that drive us to the basin a hundred times a year—"bottom line," "name of the game," "what it's all about"). I could almost say, "There ought to be a law," for if winning is "everything," then losing is "nothing," and thus to annihilate 50 percent of the thousand teams that play every week is dreadful nonsense. Of course the "everything" line may be only a worn hyperbole for "Trying to win is important" or "Winning is more fun than losing," but these are banalities or truisms that hardly require formal public statements. They are the opposite numbers of the clichés about "character building," which now happily survive, if at all, only as ironies: "character year" means "poor material, mediocre season." What is essential, and it seems hardly beyond the bounds of possibility, is that the official, ritual hoopla about football— the verbal formulas rolled out liturgically by hustlers to troops, alumni, and contributors—allow for getting beaten as a 50 percent possibility, as not intrinsically dishonorable, and as humanly survivable.

Since winning, or just avoiding destruction, depends on the talents of players who often have minor talent for education, keeping these warriors, often loosely called "student-athletes," academically eligible leads to various devices, letter-of-the-law schemes, slipperinesses, and skullduggeries that are either well known or suspected and ordinarily treated with deadpan silence or knowing winks. The mildest of these involve intra-institutional as- sists: (1) concocting courses that the lads can pass (such as "The Techniques of Football"); (2) identifying courses in the less abstruse academic fields that at best are not too impenetrable; (3) identifying instructors, whatever the fields (in one place I know about, it was Anglo-Saxon), who have kindly and vague natures given to putting the best construction possible on students' efforts; (4) employing special tutors supposedly skilled in pounding any required academic material into minds not always wholly receptive after the day's head-knocking (in the tutoring bureau in which I worked at Harvard one year, we were ordered to shout information at students during the hour or two meant to sum up the course for them). There are occasional rumors of more sinister goings-on, but in fifty years of teaching I have run into no cases of bribery and only one of attempted intimidation. This nonce-case is worth mentioning. One year a fellow alumnus of Lafayette got a job in the Washington office of intercollegiate athletics. Presuming on the Lafayette connection, he came to my house one Sunday afternoon (insufferable intrusion) to demand an end to failing grades that English instructors had been giving to Hugh McElhenny, the great running back. The nuncio said, glowering at me, "I don't think the regents of this university are going to take it lying down if the English department makes an All-American back ineligible." I don't think any other experience in a long life as department chairman made me as angry as I was then, and I am saddened that I can recall none of the verbal barbs that I would like to think I planted in this barbarian. All I can remember is sending word to instructors who did or might have Hugh as student—incidentally a rather nice guy—that naturally he would continue to receive whatever grades he earned and that if they were visited by any emissary of the athletic department, they should send the agent straight to me. None ever came. The original barbarian left the university after his first year.

No, the role of athletic officials who approached faculty—and that was a pretty infrequent event—was that of gentle salesman or defense attorney throwing a sinner on the mercy of the academic court. A more frequent experience was a sort of tearful wheedling by "student-athletes," an insinuating palpation to discover the secret entryway into your good graces, or your soft spot, or your sense of their undefined privilege (methods much more frequently used also by student-nonathletes). Once a defensive lineman at Washington, a literate man thinking of some kind of writing career, wrote me, instead of an assigned report, an account of his defensive skills. His rhetoric was that of facile journalese, with some pat parallelisms rather more sophisticated than standard undergraduate stumblebum prose. I remember a series of "I can's" that made him into a sort of giant superior to the petty needlings of class requirements. When I came to "I can read a trap," I thought, ever so smartly, "Yes, I can too, and you haven't read a book." So I stayed petty, and his grade greatly displeased him.

But one remembers such episodes because they are rather rare. The eligibility drives mostly take other forms. There is a regular curve of events in this sector. Low points of impropriety are the result of occasional doses of reform; they are followed by a rising "ARES Curve" (Academic Requirement Evasion or Simulation), as we social scientists call it. In time the curve shoots off the graph in hardly camouflageable scandals such as those of 1979–1980, when many players were found to be staying eligible through high grades in courses that they did not attend or that existed only in entrepreneurial pamphlets issued from some inaccessibly distant credit-factory making like a junior college. Then the curve takes what we call the "MARS Dip" (Moderate Awareness of Rules and Sanctions) and stays at a lower point until the "winning is everything" uproar, accompanied by a temporary siesta of once-victorious watchdogs in the doghouse, hots up the situation. Then we have another ARES upswing until the next crop of misdeeds ripens for a journalistic harvest (sheaves of profitable scandal tied up in the beautiful white twine of "Right-to-know-ism"), with resultant clangors of indignation and officials' resolves to absent themselves awhile from the felicity of innocence and to recheck the local granary of souls.

vi

It does not minimize the misdeed or deny the problems to say that what we have here is a very familiar kind of historical evolution in which two activities, lodged in the same institution or felt to be related parts of the same enterprise, develop contradictions or perhaps, as some critics believe, irremediable incompatibility. The athletics-in-academe tie-up is only one of several complex relationships that football has, as it were, stumbled or drifted or grown into. The multiple nature of football accounts in part for its expansion in, or its development of symbiotic ties with, other nonathletic institutions. Of course, the three principal ones are college, city or community, and communications. The relations may be dominantly or partly economic, but in any case the economic is greatly complicated by less tangible issues that are psychological or emotional—pride, convenience, pleasure, competitiveness. In preprofessional football the symbiosis is, as we have seen, with academe; in professional football, with consumer areas and the broadcast business. The ties may have been historical, unexpected, eyebrow raising, or paradoxical. The invariable medley of profits, probabilities, pressures, and problems is worth a look.

As far as the problems of football on campus are concerned, there are several approaches. One is the middle-ground, compromise, muddle-through approach: maintain the historical relationship by trying to adjust the machinery so that the decencies are not intolerably violated, accepting imperfections, and avoiding radical action in the hope that the imperfections will stay within bounds. Obviously this is the route that has been taken by most colleges and universities during the half century in which I have known the game at that level. It is the route of an accommodating worldliness, of democratic politics, and finally of comedy (which I may introduce because I have already likened the event in the stadium to a theatrical melodrama), with its characteristic ironic contemplation of a multifold actuality variously out of harmony with, but not determinedly antagonistic to, the ideal usually present in some symbolic way or other. It remembers both the possible and the desirable, and it has doubts about the absolute.

In contrast with this rather empirical style of keeping the old union going, however bumpily, there are several absolute therapies based on the theory that incompatibility has reached an ontological state that demands divorce. There is an idealistic absolute as well as a realistic absolute. The idealistic absolute is to throw football off the campus entirely—many of my colleagues in English would go for this[1]—or, at most, let it survive, if it can, with no budgetary life support, as an intramural fun-for-some. At various institutions the budgetary shrinking pains have led or will lead to the adoption of this absolute—the ironic influence of economics (as we all can see) upon ethics (as some see it). This mass-sterilization approach ignores, perhaps, the fact that some good may spring, as we noted earlier, from improbable loins. The realistic absolute, on the other hand, is to keep football but do away with the myth of the "student-athlete." There are two versions of this mode of divorce. One of them is, as far as I know, the brainchild of the ex–sports editor of the *Seattle Times,* Georg Meyers: his proposal is that universities establish a degree curriculum in "professional sports." This would divorce the athlete, for our purposes the football player, from the burdensome degree-requirement courses that are now the major stumbling blocks to eligibility (I never heard of an athlete's flunking a course in Coaching Football, or Teaching Football). He would spend all of his time in the lab, which for him would be the whole university. If one hesitates a little at this divorce, which still lets the parties occupy the same general premises (if not the same rooms), still one has to confess that the

---

1. After all, English teachers would remember that gross, brutal Tom Buchanan in *The Great Gatsby* was a former Yale end who had peaked at age twenty-one, that Tom was softened into nostalgic alcoholic in Brick Pollitt in *Cat on a Hot Tin Roof,* and that Biff Loman in *Death of a Salesman* had declined from star ballcarrier to bum. Later on, they could know that in Sam Shepard's *Buried Child* Tilden, once an allegedly great fullback, would in middle age seem a retarded child. An American myth of football-star-as-failed-adult seems in the making.

proposed course of study is no worse—no thinner, no less liberal, no less current-eventsy—than a number of others residing in the university. The other realistic absolute is one I formulated twenty years ago, which may have had other inventors even then, and which since then I have heard put forward by other theorists. It is this: let us regard football not as an extracurricular activity for which participants must be academically eligible, but as a university promotional activity totally divorced from classes and degrees. The only test of the participants would be the strength and skills that constitute football talent. They would have to pass nothing, for they would not go to class at all. In fact—and here is the rational ultimate of this utopian scheme—they would be *forbidden to take courses* unless they survived a five-part qualification series: (1) appearing before a notary public and filing a sworn statement guaranteeing, subject to penalty, attendance at all classes and fulfillment of all assignments; (2) appearing before a rigorous testing bureau and successfully passing severe tests of basic verbal and numerical skills; (3) undergoing a media interview and not once using the locutions, "uhh," "duhhh," and "y'know"; (4) appearing before a university moral officer and registering a monastic vow of painful dedication to the deities of learning; and (5) successfully carrying through a one-semester novitiate of one substantial course that would lab-test the potentialities indicated by success at the first four signposts, and determine whether the applicants had any vocation for learning outside of football. (The more I think about it, the more I see that such a test-and-probation series would be desirable for student-nonathletes too.)

A brief glimpse of football *in urbe,* or its symbiosis with city-and-country consumers. Among other things, football turns out to be cousin to another form of nourishment than that of mind on campus. I start with anecdote. During the long years of planning and proposing that led finally to the construction of the covered stadium, now called the Kingdome, in Seattle, we had to vote—twice, I think—on bond issues in support of the pre-ciprepellent arena. My own regular inclination to vote yes was unshared by many colleagues, especially the first-rate scholars and the right-thinking citizens who looked askance at the community's setting up a spot to dish out, well if not *panem,* or at least *circenses,* for the plebs. I tended to slink around saying little, or acknowledging my iniquity in a sort of don't-hit-me, Uriah Heepish defensiveness. Then one day a very distinguished scientist told me that he would vote for the Dome. When I had come to, he explained, "Not until we have professional sports here will we have decent places to eat." Now if I had been asked to estimate the impact of pro sports on eateries, I would have guessed: a hundred new fast-food joints, for after paying $10 to $40 for a football seat, no one would be able to afford more than dogs, burgers, and such. How naively wrong I would have been. For Seattle, once widely noted as a gourmets' Sahara, has in post-Kingdome days produced a hundred gastronomic oases, ranging from the straightforward to the elegant to the pretentious, from the native to the polyethnic, from Asiatic in a dozen costumes to, I am assured by an anti-football fancier of such cultural high spots, twenty-one French restaurants. Kingdoming and royal dining: coincidence of *post hoc ergo propter hoc?* The man who voted for covered sports to get culinary spots was a geneticist; apparently he read aright the information on the sociological genes. At any rate, here is a popcultic phenomenon that can be contemplated without any burden whatsoever of moral decision. Who cannot delight in the paradoxical fusion of functions—the Great Dehumanizer as the *Arbiter Elegantiarum?* (I pause to acknowledge lack of warmth for footballers who go around bawling about "dehumanization" and expect to be paid for their facade of ethical sensitivity. My heart leapt up when I beheld a rainbow in the rear—a bumper-sticker injunction: "Support Your Local Dehumanizer")

Finally, to move from a local to a national liaison: football and television, with television the well-heeled seducer, and football the agreeable lass who will do it any time of day or night that suits the money-macho overlord. Perhaps we should change the figure and describe TV as the "protector" who extracts money from the customers and passes some of it on to the wench football who might otherwise have to do business in a more piecework or cottage-industry style. The television intermediary has an interesting effect on the lusty consumers. It turns us from omni-sensory participants in the open air to withdrawn, dark-room voyeurs. "Do it again; I want to see it some more." The fascination of the replay, of slow motion, of the long-drawn-out satisfaction of the viewer's passion is very seductive. It makes us put up with a great deal from the announcers—the insufferable clichés, the perpetual babble, the constant failure to specify the only thing we're really interested in (down and yards), the documentary paragraph on an offensive guard's aunt's education when we're desperate to have an explanation of a puzzling penalty, the "message" that cuts off a crucial play, the fatty degeneration of language (why on earth say "they are now in a punting situation" instead of "they gotta punt"?).

vii

All these marriages and symbiotic happenings—shackings-up, live-in friendships, constant companionships, unforeseen "meaningful" relation-ships—between football and other ways of life, economic and educational

4

The Rail Way of the World

The record of passions in sports began way back, naturally. Another "way back" passion of mine had to do with railroads. In recalling it, I treat railway trips not only as a bit of past history but also as a mode of life—well, at least of the traveling life—that has something to be said for it. I willingly run the risk of being accused of nostalgia. Not all nostalgia is pointless.

I start, not way back at an ultimate beginning, but at an event that belonged to my early adult life. It was a big accident that happened early one August morning in the mid-1920s. A "DL&W" special train ("DL&W" and "Lackawanna" were oral shorthand for Delaware, Lackawanna, and Western, considered a major eastern line in the railroad age) was carrying "excursioners" from upstate New York to New York City. An excursion (*excursion* is a rare American example of the British style of using Latinate terms for common matters in the public domain) was a special-rate holiday trip, ranging in length from a day to a week (one-day excursions from Camden, New Jersey, to various seashore spots on the Atlantic coast were a great delight for youngsters living or visiting in Philadelphia). So joyous escape from ordinary life would have been the mood of the eight or ten cars of excursionists, bedded down or sitting up all night according to the price they paid, coasting through the August night toward the DL&W terminal in Jersey City. In western New Jersey some mainline tracks, at least eastbound, were being repaired, and the excursion train was detoured for a few miles over alternative DL&W trackage. Apparently no one had inspected the alternative route. There had been heavy rains, and in a cut some dirt had washed down over the rails. The wreck was one of the most spectacular in years. Scores of people were dead and mangled; ghastly end of a vacation jaunt.

I had some contact with this because I was then a reporter, and occasional copyeditor, on the *Free Press* of Easton, Pennsylvania, maybe fifteen miles from the accident scene in western New Jersey and the news center for the disaster. The on-site coverage was done by our senior reporter (almost a stage-and-novel type: he boozed, mastered dirty stories and cracks, whored, fondled the secretary, typed with a cigarette hanging out of one side of his mouth and his hat on the back of his head, raced to news scenes on a company motorcycle with a sidecar that he loved to lift off the road on high-speed turns). I did only peripheral office work on the story, but I managed to feel very close to it. It was my first experience of major disaster in the fascinating world of trains. Looking back, one might feel that one should have found some basic meaning in the event; narrative rules almost demand that one gain a more complex view of train travel, or of the risks inherent in peacetime life generally; that one have a sharper sense of possible disaster in any activities that diverge from routine. One did feel shock and pity, and one partly imagined what it was like. But one did not generalize, did not progress toward a sadder and wiser state, did not achieve a "there but for the grace of God . . ." illumination. One did not resolve to cut train travel to a minimum or, above all things, to avoid excursion trains. In fact, it was not long after this that a college classmate and I took a weekend excursion on a special Lehigh Valley train to Niagara Falls—an all-night sit-up ride to the Falls, a day at the Falls, and then an all-night sit-up ride back. Perhaps the ride itself, whatever the discomfort and weariness, was the major pleasure of the trip. One did not stay on intense guard against danger. No doubt one then felt that accidents happen to other people—not so much pure callousness as the shunting aside of reality that was possible in early years. I continued to envy a fraternity brother who had a glorious summer job as a dining car steward on the Black Diamond, the gem of trains on the Lehigh Valley. I kept looking forward to any train ride that could be justified by any reason or wish to be elsewhere. A grandmother lived in Philadelphia: one could make this trip by three different train routes or even a jolly over-hill-and-dale interurban that had most of the markings of a real train. Even in college years, when I in no way escaped the usual campus illusions of sophistication, I still enjoyed poring over a railroad map of Pennsylvania we had at home, a wall map about two and a half by five feet. Each railroad had its own color—the dominating Pennsylvania in red, the Reading (Philadelphia and Reading) in blue, the Lehigh Valley yellow, the Lackawanna brown, the Erie gray (or green?). Less extensive systems—and shorter lines were numerous then—were in black. The colors made the map a work of art (a retrospective judgment, of course); they enhanced the contemplation of geographic strangenesses, mysterious distances, unexpected relationships, all real and strong enough for one who had barely been outside the borders of the state. The curves of lines, their crossings, their occasional parallelisms—all these aspects of design were somehow pleasing, and somehow suggestive of natural conformations that had the charm of the unknown, an imaginable goal of eventual exploration in future times of expected but undefined freedom.

My addiction to this map began early—somewhere during early grade-school years. Maybe it followed an addiction to trains themselves, though there was probably a two-way effect in which one cannot assign primacy. Anyway, some quite early images of train life stay with me vividly. There were the inevitable rides on the local-line feeder train from Elizabethville, Pennsylvania, where we lived, to the main-line junction town of Millersburg, nine miles west on the bank of the Susquehanna. (I would learn of the Coleridge connection some years later, in college.) A lot of residents showed up at the Elizabethville station to greet the daily trains, four or six of them. The "chief burgess," as the town mayor was called, was to most of us a far less imposing figure than the locomotive engineer, in easy control of the half-threatening giant beneath him, leaning out the cab window, looking variously indifferent, contemptuous, or even indulgent under the visored cap that, plain as it certainly was, suggested that the wearer was at least a colonel in the railroad forces. It was our train, and it did not lack grandeur, even though its parts were only locomotive, tender, and a mixed baggage-plus-passenger car, with sometimes an extra car for passengers only. We were on the "Pennsy," as everyone called the Pennsylvania line, for us the premier line of the world. What sticks with me, from our rides on this train, is looking through the windowed front door of the coach at the rear end of the tender ahead and watching it in a sort of bobbing motion, as if the power units had independent habits of movement that still did not interfere with the steady forward movement of the whole train. There was something pleasing about that up-and-down and side-to-side oscillation; it was in some way a vital part of riding on that train. Did I unconsciously see before us a gigantic man-made version of the horse (I did not yet know the term *Iron Horse*), a creature that served us in front of the buggy but still had a mysterious, not always predictable, life of its own? Maybe.

At Millersburg we transferred to the grand main line of the Pennsy, upward bound from our one-track line to a magnificent two- or three-track affair, a world highway. On the station platform we waited nervously for the relatively long train roaring toward southeastern Pennsylvania from Williamsport, Erie, or even Buffalo, mysteriously distant worlds. Intimidating grandeur! Would we manage to climb on before the giant train ruthlessly pulled out, would we find seats together (there were five of us), would we be stuck in random singles up and down the car? Or even have to stand? Would any of us be lucky enough to have a window seat, and one on the right side where one could watch the meandering Susquehanna for a good part of the thirty-mile ride to Harrisburg? Harrisburg, as state capital, was mildly exciting—but not nearly so exciting as the Pennsylvania station there. It had several sets of two tracks each, bordered by concrete platforms at coach-door level—a delightfully sophisticated improvement on the situation at Elizabethville and Millersburg, where one had to struggle up from ground level to the almost-out-of-reach lower step of the series by which one mounted to coach-aisle level. If we were staying on the train, we could get better seats as other passengers left, and we could watch both the exciting flurry of crowds on the platforms and the movement of other trains pulling in and out. If we were going to Philadelphia, we might have to change or choose to change trains—a tense but exciting experience. If one chose, it was to leave a "local" or "accommodation" train and take instead an "express" or "limited" ("limited" seemed the ultimate in contemptuous speed, in triumph over slow motion and nonmotion; the "through" train par excellence). One sees in retrospect that "accommodation" was a skillful bit of PR for a hesitant stop-and-start train: we will accommodate all by taking all just where they want to go and pausing there, however minute the spot, to let them off (and others on).

The two- or three-hour run to Philadelphia was long enough to permit choices. If we found neighboring vacant seats, should we form a family nook by reversing one double seat (all seats were double—no single buckets then—and reversible)? Cozy, but some of us had to ride backward, which, to some hyper-raffiné characters, like me, seemed second-class citizenship. My ploy, to face forward, was to threaten carsickness, though this was more likely on an interurban with its rocking motion. Should we open a window or windows, always an enticing possibility in pre-air-conditioned days? The rushing air was great fun, especially in summertime; having a head or an arm out in it, despite warnings of decapitation or "disarming," a thrill; and cinders in the eye a worthwhile risk. And as long as elders were the laundry detail, blackened clothes and body perhaps made one feel quite adventurous. (In later unsupervised years one could feel quite devilish by standing on the open swaying platform at car-end, a bit of ostentatious boldness eliminated when car-joinings became, for passengers, internalized between accordion-pleated, quasi-leather borders of considerable griminess.) And how to resist the uniformed concessionaires (I remember "Western Union" on their caps, but this can't be right; they must have worked for some newsstand outfit—"Railway News"?) who peddled chocolate and other such goodies through the coaches? We knew how thin the family purse was. Did we beg or just yearn? Sometimes the peddler went through the coach laying a chocolate bar on each seat. Once we mistook this come-on for a handout. Discovering the truth almost spoiled the trip. But then there were the external excitements, the views, the places passed through and sometimes thrillingly announced. "Lancaster," "Coatesville," "Downingtown," sonorously rolled off official tongues, seemed to identify especially significant spots.

But the greatest of all such sounds was "Broad Street Station, Philadelphia." To detrain or entrain there was to worship thrillingly in a true cathedral of traindom. The high, arched glassed roofings created vast vertical space to match a horizontal spread great enough to accommodate a score of tracks, at least half of them always occupied by arriving or departing trains. The cathedral air was heavy with incense—steamy, some of it, but most of it the heady aroma of coal smoke. And the music was that, not of choir and cantors, but of pipe organ gods themselves, incarnate in the black reality of immense steam locomotives, vaguely felt to be benevolent (we did not play William Ellery Leonard to these locomotive gods), but always in their magnitude and power and volcanic possibilities a little menacing, as true divinities must be. They did nothing so vulgar as growl; rather they did highly rhythmical cantatas—each divinity a choir in itself—all in bass, baritone, and tenor. Resting after labor, they would breathe heavily in regularly interrupted hums: "dong-don, Cam-den, dong-don, Cam-den." But pulling out for other worlds they were in full musical glory, summoning creative strengths in slow-slow roarings from mysterious divine depths: "gorr-umph"—long pause—"gorr-urnph"—slightly less long pause—"gorr-umph"—and then gradually faster with a "groosh-groosh-groosh" and in time on to a steady deep-throat hum in counterpoint with the rapid percussion of steel wheel on steel rail. We soared in a divine polyphony.

Better to leave Broad Street Station that way than to walk out on Market Street looking for a streetcar. On the street there was plenty of clatter and gabble, but not a hint of station grandeur, such as we have now learned to call the "sacral."

Back to Harrisburg for a moment. There we might alter the adventure—a train trip was romance, never mere utility—by transferring from the Pennsylvania to the Reading. Any change of line was a glorious experience: the coaches might be of different colors, and this symbolized adventure in a wholly different world. The Reading station adjoined the Pennsylvania, and one got to it by an enclosed overhead walkway. The transfer had its own delight: it led to novelty, but one was still enclosed within the railroad world, wholly free from outside ordinariness. It was exploring the upper reaches of a cathedral, though without, as yet, any knowledge of the hunchback. Descending on the other side, we would take a train—its greenish-gray a shade less enchanting than the Pennsylvania red but still engaging because different—for Lebanon, where other relatives lived. It was less exciting than going to Philadelphia, but still a worthy train experience. Still better, when we were Lebanon-bound, was a more exotic route that wandered around in an intervening range of mountains; eastward from Elizabethville through Lykens and Tower City, and then picturesquely onward through Tremont and Pine Grove—all wonderful Alpine wilderness, followed by a descent through lesser-known backwoods country to the Lebanon valley. Besides, this route meant using some less-known local line—another touch of romantic novelty.

(Once arrived in Philadelphia or Lebanon, we gave up the thrill of movement for a standard heavy anxiety: when would the baggage come? A family group then traveled not with a battery of suitcases but with a big trunk; checked via American Express or Adams Express, it seemed always to be lost or detoured. We might wait for days. It felt like Christmas when the horse-drawn delivery wagon got to the door and made some changes of clothes possible at last.)

For some years the Lebanon grandparents lived in the country, the farm they worked maybe a hundred yards from the main line of the Reading, its double tracks announcing true worldly importance. We could sit on the dirt bank by the hour watching trains go by, enthralled by the clackety-clack of speeding passenger trains, and with the freights, which had magnitude instead of speed, counting cars and hoping always for the one hundred that somehow made our day. We had a private sense of the personalities of the eastbound passenger trains, knowing their arrival times at Lebanon and the stops they had to make en route to Reading or beyond. The weak sister of the afternoon array was the 3:27, doomed to stop at Avon, Myerstown, Womelsdorf, Robesonia, Wernersville, Sinking Spring, and Wyomissing before limping dispiritedly into Reading (not yet famous for Updike). We might have to take it because we could catch it at swanless Avon instead of going all the way into Lebanon. But what a triumphant moment when, at Wernersville, we changed to an express for the rest of the trip to Allentown or Philadelphia. It made a lordly pause at Reading, in a station whose charming design is still clear in my mind: the main building and platforms were in the center of an engagingly handsome deltoid; that is, an equilateral triangle with concave sides, each one a long, gently curving arc that was the station segment of a main Reading route (Harrisburg-Allentown, Allentown-Philadelphia, Philadelphia-Harrisburg). Back to the Lebanon countryside: the heroic trains flying east from Harrisburg were the 1:05 and the 5:10, which we could imagine slashing contemptuously through all those small towns. But the ultimate spectators' glory—in fact, the glory of the countryside—was one westbound train that seized on our imaginations, the 9:27, the Queen of the Valley, rolling along from Philadelphia to Harrisburg in the evening, all lit up like an organized host of fireflies. Once we were old enough to stay up and view the passage of the Queen, we felt that the day had an ecstatic finale, a sort of son et lumière all's well that ends well. Bed was bearable now; all was quiet on the Reading front.

It was in the country that one best heard the marvelous steam whistles; not the series of quick, sharp blasts to warn pedestrians or buggy drivers close at hand, but the protracted, piercing, giant woodwind notes, expanding in volume and then thinning out in an imploring decrescendo, a magnificent musical transcription of Arnold's "melancholy, long, withdrawing roar," and yet charming one as if a warning of disaster or a voicing of grief had become purely aesthetic, a theatrical outcry enthralling even as it faded away. In a Willa Cather short story a midwesterner, a country worker, sits on a farmhouse porch at night and hears, in such a long-drawn whistle, an announcement of distant places, lovelier scenes, a glamorous world that he will never know. For us it meant no grief; it was vaguely sad but still a wondrous and moving sound. It was a brutal letdown when the extraordinary enduring notes of escaping steam gradually gave way to the nasty, rasping foghorn grouch of the homely diesel engines, dull dwarfs, homely man-made contraptions standing in lumpishly for the old divine, or diabolic, fire dragons of high spirit (the railroads joining in the "God is dead" chorus). In recent years there have been efforts to resuscitate or at least imitate the old steam-whistle glory. This is less the result of widespread nostalgia, I suspect, than of a small minority's steering us from something intrinsically ugly to something with an objective charm that moves whoever hears it, even if he is without the benefit of memorial participation.

ii

Memorial participation: always there is the danger of inflating the pleasures of long ago, when things were fresh and glowing and one had not yet taken on the adult obligation of crimping skepticism. But for all who felt them, train delights tended to survive into later years. I've already mentioned the satisfaction of being able to go from Easton to Philadelphia by the Pennsylvania or two different Reading routes. Likewise one could go from Easton to New York by the Lehigh Valley or the Jersey Central (which seemed to be a kind of kissing cousin of the Reading). Having options was exciting; it was almost like being rich. One never thought that different lines were much alike, everything standard and predictable. And options aside, just traveling on new lines was a happy achievement. One was discovering new worlds. The first trip to New England: what a series of firsts. It was probably not my first trip by Lehigh Valley to Pennsylvania Station in New York—a cathedral of even more illustrious grandeur than Broad Street Station in Philadelphia. But there was the first underground trip across town to Grand Central Station, another memorial to an eternity of movement. There one saw the first New York Central trains, rode for the first time on the "New Haven" (New York, New Haven, and Hartford), had the first wrestle with clothes in a sleeper berth. A little later the New Haven to Boston; the joyful negotiation of both South Station and North Station in Boston; and then, novelty of novelties, a round of Arctic life—the Boston and Maine all the way up over the tundra to its northern terminus in Bangor. It was a more fundamental adventure than flying, many years later, from Seattle to Tokyo or from London to Johannesburg.

I was an adult now, but not at all into questions or ho-hummerie. Delights came, and one just took them at face value. One got jobs in different places, and getting to a new spot always opened up a new railroad world. After a summer in North Carolina, where I learned all about the Southern line, I had to get to a new job in Athens, Ohio. No one could have had greater map-and-travel ecstasy than I when I discovered the Clinchfield line that ran north from Spartanburg, South Carolina, through western North Carolina, eastern Tennessee, across the southwest corner of Virginia, and on to Elkhorn City, Kentucky. Thence north on the Chesapeake and Ohio and west on the Baltimore and Ohio—two new lines!—to Athens. The Clinchfield was a single-track line meandering through attractive upland backwoods and across two mountain ranges—the Great Smokies and the Cumberlands. The one- or two-car train—or were some freight cars also attached?—lolled along through some wonderful scenery, rarely hurrying, and once standing on a siding long enough for a trainman to pick flowers in an alpine meadow and present them to women passengers. And one could feel a little like a mountaineer when, come evening, the train stopped and all passengers trooped into a bare little hotel for the night. Rooms were lighted by a single globe on a wire suspended from center ceiling.

Living in Ohio for several years, and once having a summer job in Michigan, I had several options for eastbound travel. The best trip was by the main line of the Pennsylvania: Columbus to Pittsburgh to North Philadelphia. Since I wanted to see all the country we were rolling through, I detrained for a night in Pittsburgh—at a two-dollar railroad hotel that seemed to demand quite a hike for a person a little encumbered with two suitcases containing all his worldly belongings. The big thing east of Pittsburgh was the famous "Horseshoe Curve" near Altoona, a legendary marvel in Pennsylvania folklore. Coasting around that giant *U* was a little bit like seeing the Statue of Liberty for the first time. And on this train one could—or at least I did, perhaps violating passenger-coach protocol— venture onto the rear platform of the Pullman car at train-end, a space that could accommodate four or five light chairs under brightly colored canvas awnings. There one joined the happy few in the bliss of movement and of visible superiority to the passing scenes. Truth to tell, the awnings flapped with ear-blasting noisiness, the ceaseless air currents threatened to tear one's clothes off, and smoke and cinders were constantly sucked down and in to turn a sacred space into a sort of whirlwind inferno. On the other hand, it was here that Harry Truman stood and harangued small-town audiences on his famous whistle-stop tour of 1948. One could feel that one had, in a way, shared the spot.

I got off at the North Philadelphia station, my last contact with a fascinating scene where, in earlier years, I had often hung around for hours (after a twenty-five-block walk from my grandmother's house), passionately watching trains rushing to and from still-mysterious New York. My sister, who met me, said that my train had been sonorously announced as coming from "Harrisburg, Pittsburgh, and the West." "The West," no less. One felt like Lewis and Clark in reverse.

A more westerly West would be a reality in time. But first came a Louisiana job and, with it, initiation into a great new railroad world. Although the Missouri Pacific and the Texas Pacific ran nearby, they remained only names for travel adventures never to be experienced. But for travel to the northwest, for family visits, what choices! One could take the old Crescent Limited on the Southern, or the famous and more glamorously named Illinois Central Panama Limited to Chicago. But we had to take rather inglorious trains, the most inexpensive available, on a two-day sit-up trip to Boston in 1936—a Christmas-break quickie to the Harvard Library to check references for a book. It was Illinois Central to Memphis, then across Tennessee (by Southern?), but with a change, somewhere in Tennessee, to a new line traveled for the first time, the Norfolk and Western, a gratifying accomplishment. Then in the 1940s the hearts and imaginations of travelers were won over by the new light-metal trains, at first all sit-up affairs. The Southern's new train from New Orleans to New York became so prestigious that people who got their names in the social columns were reported to have traveled via the "Southern Belle." My own thirst "after outrageous stimulation," to apply Wordsworth in a new way, led me to discover another aluminum speedster, the Bluebird of the Louisville and Nashville line; starting from New Orleans or somewhere along the Gulf Coast, it wound around, most of the time through temptingly unfrequented hills and valleys, up through Alabama, Tennessee, and Kentucky, to Cincinnati. To ride it—what a happy Columbian exploit.

Finally the Pacific Northwest, with railroad glory everywhere one turned. One could actually go from Seattle to Chicago on great-name trains on four major lines and, with a little detouring, on two other grandiose transcontinental lines, the Canadian National and the Canadian Pacific, which climbed east out of Vancouver, British Columbia. All routes began with a brief coastal run and then spent a great twenty-four hours threading and curving their way, via tunnels and end-runs, through Rockies and desert before dropping down for the rapid skimming across plains and farm country into Chicago. In ten years of administrative travel (I had a department chairmanship at the University of Washington) I gladly used five of the six routes that rails provided. I think that the Canadian Pacific train was called the Canadian, a well-appointed and handsome aluminum train that one rode as far as Winnipeg before heading south through Grand Forks and Fargo to the Twin Cities. The only trouble with the Canadian route is that that far north the Rockies are pinched into a much narrower band than in the States, and the plains become correspondingly wider. They go on and on. Each of the four American trains had its own claim on one's irrational devotions—the Hiawatha of the Milwaukee line, the North Coast Limited of the Northern Pacific, the City of Portland of the Union Pacific (some coaches from Seattle connected with this train at Portland), and the Empire Builder of the Great Northern—which gained some glamour from being the most northerly of the routes. On the other hand, in southern Wyoming, on the Kemmerer-Rawlins-Cheyenne run of some three hundred miles, the Union Pacific tracks were consistently at least seven thousand feet above sea level. This was practically air travel.

All such trains brought one into Chicago about breakfast time. If one's goal was the East Coast, one had to get oneself to another station via one of the ten-or-twelve-passenger limousines run by the company that had the franchise. Then one had wonderful options. To Boston, one used a combination of New York Central and Boston and Albany. To Washington it was the Pennsylvania or Baltimore and Ohio (and perhaps Chesapeake and Ohio?). Best of all was the New York/Jersey City run: one could do it by New York Central, Pennsylvania, Lackawanna, or Erie, or even a combination of New York Central and Lehigh Valley. I happily managed them all at different times, enjoying the diversity of intervening towns and cities, rolling country and rivers, viaducts and long views, creaking climbs and long racing runs.

Episode reflecting pride of the transcontinental traveler: once, on a train eastbound and barely out of Chicago, a young man brought his family into the club car, lit a cigar, and announced to all (who could not choose but hear), "Oh, the joys of the open road!" "Open road" indeed. One smiled indulgently from the fullness of one's just-completed two thousand miles of open-roading across mountains and plains.

From Seattle one could go south to the Bay Area or Los Angeles—to the former by the Daylight, a testing trip of fifteen hours that one often took for the pleasure of seeing the mountain scenery in southern Oregon and northern California; or to both by the Starlight, on which one was protégé of both Union Pacific and Southern Pacific. Regret: I never managed the Southern Pacific between the West Coast and New Orleans, or the romantic Santa Fe (Atchison, Topeka, and Santa Fe) between California and the Midwest, with its famous transcontinental express, El Capitan, or the Denver and Rio Grande, said to pass through the finest mountain scenery in the country as it wound its way from Denver through Colorado, Utah, and Nevada, to Oakland.

iii

Insofar as the theme is the variety and fascinating differences of railroad lines, the tale is mainly of the past. Amtrak is so identical from place to place, so cut back and homogenized, so bureaucratically commonplace (a bureaucracy can make a once-handsome station look like a dump) that it hardly provides the satisfactions of railroad travelers during the hundred years leading up to the mid-twentieth century. In some sense there "hath passed away a glory from the earth" (to invoke Wordsworth again, and surely in a context of which he would not approve). But all is not lost, and I shall argue in time that a tale of railroads is more than an archaizing excursion trip. Still, there is no point in denying the historical aspects of the tale. Part of the charm of railroads was their having individual personalities, now probably gone forever. Another part was their fundamental alteration of the horse-and-buggy age into which they were born. Maybe this could be adequately felt only by someone who knew the horse-and-buggy age firsthand. I, for instance, can remember dreaming of the day when I would own, or at least be at the reins of, a horse and buggy by which I could freely explore areas that lay mysteriously, and invitingly, beyond the borders of Elizabethville and the three country churches that belonged to my father's parish. It would have been fun, too, to ride in what we knew as "the stage"—a horse-drawn, sizable, low-slung carriage, a two-seater with a large space between the seats for baggage and mailbags—which met trains in Elizabethville and then took off for smaller country towns to the north. How much more amply and grandly one could explore the country when, after centuries of horse and buggy, or plain horseback, railroads came in and went everywhere. (Autos are another story; I'll come back to them later.)

To recall the pleasures of train-riding (from 1948 to 1958 I made all professional trips, and they were fairly numerous, by train) is pretty likely to evoke a censorious cry of "Nostalgia"—that is, a sentimental longing for what is irrevocably gone. But that charge is clearly too simple. All over this country, for example, old runs of trackage, and old trains, are being revived for periodic trips that are usually fully booked. They may have some local utility for a tourist or two, but for the most part they hardly serve travel. They are patronized not only by people who are old enough to remember regular rail travel but by a majority who have no memory of rail travel. A ten-mile run going nowhere may be better patronized than common kinds of public transport taking one where one has to go. Clearly there is something intrinsically satisfying in the rides: they are an amusement-park simulation of an experience that is gratifying even if its practical ends are gone. Most Amtrak trains are reportedly booked heavily in advance. (In Europe, of course, natives and visiting Americans find railroads of pristine utility: fast trains going everywhere on rails that seem beautifully kept up. They please even in England, where passenger cars seem awkward assemblages of a half-score of stagecoaches yoked together end to end, and where young "drivers" can at times make one a little jittery: I remember staying excessively alert on a Leeds-London express doing one hundred miles an hour through heavy fog.) The *Great Railway Trains* series on TV was repeated regularly; obviously it drew big audiences in a post-train world. Books about trains, locomotives, and the like roll off presses steadily. Stephanie Brush, a syndicated columnist, recently published an enthusiastic column about train whistles, train rides, and our need to have again this form of "industrial poetry." Famous trains live on by word of mouth and as journalistic topics. In South Africa, for instance, I felt deprived by not having time to take the Blue Train from Cape Town to Johannesburg. The stature of famous trains is established by the tendency of some travelers to deromanticize them. Friends who took the Trans-Siberian Express complained of the difficulties more than they rejoiced in the exotic scenes they passed through. Another friend complained of the Orient Express: "It's just a pile of junk. I couldn't even plug in my razor." But I have yet to hear such denigrations of the Trans-Australian Express.

My point: train-riding provides a satisfaction that does not date—a satisfaction that is much diminished in auto travel and is nonexistent in plane travel. It is felt spontaneously by people who have been born into the automobile age and into the plane age. In other words, insofar as they do something for us, provide a certain kind of satisfaction, railroads, techno-logically superseded though they seem, do not belong to a *temps perdu*.

iv

There are doubtless different readings of the ways in which railroad travel gratifies. It has probably been praised as a means of change and escape, but such ends can be attributed to any mode of travel. (Still, one wonders if the midwestern farmer in Willa Cather's story—who, hearing the long-drawn-out train whistle at night, thought sadly of the unseen worlds it seemed to announce—could possibly be stirred to such a feeling by the sight of a plane high in the sky.) Once there used to circulate a Freudian reading (actual? quasi?) of the train as male/aggressor, but this theory applies better to automobiles, whose names frequently suggest savage attack. In its sexual dimension the theory must have made something of tunnels, lying as they sometimes do beneath pleasantly rounded hills of imaginably mammary lines (see Somerset Maugham's "Rain"), but they seem entered too easily and routinely to do much for the rampant male ego. (Since many children were frightened of tunnels, a theorist might have made something of prepubescent or pubescent sexual trepidation.)

For years I had no word for the special pleasure afforded by trains; the sense of it existed powerfully but namelessly. Then, in the mid-1950s, something suddenly came home to me. My wife and I were driving through the Rockies, probably in Colorado, and at the summit of some high pass we stopped and stretched. We were enjoying the view, this time not the standard more-or-less horizontal expanse, but a nearly vertical long look down to an irregular valley far below. Throughout that valley there shone the two rails of a single-track line curving in gentle arcs amid trees, bare spaces, great rocks, an undesigned medley of things that included a mountain stream, sometimes wide, sometimes narrow, sometimes flowing quietly, at others dashing turbulently in miniature falls. It suddenly struck me, though I may not have put it into words, that the combined view of valley and tracks was something special: that the tracks were handsomer than they would have been if one had been looking down upon them in a large, level expanse, and that the valley itself was the more attractive for the presence of the railroad line. Obviously I am on a different aesthetic track from the devotees of "unspoiled nature," but I am not advocating the introduction of railroads into all mountain fastnesses. Those devotees love a certain kind of singleness, whereas I am noting an aesthetic attractiveness in a more complex situation: an antique singleness has been modified and converted into a new doubleness that characterized what today would be called the "railroad experience."

That is, what we saw from above is a version of what one does below. On the train one benefits from, and enjoys, a kind of art, a man-made construction. But it is not art, static art, enclosed in a museum and lighted in one spot, more-or-less permanent, for display only. It is art as a composition in motion (we often hear of the "movement" in paintings and sculpture); it is an artifact whose essential character is kinetic or, to risk a coinage, dromic. Not, however, that it does not have its locus: its locus is the world of nature through which the train moves and moves us. It is our passage through that world—or, in other terms, the passage of that world past us on the train—that is indispensable to the aesthetic experience of the train ride. Motion in the abstract is nothing, has no virtue. What counts is motion amid motionlessness; it gratifies at once our instinct for movement and for the stability symbolized by the stationary. On a train we are, as it were, in an extraordinary Calder mobile, but a mobile that transcends its class by rolling locomotively rather than swinging placidly, circularly, in loco. But this art is in no way the art of "art versus nature"; that is a paradigm of war and conquest, a war of eternally uncertain outcome—a concept totally alien to railroad pleasures. The train world does not impose powers and shapes upon nature; it places one with respect to the other—two worlds with conjoined appeal. We have art *and* nature, art *in* and *amid* nature, art in juxtaposition with nature, both to be savored, relished. It is the totally ordered in juxtaposition with the unordered or less ordered. One can hardly overstress the indispensableness, to train pleasure, of that visible outer world through which the train passes. It is quasi-cinematic, but without benefit of visual technology; we ourselves are the freewheeling camera eye. Hence we can regard a train ride as a joyride, or even take it as such. But note: no one would ever take a joyride in a subway. The subway ride is utility only; artifice reigns; there is no contrast with live nature to stir senses and imagination. When trains are in tunnels, all aesthetic joy disappears; what was art-in-nature becomes a howling, technological monochrome, a threat to ease and patience. The long train ride under the English Channel will impose an endurance of harsh bare-bones utility without aesthetic dimension; it will drive the imprisoned to pills or booze.

The more the "nature" outside the train is crusted over by static human artifice, the less the pleasure of the ride. The run from city-center terminals through factory and warehouse areas was always tedious; the pleasure of motion itself could hardly overcome the rider's distaste for purely utilitarian, unlovely static artifice. The Amtrak run from Washington, D.C., to New York rarely allows a sense of cooperative nature outside the train, and the interminable structures that replace it or blot it out, far from elegant in their prime, are horrid in rusty decay. Heavily built-up areas likewise close out nature. But the human was not always a blot upon nature: the two often seemed peacefully joined in the smaller communities that trains went through or by—nature softened or domesticated rather than trampled on or deformed by relentless artifice. The attractiveness of many towns, their participation, as it were, in a contrasting nature, became doubly visible after dark, especially in places where human overcrowding was not yet. Lighted houses flicking up in twos or threes improved on the pure darkness, provided a stable contrast to our movement, guaranteed the essential train pleasure. Those lights, in their warmth, let travelers envision a stable domestic quietude that one could imagine gladly sharing. They were an anchor. We felt its pull as well as our movement.

A special case of art in juxtaposition and contrast with nature: winter weather. No doubt more for travelers from little-snow regions than for those from regular-snow regions, a snowstorm made an attractive scene for us on a moving train. This would be true as long as the story was one of art-amid-nature rather than art-versus-nature. Let a storm get overpowering, and the relations are out of balance. If the motion, the essential ingredient of the art, disappears, the experience is finished (this once happened to the Hiawatha, on which my wife was a passenger, somewhere in the Dakota outlands). The train is reduced to an inadequate hostelry, an insecure fortress, surrounded by a controlling nature now hostile and the more insidious because it is beautiful. La belle dame sans merci. Could she drive us civilized people to thinking of cannibalism?

Such a reduction of gratifying and indeed stirring coexistence to war can happen in plains or mountains. As counterpoint to movement, the plains have something on, and also lack something of, the rolling country of hills and valleys. What plains have is linear vastness, grand extent of scene: a magnificently spacious museum for this "art experience." Yet vastness can have a tincture of sameness: the challenge to the railroad designers seems too mild to bring out their best. In rolling country they have to work harder at design, and they seem to get better. Civil engineers can achieve curves by different ploys: in America the railroad seems to curve miles out of its way to avoid tunnels; in England and France the designers seem infatuated by the problem of tunnels and so curve miles out of the straight path to aim at a hill that they can tunnel. Either way, the winding around complicates and enriches the design. Hence the joy, for designers and public alike, of rising insinuatingly from lower levels to mountains—westbound, from seaboard to Appalachians in the East, and still more, from the tautology of plains to the Rockies in the West, their threateningly severe front lines backed up by every variety of reserves. Here all the artifices of the railroad are in full display in their multiform interaction with a many-sided, many-decked nature that, in its relationship with the railroad, has evolved from passive resistance to cooperative independence in a complex interplay of sculpture and dance. The train writhes gracefully around curves, eases along parapets overhanging deep mountain gashes, slithers through many short tunnels in a series, balances on narrow balconies slung perpendicularly way above disorderly streams, swings with a mild graceful lean out of a tunnel across a high bridge uniting two cliffs that nature set apart, winds down from high-pass altitudes around semicircles over broad mountain shoulders, gradually increases speed down a sloping terrain set against the looming disorder of solipsistic peaks, and finally races across a plateau way above sea level but still a deep valley in the shadow of heights just threaded through and circumnavigated and of new heights ahead to be negotiated by another burst of strong persistence and deviousness.

The curves are the main emblem of the artifice that derives glory from the contrast. They proclaim order, an order more visible in a setting of natural disorder—mixed angles, irregularities, bluntnesses, incoherencies, unmodulated successions. Not that a straight line does not announce order agreeably; connecting two points, a rulered line is better than a freehand line, inevitably wavering at least a little. But the best of straight lines seems a little easy somehow, more a casual utility than a planned work of art. Automotive or locomotive man shall not live by straight lines alone. As I look back at childhood responses, I can see that they embody perceptions that one could in no way articulate then. A rail line, if only a spur, crossing a road, was always a pleasure; ordinary dirt, seemingly shapeless, juxtaposed with a conscious design. The plainest case was a right-angle crossing; the next best, an oblique angle crossing; the most charming, a curve in the crossing line. That was art, one can say now. Whatever the visual charm of tracks, the attraction was smallest in a railroad yard, which was all tracks and no nature to fill things out. The construction of a new railroad line across the "unspoiled" farming countryside north of Elizabethville, when I was between eight and twelve, was totally fascinating. In no way was it "progress," or better transportation, or a boon to farmers, or a "getting with it." It was the delight of contrast, of a new dimension or tone in an established order of things, of art-in-nature with each constituent enhancing the other. The principle of this felicitous mingling holds even among model-railroad buffs. They start with plain oval tracks on a table or floor; add sidings, signals, stations, new trains; but finally, and best of all, laboriously fabricate irregular countrysides—hills, valleys, woods, streams—to provide that ultimate contrast, that merging of opposites, which is at the aesthetic heart of the matter.

Whether one is doing toy railroads, or just watching trains go by, or just looking pleasurably at a track layout in a natural setting where each enhances the other, or perhaps just looking at a stationary locomotive reduced to exhibition status—one is experiencing, if unaware of its nature, the delights of synecdoche. Each part has surprising power to symbolize the whole.

V

The delights of the railroad, as looked at or as fully experienced, as enjoyed unreflectively (simply an undefined thing-in-itself) from early years to midlife, and as articulated long after, lay in a combination of discordant elements in a mode of concord. In sum: it was geometry in conjunction with geology. It was not a contest but a collaboration; not a competition but a composition. It was the planned amid the random; managed order against a chance distribution of elements, objects, and shapes. Geology provided the unpolished setting essential to the drama created by the geometric design. The more drastic the geology, the more responsive and masterful the geometry. When geology is pacific rather than Pacific, the geometry relaxes into a quiescent or routine format (a geologist once assured me that "soft rock geologists" are naturally dull fellows). But when the geological world can produce giant churning plates and gross, unruly upthrusts in massive disorder, it draws out the best potential of geometry, which achieves the most graceful of dances about, and indeed with, a giant rough-hewn partner. Thus the constructive imagination energized in railroads combines the two elements of another dualism, a dualism that has been a staple of French cultural analysis: *l'esprit de géometrie* and *l'esprit de finesse*. Rich geometry and fecund geology produce distinguishable habitats that we need equally—the formed and accidental, the mobile and the static, the fluid and the fixed, the molded and the "jest grew," here joined in a consenting union.

At the end of a train trip, especially a long trip, one felt a sharp letdown, a descent into dull lassitude, into strain, almost depression. Not the relief of "mission accomplished," but the plunge into the anxiety of the ordinary (I yield to the contemporary fashion of discovering novel anxieties) from the combined stimulation and relaxation of the extraordinary movement through stasis. The burdensome trip-end flatness has several causes—not only the ending of an unusual harmony of contrasting realities, but the ending of another human experience, that of carefreeness and even invulnerability. On a train trip one does almost nothing for oneself. There is no job to attend to, no housework or homework to get through, no yard to maintain, no cooking to be done, no Joneses to keep up with, no risks to meet. One may have brought some little tasks aboard, but in this air of magically reduced responsibility, of *dolce far niente*, little tasks hardly seem tasks at all, or seem easily postponable without moral burden. Getting meals means no more than a walk to dining car or café car; no shopping, cooking, or dishwashing. No housecleaning; no laundry. No calendar of events and engagements to set up and keep up with. The trip is safe and sound and duty-free. It is travel without travail. No wonder the end of it is like being cast out of safety and pleasure into harsh reality. It is being born into the gross world of toil and trouble, and one is hit by the birth trauma. One has indeed been in a womb. But this prenatal life is special: one looks out from it at moving scenes of infinite variety, scenes that the alert traveler makes the most of, using windows far more revealing than those at home. He has been in the most remarkable of moving matrixes—an amnion with portholes, a womb with a view.

vi

Other ways of moving through stable nature offer fewer satisfactions. Horse and buggy? Hardly. For one thing, it provides less of art to contrast with nature, and less of nature to contrast with what art there is. One might protest against this quantity standard, even applied to nature, as vulgar; after all, the hostess who provides only a delicate drop of a gourmet potable announces a higher aesthetic spirituality than one whose guest's cup runneth over. But we have got used to a wider sweep. That is the way it is; no need for alassing. Besides, that old travel ambience (ah, I have made it!) was rather less amniotic than the train's: cold and heat and even moisture assaulted one brutally, and hot bricks under a blanket nursed the feet only briefly. But it is worth noting that many people—almost as many as can afford it, one assumes—keep horses to ride, not through city streets, but on bridle paths or across country, as close to unpopulated nature as one can get.

Automobiles? They are the horse and buggy become all artifice. Hence they seem to offer the same satisfactions as trains; a kind of geometry in a geological setting. But these cars are strong on utility, weak on charm. They play to the power sense, not to capacity for delight. They allow little opportunity for the detached contemplation of nature, for the museum experience of motion and motionlessness simultaneously. The driver has to concentrate on unrelenting labor; let his mind wander briefly from utility, and unpleasant things happen. The other passengers are stashed in and tied down; they have no trace of the freedom of movement that they have on a train. They are packed for transport, but unlike mute, insensate packages, they have unrelenting problems. They have to decide on, and find suitable spots for, "comfort stops." They have to agree on and find food stops. They have to agree on and find stops for the night. They have to tank up. If anything goes wrong with their contraption, they have to deal with it. All is wear and tear. There is little freedom for contemplation, for a sense of agreeable interplay between art and nature. Their car trip makes possible only one satisfaction: "our fearful trip is done." The road trip can approach the rail trip only if one does it in the John Madden way: the built-to-order house-on-wheels cared for and driven by someone else, a private train engineer. This mode may approach travel by the palatial private car of the old-time railroad baron.

Planes? If automobiles are strong on utility, planes are nothing but utility. They mean only getting there, and give no pleasure in the process. There are none of the contrasts that are at the center of railroad pleasure. Once you're off the ground—and nowadays you are holding your breath until you are airborne and have a lot of air beneath you—you have no contrast of motion and motionlessness; in the air, motion is almost identical with motionlessness. All is artifice; nature is reduced to something you feel only when its unseen essence becomes turbulent. You can rarely see the world below, and when you can, it is like looking at a map without crosshatchings and place-names. Besides, what is sometimes there to be seen can be caught, if at all, only by neck-paining twists for momentary glimpses through one of a series of minute peepholes—in contrast with the marvelous car-length windows through which train travelers have an easy full view of all geological settings. But of all the passengers on a plane, only one-third—or, on a wide-body plane, two-ninths—are able under any circumstances to look out and see what can be seen. A long plane trip is like a long train ride in a subway or tunnel, on which, as I have said, no one would ever go for pleasure. And insofar as one can catch a fleeting glimpse of what lies below, what is there is less a panorama of delightful changes than a distant enemy, all hostile gravity, ceaselessly striving to bring one down to its level, to inflict the Icarian penalty for high-flying. One is all tension and anxiety, hardly able to ignore one's awareness that planes are tending more and more to come apart in flight. (This awareness is far more disturbing than Amtrak's periodic difficulty in keeping trains on the tracks. A wreck like the one I described at the outset is so rare that the train rider hardly thinks it possible.) And whatever of consciousness is not occupied by anxiety is filled with discomfort, boredom, and sharp annoyance. Discomfort: one is stuck in a small space, a packed meeting room where the relief by movement is difficult at best and often forbidden. One is less a human being in agreeable motion—and able to move casually within the instrument of motion—than a parcel shipped for speedy delivery, and quite likely to be lost or damaged in transit. Boredom: the carrier recognizes this spiritually famished state and may counter it with a boring movie (homeopathic desperation), a small dose of illusory motion against a long draught of imperceptible motion. Annoyance, often maddening, as alternative to the above: rare is the plane flight not cursed by a male passenger who, the insentient owner of a massive, rasping penetrating voice, exercises it with proud indefatigability and thus compels a good ten rows of victims to listen to endless, awful, ear-wounding accounts of how he does business.

Hence, though one might delightedly take every possible train route available between two points (for example, Chicago to New York), one would never, never take anything but the shortest possible plane trip. The Concorde could have come into existence only as a mitigation, by diminution, of the inhumanities of air travel.

All the sufferings are in the name of triumph, a world away from the humanities of train travel, with its genial accommodation to a passing world nearly always charming. While Renaissance poets lauded the triumph of time, planes assure us of a triumph over time. In triumphing over time, we claim to save it, like explorers and missionaries triumphing over an alien race. What we do with what we save lies outside the boundaries of this discussion. Perhaps, as with most savings, we let it lie fallow—or waste it.

vii

I mean to describe, not inveigh. Planes have somewhat altered the way we look at time, and we are not likely to change that attitude for a while. Here they serve us through their provision of an enlightening contrast between pure-utility-transit and utility-transit-with-pleasure. The latter lasted for a century or more. To define its rich charms, its mingling of workaday and aesthetic utility, is not merely to "love that well which thou must leave ere long" (or, "hast left for good"). Trains have a strong double-hold that may undo or modify the apparent supersession of them by planes. Train-love may be less nostalgic than predictive. I doubt that train riders will ever echo, in whatever their own terms would be, what an Empire Builder trainman said to me as we rolled peacefully through western Dakota and eastern Montana: "When I began working for the railroad thirty years ago, it was the most romantic experience in the world. Now it is just a job." Plane travel quickly became just that. Trains cannot lose the art that enhances their utility.

II

writers
portrayed

Recollections

The four writers portrayed in this section were all colleagues of mine in one or the other of the two universities at which I spent my entire post-Ph.D. academic life. Two of them I knew at Louisiana State University—Eric Voegelin and Robert Penn Warren. Two of them I knew

at the University of Washington—the poet Theodore Roethke and the critic (also once a poet, though hardly known in that role) Malcolm Cowley. Voegelin, Warren, and Roethke were regular colleagues, presumptively permanent members of the faculties in the two universities. Cowley was in a different category. He was at the University of Washington only for a term as visiting professor, and I saw a good deal of him during that period. My account of him is less a portrayal of a gifted writer and thinker than it is a record of special circumstances attaching to his visit, circumstances that illustrate a certain period of American history and reveal aspects of university life not always well known. Although our relations necessarily had an official tinge, we became, I felt, good friends. I remember clearly Cowley's social gifts. When, some years later, we turned up simultaneously as visiting lecturers at Vanderbilt University and ran into each other (neither of us knew that the other was there), we felt like, and acted like, old friends who had been through various unifying difficulties together. I valued my acquaintanceship with him.

5

Eric Voegelin

I first met Eric Voegelin in 1940 or 1941 when he came to Baton Rouge to lecture under the auspices of the department of government at Louisiana State University. He may have given a single lecture or a series, and the subject, I suppose, was something that would be part of *Order and History,* though that large work did not begin appearing for another decade and a half. My first impression of Voegelin was of a speaker of great dignity and ease, of vast learning easily borne and not trimmed to please a general audience, of formality and yet graciousness. Here was a philosopher who had no marks of either the pedant or the popularizer; the gentleman as thinker. Despite a highly technical vocabulary and occasional, but not intrusive, problems of idiom and accent, Voegelin seemed comfortable and fluent in American English. During his stay in Baton Rouge, Eric—I use an informality that was slow to develop—attended a meeting of a faculty discussion group at which I was also present, whether as visitor or regular attendant (I am relying entirely on memory; I have no file of documents, formal or informal, to consult). I remember vividly the type, though not the specifics, of the argument that broke out there between him and several of my colleagues. The latter were depending, as faculties often do, on the fundamental rightness of the current beliefs of social and political liberalism, and no doubt Eric challenged one or more of these; it was not that he was antiliberal in principle, but that he was a vigilant challenger of the going clichés of both left and right. Perhaps his point was that Hitler and Nazism represented less a violation of American democratic ideas than an enduring disorder of a distinguishable philosophical and theological type. I do not remember the details, but I do retain a strong impression that my colleagues, several of whom were my good friends, were badly though unknowingly overmatched.

Early during the 1941–1942 academic year there came the news, exciting to all of us who had been greatly impressed by Eric during his visit, that he had accepted a position in the LSU department of government (it had not yet become the department of political science: Bob Harris, then chair, always insisted that the field was not a science) and would arrive in Baton Rouge for the spring semester. Eric's coming seemed to us a major institutional coup, another step toward LSU's realizing a potential that had become evident in various ways. One of the best agents of that potential was Bob Harris: he had an excellent eye for professional quality and, though not a theorist in the Voegelin mold, fully appreciated Voegelin's gifts. Eric would have arrived in January, and I got acquainted with him, I believe, not long after that (my uncertainty about this became an issue during Eric's naturalization proceedings in 1944, a matter that belongs to a later part of this narrative). My wife and I probably met the Voegelins through the Heberles, refugees who had arrived in 1938; Rudolf, a sociologist, had been at Kiel, and his wife, Franziska, was the daughter of the eminent sociologist Ferdinand Toennies.

My wife and I found both couples congenial socially. The men were splendid additions to the faculty, and the wives were superior people; they all remained tactfully silent about whatever differences they found between Vienna and Kiel, on one hand, and Baton Rouge on the other. We made special efforts; not only did we want them to feel at home at LSU, but we could imagine their problems in adjusting to a new culture and in having to use a new language. We thought of the daunting difficulties we would face as American refugees in Europe: the problem not only of a new culture but of trying to make a functioning daily tongue out of our graduate-school French or German. We wanted things to work out for the Voegelins and Heberles and hoped that welcoming natives might be helpful.

As northerners we too had at first felt like foreigners in Baton Rouge. We had since come to feel very much at home and no doubt felt that, as outsiders-turned-insiders, we would be useful interpreters of the Louisiana mode of American life. In one way, of course, we were doomed to failure: our academic German in no way equipped us to speak and understand the conversational language—a skill that might have temporarily relieved the refugees' burden of having to manage all communication in a second language. They would occasionally fall into German, especially if they had guests whose first language it was. When we were the only monolinguals present, we would sometimes leave early to free the rest for the pleasure of speaking their native tongue without having to be concerned about excluding the two anglophones present.

In time we came to use first names. This did not happen rapidly, for society had not yet reached today's stage of instant, obligatory informality, and as individuals we were disinclined to a stylistic intimacy that had not been earned by experience. Perhaps it was we who, as spokesmen for the native mores—we had drifted into the role without seeking it—proposed the use of first names. I mention this because Eric admitted that he found it difficult to call me "Bob," which seemed to him too trivial a vocative to apply to an adult who was at least nominally a scholar. I suppose he got used to it, but for some time he found "Robert" more bearable.

We tended to drift together at parties. As Lissy Voegelin said to me years later, "Eric had no small talk." When conversation was called for, he tended to launch into a disquisition on whatever technical issue he was thinking through as he composed *Order and History*. To an auditor not equipped for such discourse, Eric might have seemed to be exhibiting learning inappropriately or even engaging in a put-down. But anyone who read him thus was utterly wrong. Eric was a considerate man who in social circumstances—as opposed to formal debate, in which no holds would be barred—would never consciously speak in a condescending or indecorous way. He had a strong sense of the proprieties, the decencies, the observances that marked civilized people, and he was incapable of vulgarity, whether in the guise of unrestrained egoism or of simple commonplaceness. If one lacks small talk, at a social occasion one talks about the larger things familiar to him, taking for granted the adequacy of the hearer to the heard. Eric did not monologue. He would make a statement about what interested him and seek responses. He assumed the auditor's competence; he did not talk down to others by sticking to the quotidian or simplifying an issue. Responses were likely to be halfhearted or vague if Eric spoke about, say, the late-medieval origins of the concept of the Third Reich, or the spiritual breakthrough achieved by monotheistic thought, or the derivation of some current political idea from an error by Hegel. He tended to treat his colleagues precisely as if they were fellow members of the philosophy faculty at the University of Vienna. Whatever our professional competence, we were for the most part not quite up to the role. What many of us felt was less resentment than a regretful sense of not being with it, and of wanting the ease of more reassuring company. (Insofar as I may have felt that, the feeling was more than counterbalanced by the awareness of being in the presence of an extraordinary man.) Some people were so defeated by Eric's intellectual superiority that they just wished he'd go away. But he never indulged in derogation, and he tended not to introduce topics he knew would be unwelcome. He was a man of great punctilio. But if controversial topics came up, he did not hesitate to challenge the clichés he heard bandied about. After all, in Vienna he had vigorously attacked rightists even when it was dangerous to do so (in his case it had been life-threatening, and it led to exile). Here in the land of free speech it seemed natural to challenge ideas on the other end of the political spectrum when they seemed inadequate. Obviously, a man who at best was hard to understand and who dared to question long-held secular faiths was not always easy to take.

What precedes may suggest that Eric generated only negative reactions. But there were colleagues who, instead of fleeing or being captious, were admiring and devoted and willing to listen and to learn. They might not, however, always be present at parties or handy at given moments. So Eric tended, at social events, to become a solitary, not looking disgruntled or censorious or troubled or neglected, but with his ordinarily pleasant mien— he had a genial air, but with the geniality modified by a certain formality— falling into an expressionless neutrality: registering not bad temper but a sense, somewhat escaping an effort of concealment, that though this kind of sociability had its place and had to be endured (Eric always had a strong sense of obligation), it was still not the most satisfying way of spending several hours. He seemed to be masking discontent or disappointment under an air of detachment. He was not ungracious, but he was genuinely courtly, and that meant that he registered social obligations in a formal key, different from the folksy American geniality based on the exchange of uncontentious trivialities. He was not contemptuous of this American style of social intercourse, but it was not for him a natural way of doing things. Eric was always a thinker before he was a social being.

ii

All this is part of a historical picture of Eric Voegelin, but it also serves to introduce an account of my own relations with him. When I said that we tended to drift together at parties, I was not defining myself as his equal or as intellectually superior to our colleagues. In me Eric excited a respect bordering on veneration, for I recognized in him the most extraordinary intellect I had ever encountered, one I could in no way keep up with, especially in the abstruse philosophical matters that could come up spontaneously in any conversation. Although the spirit was willing, the mental flesh was weak. But my good luck was that Eric had as it were established me in a role in which I felt some competence—that, to borrow a term from anthropology, of "native informant." (This is not, of course, to claim exclusive possession of a role that was shared by Bob Harris, Cleanth Brooks, and others who had discovered some congeniality with Eric.) As a non-southerner I might be expected to understand the questions that would occur to another outsider experiencing the Deep South for the first time; in a sense we were foreigners together. But by 1942 I had been in Louisiana for seven years, and I could speak also as an insider. I could act as the interpreter of academic folkways that were unfamiliar to a European-trained scholar. And I knew members of the faculty well enough—LSU was still a relatively small university—to be able to characterize people and to make judgments on their talent, zeal, and professional accomplishment (no doubt with a dash of that free-swinging, confident finality to which one is liable in one's thirties). But the local scene was only a temporary object of inquiry; Eric was more curious about the general habits of American academe—everything from institutional governance to habits of thought to philosophical positions; types of administrative personnel and attitudes; power bases; relations to the outside world; sense of mission and sense of profit; and so on. He knew a great deal about the *materia* of various fields—the arts, music, history, literature, and of course philosophy—and he was curious about the academic management of these. He would ask about historiographic and critical practices in literature, and often about specific writers: their styles, beliefs, current status in academic esteem; and about individual works and their reputations. His knowledge of literature in English was wide, and he often asked searching questions. These questions, which showed a range of knowledge rare in the practitioners of nonliterary fields, tested the abilities of the informant, whom Eric could praise, assist, and of course challenge.

Praise: he once told me that I could and did answer questions that remained unanswered when he directed them to other professors of literature. This puzzled me, for any competent Ph.D. should have been able to deal with most of his inquiries, which by and large concerned central, mainline matters. I can still hear him saying, "They do not answer my questions." I remember his delight when he came across some work he had not known before, such as Ben Jonson's *The Alchemist:* this play indicated to him an English awareness of, or even tie-in with, the alchemical thought in which Eric had some interest as an aspect of the history of philosophy.

Assist: he asked many questions about Shakespeare, and my task was to describe the kinds of scholarly activity practiced by Shakespeareans. I made one sweeping statement—I have forgotten what—about Shakespeareans' habits, and Eric promptly asked what specific person did this sort of thing. When I could not pin down my generalization with an example, he gracefully covered for me: "Ah, it is in the air." This is a phrase I have often found convenient. Now and then, despite his moving primarily in a terminological world of European philosophical practice, he would come up with a simple and useful phrase with an Anglo-Saxon base, for example, "free-floating hatred."

Challenge: Eric had a deft way of indicating doubt about some of my judgments and procedures. In analyzing plays and novels I tended to look for the springs of human conduct—the motives, "drives," needs of characters in interplay with one another. It was distressing, then, to discover that Eric considered "psychological" analysis a distinctly inferior mode of criticism. What went on in literature was for him an interplay of philosophical issues and spiritual forces, a clash of symbols rather than a confrontation of psyches. In my later work this view may have somewhat colored my sense of what went on in narratives, but I was not really equipped to see things in Eric's way. Still, I shall never forget the air of innocent and amiable curiosity with which he raised literary questions, and his brief interpositions, ironic but not biting.

He would occasionally ask about specific writers. In the late 1940s he observed that much critical discussion of Henry James was going on, and asked what he should read by way of introduction to James. I had been teaching and writing about *The Turn of the Screw,* and I suggested it. Eric read it immediately—in one sitting, I believe—and wrote me a very long reply (an essay-length letter) interpreting the novel as a study of American Puritanism in which the dramatic actors are God, the Soul, and Ordinary Life (the uncle, the governess, and the housekeeper, respectively). He gave *The Turn* the highest possible praise when he told me that had he known it when he wrote a book about America after his first visit here, in the 1920s, the book would have been different. I say no more about the subject here because fortunately Eric's letter-essay, with modifications he made several decades later, reached print.[1]

At the same time that he was asking me questions about literature in English, he was making occasional efforts to educate me about European works; he would recommend novels available in translation. One of these was Hermann Broch's *The Death of Virgil* (I remember his especially praising a "philosophy of laughter" found in that book), and I was sufficiently struck by it to publish a review. Once he urged me to study, if not indeed to memorize, the chapter headings of a volume that would clue me in to how one went about the study of metaphysics. The captions were in German, alas, and I failed the assignment. But Eric was forgiving, and he went on acting as if I were capable of philosophical redemption, despite his inevitable awareness that I was an inadequately endowed pupil.

---

1. *Southern Review,* n.s. 7, no. 1 (1971), 9–48; reprinted in *The Collected Works of Eric Voegelin,* vol. 12, *Published Essays, 1966–1985,* ed. Ellis Sandoz (available Columbia: University of Missouri Press, 1999).

iii

Our relations with the Voegelins took a special turn in the summer of 1944, when they were in Cambridge, Massachusetts: as in many summers, Eric was working in the library at Harvard. During their absence from Baton Rouge, the rented house in which they had been living was leased or sold out from under them, this in accordance with a wartime regulation that permitted the dispossession of occupants if the premises were then to be occupied by the owners or members of their family. This must have been another severe blow to people who, after the troubles that led to their flight from Austria, might have felt they were beginning to get a foothold in America. They evidently felt that they could not contest what amounted to an eviction. It would have been costly; as "foreigners" (though naturalization was imminent, they had not yet gone through it) they would have been at a disadvantage in a legal dispute; and Eric desperately needed all the time he could get at Harvard on materials unavailable at LSU. Had they made the long and expensive trip back to Baton Rouge, they might not have been able to find other rental housing. Apparently the only solution was to buy a house, provided a suitable one could be found for sale. At this point they phoned us and asked us to buy a house for them, that is, to find one for sale, commit them to buying it, and perhaps put down (I'm not sure about this) some earnest money. This was a forbidding assignment; picking out a house for someone else could never be easy, and for people of the Voegelins' fine taste it seemed close to impossible. The Voegelins could be stuck with a house of which their undying thought might be, "Couldn't Ruth and Bob do better than this?" But however it might come out, our taking the assignment must have seemed, in the exigencies of a wartime world, a lesser evil than any other course . . . and we did take it on. Although I say "we," the task fell largely to my wife, Ruth. One reason was that I was teaching full-time in summer school (fifteen hours a week then, and no trace of the cooling systems that have since become standard equipment in Baton Rouge), an annual necessity to keep us financially afloat; the more significant one was that Ruth was much better than I at amateur realty. I no longer know what her research method was, or how long she worked at it, but I do recall that she uncovered only two houses for sale. We may have looked at both houses, or it may have been, as I suspect, that one of the two was so obviously inferior that it dropped out of consideration. The remaining one was no gem, but it would do, or rather would have to do. Because it was really the only one available, we at least escaped the burden of seeming to have made a sorry choice. We signed for it and phoned the Voegelins with the news.

Lissy came down by train to take care of the paperwork; I believe they borrowed the money for the trip as well as for the down payment (in fleeing the Nazis, they had to leave Vienna without either possessions or cash). My impression is that the house cost six or seven thousand (for comparison: I was an associate professor then, and my salary was, I think, a little more than three thousand; Eric's was probably somewhat, but not much, more than that). Later, with a frankness in financial matters that was characteristic, Eric said he had received a loan from a relatively well-off refugee, a Jewish businessman, I believe.

If Lissy's heart sank when she saw their new home, she concealed the fact well (I can imagine the Voegelins having a mental picture of a modern house on a good-sized lot in an attractive neighborhood, a house such as the Heberles had by now acquired). Fortunately, the Voegelins' fine taste was balanced by a sense of reality. The house we found was roughly downtown, on a narrow street a few blocks east of the central shopping section. The names *Canal* and *Cherry* come to mind, but I would not bet on either; whatever its name, the street on which the Voegelin house stood was wiped out by the new freeway that, curving in from the north and east, took over the area. As I remember it, the area was, if not outright crummy, at least wholly undistinguished: a sequence of narrow houses on narrow lots on a narrow street. But Lissy Voegelin made that house into a very charming place; we were occasional guests in it, and after we left LSU we once spent a week there. This was early one summer—in 1953, I think—after the Voegelins had left for what had become a standard summer research stay in Cambridge. We could see the works of art that were an important part of the transformation, and we could see (and use) the large tub in which, we were told, Eric sat for hours in cold water, smoking the cigars he was fond of and working with papers and books arranged on a board spanning the tub. Lissy contributed to his writing by trying to maintain favorable working conditions; she was a noise-abatement society of one, campaigning in particular against kids whose habitual hollering disturbed Eric's flow of thought. It must have seemed very odd, in a neighborhood where reading, if any, probably did not go beyond the daily papers and where books would have seemed strange objects stored in libraries, to be told that a new neighbor, suspect anyway, was actually *writing* a book and needed a quiet atmosphere in which to carry on this peculiar practice. You never could tell about foreigners.

Whatever problems there may have been—and I never heard any report of hostility (even during a war when the Voegelins' marked accents might have aroused suspicion in some segments of the American public)—they lived in that house from 1944 to 1958, when they returned to Europe for what would be a stay of some years.

iv

Aside from the housing problem, another significant event occurred in 1944: Eric's naturalization as an American citizen. I was his designated witness, the citizen whom the immigration authorities would quiz about the applicant's political and personal reliability. But before we got to the crucial moment of the hearing, there was a rather long period of preparation, during which Eric asked me some routine questions. One big issue did arise, having to do with a training booklet provided to would-be citizens by the division of naturalization. Eric would of course know its contents by heart. One day he asked me, "If the answers in the handbook are wrong, should I give the right answers or say what the handbook says?" Anyone with knowledge of officialdom will know what my answer was: "You say what the book says, even though you are sure you are telling a lie. If you correct an official publication of a government bureau, they will surely take you to be an unreformed Nazi, a Communist agent, or else a professional troublemaker." The situation was this: the handbook summarized various matters the candidate was supposed to know about—the Constitution, the Bill of Rights, and legislation having to do with the duties of citizenship. Eric did not rely on this secondhand version. As a political scientist, he read the originals, which of course he saw through a highly trained professional eye; hence his sense that the handbook, meant for a diverse and unread laity, fell into technical inaccuracies or at least approximations of dubious reliability.

I was present during part of Eric's naturalization interview, where he conducted himself in a becomingly low-key way and without bursts of learning that might alarm the board. He passed without difficulty. I also underwent a private questioning. In general it had to do with Eric's potential for good citizenship, and of course I could be enthusiastic. I recall few details, but I do remember one large and unexpected stumbling block. I was asked how long I had known Eric or, more precisely, just when our acquaintance had begun. The exchange went approximately like this:

RBH: Well, let's see, he came to LSU in 1942. Let's say about two years.
Naturalization Officer: You must be more specific.
RBH: Well, he came here from Alabama for our second semester. So I met him sometime in the first half of 1942.

N.O.: You must be more specific.

RBH: Since he came for the spring semester, he would have arrived in Baton Rouge in late January or early February. I met him not long after that.

N.O.: You must be more specific.

RBH: I probably met him sometime in February.

N.O.: That is too general.

RBH: Well, let's say I met him February 16.

The interrogator had the satisfied look of an examining attorney who has at last elicited an essential fact from a well-meaning but none-too-sharp witness. My last statement settled things. Later Eric told me that the officer had told him, "You had a very good witness. Professors usually aren't good about details. They tend to be vague, especially about dates. But Heilman really had the facts at his fingertips."

V

Over time, Eric had become known as a faculty member of extraordinary knowledge, insight, and depth. But he had none of the feeling for easy or popular targets needed to create the spellbinder who elicits volumes of praise from students and garners teaching prizes. He was uniformly admired by the best students rather than being widely popular. He never tried to gratify or to upset auditors; rather, he wanted to expound ideas, which might do either. His aim was understanding, not approbation or the making of converts. Once he told me of a woman student upset by his presentations of political theory; she felt that his ideas raised unnecessary difficulties and underrated a success-marked actuality. Eric gave her an opportunity to tell what she would prefer. She said she just wanted to be "happy." What, Eric asked, did it take to produce happiness? She said, "I just want to be married, and have a family and a house and a car and a radio." In reporting this to me Eric was wondering how widespread her attitude was and, if it was a sound representative of American thought, how we had managed to last as long as we had. Eric was grateful for an American refuge, and he never evinced any European snobbery; but he would never hesitate to make a point that might displease chauvinists, those who took the status quo to be the ultimate social and moral achievement.

Eric was the ideal colleague for those special cases in which a student advisee would seek not to have his requirements met as quickly and easily as possible, but to be sent to the best minds on the faculty. That sort of thing does happen occasionally in academe, and it was wonderful to have an Eric to recommend to such seekers. He was quietly admired despite the difficulty of intricate and unfamiliar concepts. I have the impression—though I have no solid evidence on this—that when Eric offered a law school course in natural law, student responses were marked by the feeling that though these ideas had the merit of unusualness and depth, their connection with litigation was not altogether clear.

Eric not only attracted the best students, but he aroused the interest of townspeople drawn by the new intellectual range. Among these were my wife (who had also audited a course given by Cleanth Brooks) and Dorothy Blanchard (a sister-in-law of Mrs. Brooks), who one year sat in on Voegelin's course in Nietzsche. I got many reports on the flow of ideas, on student reactions, and occasionally on terminological problems. Eric's English was fluent, but the language was highly technical, the idioms came from philosophical vocabularies, and now and then a pronunciation was European—a source of an occasional problem that was more amusing than deeply vexing. The class heard about the Greek divinities "Ahtaynah" and "Tsoiss," and from context soon identified them as the goddess of wisdom and the head Olympian. But an apparently common noun, "wahzy," remained an unsolved mystery for weeks. Puzzlement was widespread. Because "wahzy" seemed to have aquatic connotations, the semifamiliar *wadi* came to mind, and the association seemed fitting: the word seemed to come up in contexts of the transmission of cultural influences through desert lands. But enlightenment had to come from Eric himself, who, questioned by students, explained, "Oh, you know, a watering spot in the desert." *Oasis.*

But problems of pronunciation were transitory and minor. Eric would ask me about them occasionally, and he caught on quickly to the representations of sound, inconsistent as they are, in English orthography. We moved on quickly from such mechanical matters. My longer-term role was that of explicator of American academic English, and finally I became a sort of consultant on Eric's own formal use of English (he had started writing his books and articles in English—surely the most difficult of the leaps into the New World). In time Eric asked me to read the typescripts of articles, reviews, and the like, and finally the texts of volumes that would become parts of *Order and History*. He particularly wanted me to catch slips in idiom. In one book he kindly included a paragraph to the effect that my influence upon his English had been beneficent. I wished that might be true, but I tried to avoid deceiving myself.

Being Eric's consultant on style was flattering but difficult. My philosophical shortcomings often left me feeling insecure in suggestions I wanted to make. I would see apparent problems in idiom, phrasings not in accord with the expectations of readers in English, locutions I felt to be literal translations of German idioms that, when Englished, still did not become English; but when I broached the subject, I would find that the way he had put the matter seemed to Eric essential to the accurate communication of his thought. In such cases I was not only failing to help Eric, but also causing him the additional labor of explaining his intent to a well-meaning but philosophically defective copyeditor. What I always hoped for, of course, was conspicuous and unmistakable derangements of idiom, the correction of which would make me look competently helpful rather than conceptually hopeless. Little luck of that kind. I can still hear his "But you see, Bob . . ."

A reviewer of one of Eric's later books declared it a pity that Voegelin had given up writing in English. What the reviewer meant was that Eric's basic technical vocabulary and idioms were not always in line with standard academic English. I can understand this criticism, provided that it is aimed at stylistic mannerisms and is not used as a defense mechanism against his thought. For instance, "tension toward," a phrase Eric frequently used, seems to me not to work well because it runs counter to anglophone expectations with regard to "tension." But such views are not necessarily shared by readers of greater philosophical expertise.

I have already alluded to Eric's strong, nearly fastidious, sense of decorum. What was true of social relations was even more true of professional ones. When I dedicated a book to him—an essay on the relation of language and drama in *Othello*—he commented on the volume with a fullness, and with an appreciativeness of the intended honor, matched by no other dedicatee. His response took the form of a letter of two or three pages, single-spaced, which gave a handsome account of what he took the book to be doing. His reservations about my conclusions were so gracefully embedded in the descriptive text that I would have been able to ignore them had I wished to do so. I did not wish to, certainly, but by then I knew I was incapable of reshaping my critical praxis to make it less distant from the Voegelin ideal. I recognized that I instinctively fell into psychological criticism, of which—as I've said—Eric disapproved.

vi

In 1948 Ruth and I left for Seattle, and after that Eric and I exchanged letters regularly, if not frequently (as did our wives). The correspondence continued when the Voegelins returned to Europe in 1958. Eric had accepted the directorship of the Bavarian state political science institute in Munich. This was a professional advancement, I suppose, but it never seemed to me that Eric suffered from the institutional angst so common among American professors. He thought about his work; in no way did his status, or his sense of achievement, depend upon what post he held or what university he served in. So though the Munich post may well have seemed a promotion, I imagine that his motivating influence in taking it was the strong pull of Europe after twenty years away, and of the Voegelins' native language.

They must have crossed the ocean about the time we were returning from a 1957–1958 sabbatical. When we returned to Europe in 1964–1965, the Voegelins generously asked us to visit. Eric invited me to speak at a seminar of his, and he also managed—against what resistance I know not—to encourage the department of English to sponsor a lecture by me. The chair of English was Wolfgang Clemen, and since we had both trafficked somewhat in Shakespearean imagery, there were grounds for our finding ourselves at least mildly simpatico. Then I received a letter—a sort of warning I took it to be—from a member of the Munich faculty who had taken his Ph.D. in our department at the University of Washington, where, the gifted son of an immigrant family, he had established himself both as a superior student and as a talented one-upper. The burden of his letter—we had had no prior correspondence—was that the department of English at Munich was "sophisticated," and that a visitor would want to mind his p's and q's lest he betray provincialisms that might embarrass him. Oh dear, I thought, I am in danger of disgracing not only myself but my sponsor, Eric. Well, I spoke to Eric's seminar—a seminar in some phase of political science—no doubt on some aspect of tragedy, the subject of a book I was working on, and had a vague sense, not too illusory I hoped, of having got by without betraying an appalling failure of sophistication (even though I had to speak in English, as the students were more at ease in it than I would have been in German). Eric had told me that he wanted his students to see what a competent American academic looked like. There may have been an implied contrast with the Munich professoriat, our impression of whom, conveyed largely in letters from Lissy, was of complacent, humorless, domineering types, very different from the gentility the Voegelins remembered in their Vienna colleagues.

The story might be better if I remembered the subject of my general lecture for the department of English, but I have blacked out the formal occasion. My recollections begin with the postlecture chitchat: Professor Clemen told the Voegelins and Heilmans he had arranged no social affair, and he suggested that we take off in cars for a public park where desired refreshments could be ordered. Off we went, an unorganized and uncertain medley of faculty, students, and others; there was little or no coherence among the twenty or thirty people who made up the park delegation. Feeling ill at ease in the what-do-we-do-next air from which no one seemed exempt, I latched onto several graduate students, proposed that we sit together, and asked them to order—the bill to me—whatever beer they liked and whatever food would go with it: cheese, chips, sausages, and so on. I no longer remember whether I paid or whether Clemen stopped by to pick up the check. I was trying to make conversation while observing Eric and Lissy walking around like lost souls, she looking thunderous and Eric grinning in a most singular fashion, as if this were an especially gratifying occasion. It wasn't long before Clemen stopped by to whisper a request in my ear: if I declared I was tired, this would enable him to flee, as he would like to do, because he took no pleasure in being here and could think of other things he would prefer to do. By then I may have been a little annoyed, and disinclined to play further the role of idiot boy to all these "sophisticates," but all voluntary action was suddenly ruled out by the onset of a thunderstorm. We were sitting in an insubstantial enclosure, I think under a light cloth or canvas covering that temporarily resisted the downpour, but the sides were open, and the storm blew through. Retreat was mandatory, and everyone had to hurry toward parking areas that seemed some distance away. Lissy, who did all the driving, had to dash through the rain for their car. From somewhere there was an umbrella available for the other three of us as we struggled through the rain. We got back to the Voegelins' apartment and chatted and had drinks during the drying-out process. Lissy's displeasure with the evening now expressed itself in denunciations of a social style she saw as a violation of all European, and especially Viennese, decencies. Eric continued to smile, delighted, it seems, by an unforeseen confirmation of his suspicions. As he put it, "I knew that something was wrong with the department of English, but it is much worse than I thought."

The Voegelins were wonderful hosts and took us to see everything that should be seen by visitors to Munich—museums, churches, political and historical sites, restaurants. At all such spots Eric spoke with great ease and informality, a guide in control of all pertinent information, aesthetic and historical. One occasion brought out a response I had never seen in him: anger. A doorman or waiter was either inattentive or outright rude, and Eric grew furious. He told the man off, emphatically but not coarsely, and we went on our way. But his resentment at bad style was perceptible for quite a while.

In time the Voegelins wearied of Munich; my impression, gained from other sources, is that the disruptiveness of dogmatic student Marxists—a boorish tactic we have seen in this country—made Eric's educational mission seem excessively difficult. I never asked about this. In the late 1960s they returned to the States and made a permanent home in California. Eric was for a while a fellow of the Hoover Institute in Palo Alto. After he left the institute, Eric told me that the officials there were overly concerned with opposition to communism; Eric felt, if my inferences are correct, that this opposition committed resources and energies against an ideology he already saw as doomed. We began to see the Voegelins regularly again, for our son and his family lived in Palo Alto, and we had a pied-à-terre there. I remember well the July day in 1969 when we four were at my son's house, along with my son and his family, watching the TV broadcast of the moon landing. I had expected Eric to be uninterested or even in a skeptical or debunking frame of mind, but he seemed no less fascinated by the lunar scenes than the rest of us.

vii

Before coming to the ending of the tale, I want to record a few impressions that may not be attached to specific events. As I have indicated more than once, I lacked the philosophical equipment to engage in activities that turned on technical consideration or application of Voegelin's thought. (In contrast, Cleanth Brooks—a friend of both of us—made use of a Voegelin idea in an essay on Walker Percy.) But one kept picking up snippets that might influence one's thought or writing. I always noticed Eric's use of the word *science* in the general sense of "knowledge"; repeatedly he would say something like, "Don't let the lab boys get away with monopolizing that word," that is, limiting its applicability to the management of aspects of physical reality instead of to the treatment of essence by philosophy. Thus he was always providing his listener with conceptual tools that were not necessarily part of his systematic thought. His sense of the varieties of religious experience—he once spoke about "the atheist religion"—was always present to me as I was working out the implications of the picaresque heart of Thomas Mann's brilliant *Felix Krull*. His idea of the "deformed community" directly influenced my sense of what goes on in Walter Van Tilburg Clark's *The Ox-Bow Incident*.

What I was doing was picking up individual ideas from printed or spoken word and using them to enlighten artistic practices rather than ingesting a philosophical system and letting it determine point of view. "System": my colleague Eugene Webb once told me he had given up studying Voegelin because the latter was "not a systematic philosopher." When I mentioned this to Cleanth Brooks, Cleanth replied that if Eric heard this complaint, he would say, "I'm pursuing truth, not constructing a system." Webb has, fortunately, since resumed his study of Voegelin.

After leaving the Hoover Institute, Eric, needing income, took up the study of the stock market. (I am assuming this chronology; I cannot vouch for it.) He undertook this intense research in his sixties, when many people opt for retirement. Eric did very well in this new venture; he told me once that it took him about two hours a day to spot and keep up with the trends that dictated buying and selling, and after his death Lissy told me that she had been left in a very comfortable financial situation. A lifetime as a profound theorist did not diminish his awareness of how the ordinary world goes and of how to survive in it; he accepted, so to speak, the ways of the world, as long as that acceptance did not run counter to his sense of what was fitting. Once Lissy got the notion that one had to be a church member to undergo funeral rites; Eric said, matter-of-factly, "All right, we will join a church then."

Although he could be sharply critical of American ways of doing things, Eric did not stint on praise when he felt it was due. He thought, for example, that American medical practice was superior to European. In the late sixties or early seventies, after he and Lissy had both had major surgery in Palo Alto, he said, "If we had stayed in Vienna, we would both be dead by now." After Lissy's surgery, Eric dashed to the hospital with the most elaborate bouquet he could find; he had laid hands on it at a florist's where it was part (it was an artificial bouquet) of the shop's permanent decor. He presented it with as ardent a speech as might have been delivered to a dying spouse in a Victorian novel. His words apparently implied that her situation was terminal; Lissy made clear that she was doing quite well, thank you, and expected to be around for a while.

Lissy had a great sense of humor and a nice touch of American slang, which showed up charmingly, mingled with an Old World style that was more literary than epistolary, in her letters to Ruth. Those letters nearly always ended with "So long, Ruth." Lissy and Ruth had occasional phone calls, and I would always hear my wife's laughter at the jests that came over the wire.

In Palo Alto the Voegelins put together a home of great elegance in both furnishings and ornament. I remember especially a large Kokoschka and a Japanese screen, which I believe Eric brought back from a trip to Asia (he had become interested in Eastern philosophies, and had made some progress in learning Chinese). There were no photographs in evidence; they did not go for the American practice of devoting wall space to a photographic family history. They lacked family, in the usual sense, and this was a source of some sadness. Relations with Lissy's family in Vienna were difficult, and may indeed have ended because her relatives were businesspeople who had welcomed the Nazi regime. Perhaps there were no survivors in Eric's immediate family. At one time, however, the Voegelins had welcome contact with—visited and were visited by—a niece of Eric's for whom they felt considerable affection. My notion is that the geographical separation prevented the development of an enduring relationship. The Voegelins spoke once or twice about having or adopting children, but it may be that by the time they were financially secure, age had become a bar to parenthood. They had a pair of dogs, of which they were, or at least Lissy was, very fond; these beasts seemed not to welcome our visits and adopted a frighteningly yapping and snarling style, in which they were reminiscent of the dreadful Caesar, who regularly alarmed guests at the Brooks home in Baton Rouge back in the forties. The Voegelins had cars, handsome ones; and as I've said, Lissy did all the driving. Eric had driven when they first had a car, I was told, but a mishap when he was at the wheel had led to Lissy's permanent assumption of the chauffeur's duties. This was not one of those cases I have known in which an intellectual's professed inability to drive seemed less an admission of incompetence than a claim to talents that rendered him superior to such mechanical activities. (Obviously I write as one who likes to drive.)

When Ruth and I visited our son and his family, we regularly called on the Voegelins, sometimes to share a meal and sometimes just to talk. The last time the four of us were together was in December 1984. Eric, who had been in failing health, was bedridden. We talked with him as he lay, in pajamas and a bathrobe, on a daybed in a smaller room (not primarily a bedroom, I think) down the hall from the main living room. I remember that his white hair was unusually long. He took pleasure in biblical readings—the books were mentioned, but I can't recall them—these often done by an attendant. One event during this visit stands out in my memory. Eric said, in a peaceful and unemotional way, without a hint of this-is-it heroism: "It is time to die." Lissy responded sharply, almost angrily: "But you do not think of me. What am I going to do?" We had never heard her use that tone with Eric, though she was always as independent as she was devoted.

Eric died about ten days later. He died on the same day as Charles Hyneman, formerly a political scientist at LSU, whom I am glad also to claim as a longtime friend. Charles was a sedulous student of practical American politics and thus presented a contrast to Eric, the theorist and philosophical historian. The *American Spectator,* founded by former students of Hyneman's at Indiana, remarked that the deaths of Voegelin and Hyneman had "lowered the intelligence level of the nation."

During visits to the Voegelins in Palo Alto we might, as I have said, dine together, or we might chat. Occasionally Eric would say, making a rare dip into colloquialism, "Bob and I must have some boy-talk." Off we would go to a restaurant, and by way of boy-talk Eric would hold forth on whatever topics he was currently exploring in his reading and writing. I have already mentioned Lissy's comment that Eric "had no small talk." I had plenty of it, but it seemed too small for the occasion. So I tended to be listener only, mortified by my incapacity to deal with the subjects on which Eric spoke easily and eloquently, and mortified too by the flattering implication that I was an equal partner in the conversation. I fell into the category that Peter Shaffer, in his 1968 play *The White Liars,* called "Takers" (as opposed to "Givers"). I have long remembered an aphorism of Eric's at one of these occasions: "Of course there is no God. But we must believe in Him." I understood, I thought, the concept of the indispensable symbol.

The disparity between the Giver and the Taker roles led, as it seemed to me it must, to a thinning of our relationship. My original duties as native informant virtually disappeared as Eric came to know more and more about America. He had read widely in literature in English, and he was a more than capable critic of what he read. Listening, however enthusiastic, was not enough. I knew Eric felt pressed by the vastness of the intellectual tasks in which he was engaged, and by the sense of a rapidly diminishing time in which to carry them out. I came to feel that I could be most helpful by not taking up time he could use more profitably in his study. We gradually reduced the number of our visits to the Voegelins, but there was never any diminution of their wonderful cordiality.

After Eric's death the matter came up in a conversation between Lissy and me. Perhaps I brought it up, wanting to explain myself, no doubt hoping to have been seen as considerate and helpful rather than indifferent or unfriendly. Lissy's comment went something like this: "Yes, Eric noticed that you weren't coming over as much. He wondered why. He was very sad about it. He was very fond of you." I wondered whether, as often happens with good intentions, I had blown it.

6

Robert Penn Warren

When I began to put these notes together,[1] I was struck by a geographical irony. Here was I, a native Pennsylvanian, writing literally on an island shore in Puget Sound, about a Kentuckian whose colleague I was forty years ago in Louisiana and who has long lived in Connecticut. What we had shared, for a few years, was a Deep South which we had both left in the 1940s, and which no longer is what it was then. Yet that past still asserts its vitality for me in our now-distant present.

My glancing back, in a Kentucky scene, to that old Louisiana reality reminds me, if only faintly, of Red Warren's going back to Todd County to see again the Jefferson Davis monument, begun long before, finished much later, and then in 1979 a key point in a Davis commemoration. It should be amply clear that I am not a Warren—that most of us here are not Warrens—and that he is not a Jefferson Davis. Granted that, rough parallels between the backward looks, or the absence of them, will come to mind. I can start with no childhood images to be partly unlearned and partly confirmed later on, though I might seek a parallel by claiming that my first images of Red, forty-five years ago, were products of my professional childhood. But my early images came, of course, not through a grandfather, but directly from the subject; they were tentative rather than decisive; they were to be added to rather than revised or justified. And the native Kentuckian who is the center of our rites is happily not at the stage at which stone monuments are the required idiom. Or better still, he has been building his own monument, not quite so localized as the Davis one, a little longer in construction, and visible in all scenes and at all distances. So in our present

---

1. The sketch of Robert Penn Warren was originally a talk delivered on the morning of October 29, 1980, in the Department of Special Collections, King Library North, at the University of Kentucky's Robert Penn Warren seventy-fifth birthday symposium.

pageantry we can see both man and monument. In 1979, Red Warren, glancing back over a century and a half, could meditate a little on the passage of things and even, in the totally dry-eyed way that marks his style, on the *lacrimae rerum*. One might be tempted to borrow that mode here, even with less than half a century to think about, and to record the sense of something gone besides the years. But that sounds like standard septuagenarian mournfulness, which I do not feel. As to what slides away, then, better to borrow the silence that held between the Warren brothers as they looked at markers of time past.

So on to bare annals. When I arrived at LSU in September 1935, Red seemed like some kind of old-timer there. He was well along at thirty, and I was a mere twenty-nine. To me, a new instructor with a new Ph.D. and old debts, an old-timer was almost anybody up ahead; there they all looked secure and entrenched. Red was an old-timer of a year or two, and what is more, an assistant professor. From where I stood and waited, it seemed an exalted status. At that time one was not spotted in advance as a period man or a type man (say a medievalist or semiotician); one was just signed on to teach freshman English and the peripheral goodies in literature, if any, that might drop into one's lap when and if the fates were kind (that is to say, unkind to someone ahead of one in the pedagogical chow line). So I had only extreme juniority, an everyman's generalized teaching role, and no record of any kind to make me an identifiable individual. Established assistant professors seemed a different breed to whom one spoke only if spoken to. Besides, this was the Deep South, and my first sight of it; all was foreign, and anything one said might be a goof. Too, this redheaded assistant professor was a strange duck who had the most extraordinary accent, not the Louisiana speech I was learning to hear, and with no trace of the Oxonian which sometimes sweetens the tongue of old Rhodes boys. For such reasons it was quite a while—perhaps a year—before I began to get acquainted with Red at all.

As seasons of mists and mellow fruitfulness go, that autumn of 1935 was an unusual one, with an ironic ripeness at the core, and even fumes of poppies of a sort. Huey Long was shot on the Sunday after Labor Day and died two days later. These somewhat Shakespearean events took place during my wife's and my first nine days in Baton Rouge, and we were in the visitors' gallery of the lower chamber in the State Capitol when the shots snapped out just below us. We could hardly know that, in being on hand at the spectacular cutoff of a spectacular career, we were standers-by of an ending that was also a beginning. This rounding out of a life made it visible as a whole, the raw material available for transmutation, a decade later, into the different life of one of the great American novels, as I can say with assurance, of our day. Was Red Warren's imagination already beginning to play tentative games with that life, brief but now complete, and to see it extending into a mythic existence beyond time and place? I wish I could report that I had spoken with Red about such matters, but I cannot. There are always large vacant spots in one's past luckiness. Still, just being a bystander when shots bloodied the statehouse floor seems a little like having been a passerby where the Daulia road meets the Delphi-Thebes road—they still point the alleged spot out to tourists—when an arrogant old man ordered a young chap off the road and got hacked down. Out of such brief episodes come, in time, works you don't forget. One knows this, alas, only through hindsight and not at the hot moment.

Did Huey's death raise any qualms in the editors of the *Southern Review,* which was just aborning? The editors might well have wondered whether the budget for the *Review,* a paradoxical product of the very complex Long era, would survive in a new post-Long regime. If the question had occurred to me at the time, I would not have been up to asking it, and I never thought to bring it up later. A casual retrospective observer might see, in the coincidence of Huey's death and the *Review*'s birth, a simplistic symbolism: ring out the old, ring in the new; down politics and up culture. The truth, happily, deserts such obviousness for irony: the *Review* did not meet its death until seven years later, and then during a reform administration in the state.

Well, Huey died, and a few weeks later the second issue of the *Review* came out. Assistant Professor Warren, as I have said, seemed an entrenched old-timer. He had been at LSU long enough to have engaged in the preplanning—they did a year's work in six months—needed before the first *Review* could come out. On the literary side it seemed, I guess, a rather strange beast to the majority of us who had been brought up, in college and graduate school, in the old historical tradition. Some of us wouldn't buy it at all—I use *buy* in the figurative sense, since purchasing anything but necessities was a slender practice in those Depression days—and some of us were teased into its orbit despite ourselves. To some it was a freak, to others invisible, to others a godsend. In general the usual distrust of the new and the usual envy of growing success were in time more than matched by a sense of the class of the *Review* and hence by local pride in it. Surely no one foresaw, however, that in a brief septennium the *Review* would become memorable, would take such almost unknowns as Eudora Welty at least through the vestibule of the house of memory, would give some glory to its university, would help qualify its editors for major posts in distant states, and incidentally would send forth its first two business managers into notable editorial careers elsewhere. Again, as with Huey's death, how comforting is hindsight.

After I became acquainted with Red Warren and Cleanth Brooks, I got the impression, more from chance remarks of theirs than from outright assertions, that they saw pretty much eye to eye on contributions, or could argue vigorously but peaceably; that their tastes sometimes differed sharply from that of Charles Pipkin, the political scientist who was nominal headman at the start; that some editorial agreement was necessary for acceptance of a contribution, but that two tepid yes votes were not enough. One strong yes was essential. But still, these are impressions that may be sustained, modified, or demolished by the principals who can speak from knowledge instead of impressions.

Time-consuming as the *Review* must have been, it was only a fraction of Red's life. I do not know, as I have said, whether his imagination was already beginning to work out from the Huey Long story. His imagination had to be at work, if not in 1935 at least pretty soon after that, on the Kentucky tobacco wars, for *Night Rider* would appear in 1939. *Night Rider* began his long series of treatments of middle-South subjects, especially those of Kentucky and Tennessee; if Nashville was not quite his Dublin, still the analogy is suggestive. Memory of where one is not is the catalyst; after all, the Louisiana story came into its transformed fictional life only after Red had moved to Minnesota. Unless my memory, with customary fidelity, is deceiving me, Red's decade in Louisiana did not generate fictional themes beyond the large one of *All the King's Men.*

Back to the late 1930s, when *Night Rider* was in gestation. These were incredibly productive years, even in the context of a long life never exactly torpid. For Red was working on both stories and poems (his second volume of poems appeared in 1935, that wonderfully full year), coediting the *Review,* collaborating with Brooks on two textbooks, *Approach to Literature* and the more famous *Understanding Poetry,* both of which appeared in the later 1930s. And then of course there was *Understanding Fiction,* and along with it the second novel, *At Heaven's Gate,* both in 1943. All this is in the public record, though the casual reader of the record might not envisage the great gushing forth of intellectual and imaginative energy. But like most of its kind, that public record is incomplete. It does not reveal, though it may imply, that Red was teaching full-time (the full-time probably included some nominal allowance for editorial work). It does not reveal that the teaching was more than providing the casual classroom semi-presence that some scholars and writers think is enough. It does not reveal that he was busy in department life, first in helping shape up a new Ph.D. program (not to mention working on examination committees for M.A. and Ph.D. applicants), and then in that busyness of correspondence, caucus, and corridor that broke out when the department faced a change of chairman and was shaken by the urgent campaigning of one candidate who to many of us seemed a walking anthology of administrative disabilities. Nor does the record reveal that Red was one of a relatively small faculty group who, when the post-Long scandals broke out in 1939 to festoon the state like the decor of a colossal musical comedy, tried to make hay by pushing for some small betterments of the university. All these doings not on the record prove a large conscience in university affairs—the kind of conscience often choked off at birth by scholars, and rarely even a gleam in the eye of writers, who are rarely seduced into institutional citizenship. Put together the doings on the record and the unrecorded doings, and they give a picture of Warren's work fantastic in its variety and quantity. It was an early model of the diverse creativity—which extended of course to social criticism—of that rare being, the full-scale man of letters.

If only I could claim that, as a colleague of Red's from his thirtieth to his thirty-eighth year, I foresaw the future achievement. But I can assert only that I did spot him as an unusually able figure in the English department and university. At the same time the man of talent and the nonstop worker was a very attractive human being. Let us not, however, shrink him into a standardized charm-school midget, smiling his way into all unjudging hearts around. He had a deadpan, almost stern, mood, a sort of flat withdrawal or uncommunicativeness that could make one wonder, "What have I done?" Then there was another style that seemed to go naturally with the lined face and hard-bitten look that were there early—a skeptically ironic twist of expression and of speech that could effortlessly deflate any foolish ideas, or for that matter popular ideas, that might be floating around without getting many questions. It neither reflected a suspicious nature nor fell into easy sarcasm; it was rather a natural inquisitiveness of one not easily convinced or converted—a sort of Kentuckian Missourianism. His critical curiosity seemed to issue from near the corner of the mouth, without drifting into what a college teacher of mine called "sidemouth philosophy." Perhaps in his close look at things there was also a touch of that strong wariness of sentiment which helps toughen up the fiction. Then finally there was the joyous and laughing Red, whose full face crinkling into merriment meant a fine display of teeth and that long little suck or hiss of breath, an inbound or outbound sibilance, that somehow doubled the sweep of delight. I thought of this aspect of Red while reading Eudora Welty's comment, in a recent interview, on a visit from Red: they just "sat around," and he, leaving, said, "I have never laughed so hard—not a serious word all evening."

And that brings us to the gregarious or social Red. *Social* is probably the better word, since *gregarious* connotes a habitual search for company, as if solitude were a kind of flu, whereas I'm talking about the basic hard worker, who has to be solitary, and then the variations on that base. Whatever his working schedule inevitably was, Red was a better-than-average social being, as a guest ready for whatever fun and games would break out, and as a host easy, amiable, and generous. He was a mean gunner in a battle of charades; it was easier to be on his side, and not to have to face his look of the unmoved mover, pitying, condescending, amused, and a little amazed at the obtuseness of the interpreters. I remember him as a host at occasional big parties, the guests a wide spread of gown and some town, making each guest feel sought after, and seeing that the supplies of food and drink were located and utilized by the guests. I don't mean, of course, that Red really came up to Colonel Sanders, though within the last few days he seems almost to have made it here in Kentucky.

In those spring years one could eat and drink with more abandon, and with little hint of the watchfulness that would later overtake us. I still have a clear picture of one Warren guest, an instructor in English, standing there with his back against the wall, a little cross-eyed by now, like a happy late-nighter in a cartoon, suddenly starting to slide gently down the wall, his feet moving slowly forward and outward until, never losing contact with the wall, he was seated solidly on the floor, his legs making a big V, and his face coming apart in a slightly puzzled gaze. The Warren party air, though not intent upon such a fall, was comfortable with it; first aid and a comic sense were both there in suitable measure. At such a time all the king's men could reassemble the wall-fall guy.

Red was not only a ready party man, and an apt host, but a great entertainer. In him I saw and heard, for the first time, the southern storyteller, who is what he is, I guess, because he does not live by the punch line alone but has equal zest in the spread of detail along the way, the filling-out of scene and action that have their own life and are not to be hurried over as mere props for the finale. Not that the finale is trivial, but that it completes a structure instead of being merely the pop for which alone the popgun exists. I heard him do the great tale of the mountain folks' big family bed, the sleeping place for pappy and mammy and their large brood, the brood all equipped with coonskin caps, which they kept losing at moments of crisis during the long night. Perhaps the best of Red's tales—which by the way he credited to Andrew Lytle—was the one of the city-slicker salesman who came to a southern hamlet, snatched the local belle from the arms of her less crafty village swain, and then threw a big wedding dinner. It reached a climax in prose epithalamia by the male leads. We listeners rejoiced in a wonderful archetypal contrast in rhetorical styles as winner and loser worked with a common image of bridal loveliness. I stole the tale and for years presented it, without demand but with byline, once winning a large acclaim with it at a dude ranch near Kerrville, Texas. But my version was no Warren work of art; Red invested it with a fullness of body and ornament that an alien amateur narrator could never come up with.

It is surely clear by now that the rising academic man, the oncoming literary man, and the instinctive social man was a very likable human being—not a personality boy, never a gusher, rarely without some reserve, having a sharp edge when needed, capable of impatience, but never self-assertive, and always unostentatious, decent, and courteous. He was a rare denial of the four-letter definition of literary people which, a decade or two earlier, T. S. Eliot had vented at a luncheon with Conrad Aiken, and he was a negative answer to Osip Mandelstam's inquiry, "Might there not be some inverse ratio between the moral and dynamic development of the soul?" When I first came across Thomas Mann's wrestling with the problem of bohemian and bourgeois, I felt that Red had solved it by combining the virtues of both, or, if you will, of writer and citizen, or better, artist and gentleman. From Red I learned so early in life to associate good art and good manners that over the years, when my academic job involved me in regular contact with poets and fictionists, and of course professors, I found myself impatient with those who took tantrums for talent, or boorishness for genius. When Red came to Seattle to do the Roethke memorial reading a few years ago, he was one of our best visitors, famous now, but a wonderful trouper, tired from travel and performance, but amiable and even jolly with scores of introducees. Early and late, he has been essentially modest—not unconfident, not muddied with mock humility, but open to the rest of the world, as good a listener as he was a talker, talking about things out there and not in here, ready to belong rather than dominate, and dominating, when he did, only by others' sense of quality in the man. There was no side, no knowing insidership, no need to go by current standards, no affectation of high-toned with-it-ness. He once told me that he couldn't read Thomas Mann. Maybe that changed later; I don't know. Anyway, it enabled me to take the risk of saying I couldn't read *Finnegans Wake,* that polymorphously perverse anagram, fitter for dissertations than for delight. He once claimed to be tone-deaf and thus to shun all musical events. I heard him say this at a time when an artist friend of ours was showing especial delicacy of ear by insisting that even symphony was too noisy, and that only a quartet was fit for civilized listening. Well, Red's alleged absence of musical ear made me less cringing when, in a community of opera buffs, I finally realized that I simply did not like opera. Red would listen patiently to criticisms of points in the textbooks. He sent me the typescript of a novel—*At Heaven's Gate,* and perhaps later *World Enough and Time,* though incredibly I am unsure of this—and asked for comments. This was genuine modesty, as was his handling of my doubtless square responses. He would say, "Yes, I'll have to do something about that," or, more often, "No, I think I'll have to stick with that; you see . . ."—as usually I hadn't seen. A reader of my present memoir wondered whether Red's work might have been influenced by the comments of such manuscript-readers as myself. I doubt it very strongly. Perhaps an occasional point made by a reader led to some local modifications, but spurring local modifications is not quite exerting influence. Anyway, most of Red's career has been in the years since I was in close touch with him, so I am an incompetent witness on this point.

Perhaps his ultimate modesty is the willingness and ability to write the lucid and unaffected prose that has always dominated his critical work—a prose often imaged and allusive, yes, but with no touch of the Byzantinely opaque mode that now and then rampages in academe, unhousebroken. He took the risk implicit in an Oscar Wilde character's observation: "Nowadays to be intelligible is to be found out." And then there is that comment in a recent interview: "I am trying to be a good poet"—this by a senior writer a little later to be called, in *Newsweek,* "America's Dean of Letters."

But I must stick to my role as recording nonangel of an earlier phase in the three ages of American man—minority, middle age, and Medicare. (I do not include "maturity," which may happen in minority but may not happen in middle age.) Most of my memories are miscellaneous, but three of them naturally fall together to show Red in combat. I take them in anticlimactic order. The scene of the first is a conference on southern affairs hosted at LSU. The only aspect of this event that I remember is Red's rising in the middle of the audience and rebuking the conference. The conference was on the wrong track, it had no idea of the true South, and no decent picture of its future. Although this occurred during general discussion, Red was reading his remarks from the back of what looked like a large manila envelope—a great comfort to us who can extemporize only from a prepared text. Well, this injection of an alien view seemed very brave to me; alas, I cannot recall what followed. In the second episode, the main character was a student caught in, or at least charged with, some kind of theft. Authorities were about to throw the book at him, and he was a likely target, for he was not a very lovable lad—perhaps a 1968 type born too soon. But he was evidently a good student, and that is probably what brought Red into a sturdy defense that was not altogether easy. A scholarly youth should not be treated with a severity unlikely if the culprit were a football player. Anyway, it took some conviction and guts to be on the boy's side. But with my unusual faculty for forgetting the next chapter, I cannot report who won. The scene of the third episode is again a bar, not of justice this time, but of a convention hotel. A number of us were sitting around a table, the boy brought the drinks, and Red exclaimed quickly, "But they forgot to put the whiskey in mine." I didn't know whether that was a literal statement of an accidental omission, or a metaphor for a slick barman's cheating half-jigger. Whatever it was, Red spoke firmly to the Ganymede of the place. Although I said that I would use anticlimactic order, I am now hedging, for this was the only one of the three episodes of bold dissidence that could invite the attentions of a bouncer. But there was no bouncing; bourbon was brought; and whether the bill grew, I don't know.

A medley of images is scattered about in the frail storage room of memory. If only they were ordered in an assiduous diary; if only one had had the wits to be a Boswell when there was much Boswellizing to be done. But my images are random and chancy, relics tumbling from a messy attic room when one opens the door in search of old gold. The real gold is one's memory of an association, which isn't kept in the attic. But the attic has the purse trimmings, those signs that the real thing is there. One trimming: the time when Red was first teaching a course in Shakespeare. For some reason this involved the splitting of a class assigned to senior professor John Earle Uhler. Maybe it was just that the class suffered from overpopulation, since Dr. Uhler was quite a drawing card on the classroom stage. Be that as it may, Dr. Read, the department head—in those days having a head was not considered a piece of gratuitous tyranny—told Dr. Uhler to divide his class equally and send one half to Mr. Warren, who would be waiting in another room in Allen Hall (the arts and sciences building named after Governor O. K. Allen). Dr. Uhler went back to Dr. Read and reported that alas he could not split the class because no one would leave. Although Dr. Read was aged and fragile, his Virginian eyes sparkled, he grasped his cane, he snapped, "Well, if you can't split the class, I can," and he limped off to do battle. Thus began Warren's career in teaching Shakespeare, a subject in which he has never known a shortage of students.

A junior colleague told me once that Red had wanted to swim—a bit of a problem in Louisiana, where the thick brown waters are generous hosts to moccasins and alligators. The young man provided the swim spot at a country place, either a pool of sorts or a river eddy relatively safe from unseen currents and water wild beasts. He reported to me, "Red put plugs in both ears, waded in, and swam madly in a little circle for five minutes, and that was it." Not much hot-tub indulgence there. I do not know if this whirlpool style was altered in later years and other climes. I move on from warm water to ice tea. In the Deep South summer most of us got addicted to Coke or ice tea; I swilled both, but especially ice tea, and the habit clung even in the off-season. It seemed a bit of a secret vice, like sherry in the office-desk drawer. I confessed it to Red, the kind of man who would understand weaknesses. He said, "Live on ice tea? I work on it—and all year round. I couldn't write without a pitcher of ice tea." Saved again; one no longer had to justify guzzling ice tea in winter. In the hot and humid months I would drink about a quart and a pint at the evening meal, an intake made simpler when my wife found some ice-tea glasses that actually held a pint. I told Red once, "At supper we have only two things—ice tea and salad." "Good God," said Red, "if I came to the table and found only salad to eat, I'd just sit down and cry." I don't know whether forty subsequent years have either reduced the tears or removed all such occasions for them. I move on to a third liquid, and it happens also to be my third drawing on it—whiskey. This time Red is narrator. He was good not only as tale-teller but as reporter on persons, places, and things. The person in this story was Tom Wolfe—the Eugene Gant one, that is. The place, I think, was a writers' conference somewhere in Colorado. The time—an after-work-hours party. Wolfe arrived in a capacious jacket—or maybe topcoat, but jacket makes a better story—with large sidepockets, each one stuffed with a fifth. He was costumed with the ammunition for a bull-shooting that was to last most of the night. Wolfe was evidently a Gargantua in monologue. Red, as I have said, was a good listener, and this time his listening system must have got an extraordinary workout. No complaints, though; only lively details of the roaring boy on stage.

From fluids to dry goods. As dresser, Red could be equally colorful and constant, occasionally shiny but more generally old-shoe, never one to turn out an old faithful. Any other Louisiana relics will probably remember as well as I do an old reliable jacket, a jacket that went on and on. It was of a reddish-brickish-orange-ish hue, with touches of two geranium shades, and maybe a dash of horse chestnut. At first it riveted the eye in those precolor days of haberdashery, and then it stuck with one like a mistress dwindling into a wife. One noted it invariably, but inattentively, as one does a spectacle, like hijacking, that has become daily news. Maybe it was an indestructible tweed of Oxford provenience. It gained a special bouquet from Red's habit—I report this secondhand—of sticking a not-yet-dead pipe into a pocket and thus setting up a double smoke. John Palmer once said that the beast had seen its best days and, like the horse in *Animal Farm*, was ready for the knacker. Only a good friend could be so inhumane.

From dry goods to dry statements. The subject was the Civil War. Red said of a southern general (I'm too uncertain of his identity to mention the name that comes to mind), "Lee should have had him shot." It was my first experience of so uncompromising a judgment of a member of a class that somehow seemed exempt from stern censure, though in this matter, times are much changed. And for me, in my parochial naïveté, it was also very early evidence that southern loyalty did not mean unqualified admiration of everyone in southern ranks. I insert a more trivial moment, this one after Red had moved to Minnesota. It was a meeting early in the fall, maybe in Chicago. As we were breaking up, Red said, "Well, nothing to do now but go back to Minneapolis and wait for the first blizzard." It was his only comment on that city that I remember. Another dry statement later on, in a probably less trivial moment: "Some of my friends want me to become a Catholic, but I haven't the vocation." What his vocation was had long become clear. As for the products of that vocation, I have written about one or two of them. One of my happiest assignments was reviewing the reviews of *All the King's Men,* for rarely did one find so many big guns, commingled with various small side arms, cannonading such downright nonsense. I found that nonsense appetizing in two ways. One, it relieved any fears one might have that criticism was getting too rational. Second, it was the kind of nonsense that positively made one salivate epithets; abuse came flowing out like automatic writing. These victims were fun, however little fun their victim might have got out of that extraordinary flux of astigmatic holier-than-thou judgments.

Once I planned to write something about a poem of Red's—"The Ballad of Billie Potts." When I first read the "Ballad," probably some time after it came out, I recognized the plot as very much like that of two plays, George Lillo's *Fatal Curiosity* (1731) and Camus's *Le Malentendu* (1944). Obviously the story that Red had picked up from an elderly relative in Kentucky was one branch of a mythic family that had migrated widely. This kind of parallel or relationship interests me, and I mentally outlined an article on the literary history of unwitting filicide; I think I was going to call it "Laius Acts First." I mentioned the plan to Cleanth Brooks, who said, "Go ahead. Red will be glad to play dead." Somehow this chance phrase made the historian of filicide seem like an unwitting homicide, and I let almost three decades pass before outlining the worldwide travels of the Billie Potts myth. Meanwhile, others had got into the act. My sketch of the myth, and of its other sketchers, is now embalmed in a long footnote on page 346 of a book I published in 1973 (*The Iceman, the Arsonist, and the Troubled Agent*).

It seemed like filicide and homicide when a misunderstanding—this is my guess—resulted in Red's departure to Minnesota in 1943. Maybe departmental suicide would be the better term. We felt the loss in many ways. Doubtless Cleanth would leave next. Fortunately he stayed another four years. My own departure, a few months after Cleanth's, is a small footnote to this memoir. The University of Washington was looking for a chairman of English. One of the people they asked for nominations was a man who had been a visiting professor there—Joseph Warren Beach. Beach, of course, was at Minnesota. Maybe he couldn't think of anyone; maybe he just wanted more names. Anyway, he met Red Warren in the hall one day and casually asked him if he could think of anyone. How many names Red gave him I don't know, but one of them was mine—a gutsy gamble by him, and then by Washington. And so off to Puget Sound, about as far away as possible from New Haven.

A final word on the subject from which I have slid off into parentheses—Red's vocation. Two products of it, in some ways alike but both different enough from the expectable elements of a literary career to prove an extraordinary creative range, are beautifully spaced just about fifty years apart. One might call them the alpha and omega of the writer's life, except that the omega time is not yet. The study of John Brown in 1929 is surely the alpha, but the study of Jefferson Davis in 1980 is hardly a terminus. How nicely these studies balance out—the history of the northerner who hoped to start a revolution but died before the war he helped precipitate, and the history of the southerner who, unfitted though he was for the task, had to "manage what was, in one sense, a revolution," and a war; and to survive it, with little happiness, for a quarter of a century. And how nicely, too, the characters balance out—the fanatic and the logician. Ironically enough, the logician survives better in memory; the fanatic, who knows no law but his own will, exhausts his imaginative impact in his own time. Red's work on Brown might be called "The Unmaking of a Martyr." In a quite other way Red reversed his first subject: the Browns came from Connecticut, and John got to the South via the Midwest. I wish I had read the Warren *John Brown* when it first appeared—just a year after Stephen Vincent Benét's *John Brown's Body*. It just might have added something to my presentation of the Benét work, which in the early thirties was required reading in our freshman course at the University of Maine.

It may seem a combination of excessive persnicketiness and sheer banality to say that the *John Brown* is not as good as the *Jefferson Davis*. Yet even in the earlier work there is much of the echt Warren—the dominantly direct narrative style, with nothing purple or pretentious; the concretely imaged scenes and looks of people and things; the occasional magnificent description, such as that of Brown's prosecutor; the dry observations; the ironic perceptions; the snatches of wit, with now and then, cliché though the combination is, the wisdom that one wants to feel is beyond the writer's years. (And speaking of years, I was delighted to see Red calling Brown, then in his fifties, an "old man.") There is always the penetrating moral sense that never announces itself with a fanfaronade, and the grasp of the convoluted self-deceiver in Brown which restrains what might be pure polemic. Good as this first work is, we miss a steady control of style and form: the writing is not always graceful, the focus slips, the historical narrative is not always clear, the structural lines are at times more bulgy than crisp.

It is by the control of form that the Davis piece achieves excellence and I believe distinction. It is not merely that it comes fifty years after *John Brown;* that is too simple. Its virtue—any work's virtue—is not an automatic product of half a century, a fiftieth-anniversary gift of the gods. Time does not guarantee grace. Red might have peaked at twenty-four, as many do. In the Davis narrative there is rather an achieved quality, the spontaneous imagination nurtured by experiences, yes, but more than that, governed by disciplined striving. Well, these words may be a more than usually futile effort to describe quality. In brief, Davis, a very complex man, is portrayed by an equally complex art. Warren multiplies perspectives or context or framework; there are more points of view than in *Wuthering Heights,* but they all belong to one narrator. They are all on leash. There is the frame of the young boy listening to a grandfather who is seen in his local context. There is the frame of the second Jeff Davis, the sad hometown ne'er-do-well. There is the frame of Guthrie and its ways of creating the narrator's "uninstructed southernism." There is the frame of the monument story, which began when the narrator was ten or eleven and went on for many years. There is the meditative frame: what are monuments for? There is the frame of World War I. Take away these frames, of which the reader is periodically reminded, and the direct portrait of Davis is a different thing, perhaps a lesser thing. And then within the portrait itself there are other framings, improbable as my imagery may sound: the sketches of Lincoln, of Lee; the ironic linkages with Simon Buckner, Zachary Taylor, John Brown, Gerrit Smith, and others; the national context, the minglings of attitude in both South and North; the frame of the twentieth-century line of vision, of political principles and wartime practice, of conflicting theories of war; and finally back to the first personal frame of the narrator, now merged with the new frame of the modern celebrations that only thinly echo the celebrated; and then the new personal frame, that of the family graves. I sink into catalog, I fear; I do not try to show how these diverse perspectives work; I omit much that is important; I only assert the unity. Well, if I am lucky, this sketch of what I take to be the *unum e pluribus* may suggest something of the combined substance and elegance of the Davis study.

But I must return, for a closer, to my assigned subject, which is not so much the work as the man, and indeed the man in that distant no-man's-land, or everyman's growing land, between minority and middle age. In my recollections of the man I fear I have been mostly knee-deep in trivia.

But when the trivia concern a big man, they lose, I hope, something of their triviality. And I hope that, however peripherally, they may help evoke the image of a young man who at the time seemed a little more than the common man celebrated in modern myth. In retrospect we can see clearly what we did not all spot at the time—the creative energy that would still be surging long beyond threescore and ten. He was, and is, the gentleman who has an uncommon sense of the ungentleness of the human tribe. Know what he may, he still remains among the artists that, in Elizabeth Bowen's words, "were intended to be an ornament to society." But not through not seeing through it when it needed seeing through. And not only society, since it is for all of us that he can ask, in that summer-afternoon hypnotic state that brings certain truths to the surface, "Was this / The life that all those years I lived, and did not know?" So one remembers John Stuart Mill's claiming for himself a "large tolerance for one-eyed men, provided their one eye is a penetrating one: if they saw more, they would probably not see so keenly." Red saw, and sees, not only keenly, but more.

7

Theodore Roethke

Anyone who has listened to or read descriptions of Theodore Roethke cannot have failed to notice that one image is used repeatedly to portray the physical being: "great bear of a man." It is good enough down to a certain point, but not below it. Around the middle he was expansive, even fat if he let his stomach get away from him. He had a barrel-like upper trunk, widening out still further into great shoulders that made a vast prominent mound because the head, large and striking as it was, was forward and slightly low, as if fixed there like that of a very tall woman always trying to seem, even on a grand scale, petite. A man over six feet in height, he seemed to be slightly hunching; and he could easily and quickly squeeze into a crouch in those moods when, with self-critical humor or a challenging earnestness, he liked to fancy himself the prize-fighter. His walk was rather ungainly; it had an uneasy swaying effect, as if the feet were heavy. If he wanted to hurry, his motions reminded one of a person in a dream, making great efforts but held back by some intangible weight or marshy ooze.

So much for the bear. What that image, useful as it is, does not reveal is that, for all of a kind of sad laboriousness in the walk, the legs were long and relatively slender. They were far apart, and his feet toed in a little. This, together with the characteristic loose and baggy clothes that had the effect of extending his general paunchiness downward, helped disguise the fact that in his physique there was as much of the ostrich as of the bear. He had to be in shorts for this to be seen. One might have guessed it, though, even without seeing him specifically at tennis or badminton (in which he was an intense competitor without mercy for others or, more significantly, for himself). For along with his heaviness, sometimes that of the sack of vegetables, sometimes that of the monument, was a remarkable latent agility, a capacity for high-speed controlled movement, an instantaneous motor response to stimuli. Once, when Roethke was in

117

the English office, someone's lighted cigarette falling off an ashtray set afire a mass of papers on a desk; while the rest of us gaped and uncertainly tried to think what to do next, Roethke whipped into a supply room, snatched a fire extinguisher, and in what seemed less than a second was the only effective fireman in the lot of us. The massive shambling man was suddenly the quick getaway man, with the fast reaction time that means high cooperation between speedy thought and utterly responsive muscles. Here, of course, the ostrich figure breaks down; it gives the right physical image, but it also suggests the long-paced cross-country racer, which Roethke was not. He was not a straightaway runner, not a trackman, but rather a man of lightning footwork, a short-paced skipper and dodger, a stage or ballroom dancer. At parties, I've heard women say, he was as good a dancer as he chose to be, light-footed and rhythmic; it depended on whether he wanted to yield to the music or seize stage, be a participant or a dizzying star—or toy with his partner in a jocose or even raucous elephantine amorousness that betrayed more a sense of spotlights than a Don Juan intentness on results. He liked looking like a naughty boy and was inclined to take looking for being; in any little enterprise à deux his eyes, registering delight at his deviltry, were as likely to be seeking applause from observers as consent from the woman in hand. (Some women found him, with his unsubtle hands and mountainous verbal coynesses, bothersome and boring; some were charmed, some fascinated; some were matter-of-fact, some found the sparring fun; some dutifully disliked the passes, others hated to be passed over; and veterans of dining-table and parlor skirmishes could always be relieved by new volunteers, half-ready to bare a breast to the enemy charge, half-ready for the purple heart, and always able, if the pressure was too severe, to retire upon reserves of husbandly strength. The reserves had styles ranging from suitable indignation, fired from heavy batteries of propriety, to an insouciant "You know your way around the course, dear. Don't lean on me.")

The large head was the more impressive for the thinness of the blondish, light-brown hair that left him close to bald. The blue-gray eyes, rather far apart, were rarely mild; if he was angry, or strongly moved in other ways, his glance took on an intimidating intensity. He had a large mouth that spread far and opened wide for the belly laughs that were the most characteristic expression of his gay moods; there were fewer of these in later years. An ordinary social smile was difficult for him; the uneasy flash that he managed was a cross between a nervous simper and a grimace, as if he simply did not know how to do it or was fixing the lines of his face like an unimaginative actor responding mechanically to a director. Hence, if he was not roaring and gargantuan, he tended toward a severity of expression that betokened, however, less a we-are-not-pleased stance than a limited capacity for easy and casual amiability. In the face one was less aware of the bony structure than of the ample fleshiness; if he was not well or did not take care of himself, it took on a somewhat sodden cast. Indulgence could make it, at times, flabby and gross. Yet what looked like a heavy sulkiness could be transmuted, as quickly as his lumberingness of body into alert action, into a variety of different strong and lively expressions: a snarl of contempt, a wide-eyed and even slightly pop-eyed burst of approval for an act of style he admired, an intense high-voiced excitement of a maker of plans, or even a grin and great chuckle of self-irony, with a pleasing medley of sharpness and good nature.

In photographs this face, more coarse than delicate, more violent than ordered, more commonplace than distinguished, invariably took on a perceptiveness, a thoughtfulness, a true and profound solemnity from which it is difficult to withhold the word *noble*. In no sense did the photographs fabricate, in no sense do they lie. They seem rather to catch, with impressive unanimity, an essence that did not easily break through the features presented to us in everyday life. The nobility that they discover has its roots in suffering—in suffering endured, dreaded, inescapable, and yet survived and, in an ever maturing art, surmounted. The photographs give us the face of a man who has seen a terrible vision, who has been unalterably marked by it, made permanently somber and doomed to the valley of the shadow; yet not crushed or deadened or rendered pathetic, but endowed with knowledge that is a burden to the man but a boon to the artist. He has known la belle dame sans merci and has found, instead of listlessness and disillusion, a graver wisdom. It may be that such a speculation derives mainly from one's knowledge of Roethke's medical history, but I am inclined to think that what the photographs reveal is likewise revealed by the poetry, with its progress, through an indefatigable experimentation in modes, to a contemplative, philosophical range that, without repudiating them or ceasing to make use of them, has gone beyond lyrical topicalities, surrealistic discords, and nightmare intensities.

If a conventional social style was not Roethke's forte, it was that his instinctive manner, or, as he might have put it, his "rhythm," was a special one, not that he disdained the amenities. Whatever of the bohemian there was in some of his habits (with night as the major time of serious work, as well as of madcap play from which he wanted always to be the last to retreat to bed; with a fondness, at least in anecdotes, for dives, bums, the offbeat; with a natural and easy kinship with artists in other media), his sensibility was markedly bourgeois. He liked the well heeled, the well got up, the well bred; he liked to have a big salary, big fees, a big house; he liked big guns, big wheels, powers on and behind thrones. He dreamed of Maecenases, he was candid to his chosen candidates for Maecenasships, for truth was his jovial ploy; and he did achieve, if never a Virgil's patronage, at least some satisfying fringe benefits. But he was not really calculating, and he was no plutocracy snob; he could like men who were not luminaries in the world or in anything else, and "sweet man" was a phrase he often used to describe human quality. He went fishing with impecunious graduate students as well as with downtown lawyers. Hence he was an invaluable link between the university and a large nonacademic community where professors are often suspect, or, because they are either too modest or too magisterial, do not represent their world effectively. As a gown amid townsmen, he could be offhand, gauche, grumpy, occasionally quarrelsome, and even boorish; he took some tolerating, though of a different kind from that exacted by a pure academic of the contentious or self-righteous breed. But he was not really contentious and not at all self-righteous; in the end what came through was a very strong, special personality and a sensed genius joined with a willingness to like quite different men and a desire to be liked by them. Along with the complex and sophisticated imagination there was a real strand of naïveté in the personality, and it was appealing; it provided lesser men with a counterbalance to their own limitations, so that they needed not merely to succumb to greatness but found, to ease the mind, an intimation of equality. They could smile a little when he elaborated great plans for profit, for utopias, for revolutions against incompetence *in urbe et orbe* (not to mention *in universitate*), for new institutions, and daring enterprises; or in intimated triumphs in the profession (bigger advances, larger prizes coming), in love (eager partners queuing up), in war (foes literally flattened, falsities unmasked, arguments demolished). Then they could the more easily grant him unusual immunities, unreservedly admire the extraordinary talents, and wholeheartedly rejoice in the procession of real triumphs. In guessing about some of the subtleties of interplay in such relationships, I by no means cynically imply a psychological and moral quid pro quo, a yielding of esteem only when there are the mechanics for a token of self-esteem. Many lesser men do not—and did not—fail in the esteem deserved by a greater. No death in the university community, I think, ever evoked a greater sense of loss in the city.

About people he had an odd union of perceptiveness and naïveté— though no odder, perhaps, than that of the rest of us. The naïveté appeared in his tendency, by no means a unique one, to value above the market rate critics and scholars who were showing a special interest in his own work and to urge that we try to recruit them for the staff. Otherwise he was acute in estimating personalities. In earlier years he would leap to unqualified judgments (though rarely without a general rightness) and put them in vigorous and pungent words, but he could always reassess when his eye caught something it had not seen before. Although often distributing abuse was for him a kind of game, a metaphor of discontent, a release of tensions, an excuse for verbal pyrotechnics, he was not an angry man, an arrogant contemner of others. He could be very generous. But he was often ahead of the conventional or the going evaluations of people: he had a very sensitive intuition of ultimate quality—of sickness, or coarseness, or ambiguity, or largeness; of whatever element did not readily meet the eye.

Yet one might hear him spot a basic, generally invisible flaw in a man, and then learn that he had asked the man's advice about a poem he was working on. What looks like an inconsistency is not a real one. Roethke might identify a shrunken soul and yet along with it spot a taste that in a certain context he could rely on. More than that, the man who could at one moment insist that he was the greatest living poet could at another moment be very modest about his creative tact and hence entirely willing to learn from others. He might formally think a response untutored and yet respect it. At one moment he might think of academic colleagues as pedantic; at many more moments he was likely to value, even to overvalue, their learning, and hence be ready to draw on it. The point is that he was willing to learn from everyone. He had no false pride here, whatever pride he had elsewhere. Behind this point lies the still larger one that he had a vast conscience about his work. He never ceased revising, fiddling with a line or word, trying it a dozen different ways; for nearly every poem he produced a sizable informal variorum, as future editions will show. He would never let anything "go" until it was "ready." With him the withholding of the final judgment of readiness was an invariable sign of health. In illness he was quickly enthusiastic, even about inferior work.

He had an equally goading conscience about readings. He wanted to be paid well; he had a Byronic disinclination to give anything away. But then he wanted to put on the best show the audience had ever seen and heard; he had in him none of the languid youth on the poetry circuit, listlessly dropping pearls before swine unaware of their good fortune, nor of the turtleneck-sweatered adolescents using unkempt mien and verse as instruments of retaliation against an unheeding world. Roethke wanted to delight, move, "send," overwhelm the audience. He gave everything he had lavishly—of voice, variety of pace, mimetic talent, gesture, of energy rushing out as it were over and above its physical channels, as though he were forcing life into an audience, bringing them to a new height of vital participation and excitement. The strain was exhausting; he came to know that he could not accept a third of the invitations that kept coming to him. Weeks before a reading, he would begin to tense up. He told me that sometimes he vomited twice before a public appearance. He planned the "show" carefully; he did not drift around as though he did not know what was coming next. He wanted to be the ultimate showman, to read as soaringly as Dylan Thomas—or better—and to combine the reading with a vaudeville or nightclub act. He strove to be a great public entertainer, a combination of powerful, sublime reader with comedian and humorist and even satirist. In the latter role his judgment was unsure, and his consciously funny topical verses, quips at the audience, topical references, and jokes about others and himself often fell below his best level of private spontaneous humor, not to mention his bardic performance. But whatever faults of this kind he may have had, if faults they were, were intimately attached to the extraordinary virtue of commitment to the maximum excellence of the poet holding and enthralling his audience.

As a teacher he had the same unpacifiable conscience. He never had the vanity, common among both writers and scholars, of thinking that the classroom work was only a necessity of existence, a nominal reason for rewarding his genius, but a task that properly belonged to lesser men. He always taught a regular department schedule. He did want to teach less, but this was because teaching took a great deal out of him; in class he felt almost the same strain that he felt in public readings. But he never ducked classroom duty; when he went away on readings he rarely failed to say something like "Look, Pa, I'll make it up with extra meetings." But these matters are peripheral. At the heart of the matter was that teaching took a great deal out of him because he put into it everything he had. He was apparently incapable of doing less. Once he told me that a doctor had told him that he must make an effort to slow down in class, to avoid "revving up." He said wryly, "Low-gear Roethke." I doubt that he got down even as far as second gear. I don't know what he actually did in class; I do know that his students always thought it superb teaching. Some of it, perhaps most of it, was "nature"; but it was always abetted by "art." He thought a great deal about teaching; he kept elaborate notes on classroom procedure. He could ask, "What did I do wrong?" From his conviction, his energy, his imagination, his sometimes—I'm guessing—inarticulate pushing outward of intuitions and intense feeling, as if they were palpable essences, his students got a sense of light, of elevation, of power conferred. But besides his instinctive giving and giving out in this way, he did a great deal of planning of methods for training in craftsmanship. If his soul was Longinian, his mind was Horatian. He assigned all kinds of finger exercises in composition; three-beat lines, four-beat lines, couplets, quatrains, set rhyme schemes, assigned images to be developed. He would give out the rhyme words and make students fit verses to them—kindergarten sestinas, as it were. He valued discipline highly. The marriage of spirit and mechanics was peerlessly effective. It worked for many students who became publishing poets. It worked for many who were not to be poets but who from him got a great inside knowledge of poetry. The pure impressiveness of the man made a mark that not many teachers make. Students' devotion was unlimited. And in his times of illness their understanding was that of the most mature and experienced adults.

He had a vast conscience as a host. Entertaining, I'd guess, was not easy for him, but he was more than dutiful about it, more than generous. When he embarked on a party, he wanted it to go, or still better go off with a bang. Sometimes he supervised the cooking; he had some kitchen talents. He could bellow immoderately at his wife if things seemed to him not split-second, spit-and-polish, according to the book as he pleased to read it at the moment. (He was immensely devoted to her, and she took his drill-sergeant shouting or sarcasm in stride: "Oh dear, there goes Ted again.") He was a bartender of reckless elbow and overbearing insistence; he considered continuing sobriety among his guests a case of challenging bad manners, and he was prepared to grind it down; guests might well fear that, if necessary, he would hold their heads under pools of drinks, for he was big and strong and gave the impression of not bowing to petty inhibitions. Before dinner or in the early hours of an evening party he would be an unsmilingly earnest pusher of drinks which were always tanned in complexion, never pale; he was like a churchwarden rigorously and even harshly urging a bigger dose of the gospel upon backsliding Christians. With a mixture of unease and censoriousness he would anxiously demand that guests instantly shed their anxieties and break into boisterous gaiety. Eventually he would ease up himself and take the lead in genial noise, in guffawing, in frolicking fancies; and he loved to get a dance started. When guests began going home he would look incredulous, aggrieved, hurt, unloved; for them to go before 4 or 5 A.M., before an early breakfast, was a blow to the host, a failure of respect, a vote of lack of confidence, an accusation of inadequacy. No doubt he never did say piteously "What have I done?" but the image of his doing just that best describes his air of anguished disbelief as we weaker sisters took off.

As a colleague he was a man of great conscience. He was not useful in ordinary ways in the department or the university; he was not a committee man. But he was not aloof, indifferent, a great man who could not be bothered. He was profoundly concerned about the department, more so, perhaps, than some people who took their own good citizenship for granted. He thought about colleagues much more than most of them knew. He had fantasies of demoting and ousting those who he thought did not contribute. But more important, he had a keen eye for quality, or rather, a passion for it. His eye might err, but he did not disdain the lenses of new evidence. He could sound ferocious about those who seemed untalented or lacking in some way or who seemed to be pursuing only private ends, and yet have a very kindly feeling for someone in whom he sensed a warmth and the right devotion. He wanted to make the people of quality effective, influential, powerful. He developed an increasing range in his sense of quality. Years ago he said to me, "We need more screwballs in this department." Later he came to admire men whose solid virtues were as far as possible from screwball. But he not only cried for quality, he relished it; he was delighted when colleagues turned out superior work; more and more he came to have a picture of the department as an assemblage of highly gifted people in whom he took great pride. Privately he might rage about people who did not measure up; publicly he was given to hyperbolic praise of the department, as if a larger than average number had measured up. He traveled more than most of us, and in this country and abroad he sang our praises without stint.

He was not a shrinking violet. He knew the extent of his own contributions to department and university, and he did not leave them unrehearsed. He fully reported all recognitions, achievements, honors, glories, always prefacing the record with "Look, Pa, I don't mean to pull the I-love-me pitch." He wanted due rewards from us; he had a little of some professors' itch for special prerogatives that will assure them from without, when the inner voice begins to crack and lose strength, that they are not as other men. Yet he had far less willfulness than some other men, often less gifted ones, have; he really did not equate the gratification of his ego with the course of justice. He had in him something of the promoter, but he did not substitute self-promotion for ability and the hard practice of his craft. He naturally caught and held the eye of others, he could be jealous of rival attractions, and he relished attention, but he did not use base devices to get it. He was not a peddler of easy shocks, a calculating upsetter of others' nerves, a shoddy middle-aged *enfant terrible*. In good health he could be a lively playboy of the western world, a mischievous needler; yet he had the kind of essential maturity that goes with authentic talent. The roaring-boy fantasies of gangsters and gunplay that usually betrayed ill health may have connoted an outsider's resentfulness or even revengefulness, for widespread recognition came to him late; but in his general style there was little aggressiveness beyond that of verbal games. For a big and frequently noisy man he was remarkably mild. Whatever anguish there may have been as an inseparable accompaniment of serious creative life, I had the impression that beneath all fluctuations of mood and demeanor he felt a rather substantial security in his gifts. He could rage about other poets, but he rarely sounded petty or meanly envious; challenged about a diatribe against a big name he could say quickly, "Oh, I know he's a great man," and he praised many of his contemporaries. He took immense pride in the work of his students; he did not feel challenged or get anxious lest his own light fade when they shone. He must have been sure of himself, it seemed to an observer like me, because he had an aura of genius. It is hard to put a finger on, but most people who had contact with him felt that they were or had been with an extraordinary person. A strange force emanated from him. Even before fame had come to him, people in the university began to feel that he was worth some special treatment. His personality was charismatic; along with the magnetism of felt special gifts there was a drawing power to which many different kinds of people yielded. It was not charm in any conventional sense; the style was offbeat, and he was often difficult, clumsy, rude. Without trying he could make others feel ignored or belittled, sometimes repelled and even, once in a while, outraged. Yet I have heard more than one person speak of him as a "wonderful human being." There was a center of power in him that drew people; in the end he was, in his own way, a winning person.

Of this there is no better evidence than his impact on the secretarial staff of the department. In a burst of impatience he could reduce a young woman to tears; he wanted a good deal of service, and his often lumbering way and imprecise communicating of just what he wanted made him not the easiest taskmaster, especially to one only modestly endowed with extrasensory perception; he had a way of settling down in the office and blocking both passageway and ordinary proceedings like the immense tycoon that, with some part of his being, he always wished to be. Yet the secretaries came to do everything they could for him; they were truly devoted. To give this point the emphasis it needs, I should stress what is known only by someone who has worked in an office: a secretarial staff knows a very great deal about department members. It gains this knowledge willy-nilly because in front of the secretaries most faculty members are off-guard, and willy-nilly they either prove or betray themselves. While some unknowingly reveal themselves as bad-mannered or bad-tempered, self-important or self-seeking, pompous or wheedling, demanding or tricky, Roethke won, by whatever intangible quality it was, a desire to help him. At any given moment he might frighten or even disgust, but such moments were forgiven because they seemed deviations from a real nature that made the staff willing to do all it could for him.

Perhaps, for all of a sometimes peremptory style, there was a kind of helplessness that made the staff helpful. He was frank, unpretentious, even rather innocent; stratagems and calculations were beyond him. He did not substitute talk for work. In trouble, he won sympathy; when he joked, laughter broke out. He had a wonderful capacity for self-criticism that would undercut all euphoric flights and grandiose dreams. He could jest richly about his own illness. Once, in well-being and good spirits, he looked back on a recent "high" period when he had been hospitalized, and roared gleefully, "Bet-a-million Roethke will ride again." At such moments he was irresistible.

He was always compelling. It was part of the good luck of my own life to know him well, for fifteen years, this witty and imaginative man, sometimes troublesome but more often troubled, sometimes combative but more often playful, yet always of high earnestness and conscience in his double vocation of teacher and poet—a man in whom I felt something that, I came in time to know, was to be called greatness.

He died in 1963, and thirty-five years later he is remembered so clearly as a department star that it was almost as if he were still alive.

8

Malcolm Cowley as University Professor

The worries and conflicts preceding Malcolm Cowley's stint as visiting professor at the University of Washington early in 1950 have been pretty well described by Jane Sanders and by Cowley himself.[1] But some details of the Cowley episode do not enter into their published accounts, and history may be served by spelling out these details. They should add some color, and may even add a little bit of body, to an episode of more than forty years ago. I write, however, not as a formal historian, but as a participant working primarily from his recollections of happenings in 1949 and 1950. This report belongs, then, to the realm of journalism rather than to that of scholarship.

Few nonparticipants and nonspecialists, even those living in the Northwest, will remember events in the state of Washington in the late 1940s, however much these events were big headliners in their day. So it seems sensible to establish several contexts for the attempted blocking of Cowley's appointment as a visiting professor at the University of Washington.

The national context: The postwar fear of Russia was great; the House Un-American Activities Committee was feeding on this fear and no doubt increasing it; this double process was to reach extremes a little later in the prosecutorial style of the McCarthy committee in the Senate.

The state context: The Canwell committee, a state predecessor of the McCarthy committee at the national level, had been on a Communist hunt for several years and had unearthed several former or supposed members of the Communist Party on the University of Washington faculty. University hearings in 1948 had led to the dismissal of several faculty members and the placing of several others on probation.

---

1. Jane Sanders, *Cold War on the Campus: Academic Freedom at the University of Washington* (Seattle: University of Washington Press, 1979); Malcolm Cowley, "Gammon for Dinner," in *The Flower and the Leaf,* ed. Donald W. Faulkner (New York: Viking, 1985).

The university context: The administration was caught in a difficult situation between outer pressures to move against supposed Communists and faculty pressure to resist all outside pressure (and there were splits within the faculty itself). The administration was also caught between these political pressures and its desire and efforts to enhance the scholarly status of the university and to push it on from regional activity into a larger participation in the national scholarly scene.

The department of English context: There was great psychological turmoil because of the Canwell committee attacks on various members of the department, attacks that led to the dismissal of one staff member and the placing of another on probation. An immense amount of energy went into discussion of the Canwell hearings, university policy, and the style that others thought appropriate for those summoned to testify before the Canwell committee and before the university committee that heard charges against faculty members. The targets of the Canwell investigation were generally well liked and were regarded as totally incapable of any action harmful to the country; there were amazement and indignation at the apparent belief that their presence intimated a Russian infiltration of the university. At the same time we were inaugurating a program, one that has become more extensive over the years, of importing writers (fictionists, poets, critics) as visiting professors for periods ranging from a week to a term to an academic year; this was one aspect of a general movement toward a wider participation in the literary and scholarly life of the country. (We secured various writers for what were their first teaching jobs: Cowley, Richard Eberhart, Vernon Watkins, Elizabeth Bishop.)

Such was the background for the department's invitation to Cowley to be a visiting professor during the winter quarter (January to March) of 1950. I recall no opposition within the department, no raising at all of the question of politics. Cowley was widely admired as a literary critic, and no one thought of him as either a political liability or a political prize. The first raising of the political issue was by Cowley himself. His letters to me showed that he was aware of the doings of the Canwell committee during the past several years and of the possibility that such bodies might want to feast upon his political activities back in the 1930s. He spelled out the facts that some right-wing group might want to use against him. His character showed in candor rather than concealment. I of course included all his statements of this kind in the vast intra-institutional correspondence that led to approval of the appointment by the appropriate internal agencies and then brought the recommendation for the appointment to the Board of Regents. Ordinarily, board action on such recommendations would be automatic, but strong opposition by one board member evidently created enough doubt to slow things down. The board did not act at the first meeting at which the Cowley appointment was on the agenda, and I was summoned to testify. My chief recollection of the board meeting is that the atmosphere was comfortable, not confrontational, and that I was not so much challenged as asked to explicate. I also recall an impression that, to my surprise, some of the most intelligent questions and comments were those of board member Dave Beck, the already famous head of the Teamsters. I assume that the date of this meeting was May 13, 1949, which official correspondence shows was the date on which the board approved the Cowley appointment. The chief opposition was by Regent George Stuntz. When all hell broke loose in December 1949, Stuntz was listed in the press as one of the Cowley opponents, and a news story contained this statement: "Stuntz said he had opposed Cowley's appointment in two meetings of the Board of Regents, 'but faculty members talked me down.'"[2]

During the next six months anti-Cowley forces were busy looking for facts supposedly to his discredit and circulating them. Cowley evidently got wind of this (in letters from me? The official file contains no such letters), and in November he sent me a very long account of all his political activities in the past and authorized me to use these facts in any way that might clarify the situation. I sent his statement, along with several of my own, to the president's office for use in answering complaints about the Cowley appointment. But things went on getting worse rather than better, until there was a public uproar in late December, just a week or two before Cowley's scheduled arrival. Up to this point the public story has been well told in Jane Sanders's *Cold War on the Campus*. I summarize the main facts only as background for my own account of one or two behind-the-scenes events. Cowley's essay says something about these, but not in preemptive detail.

ii

Sometime in December 1949, the university's president, Raymond B. Allen, phoned me to talk about the welling up of opposition to the Cowley appointment, and the problem of dealing with growing complaints that would probably eventuate in a public outcry. He made no suggestion

---

2. All matters of fact (names, dates, statements, and the like) not clearly deriving from my own recollections I have secured from the Heilman Papers, Box 11, Folders 9 and 10, in the University of Washington Archives.

whatever of backing down; obviously we were going through with the appointment. But he had some ideas about action, and I have, even now, a very clear recollection of his putting several options before me.

"We could just tell these characters downtown that it's none of their business, and then stonewall it. [I know that "stonewall" is of later provenience, but it best describes the style that Allen saw as a possibility.] Of course then there will be a terrible outcry, they will make life miserable for Cowley, and the teaching situation will be tough. Besides, our long-run problems will be greater. We'll look as if we didn't give a damn for the public, and like it or not, we have to go to them for support."

He then asked me if I'd be willing to try an educational alternative. Would I talk to some local group of objectors and try to persuade them that all was well, that Cowley's visit was a good thing rather than a bad thing? Try to defuse the opposition rather than ignore it and hope it would go away?

Allen meant, I am sure, to present real alternatives. I felt no compulsion to accept the second option. His manner was easy and even jesting. He knew that faculty members characteristically tend to resent having to explain anything to nonacademics. I was sure that if I opted for stonewalling, with all the difficulties that he outlined, I would not be classed as an enemy of the administration, and I'd have as much support as he could give. Well, the proposed procedure was a new one: explaining a course of action to its opponents rather than insisting on one's professional and moral right to follow it without interference. In part I was inclined to accept Allen's proposal because he knew the situation—by now citywide and perhaps even statewide—far better than I. I was a newcomer to the state, and I was only in the second year of my first administrative job. I did not have an a priori conviction about some absolute line that I ought to follow. Besides, riding white horses was, to mix a metaphor joyously, not my dish of tea. And I may have already been learning a lesson that later experience was to enforce, namely that in matters involving controversy, one achieved desired ends less by public gesticulation and noisy pronouncement than by quiet, private discussion. At any rate, I told Allen that I'd go along on the tactic of attempting persuasion.

He explained how he would put the decision into action: "There are several organizations that seem to be spearheading the opposition to Cowley. Obviously we cannot deal with all of them. I'll scout around and try to identify a key group. Then we'll see if we can have a talk with them." He called back several days later and said that he had indeed located the central opponent: it was the American Legion, acting through its Commission on Americanism. He had made an appointment for us to meet with them. That would be on December 27.

In one of these phone calls Allen broke some surprising news: the opposition had taken a new turn or at least had found a new weapon. A little later, on December 29, Allen, replying to a letter from a realtor, G. E. McCormick, would state that "apparently someone has circulated a group of excerpts from Mr. Cowley's poetry fairly widely through the community."[3] This act had led to a series of indignant phone calls and letters to the president and also to members of the Board of Regents: Cowley was now not only a Red or a Red-sympathizer but also a dirty poet. Such a user of foul language should not besmirch the University of Washington. It looked as if this was now to be the main line of opposition. This was an astonishing development. In retrospect most of us who had some part in these events came to this conclusion: the vigilantes had combed all of Cowley's writings, had found nothing that would substantiate their faith in his political infidelity, but then in the poetry had come across some words that surprised them—or that they chose to be surprised by—and leaped happily at this language as a justification for the opposition that had begun on other grounds. They had got so strongly committed against Cowley that they had to have grounds for it; retreat was unthinkable. Hence, thank God for dirty words. Be that as it may, it was agreed between Allen and me that my efforts before the committee would be devoted largely to the dirty-language issue. After all, a great deal of evidence on Cowley's political activities and beliefs had been widely circulated; in that area there was not much more to be said. But on the literary issue, I could be a witness with presumptive technical expertise. My being executive officer (as the chair was then called) of the department of English naturally guaranteed, at least for outsiders, my professional authority.

The phone talks with President Allen must have taken place no later than midmonth, since under the best circumstances I would need several weeks to get ready for the meeting with the Legion committee. My research was especially difficult because the anti-Cowleyites had obviously been reading Cowley like mad, and both the university and city libraries were practically denuded of their Cowley holdings. I had to get Cowley's two volumes of poetry (published in 1929 and 1941) by interlibrary loan. Reading through two volumes of poetry looking for dirty words was rather a new exercise in literary research. And the job was mainly of the "imagine my surprise" variety. Unless my memory is even more faulty than I know it to be, I found only one four-letter word, namely *turd*. Otherwise the only diction that the vigilantes could have believed to serve their ends was standard

---

3. In "Gammon for Dinner" Cowley refers to this someone as "Albert." He may have been told who it was. If I did learn the identity at the time, I have forgotten it.

oaths such as *God* and *Christ*. I probably also made a note of the presence of the word *bastard;* though it was used routinely in the literal rather than the metaphorical sense, my audience might well wish to cite it as a swear word. The poetry had no scenes or events that came within miles of what today is standard sex and elimination fare. Fortunately I quickly recalled that *turd* was used more than once by Chaucer, and I found one use of it in Shakespeare. I'm sure I checked through the *O.E.D.* to find four-letter words in "respectable" literary quarters. Eric Partridge's *Shakespeare's Bawdy* had come out in 1948, and it was great help in finding useful illustrations. I must have made ample notes on Shakespeare's frequent games with the word *die*. This was, of course, a vast amount of heavy artillery to assemble in defense of a small body of work that was on the whole so mild that it was difficult to imagine hostility toward it by even an ignorant bigot or a passionate prosecutor.

While I was privately struggling with my pro-Cowley brief, things were heating up politically. On December 22 the *Seattle Times* ran a column-long story under the headline "Vet Groups, Others Fight Appointment"; it listed various opponents. Charles C. Ralls, identified as national senior vice-commander of the Veterans of Foreign Wars, was quoted as saying that "some of Cowley's poetry is of the lowest barroom variety." The next day, December 23, the *Post-Intelligencer* ran an eight-column headline on the front page: "Poet to Lecture at U. Despite Protests." The story occupied half a column on the front page, and its continuation, plus allied stories on other pages (one of which listed numerous allegedly Communist front organizations to which Cowley was said to have belonged), would almost have filled an eight-column page. The front-page story listed the official opponents of the appointment: Ralls and regent George Stuntz, both quoted above; George Flood, a member of the American Legion's national legislative committee; Pro America; State Representative William D. Shannon; "P.T.A. Groups"; "a special American Legion committee in Seattle"; and "others."

In retrospect some of this seems rather Gilbert-and-Sullivan-ish, but it hardly did then. On December 12, President Allen had written a long letter in defense of the appointment to the Congressman Shannon listed on December 22 as an opponent. Later he wrote other such letters: on December 27, to the Reverend Dwight L. Cart, pastor of Plymouth Congregational Church, who had complained that Cowley's poetry was all "trash and morbidity"; on December 28, to Miss Gertrude L. Apel, general secretary of the Council of Churches and Christian Education, who had characterized Cowley as a person of "low ideals and immoral thoughts"; on December 29, to Harold C. Herman, of the same organization, countering the view that Cowley "delights in devoting his attention to the obscene and the frailties of life"; on December 29 to Mrs. John L. Welborn, denying that Cowley was a Communist. On December 28, Ross Cunningham, an editor of the *Seattle Times* and I suppose one of the most influential journalistic voices in the region, devoted a column to attacking Cowley and the university for offering him an appointment.

iii

Such facts reveal something about the atmosphere of that Christmas season —the atmosphere in which the American Legion committee met on December 27 to hear the university case. The university representatives were three: President Allen, Donald K. Anderson, the director of public relations, and I. We drove to a downtown building that I can no longer identify and met in a room that seemed much too large for six people. Allen made some gracious introductory remarks and then turned the meeting over to me. The two-hour meeting was surprisingly mild. I cannot remember hostility in the questioning, vigorous cross-examination, or any effort to put me down. Indeed, I cannot remember very much questioning, and I believe I had some sense of lecturing to a class that was not too much interested in the subject. I was, of course, determined not to talk down, to look aggrieved, or to be a humble suppliant for favor, but to be, instead, an independent, good-natured expositor, eager to explain an issue that was of great interest to him, and counting on the auditors to share that interest and to sympathize with the critical point of view. My discourse must have occupied most of the two hours. I cannot remember saying anything about the political issue, though I suppose I must have referred to the voluminous material on it that had surely reached the committee members. My "lecture" about the poetry turned on three points. The first was that any words thought to be naughty had to be seen not in isolation but in context, and that one had to consider the tone and import of the whole poem; from that point of view, Cowley's work was far as could be from the pornographic. I subjected the audience to a good deal of *explication de texte* applied to various Cowley poems. The second point was that we ought to look at one man's work—nowadays one would say *oeuvre,* a term it is just as well was not available then—not in isolation but in the context of the work of writers generally. This is where I introduced all the evidence of dirty verbal doings in Chaucer, Shakespeare, et al. Third, in such matters taste changes, and I believe I held forth on the relative candor of the Renaissance, the development of greater reticence in the eighteenth and nineteenth centuries, and the twentieth century moves back toward an earlier freedom.

Sometime within the next day or two Allen phoned me to say that the Legion committee had acted favorably and that we were in the clear. The committee hearing might have led to further condemnation; since that did not happen, I suppose we assumed that a sort of pro-Cowley grapevine would counteract the continuing public criticism. We felt better. Whether my disquisition to the committee had any influence I don't know. I suspect that the strongest pro-Cowley argument was Allen's steadfastness throughout, and his physical presence at the committee hearing. He had a record of anti-Communism and, a big, genial, unpretentious man, got on well with nonacademics; a doctor of medicine with a fund of stories, he could be one of the boys better than the ordinary Ph.D. (He was a urologist. Another medical man told me that urologists were famous as bottomless wells of honey-bucket humor. One has to hope that that description applied to Allen, since it would add such a nice ironic touch to the defense of Cowley.)

On January 5, Allen, expressing appreciation of the work of the committee "in this important matter," wrote letters both to Jack Schrader, chairman of the Americanization Commission of the Legion (the parent body of the committee that held the hearings), and to Stephen F. Chadwick, the chairman of the three-man committee. Aside from the statements of gratification, Allen makes interesting mention of two other interrelated matters. One is that Mr. Chadwick did not want the committee action made public. Allen was willing to go along with this, but at the same time he expressed concern that in the press the Legion continued to be listed as an opponent of the appointment. It is hard to avoid the impression that the Legion was having it both ways: showing good sense in private, but in public hanging on to an opposition that, for whatever reason, looked desirable. Allen's labors on the case did not end here. On February 2 he had to write a defense of the appointment to Mrs. Larry F. Miller, corresponding secretary of the Seattle Council of Parent-Teacher Associations, and, as late as February 21, seven weeks after Cowley's arrival, he wrote another to Mrs. Darcy Dayton of Tacoma.

The public uproar over the appointment continued through late December and on into January. On the cold morning of January 2 the Cowleys arrived in Seattle by transcontinental train, and I met them at the station amid a flock of reporters and photographers. During the next twenty years I was to meet a series of visiting eminences (Bellow, Berryman, Fiedler, and others), but not one of these attracted even a small fraction of the public attention that Cowley's arrival drew. Photographers called for us to shake hands, and a shot of the pair of us, in smiling fraternity, appeared on the front page of the *Times*—another once-in-a-lifetime experience for me.

Cowley was wonderfully gracious and urbane throughout the questioning by reporters. One statement from the *Times* is worth quoting. After reiterating his opposition to Communism, Cowley "expressed amazement at the added charge that his poetry is smutty. . . . 'Those who say it is must live at a very high altitude.' "

iv

I want to go back, briefly, to the meeting of the Legion committee where I presented our defense of the Cowley appointment. I do not remember the names of two members of the committee. They did not seem very formidable, they did not have much vitality, and I was not sure that they were with the whole business. If they suspected academics on principle, they did not show much prosecutorial zeal. It may be that my long disquisition on words and poems and their ways won some points just by boring them to death; a defense of real evil could not be as tedious as this. Still, they might vote against the person charged just because charges had been made. But the chair of the committee, Stephen F. Chadwick, was in a different category entirely. He was a big gun locally and indeed beyond local borders—head of a law firm, always active in politics, and a conspicuous figure in military and veterans' affairs. He had run once for congress and twice for a party nomination for the Senate, once as a Democrat and once as a Republican. In World War I he had served in Siberia and had received a French decoration—commander of the Legion of Honor. He had been national commander of the American Legion (1938–1939), and he was secretary of the army (1947–1954). He was commander in chief of the committee, and the other two were not very talented foot soldiers. Chadwick was worldly wise, and, as I was to learn, he had an ironic sense.

What on earth was he doing here? There was a good deal of speculation about this. He could not possibly, we all felt, have thought Cowley could be a threat to the political or moral well-being of the region. The interpretation by the more cynical observers was that of course he "knew better," but he saw some profit in playing the role of community guardian. One theory was that he wanted to run for political office again, and his sharing in the publicity of the Cowley kerfuffle would be a booster in a campaign. Politicians know what plays in Puyallup (Washington's Peoria). It is a possible scenario, but still not wholly creditable. My own guess—and I have nothing to go on but my own sense of Chadwick's personality—is that the story was more complex. I, too, like to think that he "knew better," but it is also possible that, like a good many people who were by no means in the vigilante class, he was somewhat influenced by the extraordinary fears that often made our society act irrationally in the decade following the war. Then there is a subtler possibility: that Chadwick indeed knew that Cowley was not guilty as charged but, since the charges were made or supported by the organization with which he had long been affiliated, and of which he had been the national head, it was extraordinarily difficult for him to tell the brotherhood that they were all off base and that this would never do. So he went along with the procedure dictated by their worries, but he managed it in such a way that, as hindsight apparently makes clear, the outcome expressed the duality of his impulses: he saw to it that the committee action came out right (that is, it did not support the Legion preconceptions), but he did not want this publicly known. The Legion continued to be named in the press as anti-Cowley, but its nationally known figure had privately blessed the appointment. Thus Chadwick was neither a defector from the Legion nor an enemy of the university community.

These surmises may be supported by a later episode in which I was a participant, and indeed I have gone into the Legion committee scene mostly as background for the subsequent event. Sometime in January 1950, a member of the English department, Mrs. Geraldine Leota Willis, known as "Jerilee," gave a big cocktail party in honor of Malcolm and Muriel Cowley. Since Jerilee had once been married to a member of a prominent Seattle family, she knew many local people; hence her parties often had an unusual mix of town and gown. Such a party was the natural meeting ground for Cowley and Chadwick. I was sort of propelling Malcolm around, and I may have introduced the two. At any rate, I was with the pair for quite a while, as participant in or listener to their chat. Drink flowed, and in time they fell into that delightful activity of little male knots at parties, exchanging naughty stories. I was charmed to see this common ground between the resident bourgeois guardian and the transient bohemian disturber of the peace.

Later in the party, perhaps just as he was leaving, Chadwick said to me: "I knew that this wasn't a very good appointment. Cowley is just a traveling minstrel." No need to refute that singular misjudgment. What is at the heart of the matter is not the intellectual quality of a foolish disparagement, but the meaning of it: clearly Chadwick was trying to hang on to whatever opposition he had shared in as a Legionnaire and as a creature of the public uproar, but at the same time to make the opposition intellectually respectable by detaching it from mere popular prejudices and neuroses and grounding it instead on professional qualifications. He was turning academic. It is hard not to have some fondness for such an effort to change spots.

Cowley was a good academic visitor. In two ways he was different from most visiting literati, of whom I was to see a great many in the next two decades. He had an easy amiability quite different from the dour or impatient egocentricity of many imports, and, a great companion in restaurants and pubs, he had a remarkably quick hand for the check. Students who wanted to take his lecture course were more numerous than the seats in the large lecture room to which the course had been assigned, and student reports on the course were all favorable. There were no complaints of subversion or pornography. Cowley's five public lectures went well, too. Attendance fell off somewhat, though, when it became apparent that a supposedly dangerous ogre, instead of being an exciting threat to political and moral well-being, was simply a quiet and detached commentator, wise and humorous but not spectacular, on the American literary scene of the twentieth century.

III

literary
types and
problems
inspected

Shakespeare

To begin with Shakespeare has a chronological advantage: he is the earliest of the writers
to be discussed. Through this ordering of the
materials we can have some sense of moving
forward in time. But the three plays on which
I comment have other advantages. One of the
plays is very well known: *The Taming of the Shrew*. Hence readers will be able to
make their own judgments of the different readings of the play that I summarize.
The other two plays are less well known, and hence, perhaps, make good materials
for the discussion of the dramatic forms they aspire to or achieve: "romance" and
"tragedy." Obviously it is my conviction that a consideration of these traditional
forms is a good way into the character of the individual plays.

9

Farce

The Taming of the Shrew

For some three hundred years Shakespeare's *Taming of the Shrew* was generally accepted as being about the taming of a shrew. Kate was a shrew, Petruchio was a tamer, and he tamed Kate. He was the "good guy," and she was the "bad guy" in need of reform. In the theater the taming developed a long tradition of boisterousness and rowdiness; Petruchio did a good deal of roaring about and even cracking a whip. Indeed for three centuries audiences so relished Petruchio's gaining his mastery that they rarely saw the full Shakespeare in the theater but were content in its stead with a series of raucous shorter plays, one by Garrick himself, that offered much coarser and less adult transactions between the tamer and the shrew.[1] No one seems to have been distressed by this or moved to deny that Kate was at first an insufferable woman and that Petruchio dealt with her in sound fashion. As late as 1904 R. Warwick Bond could say that Kate's early style "contradicts natural law and the facts of life," that Petruchio "demonstrates [to her] the misery of life without self-discipline," and that Kate acknowledges "the justice of the lesson"; his concluding statement is that "it will be many a day . . . ere men cease to need, or women to admire, the example of Petruchio."[2] In 1928 Sir Arthur Quiller-Couch could remark, rather touchingly, "one cannot help thinking a little wistfully that the Petruchian discipline had something to say for itself."[3] A decade later H. B. Charlton could treat the play as strictly antiromantic, Petruchio as a "madcap ruffian," and Kate as simply a shrew;

---

1. See Harold Child's "The Stage-History of *The Taming of the Shrew*" in the Cambridge edition of the play, edited by Sir Arthur Quiller-Couch and John Dover Wilson (Cambridge: Cambridge University Press, 1928, 1953), 181–86.
2. Introduction to the Arden edition of the play (London, 1904), lvi, lvii, lix.
3. Introduction to the Cambridge edition, xxvi.

in fact, Charlton is so convinced of her exclusive shrewishness that he sees only inconsistency in those passages in which she complains, laments her fate, speaks of tears, and actually sheds them.[4] When modern editors insist, as many of them feel compelled to do, that Petruchio should not brandish a whip on the stage, they are not denying his role as a tamer, but pointing out that such methods are not called for by the text.

Yet at the same time they are consistent with a certain modern revisionism in the interpretation of the play, primarily of the relations between Petruchio and Kate. Perhaps in reaction against the rowdy Petruchio of the popular plays based on Shakespeare, critics have tended, for at least sixty years, to insist that Petruchio is a much subtler tamer than he had once seemed, that he is not a slam-bang wife-beating type, but a generous and affectionate fellow whose basic method is to bring out the best in his fiancée and wife by holding up before her an image both of what she is and of what she can become. But historically this moderating of the boisterous Petruchio is less than a tremendous revisionary leap that occurred after World War II. Of this leap, there were actually a few intimations long ago. Even Bond, who thought Petruchio an example for us all, feared that Petruchio's order to Kate "to throw off her cap and tread on it" was a "needless affront to her feelings" (lviii). Before Bond, however, there had been a still stronger outbreak of modern sensibility. As early as 1890 George Bernard Shaw, without questioning the basic relationship of tamer and shrew, had nevertheless declared that a modern gentleman, if he attended the play with a woman companion, was bound to be embarrassed by Kate's long speech of submission near the end of act V, scene ii. The scene, he said, is "altogether disgusting to modern sensibility."[5]

The first step in revision, then, is to back off from the play as it stands and to find Shakespeare out of line with modern feeling: women do not and should not submit. Sir Arthur Quiller-Couch acknowledged, though reluctantly, that Shakespeare is in some respects passé, that "Petruchio's [method] was undoubtedly drastic and has gone out of fashion" (xxvi). Yet this is a mild demurrer compared with the second step, the leap as I have called it, that began some thirty years ago: the real and more astonishing revisionism, far from declaring Shakespeare out of line with modern sentiment, is to declare him actually consistent with it but in ways appreciated only in the twentieth century. In brief, he has really presented Kate, not as a shrew, but as a modern girl. This new being has only

---

4. *Shakespearian Comedy* (London: Methuen, 1938), 97.
5. Edwin Wilson, ed., *Shaw on Shakespeare* (New York, 1961), 188.

"developed the defensive technique of shrewishness" against her "horrible family"—that is, a father ready to "sell" her to "the highest bidder," and "her sly little sister." This is from Nevill Coghill in 1950. According to Coghill, Kate triumphs not only over that family but likewise over Petruchio himself, though, "like most of those wives that are the natural superiors of their husbands, she allows Petruchio the mastery in public."[6] This remarkable view found confirmation and elaboration a year later in the work of the late Harold Goddard. To him, Kate's "shrewishness," a term he declared applicable only "in the most superficial sense," is "the inevitable result of her father's gross partiality"; Kate is no more than "a cross child who is starved for love." Baptista is a "family tyrant," and it is Bianca who is more nearly the shrew.

> And the play ends with the prospect that Kate is going to be more nearly the tamer than the tamed, Petruchio more nearly the tamed than the tamer, though his wife naturally will keep the true situation under cover. So taken, the play is an early version of *What Every Woman Knows*—what every woman knows being, of course, that the woman can lord it over the man so long as she allows him to think he is lording it over her.[7]

The modern Petruchio is now simply the man who is fooled. In 1958 Margaret Webster—whose great-grandfather Ben Webster in 1844 had restored the original Shakespeare *Taming* to the stage as a rival to Garrick's shorter and simpler version—carried on from Coghill and Goddard. To her, Kate is "a 'modern' woman, of intellect, courage, and enormous energy of mind and body, shut up in a society where women were supposed only to look decorative." It is as if Shakespeare's script had been rewritten by Ibsen. This Kate, unlike Goddard's, does not want to get married; she thinks the local boys "beneath contempt"; she "despises her father . . . and her silly, pretty, popular, horrid little sister. . . . She takes exasperated refuge in terrifying everybody in sight."[8]

So much for the unusual development of Kate, for the complete turn of the shrew. Let us look for a moment at her final speech of submission, which Shaw was the first to find distasteful. It has been variously read. Mark Van Doren was the first recent critic (1939) to help establish the modern trend. This long speech, he says, "would be painful to us were she

---

6. "The Basis of Shakespearian Comedy," in *Shakespeare Criticism, 1935–1960*, ed. Anne Ridler, Oxford World Classics (London: Oxford University Press, 1963), 207–9.

7. *The Meaning of Shakespeare* (Chicago: University of Chicago Press, 1951), 1:69, 68.

8. "Director's Comments," in the Laurel edition of *The Taming of the Shrew*, gen. ed. Francis Fergusson (New York, 1958), 21–22.

a person as Portia and Imogen are persons."[9] That is, she is less a human being than a mechanical figure in farce. On the other hand Donald Stauffer, even while making a rather modern reading of the play ten years after Van Doren, reminds the reader, "No less than Milton, Shakespeare accepts the natural subordination of woman to man in the state of marriage."[10] In the next year (1950) Nevill Coghill, who as we have seen starts Kate's career as a clever modern girl, acknowledges that the concept of wifely obedience is "generously and charmingly asserted by Katerina at the end" (207). A year later George I. Duthie felt constrained to issue a warning that the play is "liable to be seriously misunderstood by the modern reader" and to insist, "Katharine's last speech in the play is an enunciation of the doctrine of order as applied to the domestic milieu. . . . An insubordinate wife corresponds to a rebellious subject."[11] But in that same year (1951) Goddard exclaims violently over the submission speech, "How intolerable it would be if she and Shakespeare really meant it (as if Shakespeare could ever have meant it!)" (1:71). And seven years later, in 1958, Margaret Webster treats the speech outright as an ironic jest by Kate; it expresses her "delicious realization . . . that to 'serve, love, and obey' in all outward seeming is the surest road to victory" (23). So judicious a critic as Francis Fergusson suggests that the speech might be used "to return us to the sadder and wiser human world," but his key phrase about the speech is "ironic as it is."[12] The ironic follow-up to this is Peter Alexander's remark three years later, in 1961. Kate, he says, "shows strength and independence that make us wish that Shakespeare could have contrived in the end to show more clearly that she stoops to conquer."[13] There is something almost shocking about Alexander's restraint. While others boldly modernize Kate, Alexander merely wishes that Shakespeare had modernized her.

After three centuries of relative stability, then, Petruchio has developed rather quickly, first from an animal tamer to a gentleman-lover who simply brings out the best in Kate, and then at last to a laughable victim of the superior spouse who dupes him. Kate, at the same time, develops from a shrew to a mistreated and lovelorn daughter to a fighting young feminist

---

9. *Shakespeare* (New York: Henry Holt and Co., 1939), 52.

10. *Shakespeare's World of Images: The Development of His Moral Ideas* (New York: Norton, 1949), 44.

11. *Shakespeare* (London: Hutchinson's University Library, 1951), 57, 58–59.

12. Laurel edition, 13.

13. *Shakespeare's Life and Art* (New York: New York University Press, 1961), 67. Richard Hosley, though more under the influence of modern revisionism, is also restrained: "Kate's speech . . . was probably, without denial of the validity of its basic doctrine, as susceptible to an ironic interpretation in Shakespeare's day as in our own" (introduction to the Pelican edition of *The Taming of the Shrew* [Baltimore, 1964], 16).

who defeats both family and husband. Not only have we tamed the tamer; we have been taming *The Taming* itself. We have been hacking away at its bounding and boisterous freedom, and, with inclinations that would doubtless be called liberal, have imprisoned the play in a post-Ibsen world modified by the Wilde of *The Importance of Being Earnest* and the Shaw of *Man and Superman*. We have domesticated a free-swinging farce and made it into a brittlely ironic closet drama, the voice of a woman's world in which apron strings, while proclaiming themselves the gentle badge of duty, snap like an overseer's lash. We have, as I shall try to show, got too far away from the text, or at least from some of it. We have done so, in the main, because, perhaps out of some unrecognized aesthetic snobbery, we have gradually become less willing to recognize *The Taming* as a farce. It is true that most critics of the play have continued to use the term *farce,*[14] and relatively few have made an issue of wanting to qualify or do away with the term.[15] But even when the term itself is used, there is an underground tendency to move away from the concepts normally implied by it. Further, the flight from farce, if we may call it that, reflects a rather hazy idea about the nature of farce, and this haziness has naturally not increased the clarity of discussions of *The Taming*.[16] We tend to take farce simply as hurly-burly theater, with much slapstick, roughhouse (Petruchio with a whip, as in the older productions), pratfalls, general confusion, trickery, uproars, gags, practical jokes, and so on. Yet such characteristics, which often do appear in farce, are surface manifestations. What we need to identify is the "spirit of farce" that lies behind them. We should then be able to look more discerningly at *The Taming*—to see in what sense it is a farce, and what it does with the genre of farce.

ii

A genre is a conventionalized way of dealing with actuality, and different genres represent different habits of the human mind, or minister to the human capacity for finding pleasure in different styles of artistic representation. "Romance," for instance, is the genre that conceives of obstacles, dangers, and threats, especially those of an unusual or spectacular kind,

---

14. For example, Stauffer, Fergusson, Webster, and Mark Van Doren. Charlton employs the concept although not the word.

15. See Hardin Craig, *An Interpretation of Shakespeare* (New York: Dryden Press, 1948), 90–91. Goddard refers to scenes "where farce and comedy get mixed" (1:70).

16. The one critic of *The Taming* who makes an implicit definition that goes beyond the external phenomena and essays to grasp its spirit is Van Doren (*Shakespeare*, 48–52).

as yielding to human ingenuity, spirit, or just good luck. On the other hand "naturalism," as a literary mode, conceives of man as overcome by the pressure of outer forces, especially those of a dull, grinding persistence. The essential procedure of farce is to deal with people as if they lack, largely or totally, the physical, emotional, intellectual, and moral sensitivity that we think of as "normal." The undying popularity of farce for several thousand years indicates that, though *farce* is often a term of disparagement, a great many people, no doubt all of us at times, take pleasure in seeing human beings acting as if they were very limited human beings. Farce offers a spectacle that resembles daily actuality but lets us participate without feeling the responsibilities and liabilities that the situation would normally evoke. Perhaps we feel superior to the diminished men and women in the plot; perhaps we harmlessly work off aggressions (since verbal and physical assaults are frequent in farce). Participation in farce is easy on us; in it we escape the full complexity of our own natures and cut up without physical or moral penalties. Farce is the realm without pain or conscience. Farce offers a holiday from vulnerability, consequences, costs. It is the opposite of all the dramas of disaster in which a man's fate is too much for him. It carries out our persistent if unconscious desire to simplify life by a selective anaesthetizing of the whole person: in farce, man retains all his energy yet never gets really hurt. The give-and-take of life becomes a brisk skirmishing in which one needs neither health insurance nor liability insurance: when one is on the receiving end and has to take it, he bounces back up resiliently, and when he dishes it out, his pleasure in conquest is never undercut by the guilt of inflicting injury.

In farce, the human personality is without depth. Hence action is not slowed down by thought or by the friction of competing motives. Everything goes at high speed, with dash, variety, never a pause for stocktaking, and ever an athlete's quick glance ahead at the action coming up next. No sooner do the Players come in than the Lord plans a show to help bamboozle Sly. As soon as Baptista appears with his daughters and announces the marriage priority, other lovers plan to find a man for Kate, Lucentio falls in love with Bianca and hits on an approach in disguise, Petruchio plans to go for Kate, Bianca's lovers promise him support, Petruchio begins his suit and introduces Hortensio into the scramble of disguised lovers. Petruchio rushes through the preliminary business with Baptista and the main business with Kate, and we have a marriage. The reader is hurried over the rivalries of Bianca's lovers, making their bids to Baptista and appealing directly to the girl herself, back to Kate's wedding-day scandals, and out into the country for the postmarital welter of disturbances; then we shift back and forth regularly from rapid action in the Kate plot to almost equally rapid action in the Bianca plot. And so on. The driving pace made possible, and indeed necessitated, by the absence of depth is brilliantly managed.

In the absence of depth one is not bothered by distractions; in fact, what are logically distractions are not felt as such if they fit into the pattern of carefree farcical hammer and tongs, cut and thrust. At Petruchio's first appearance the "knocking at the gate" confusion is there for fun, not function (I.ii.1–45). The first hundred lines between Grumio and Curtis (IV.i) are a lively rattle, full of the verbal and physical blows of farce, but practically without bearing on the action. Kate is virtually forgotten for sixty lines (IV.iii) as Petruchio and Grumio fall into their virtuoso game of abusing the tailor. Furthermore, action without depth has a mechanical, automatic quality: when two Vincentios appear (V.i), people do not reason about the duplication, but, frustrated by confusion and bluffing, quickly have recourse to blows and insults, accusations of madness and chicanery, and threats of arrest—standard procedures in farce from Plautus on. Vincentio's "Thus strangers may be halèd and abused" is not a bad description of the manners of farce, in which incapacity to sort things out is basic. Mechanical action, in turn, often tends to symmetrical effects (shown most clearly in *The Comedy of Errors,* in which Shakespeare has two pairs of identical twins): the lovers of Kate and Bianca first bargain with Baptista, then approach the girls; Hortensio and Tranio (as Lucentio) resign their claims to Bianca in almost choral fashion; Bianca and the Widow (Hortensio's new spouse) respond identically to the requests of their husbands. In this final scene we have striking evidence of the manipulation of personality in the interest of symmetrical effect. Shakespeare unmistakably wants a double reversal of role at the end, a symmetry of converse movements. The new Kate has developed out of a shrew, so the old Bianca must develop into a shrew. The earlier treatment of her hardly justifies her sudden transformation, immediately after marriage, into a cool, offhand, recalcitrant, even challenging wife. Like many another character in farce, she succumbs to the habits of the generic form. Yet some modern critics treat her as harshly as if from the start she were a particularly obnoxious female.

All these effects come from a certain arbitrarily limited sense of personality. Those who have this personality are not really hurt, do not think much, are not much troubled by scruples. Farce often turns on practical jokes, in which the sadistic impulse is not restrained by any sense of injury to the victim. It would never occur to anyone that Sly might be pained or humiliated by acting as a lord and then being let down. No one hesitates to make rough jokes about Kate (even calling her "fiend of hell") in her hearing. No one putting on a disguise to dupe others has any ethical inhibitions; the end always justifies the means. When Kate "breaks the lute to" Hortensio, farce requires that he act terrified; but it does not permit him to be injured or really resentful or grieved by the loss of the lute, as a man in a nonfarcical world might well be. Verbal abuse is almost an art form; it does not hurt, as it would in ordinary life. No one supposes that the victims of Petruchio's manhandling and tantrums—the priest and sexton at the wedding, the servants and tradesmen at his home—really feel the outrageous treatment that they get. When Petruchio and Hortensio call "To her" to Kate and the Widow, it is like starting a dogfight or cockfight. Petruchio's order to Kate to bring out the other wives is like having a trained dog retrieve a stick. The scene is possible because one husband and three wives are not endowed with full human personalities; if they were, they simply could not function as trainer, retriever, and sticks.

In identifying the farcical elements in *The Shrew,* we have gradually shifted from the insensitivity that the characters must have to the mechanicalness of their responses. These people rarely think, hesitate, deliberate, or choose; they act just as quickly and unambiguously as if someone had pressed a control button. Farce simplifies life by making it not only painless but also automatic; indeed, the two qualities come together in the concept of man as machine. (The true opposite of farce is Čapek's *R. U. R.,* in which manlike robots actually begin to feel.) There is a sense in which we might legitimately call the age of computers a farcical one, for it lets us feel that basic choices are made without mental struggle or will or anxiety, and as speedily and inevitably as a series of human ninepins falling down one after another on the stage when each is bumped by the one next to it. "Belike you mean," says Kate to Petruchio, "to make a puppet of me" (IV.iii.103). It is what farce does to all characters.

Now the least obvious and at the same time most fundamental illustration of the farcical view of life lies not in some of the peripheral goings on that we have been observing, but in the title action itself: the taming of the shrew. Essentially—we will come shortly to the necessary qualifications—Kate is conceived of as responding automatically to a certain kind of calculated treatment, as automatically as an animal to the devices of a skilled trainer. Petruchio not only uses the word *tame* more than once but openly compares his method to that used in training falcons (IV.i.191 ff.). There is no reason whatever to suppose that this was not meant quite literally. Petruchio is not making a great jest or developing a paradoxical figure but is describing a process taken at face value. He tells exactly what he has done and is doing—withholding food and sleep until the absolute need of them brings assent. (We hardly note that up to a point the assumptions are those of the "third degree" and of the more rigorous "cures" of bad habits:

making it more unprofitable to assert one's will or one's bad habits than to act differently.) Before he sees Kate, he explicitly announces his method: he will assert, as true, the opposite of whatever she says and does and is, that is to say, he will frustrate the manifestations of her will and establish the dominance of his own. Without naming them, he takes other steps that we know to be important in animal training. From the beginning he shows that he will stop at nothing to achieve his end, that he will not hesitate for a second to do anything necessary—to discard all dignity or carry out any indecorous act or any outrageousness that will serve. He creates an image of utter invincibility, of having no weakness through which he can be appealed to. He does not use a literal whip, such as stage Petruchios habitually used, but he unmistakably uses a symbolic whip. Like a good trainer, however, he uses the carrot as well as the whip—not only marriage but also a new life, a happier personality for Kate. Above all, he offers love; in the end, the trainer succeeds best who makes the trainee feel the presence of something warmer than technique, rigor, and invincibility. Not that Petruchio fakes love, but that love has its part, ironically, in a process that is farcically conceived and that never wholly loses the markings of farce.

Only in farce could we conceive of the occurrence, almost in a flash, of that transformation of personality which, as we know only too well in modern experience, normally requires a long, gradual, painstaking application of psychotherapy. True, conversion is believable and does happen, but even as a secular experience it requires a prior development of readiness, or an extraordinary revelatory shock, or both. (In the romantic form of this psychic event, an old hag, upon marriage to the knight, suddenly turns into a beautiful maiden.) Kate is presented initially as a very troubled woman; aggressiveness and tantrums are her way of feeling a sense of power. Although modern, the argument that we see in her the result of paternal unkindness is not impressive. For one thing, some recent research on infants—if we may risk applying heavy science to light farce—suggests that basic personality traits precede, and perhaps influence, parental attitudes to children. More important, the text simply does not present Baptista as the overbearing and tyrannical father that he is sometimes said to be. Kate has made him almost as unhappy as she is, and driven him toward Bianca; nevertheless, when he heavily handicaps Bianca in the matrimonial sweepstakes, he is trying to even things up for the daughter who he naturally thinks is a poor runner. Nor is he willing to marry her off to Petruchio simply to get rid of her; "her love," he says, "is all in all." On her wedding day he says, kindly enough, "I cannot blame thee now to weep," and at the risk of losing husbands for both daughters he rebukes Petruchio (III.ii.99 ff.).

(The Baptista that some modern commentators think they see would surely have said, "What do you expect, you bitch?") We cannot blacken Baptista to save Kate. Shakespeare presents her binding and beating Bianca (II.i.1 ff.) to show that he is really committed to a shrew; such episodes make it hard to defend the view that she is an innocent victim or is posing as a shrew out of general disgust.

To sum up: in real life her disposition would be difficult to alter permanently, but farce secures its pleasurable effect by assuming a ready and total change in response to the stimuli applied by Petruchio as if he were going through an established and proved training routine. On the other hand, only farce makes it possible for Petruchio to be so skillful a tamer, that is, so unerring, so undeviating, so mechanical, so uninhibited an enforcer of the rules for training in falconry. If Petruchio were by nature the disciplinarian that he acts for a while, he would hardly change after receiving compliance; and if he were, in real life, the charming and affectionate gentleman that he becomes in the play, he would find it impossible so rigorously to play the falcon tamer, to outbully the bully, especially when the bully lies bleeding on the ground, for this role would simply run afoul of too much of his personality. The point here is not that the play is "unrealistic" (this would be a wholly irrelevant criticism), but that we can understand how a given genre works by testing it against the best sense of reality that we can bring to bear. It is the farcical view of life that makes possible the treatment of both Kate and Petruchio.

iii

But this picture, of course, is incomplete; for the sake of clarity we have been stressing the purely generic in *The Shrew* and gliding over the specific variations. Like any genre, farce is a convention, not a straitjacket; it is a fashion, capable of many variations. Genre provides a perspective, which in the individual work can be used narrowly or inclusively: comedy of manners, for instance, can move toward the character studies of James's novels or toward the superficial entertainments of Terence Rattigan. Shakespeare hardly ever uses a genre constrictively. In both *The Comedy of Errors* and *The Taming of the Shrew,* the resemblances between which are well known, Shakespeare freely alters the limited conception of personality that we find in "basic farce" such as that of Plautus, who influences both these plays. True, he protects both main characters in *The Shrew* against the expectable liabilities that would make one a less perfect reformer, and the other less than a model reformee, but he is unwilling to leave them automatons, textbook types of reformer and reformee. So he equips both with a good deal of intelligence and feeling that they would not have in elementary farce. Take sex, for instance. In basic farce, sex is purely a mechanical response, with no more overtones of feeling than ordinary hunger and thirst; the normal "love affair" is an intrigue with a courtesan. Like virtually all Renaissance lovers, Petruchio tells Kate candidly that he proposes to keep warm "in thy bed" (II.i.269). But there is no doubt that Petruchio, in addition to wanting a good financial bargain and enjoying the challenge of the shrew, develops real warmth of feeling for Kate as an individual— a warmth that makes him strive to bring out the best in her, keep the training in a tone of jesting, well-meant fantasy, provide Kate with face-saving devices (she is "curst . . . for policy" and only "in company" [II.i.294, 307]), praise her for her virtues (whether she has them or not) rather than blame her for her vices, never fall into boorishness, repeatedly protest his affection for her, and, by asking a kiss at a time she thinks unsuitable, show that he really wants it. Here farce expands toward comedy of character by using a fuller range of personality.

Likewise with Kate. The fact that she is truly a shrew does not mean that she cannot have hurt feelings, as it would in a plainer farce; indeed, a shrew may be defined—once she develops beyond a mere stereotype— as a person who has an excess of hurt feelings and is taking revenge on the world for them. Although we dislike the revenge, we do not deny the painful feelings that may lie behind. Shakespeare has chosen to show some of those feelings, not making Kate an insentient virago on the one hand, or a pathetic victim on the other. She plainly is jealous of Bianca and her lovers; she accuses Baptista of favoritism (in my opinion, without justification); on her wedding day she suffers real anguish rather than simply an automatic, conventionally furious resolve for retaliation. The painful emotions take her way beyond the limitations of the essentially pain-free personality of basic farce. Further, she is witty, though, truth to tell, the first verbal battle between her and Petruchio, like various other such scenes, hardly goes beyond verbal farce, in which words are mechanical jokes or blows rather than an artistic game that delights by its quality, and in which all the speed of the short lines hardly conceals the heavy labors of the dutiful but uninspired punster (the best jokes are the bawdy ones). Kate has imagination. It shows first in a new human sympathy when she defends the servants against Petruchio (IV.i.159, 172). Then it develops into a gay, inspired gamesomeness that rivals Petruchio's own. When he insists, "It shall be what o'clock I say it is" (IV.iii.197) and "[The sun] shall be moon or star or what I list" (IV.v.7), he is at one level saying again that he will stop at nothing, at no irrationality, as tamer; but here he moves the power-game into a realm of fancy in which his apparent willfulness becomes the acting of the creative imagination. He is a poet, and he asks her, in effect, less to kiss the rod than to join in the game of playfully transforming ordinary reality. It is the final step in transforming herself. The point here is that, instead of not catching on or simply sulking, Kate has the dash and verve to join in the fun, and to do it with skill and some real touches of originality.

This episode on the road to Padua (IV.v.1–49), when Petruchio and Kate first transform old Vincentio into a "Young budding virgin, fair and fresh and sweet," and then back into himself again, is the high point of the play. From here on, it tends to move back closer to the boundaries of ordinary farce. When Petruchio asks a kiss, we do have human beings with feelings, not robots; but the key line, which is sometimes missed, is Petruchio's "Why, then let's home again. Come, sirrah, let's away" (V.i.152). Here Petruchio is again making the same threat that he made at IV.v.8–9, that is, not playing an imaginative game but hinting the symbolic whip, even though the end is a compliance that she is inwardly glad to give. The whole wager scene falls essentially within the realm of farce: the responses are largely mechanical, as is their symmetry. Kate's final long speech on the obligations and fitting style of wives (V.ii.136–79) we can think of as a more or less automatic statement—that is, the kind appropriate to farce—of a generally held doctrine. The easiest way to deal with it is to say that we no longer believe in it, just as we no longer believe in the divine right of kings that is an important dramatic element in many Shakespeare plays.

But to some interpreters Kate has become such a charming heroine that they cannot stand her being anything less than a modern feminist—hence the claim that in the submission speech she is speaking ironically. There are two arguments against this interpretation. One is that a careful reading of the lines will show that most of them have to be taken literally; only the last seven or eight lines can be read with ironic overtones, but this means, at most, a return to the imaginative gamesomeness of IV.v rather than a denial of the doctrine that she is formally asserting. The second is that some forty lines of straight irony would be too much to be borne; it would be inconsistent with the straightforwardness of most of the play, and it would really turn Kate back into a hidden shrew whose new technique was sarcastic indirection, side-mouthing at the audience while her not very intelligent husband, bamboozled, cheered her on. It would be a poor triumph. If one has to modernize the speech of the obedient wife, a better way to do it is to develop a hint of Goddard's: that behind a passé doctrine lies a continuing truth—that there are real differences between the sexes, and that they are to be kept in mind. Such a view at least does not strain the spirit of Kate's speech.

The Katolatry that has developed in recent years reveals the romantic tendency to create heroes and heroines by denying the existence of flaws in them and by imputing all sorts of flaws to their families and other associates. We have already seen how the effort to save Kate has resulted in an untenable effort to make Baptista into a villainous, punitive father and Bianca into a calculating little devil whose inner shrewishness slowly comes out. But it is hard to see why, if we are to admire Kate's spirit of open defiance at the beginning, and her alleged ironic defiance at the end, we should not likewise admire the spirit of Bianca and Hortensio's widow at the end. It is equally hard to see why we should admire Kate's quiet, ironic, what-every-woman-knows victory, as some would have it, over an attractive man at the end, but should not admire Petruchio's open victory over a very unattractive woman earlier. In fact, it is a little difficult to know just what Kate's supposed victory consists in. The play gives no evidence that from now on she will be twisting her husband around her finger. The evidence is rather that she will win peace and quiet and contentment by giving in to his wishes, and that her willingness will entirely eliminate unreasonable and autocratic wishes in him. But after all, the unreasonable and the autocratic are his strategy, not his nature; he gives up an assumed vice, while Kate gives up a real one. The truth is that, with Petruchio's help, Kate's great victory is over herself; she has come to accept herself as having enough merit so that she can be content without having the last word and scaring everybody off. To see this means to acknowledge that she was originally a shrew, whatever virtues may also have been latent in her personality.

What Shakespeare has done is to take an old, popular farcical situation and turn it into a well-organized, somewhat complex, fast-moving farce of his own. He has worked with the basic conceptions of farce—mainly that of a somewhat limited personality that acts and responds in a mechanical way and hence moves toward a given end with a perfection not likely if all the elements in human nature were really at work. So the tamer never fails in his technique, and the shrew responds just as she should. Now this situation might have tempted the dramatist to let his main characters be flat automatons—he a dull and rough whip-wielder, and she a stubborn intransigent until beaten into insensibility (as in the ballad that was perhaps a Shakespearean source). Shakespeare, however, makes a gentleman and lady of his central pair. As tamer, Petruchio is a gay and witty and precocious artist and, beyond that, an affectionate man; and hence, a remarkable therapist. In Kate, Shakespeare has imagined not merely a harridan who is incurable or a moral stepchild driven into a misconduct by mistreatment, but a difficult woman—a shrew, indeed—who combines willfulness with feelings that elicit sympathy, with imagination, and with a latent cooperativeness that can bring this war of the sexes to an honorable settlement. To have started with farce, to have stuck to the main lines of farce, and yet to have got so much of the suprafarcical into farce—this is the achievement of *The Taming of the Shrew,* and the source of the pleasure that it has always given.

If we can see *The Taming* in this way, we can have it untamed, freed from the artifices of a critical falconry that endeavors to domesticate it within the confines of recent sensibility; and we can have a return of the shrew without turning Kate into only a shrew.

10

Romance

Cymbeline

In *Romeo and Juliet* (ca. 1595) Romeo, believing that Juliet is dead, enters her tomb, takes poison there, and dies. Upon awaking and finding Romeo dead, Juliet stabs herself and dies. In *Antony and Cleopatra* (ca. 1607) Antony, believing that Cleopatra is dead, falls on his sword and thus brings about his death. In consequence, Cleopatra resolves on death by the poisonous bite of the asp. Compare these roughly similar situations with certain events in *Cymbeline* (ca. 1609–1610). Imogen, recovering like Juliet from a drug that has brought about her apparent death, opens her eyes upon a corpse she believes to be her husband's. But, though she faints, she neither takes her life nor thinks of doing so. When Posthumus receives apparent evidence of Imogen's death, he too goes on living, though he has the added burden of remorse; true, he thinks of death, but only as a natural hazard of the war that he chooses to enter.

To be sure, different lovers have different personalities. But behind the variations of personality lie literary factors that influence the strikingly different outcomes of situations up to a point strikingly alike. Different conventions are at work: in *Romeo* and *Antony,* those of tragedy; in *Cymbeline,* those of dramatic romance. As it is used here, *convention* does not mean a formula, stereotype, or constricting rule, but rather a certain point of view, a way of perceiving human behavior, of understanding it and responding to it emotionally. A convention is a bond, though a flexible one, between playwright and audience; it involves a loose, unspoken agreement about attitude and procedure; it is rooted in shared expectations, though these may be unarticulated, general rather than specific, and open to great imaginative transformation by the artist. The tragic convention interprets life as a clash between, on the one hand, transcendent principles of order

155

and, on the other, urgencies of desire and intensities of feeling that, once they are in play, lead inevitably to destructive encounters and somber catastrophes. The convention of romance approaches life in terms of the ultimate reconcilability of desires and circumstances; though ambitions and needs may be great, they tend to fall within a realm of moral possibility; and circumstances, though they may be antagonistic for a long period, eventually yield to meritorious humanity. The tragic involvement is total, reckless, irremediable; the protagonist is wholly committed to a situation that seems to enfold all of life's possibilities. In contrast, in the convention represented in *Cymbeline* the personal impulse does not become identical with, or aspire to dominate, all of reality; beyond the individuals there is an independent life that makes legitimate claims or offers alternative possibilities. For Imogen and for Posthumus, the loved one does not become the only way, a sine qua non; Imogen, though grief-stricken, can cling to life, and Posthumus can fight for his country. Thus both survive for an unraveling of circumstance that offers them, in the end, satisfactions unforeseen at the moment of apparent disaster. (In the matter of circumstances romance may be contrasted with two later conventions that reacted against it: whereas romance treats circumstances as being ultimately malleable or beneficent, realism regards them as independent and subject to their own laws, and naturalism treats them as either indifferent or positively hostile to human endeavor.)

In both tragedy and romance human beings are reservoirs of strong passions. Yet romance has a greater sense of limits—of the decorum or principle or rational endowment or even pragmatic awareness that balances off the passion and holds it back from the irretrievable. Tragedy is more attuned to extremes and depths, to profound conflicts within personality (as in Macbeth, Othello, and Lear). Cymbeline, caught between the Roman Empire and British loyalty, between wife and daughter, between his dynastic plans and Imogen's emotions, is potentially a tragic figure; but Shakespeare does not portray him as destroyed by irreconcilable forces. Romance either does not see the painful inner conflict or treats it as reparable this side of catastrophe; for the clash of impulses it will most often substitute the clash of persons—sometimes simply of the good ones who come out all right in the end and the bad ones who go down. Cymbeline's Queen is all unscrupulousness; she has none of Lady Macbeth's capacity for destructive inner stresses. Cloten is self-seeking and vengeful, but as a character in romance he is not credited with the brains or drive to do permanent damage. Again, the Cymbeline-Imogen relationship has interesting resemblances to the Capulet-Juliet and the Lear-Cordelia relationships. Capulet and Cymbeline both want to impose unwelcome marriages on their daughters: in the tragedy, the father is relentless and hence contributes to the daughter's despair and to his own bitter grief; in the romance, the father is unpleasant enough, but he temporizes and hopes rather than attempts force, and hence does not push things beyond repair. In response to a daughter's independence, Cymbeline banishes a son-in-law—a sentence that need not entail disaster and that can be revoked; but Lear turns political power over to forces of unlimited ruthlessness and thus tears a whole kingdom apart.

A very clear view of the ways in which tragedy and romance diverge is provided by the striking resemblances between *Cymbeline* and *Othello*: in each play an extremely clever man, for his own purposes, uses circumstantial evidence to persuade a husband that his new bride has been unfaithful, and the bitter and vengeful husband resolves to punish his wife by death. Although romance does not ignore evil, its vision does not include the fearful malice that, like Iago's, destroys one victim after another; instead, Iachimo's deception of Posthumus, indecent and dangerous though it is, is still a game rather than a revelation of human depravity. Romance may deal with a murderous impulse, but it does not give that impulse sole and final authority; whereas Othello in his mad error goes right to work and commits murder, Posthumus uses an agent who saves him from the consequences of his own fury. It may be that Posthumus is simply lucky in having to use an agent, but it is also possible to suppose that he unconsciously chooses an unreliable murderer. In either case—cooperative circumstance or secret intent—the survival of Imogen illustrates the view, almost invariable in romance, that the hate and violence of which people are capable, however great these may be, do not necessarily achieve their destructive ends.

Romance is not watered-down tragedy; it is another way of looking at conduct and experience. It is equally aware of serious dangers to life and well-being and of preventives, safety devices, the means of return from the shadows. It does not fall short of something that might be expected of it; rather it adopts a different perspective, and the better the individual romance is, the greater its ability to persuade us of the validity of its perspective. Romance can move toward theatrical (and subliterary) hackwork, or toward dramatic (and literary) excellence. Because it affirms the saving graces of life, it may either drift toward hackneyed, mechanical happy endings or struggle toward a peace and reconciliation that have been won by hard experience. (In the present example Cymbeline, Belarius, and Imogen have suffered; Posthumus has had to undergo a painful self-contemplation.) Since "entertainment" regularly plays up the comforting aspects of character and events, romance has strong affiliations with the world of entertainment: as such it can either provide standardized gratifications or require the spectator and reader to respond sharply even amid apparently familiar fare.

Traditionally, romantic entertainment includes much movement and variety, distant scene and change of scene, combat, disguise, plotting, patriotic appeal. *Cymbeline* gathers all of these in a rich amalgam of many sources. Yet out of this rather astonishing medley comes not so much formula entertainment as an entertaining but not inadequate or falsifying view of reality.

After his period of great tragedies Shakespeare turned, in his latter years in the theater, to romance: he appears to have written *Pericles, Cymbeline, The Winter's Tale,* and *The Tempest,* roughly in that order, between 1608 and 1612. Dr. Simon Forman saw a performance of *Cymbeline* at the Globe not long before September 1611, as we know from a description of it in his manuscript "Bocke of Plaies and Notes thereof. . . ." The play need not have been new when he saw it, but the consensus of scholarly opinion, based upon its style and type, places the anterior limit of date in 1608–1609. Certain elements in the late plays—the maturing of main characters, conversion or even rebirth, the triumph of justice in harmony with nature and divine ordinance—suggest to some readers that Shakespeare had personally come through a period of anguish into relative hopefulness and serenity. Although the interpretation is not implausible, we have no biographical evidence to substantiate it. What is established is that the romances were in tune with a theatrical fashion that grew strong from about 1608 on, representing in part the continual quest for novelty, in part a new exploitation of an older dramatic mode that had not been fully developed, and perhaps most of all a response to the more specialized taste of genteel audiences that for various reasons became influential at this time. Shakespeare was clearly writing in this new mode, but he developed the mode differently from the very popular John Fletcher and Fletcher's part-time collaborator, Francis Beaumont. Although *Cymbeline* itself and the Beaumont-Fletcher *Philaster* have resemblances that suggest influence in one direction or the other (a moot subject; the evidence is not conclusive), the Beaumont-Fletcher method is in general to decrease the seriousness of the political plot and to exploit to the utmost the private emotional life, sometimes by shocking events and strained or even morbid situations, and regularly by an intensified and prolonged presentation of feelings (pathos, shame, jealousy, humiliation, horror, and so on). In Shakespeare the situations, allowing for all the departures from everyday reality that are sanctioned by romance, are much less eccentric and much more representative, and the emotional life presented is not an end in itself, magnified for a slow savoring, but a natural unexpanded accompaniment of the action.

The customary procedures of romance, then, may lean toward either of two extremes: one, the escapist patterns and routines, where entertainment is expected to have no ties to truth; the other, a sophisticated sensationalism, where putting the audience through an emotional wringer drifts naturally toward off-center functionings of personality. Shakespeare's later romances are in a middle position: they stay away equally from the pure stereotypes that give little sense of what human character and experience are like and from the whipping up of emotional states by strange situations and prolonged displays of exacerbated feeling.

Cymbeline has won, on the whole, less praise than *The Winter's Tale* and *The Tempest*. In *Cymbeline,* some readers believe, Shakespeare reveals a less sure control of his "later style": metrically looser lines, with extra syllables and more frequent feminine endings; a tendency toward solid blocking in dialogue, with more syntactic denseness and grammatical ambiguity; random outbreaks of somewhat mechanical rhythm. (There is still active dispute as to whether certain parts of the play, notably V.iv.30–122, are authentic.) Some critics have argued that the plots are not well integrated, that Belarius is too sententious, that there are too many awkward expository soliloquies, that the characters are too neatly divided into black and white, that the gratifying conclusion lacks metaphysical support. On the other hand, few have failed to admire the characterization of Imogen and the ingenious construction of the last scene (V.v). Even allowing for the susceptibility of male critics to so charming and devoted a creature as Imogen, whose attractions, ranging as they do from sweetness of affection to sharpness in repartee, from blind fidelity to keen insight into motives and character, from cookery to courage, make her virtually a dream girl, there is no doubt that she is one of the most substantially characterized, and hence convincing, of Shakespeare's romantic heroines. The final revelation scene, with its unbroken, energetic, unforced movement from one disclosure to another, is one of the most skillful in all drama. Unlike Fletcher, Shakespeare does not secure his effect of almost continuous surprise by playing tricks upon the spectator, keeping him artificially in the dark and then shocking him with sudden new light. The spectator, on the contrary, knows about everything that is taking place; his surprise is simply the surprise of the characters as they make major discoveries; yet he always understands the characters. His role is not that of naive curiosity as to what is going on, or naive wonder at novelties he has not foreseen, but adult contemplation of the diverse possibilities of human nature.

The characterization of Imogen and the management of the final scene are key elements: the merits of the play lie in characterization and craftsmanship. These reveal, as the play goes on, a view of reality that carries the romance far beyond the expectable delights of painless and thoughtless entertainment.

The play is long, and an occasional scene, such as I.iv, may be somewhat drawn out, but there is an overall vigor of movement. Although the exposition in I.i lacks finesse, the situation is introduced, and action is started, rapidly; scenes ii and iii speedily complicate the problems to be solved. In II.iii there is a good example of a scene not only providing drama in itself but pointing ahead naturally to other action: in the midst of fighting off Cloten, Imogen misses her bracelet, so that a new problem comes into view before she is finished with the one presented by Cloten. In I.vi and II.iv, which Iachimo dominates as he first tries to "seduce" Imogen and then deceives Posthumus, excellent pace and tension are created by Iachimo in his skillful maneuvers from one strategy to another. The energetic movement is supported by variety of scene; in changing locale Shakespeare can often change mood or confront us with another point of view. From the touching scene in which Pisanio tells Imogen of Posthumus's departure (I.iii) Shakespeare makes an abrupt leap to the sophistication and skepticism at Rome (I.iv), and from that back to the heavy-handed machinations of the British Queen (I.v). The courtly polish of the scene in which Imogen, in her faithful love, resists the specious appeals of Iachimo (I.vi) is followed by the rough outdoor comedy of the loutish Cloten (II.i), and this in turn by an utterly different action in Imogen's bedroom, in which danger, evil calculation, and sexual feeling are ingeniously mixed (II.ii). From the private intrigue in Rome (II.iv, v) we are thrown back to a public scene of imperial politics at the British court (III.i), and from the royal palace to an outlaws' cave in the Welsh mountains (III.iii). From sudden battlefield reversals we shift to a supernatural vision, from divine promise to death-cell ironies, from readiness for death to a reprieve (V.iii, iv).

Nothing lags; nothing stands still; the action lines hurry on, pressed by their own inner dramatic force and intermingled so expertly that something new constantly flashes into sight to alter the perspective and undercut the obvious. This is of course good entertainment in the style of romance, but it is more than that: it is a way of countering the stereotypes into which romance may slide, of announcing the variety of possibilities in human experience, and of contemplating and accepting this variety. Although variety itself may become a cliché, variety rooted in a sense of the real alternatives in feeling and action is a denial of cliché. Even in the introductory scenes Shakespeare is not willing to let Cloten be merely the clownish butt, but instead shows him through the eyes of two commentators (I.ii, II.i), the witty observer and the straight man; aside from the drama of contrast, Cloten implicitly has enough substance to attract one follower, if only a politic one. Iachimo is the treacherous Italian dear to the Elizabethan heart, but Shakespeare modifies the conventional concept of Italian character by introducing the civil and decent Philario. The vision scene in V.iv might contain only a static, decorative theophany, but Shakespeare gives it dramatic life by having the spirits attack Jupiter almost rebelliously. Belarius and his "sons" might easily be a solid family unit playing a conventional role of rustic virtue. Belarius does voice trite sentiments about the contrast between vice at court and nobility in the mountains, but in almost their first words the young men disagree; to them their cave is a prison from the world of action and knowledge (III.iii.27 ff.). When Guiderius kills Cloten, Belarius is less laudatory than fearful (IV.ii); when Belarius wants to play safe and wait out the war, the boys override him (IV.iv). Even the boys themselves are set partly in dramatic opposition: Guiderius, the more direct and active, criticizes Arviragus, more given to savoring words and feelings, for playing Belarius's "ingenious instrument" and for drawing out his elegy for Fidele (IV.ii).

It is in the treatment of his principal characters that Shakespeare most conspicuously avoids the expected and the obvious. As masterful wife, unscrupulous mother, and sinister stepmother, the Queen is a very old and familiar character; yet Shakespeare makes her also an authentic voice of British patriotism (III.i, v). He alters the conventional villain by giving her a generally acceptable emotion; he modifies romance by observing that malicious double-dealing at court does not bar political right feeling. Cloten is defective on nearly every count: as objectionable lover, laughable "ass," and oafish courtier of dubious principles. But he too is a patriot, even though an ungraceful one (III.i, v). He is rude and overbearing to Belarius and the King's sons, but he certainly believes that he is acting in the name of the law, and he is not a coward. His dependence on his position is ludicrous, but somehow he always needs reassurance; there is a distant touch of pathos in his incompetence and hope for security, and perhaps even in his grotesque "dreams of glory" (III.v, IV.i). He tries to think, as when he expounds the cynic's view of the gold standard in moral life (II.iii.67 ff.), or wrestles with the paradox of love and hate (III.v.70 ff.). In other words, Cloten is complicated enough to demand more than a stereotyped response; hence the beheading may seem excessive, unpleasantly shocking. Shakespeare wants to give the audience a quick justification for the beheading; so he has Guiderius say, "Yet I not doing this, the fool had borne / My head as I do his" (IV.ii.116–17).

Posthumus turns out to be much more than the victim of an angry king, or than the conventional romantic hero, though he is obviously to be taken as such a hero. What interests Shakespeare more than his eligibility as a lover, or his unjust banishment, is his capacity for unheroic, indeed evil, behavior: Posthumus quickly loses faith in his wife's fidelity, and then tries to arrange her murder. Romance is made to accommodate more than a little moral reality: we see both the drive for the revenge and afterward the bitter remorse. Imogen might be no more than faithful bride and pathetic victim, but Shakespeare gives her an intelligence, a spirit, and an imagination that make her seem to earn, rather than passively inherit, the good that comes her way. But he goes beyond even this achievement and at one point regards Imogen with amused detachment that creates the most delicately ironic scene in the play. As the convention of disguise requires, Imogen takes Cloten's body for that of Posthumus, but instead of dropping the confusion at this point, Shakespeare has her go on to identify one part of the body after another as Posthumus's. Along with all the charm of her tenderness and the pathos of her apparent bereavement, there is something exquisitely comic in her assurance in her misidentifications: no one is beyond errors that evoke smiles, Shakespeare seems to say, and this implicit view makes possible a richer humanity. The impulse to humanize by cutting back a general idealizing process appears again in the final scene when Shakespeare has Imogen coolly turn her back on Lucius ("your life . . . / Must shuffle for itself," V.v.104–5), to whom she is indebted and who is embittered by her suddenly dropping him for her own business. Shakespeare is looking at the actual ways of human nature, not at pure stereotypes. Hence, though at the end he lets Cymbeline acquire greater wisdom and dignity, he makes the King a faulty enough human being, doting on his wife, misled, capable of folly and great harshness.

Iachimo appears first as an Italian rascal, a conventional source of agreeable shudders in Renaissance England, and then apparently undergoes a pleasing conversion from skepticism to faith in chaste love. This sounds like pure theatrical hokum, but the fact is that Iachimo is a fresh and lively character. Iago, whom Iachimo strikingly resembles, has a histrionic side that is a key to Iachimo: though Iago's main pleasure, of course, is in working out his malice, he also delights in working out the different roles that he assumes. Iachimo does not have Iago's malice, but his passion for the stage is even greater than Iago's. He loves to adopt a role and to succeed in it; he is a subtle union of actor and confidence man. Having adopted the role of disbeliever in woman's virtue, he must carry it to an extreme and conquer in it; in working on Imogen, he shifts from role to role with the agility of a born actor; in working on Posthumus, he arranges his presentation like a tight one-act play, moving from quick exposition through deepening tension to one climax and then another. Finally he chooses a very popular role, that of guilty man confessing, and here he seizes stage with an elaborate and attitudinizing self-condemnation. Even in his final six lines (V.v.412–17) he manages to act the guilty man with a histrionic sweep, and to attract attention by praising Imogen hyperbolically.

In adopting the genre of romance, then, Shakespeare exploits all its potential variety, at one level by an always lively movement of scene and plot, and in a more fundamental way by examining characters with either an amused detachment or a fullness that stops just short of tragic complications. Although the genre commits him to solutions short of disaster, he does not impose an arbitrary happy ending. His characters are complex enough to be more than flat figures of evil that go down, and of good that triumph. The characters that survive have not been merely lucky; they have been modified, have learned somewhat better or wiser ways of confronting the unexpected. The initial mood of the play is created by a widespread impulse to act resentfully and vengefully: the Queen plots deaths, the King is quick to banish, Posthumus wants Imogen killed, and Rome must punish Britain. But the closing mood is one of forbearance and generosity. Jupiter signals the change in V.iv when, though bitterly assailed by Posthumus's family, he waives his power to act punitively and actually gives promise of relief. Cymbeline can acknowledge that his trust in the Queen "was folly in me"; Lucius can rise above the harshness of the death sentence and generously ask that Fidele be saved; Cymbeline can give up a conqueror's rights and grant this request. When Iachimo confesses, Posthumus attacks himself more sharply than he does Iachimo; by relinquishing the easier course of blame, he forestalls an outbreak of recriminatory bitterness. And if the earlier Cymbeline crops up again in the royal impulse to punish Guiderius on the spot, at least now the King can wait until he knows a little more of the truth. Belarius yields up the King's sons to their father, though he is in tears at the loss of them, and Cymbeline calls Belarius "brother." The new spirit is summed up in Posthumus, who once wanted to inflict the death sentence on his wife, but who now says to Iachimo, the cause of his mad rage, "The malice [I have] towards you [is] to forgive you." It is the key line of the latter part of the play. Moved by it, Cymbeline pardons the Roman captives and then, under the further impetus of the oracle, volunteers to pay the tribute to Rome. Since the history upon which Shakespeare drew is very shadowy, and since he follows it very loosely at best, there is no reason he should not have chosen to finish off his romance with a patriotic note of triumph that would be sure fire theater. Yet he chose, not to make this easier, but instead to ask the audience to respond in a more mature and less obvious way—to approve the acknowledgment of a national obligation to a foreign conqueror. Cymbeline's decision, since in effect it says, "We have all been wrong in Britain," is an act of humility. It marks the general triumph of magnanimity—the ultimate value dramatically espoused in the play.

But magnanimity is not unveiled in a last-minute surprise whose power to please depends upon our indifference to probability. It is rather an extension of a certain generousness that, though at times inactive, has been recurrently present. The court scenes with Lucius have always an air of courteous consideration that survives the political dispute; once even the rude Cloten approaches civility (III.i.76 ff.). Belarius, though he kidnapped the King's sons when he was unjustly banished, did not injure or kill them; instead he brought them up in a way that could give great pleasure to the King. Belarius and Posthumus did not avenge themselves upon Cymbeline, as more persistently resentful characters might, by fighting against him in war; instead they became the instruments of his victory. Imogen has much to forgive, but she seems not even to think of the need for forgiveness.

Shakespeare defines a world in which a certain discipline of the self—which may appear as forgiveness or forbearance under provocation, or as considerateness and graciousness even in difficult relationships—is always possible and can in the end triumph, though the impulse to inflict punishment and to achieve revenge is also strong. Civility, generosity, magnanimity—such qualities mark the improved way of life that drama reveals. It is perhaps significant that these are the virtues esteemed in another dramatic genre that was just emerging in Jacobean England and would reach its fullness three quarters of a century later—comedy of manners. We began by discussing the relation between *Cymbeline* and tragedy (the play is entitled *The Tragedie of Cymbeline* in the folio of 1623); we end by noting its affinity to comedy. The genre to which it belongs is sometimes called tragicomedy. Whether it be called tragicomedy or romance, the important point is that, in a convention that lends itself easily to an entertaining escape from reality, Shakespeare always keeps a sure foothold in human reality; that where variety is a great theatrical value, he follows the fashion brilliantly without falling into banalities; that where abnormal tensions and sensationalism could, and often did, take over, his own portrayal of violence and strong emotion did not deflect him from representative impulses and motives; and that where the popular expectation of final relief might lead to mechanical repair of disorder and restoration of well-being, Shakespeare never entirely closes off our sense of the human capacity for ill-doing. Above all, he characteristically represents an improvement in life, not as a miraculous gift to make people easily happy, but as a possession earned by the mastery, in crises, of such virtues as forbearance and magnanimity.

11

Timon in Context

The problem of self-knowledge is one that may take us somewhat closer to the issue of quality in *Timon of Athens* than do other matters that have been much discussed, such as its structural defects, technical slips, and allegorical stiffness. In exploring the problem of self-knowledge, we can make use of four contexts that throw light on the art of *Timon*.[1] The first context is historical: Renaissance thought on the subject of self-knowledge. The second is the great tragedies: if one avoids the obvious conclusion that the greater make the lesser look still smaller, there are still differences in conception of character that are illuminating. The third context is that of the chronologically nearby plays—*Antony and Cleopatra, Coriolanus,* and *Cymbeline;* they illustrate *Timon's* problems best of all, and therefore I give them fuller treatment than the great tragedies. Finally, there is the unusual context of other plays in later times: they help clarify the *Timon* theme and even make Shakespeare's play look ancestral.

As for Renaissance thought, two studies give useful information. Paul A. Jorgensen's *Lear's Self-Discovery* (1967) and Rolf Soellner's *Shakespeare's Patterns of Self-Knowledge* (1972) have summarized fully the extensive Renaissance ideas on the discovery, knowledge, and awareness of the self—the injunction *nosce teipsum* or *gnothi seauton,* and the experience *anagnorisis,* to use the term, as many do for convenience, in a more limited sense than Aristotle did—and have explored various plays through the medium of these ideas. We need not go into those background materials; the point is that Jorgensen and Soellner have provided a historical justification for criticism that deals with the self-knowledge of tragic protagonists and treats it as essential to their having a "proper magnitude."

---

1. Another context, that of theatrical history, has been well dealt with by M. C. Bradbrook: "Blackfriars: The Pageant of *Timon of Athens,*" in *Shakespeare the Craftsman,* The Clark Lectures, 1968 (New York: Barnes and Noble, 1969), 144–67.

Jorgensen remarks perceptively, "If *King Lear* is an ultimate drama of self-discovery, this may help to explain why it is also perhaps the most totally compelling of all Shakespeare's plays" (2). Indeed so. Other tragedies seem equally compelling to critics who are convinced of the protagonists' self-knowledge, less compelling to critics who believe it is incomplete. One persistent interpretation of Othello has been that his bias is more toward self-justification than full self-recognition; this has stirred up defenses of his moral self-awareness that seem now to be on the ascendant in the critical sky. Various critics (Kenneth Muir, for instance) have noted a kind of limitedness in the later parts of *Macbeth;* one way of accounting for this is a marked constriction of the moral awareness that made the earlier Macbeth a figure of genuine representativeness and magnitude. Yet here again we find contradictory opinions. Some critics detect, in the brilliant metaphorical flights of Macbeth in his later downhill days, a true awareness of his moral course. To others his poetry seems to describe the results of his deeds rather than perceive their quality, to paint an existential wasteland rather than confront its only begetter. In all these judgments, however, the issue of self-knowledge is important.

I have moved over from the historical context of ideas to the context of the major tragedies, and I now want to proceed in two ways from the context of the major tragedies to the context of the late tragedies. The first transition is via the dramatist's attitude that makes many people respond similarly to dramas in both periods. Shakespeare characteristically tends to present everything that can be said for his protagonists. Hence, even when these figures are or become more constricted in consciousness, less completely aware of what they have been and done and are, they still tend to make us focus on what is admirable in them and be less attentive to other aspects of their being. Thus in Macbeth we see primarily the fighting spirit of the trapped man; in Antony, a figure of magnanimity (the view of Dorothea Krook and others) and a partner in a love that, in transcending all other values, transfigures him; in Coriolanus, the ultimate man of integrity; and in Timon, the truly generous, self-forgetful man. On the other hand, such readings are not unchallenged; qualifications or doubts creep in from other quarters. Some readers argue that Macbeth hardly acknowledges the evil that he has done, that Coriolanus remains immature and blind to political reality, and that Timon's misanthropic outbursts are tedious and self-serving. Probably Antony calls forth most diversity of response: true, almost no critics support the Roman view of life, but still there is some suspicion that the glorified Egyptian alternative does not quite escape a night-on-the-town triviality. A. L. French thinks that Antony's character is not up to the poetry that Antony speaks and that others use in speaking about him, and H. A. Mason similarly argues that Shakespeare magnifies Antony by "telling" rather than "showing," but Janet Adelman believes that the poetry triumphs over our disbelief. Norman Rabkin, usefully introducing the doctrine of "complementarity," rejects pro or con interpretations: we must live with contradictory impressions, calling on our "negative capability." To apply this doctrine in a slightly different way, we have to be aware both of the force and impressiveness of certain protagonists and of their limitations—in my view, a self-ignorance that holds them short of a possible magnitude.

The other transition from the major tragedies to the later ones lies in a contrast of motives. Lear, Othello, and Macbeth have in common a powerful egoistic passion, either foolish or evil, which drives them into disastrous actions—punitive, aggressive, or destructive—against others. They make us judge them as they compulsively strike savage blows, and so close off the possibility of becoming wiser without being sadder. Thus there is an immensely significant difference between them and the later heroes. For Antony, Coriolanus, and Timon believe—and partly or wholly persuade us to believe—that they possess, or represent, or practice a good that takes precedence over all other values. They are obsessed, as it were, with virtues that seem absolute, subject to no contingencies—in Antony, an erotic attraction apparently self-justifying and indeed salvationary; in Coriolanus, a military sense of honor that can ignore political reality or expect it to be acquiescent; and in Timon, a give-away impulse that can forget two problems, the limits of his distributable resources and the moral quality of beneficiaries.

ii

Of these late heroes—the third context for a comment on *Timon*—Antony has most range: he can have glimpses of himself as failed general and statesman, as petty in honor and jealousy, as self-indulgent playboy. But he always hurries on; at no time does he say anything as plain and decisive as Enobarbus's "I have done ill," "I am alone the villain of the earth" (IV.vi.18, 30). He cannot speak thus because, I suggest, he is at bottom the man of charm, that is, the man whose energy goes mainly into his impact on others. He charms all about him and, through them, us; then we unconsciously translate the quickly attractive into the durably laudable. The goal of this interpretation, however, is not to diminish Antony but to see that in him Shakespeare is exploring a certain kind of figure—the secular charismatic man. The implicit issue is: does the man of charm ever look within? Dare he? What substance might he find by which to estimate the thing done, the life lived? Or is charm itself a free-floating way of life, a slipping of all anchoring fixities that ordinarily define character and that might appear in one character as stabilities, in another as rigidities? Can he look within? The flow of his psychic energy is all outward; he is a kind of mesmerist. It is very difficult to imagine Antony looking inward and pondering the claims of this life or that life upon him, the authority of this imperative or that. An instinctive exciter of warm responsiveness can hardly inspect or challenge himself fundamentally, though he may briefly see that so visible a deed as the flight at Actium does not provide an image of great-mindedness. Further, the man of charm is himself charmed, by a woman who is all instinct and who embodies, better than any other Shakespeare heroine, an intuitive sense of how to achieve her ends.

In this remarkable union of charm and instinct there is, as it were, an autonomous realm, resistant to the reflective, to self-assessment; it simply is; it asserts itself by zest and magnetism; it is self-conscious only with respect to its own splendor and to unfriendly fortunes, not at all in the matter of how it may be placed by an assay of what lies beneath the dazzling surface. Shakespeare is here imagining a world where all vital powers conspire against self-knowledge. To say this may give some clue to a particular charm of the play, to the hypnotic effect of an *is* beyond reflection. When self-knowledge is present in a drama, it may pass like a disturbing current from characters to spectators. But when it is absent, its very absence gives spectators an extra measure of freedom to share in the gay abandonment, the brilliant unconcern of these special creatures who in a chosen, hedonistic island escape the cool and ordered central establishment of Caesar and Octavia; it frees us to join in all intoxications and in a rare union of disparate gratifications; to command the luxuries of the palace and yet dwell unfettered in bohemia, in a unique bohemia that grasps at cosmic unlimitedness and believes in its transcendent glory; and thus, gliding over the crude evidences of ordinary disaster, to mount to a final gilding in death and to discover, in despair of life, an erotic/aesthetic triumph beyond mortality. Behind the facade of a lost world, sometimes a theme for sermons, flames a glittering life which, undisturbed by self-knowledge in the inhabitants, is warmly inviting to the romantic sensibility. The play all but enforces a romantic response. What is most bewitching, perhaps, is the brilliant "gypsy," Cleopatra. Amid her exotic splendors and rare mingling of playfulness and passion, there is subtly embedded the ultimate creation of the male erotic dream as fantasy of achievement. That dream is only secondarily of the enumerable charms, the intimated skills, the vital unpredictability, and the infinite variety; its essential image is the soul of the promiscuous woman faithful, in the end, to oneself alone.

iii

There is a line of continuity from Antony to Coriolanus; both are military men, and Coriolanus has something of the personal power that we have seen in Antony. The patricians feel it, even the snubbed Roman plebeians feel it, and the Volscians are strongly moved by it; the tribunes of the people feel it, and Aufidius feels it (and in a noticeable structural parallel, the tribunes and Aufidius act to sterilize it). But whereas Antony is the man of charm, Coriolanus is the man of force; he is the warrior, intrepid, furious, able to take it, readier than most men to risk life in a cause. Antony, so to speak, has too little "character"; Coriolanus has too much. Whereas Antony is hedonistic, Coriolanus is ascetic—hardy in endurance (his most self-possessed moment is his departure into exile), a taut guardian against common self-indulgences, with a prophet's quickness to rage at and smite down what he sees as evil. Antony is equally at home in army tent, court, pub, or brothel, everywhere falling naturally into camaraderie; Coriolanus's taste is for battle alone, and he instinctively converts all life into a battle, with himself as the captain of rectitude triumphing over policy, pusillanimity, and perfidy—which are what he sees mainly in other men. He becomes a rigid Puritan Hotspur, a heroic tilter turned scourge and revenger. If Antony is the charmer, whose very stock-in-trade inhibits, despite his considerable stock of knowingness, persistence in self-knowledge, Coriolanus is the warrior whose unvarying military stance obstructs not only self-knowledge but the very awareness that there is anything to be known.

In battle Coriolanus is all but a parody of the hero, with his bloodiness, frenzied pursuit, noisy words of hate, and indifference to wounds. "My work hath not yet warm'd me" (I.v.18), he says, in words that actually echo Prince Hal's burlesque of Hotspur ("he kills me some six or seven dozen Scots at breakfast, washes his hands, and says to his wife, 'Fie upon this quiet life. I want work.' 'O my sweet Harry,' says she, 'how many hast thou kill'd today?' 'Give my roan horse a drench,' says he, and answers, 'Some fourteen . . . a trifle, a trifle'"—II.iv.115 ff.). He is even more excessive when he rejects spoils and compliments (I.ix.37–53); as he keeps harping on his distaste for praise (II.i.185–86; II.ii.76, 81), the selfless man becomes self-conscious; his ascetic rejection of adulation is strained, finally self-adulatory. So in his revulsion at political campaigning and in his tactless candor to the plebeians we can see integrity, yes, but interlaced with stubbornness and complacency, the pride that hates to flatter confounded with the pride of stiff-necked self-will. He supposes that he is exempt from the ritual humilities essential to political and indeed social existence; he has an illusion of immunity to custom. Character is made brittle by egoism.

When we are not in our pragmatistical mood, we spontaneously applaud the uncalculating, straightforward man of strength, identify with the pride that will not truckle, rage at imperfect actuality, condemn fickle mob and slick demagogue, find relief from the ways of the world by exploding into unreserved free speech. Basically, Coriolanus acts in ways, and possesses qualities, that humanity values or admires or even envies. In his crisis we see the perennial confrontation of the good man and political reality. But this good man is a special case: he is intransigent in his self-asserted rectitude; his sense of an absolute moral "I" is fortified by his warrior's assurance that every antagonist is evil, his integrity is hardened into willfulness, his honor is turned macho. His "virtue" is literal and traditional—"manliness." What constitutes manliness? For Coriolanus it is manifested only in cut-and-thrust direct attack. For his mother, Volumnia, however—the woman who, ironically, managed to stunt her son's growth at military-academy level—manliness can encompass various courses: if primarily it means bloody conflict, still it need not deny actuality, and it can permit forgiveness. Except for a fleeting moment or two, Coriolanus cannot accommodate such a trinity of alternatives. In him Shakespeare explores the way in which single-mindedness can mean a single-track mind. A grasp of complexity is one fruit of maturity; Coriolanus never ripens into such an awareness. Aufidius, of whom Coriolanus thinks only as a manageable instrument but who reflects a great deal on Coriolanus's nature, sums him up aptly in his final epithet, *boy*—the right term for a man whose experiences have all been single-valued and whom they have left unable to grasp ambivalent reality. In Coriolanus, Shakespeare studies the man of honor whose self-conscious virtue prevents his knowing either others or himself. This man understands the responses of others so poorly because he cannot look within to learn something about human motive and attitude. His own uncriticized feeling makes up all his knowledge; it does not dawn on him that his own half-truth view of life has made it possible for enemies to attack him with half-truths. He does not suspect that he has misunderstood the nature of political life, betrayed himself to demagogues, betrayed Rome, and then betrayed his commitment to the Volscians; least of all does he glimpse the self projected in all these passionate steps.

iv

So much for the several contexts that in different ways prepare us for the problems of *Timon*. Timon, as we have seen, shares with Antony and Coriolanus a conviction of possessing or practicing a good, one that is uncontingent and self-justifying and hence seals off an awareness of other values that may have some claim, of the nature of the humanity with whom he deals, and of other motives that may complicate his own actions. Timon and Antony are both outgoing; by a union of instinct and will they please others, Antony through a charm that everyone else feels, Timon by an easy generousness that nearly everyone enjoys. Antony loves loving, for which he gives up all; Timon loves giving, and he gives all. But Timon has still more in common with Coriolanus, different as are their surface styles. Both are givers, one of blood, the other of money; each one considers himself a creditor; each is convinced that his fellow citizens dishonorably reject his claims, berates them furiously, goes bitterly into exile, and is willing to see a military revenge upon his own city. If *Timon* was the earlier play, it could be a sketch for *Coriolanus,* which treats both the hero and his adversaries more complexly. If *Timon* was the later play, it represented either a decline in Shakespeare's artistic skill or, quality aside, his attraction to the problem of what happens to the benefactor who, when he is disillusioned, has a longer time to feel the impact of disillusion. In both plays, of course, Shakespeare reduces the range of his character by allowing him virtually no self-awareness. Hence the vitality of each play derives, not from the growth of moral perceptiveness in the hero, but from the hero's extraordinary energy in the quite human activity of thinking well of the self instead of thinking truly of the self.

To return for a moment to the context of the greater tragedies and its usefulness for the study of the later group. In both groups, of course, all the protagonists are "good" men, not ones we draw away from because of some central evil in makeup; they are tragic heroes in the Aristotelian sense. But there is one marked difference between the men in the earlier group and those in the later group. Lear, Macbeth, and Othello all carry out actions that are evil or lead to evil, and Hamlet desperately wants not to do an evil deed. On the other hand, Antony, Coriolanus, and Timon are all presented, initially or throughout, as possessors or practitioners of a good (a transforming love, patriotism and integrity, generosity). Lear, Macbeth, and Othello must all recognize, as best they may, that they have done evil. But Antony (with brief intermittent exceptions), Coriolanus, and Timon rest fairly secure in the conviction that they have found the right path and embody genuine virtues (as Hamlet struggles desperately to do) and that when things have gone wrong, loss or disaster is due to some inadequacy or failure of the world in which they live. Finally, and most significantly, the major tragedies are wholly unambiguous in presenting wrong actions, whereas the later tragedies are ambiguous in presenting actions that are deemed by tradition or by those who perform them to be good. Up to a point, of course, the plays affirm the values enacted or accepted. But the plays as wholes inhibit our total assent to what appears to be affirmed. We are not invited unquestioningly to accept romantic love, valorous independence, and material openhandedness as absolute or transcendent virtues, or even to be sure that they are possessed in pure form—hence, of course, our inconsistent responses to the heroes as exemplars of virtue. In one reading, Timon is admirably generous, his friends are execrably greedy, ungrateful, and unreciprocating, and his inevitable turning upon them generates a brilliant rhetoric of excoriation. Other readers find Timon silly, his polemics tiresome, and his history all too allegorical; that is, his sudden conversion from philanthropic man to violent misanthropy is pat and mechanical.

The weakness of the play, however, lies in Timon's long-winded obtuseness rather than in his turnabout in mid-drama. Shakespeare is not wrong to convert philanthropy into misanthropy; what connects these attitudes psychologically is that both are univalent and therefore uncomplicated. One simplicity does easily change into another. Love, as we know, is quickly metamorphosed into hate; extremes meet. Timon's misanthropy is plausible but is overpresented, as if the dramatist had become addicted to it. In vituperation Timon goes on and on. Why? Because abuse is very necessary to him. Compare Lear: as long as he can flay Goneril and Regan, he can avoid acknowledging his own responsibility for decisions that have turned out disastrously. But in time Lear goes beyond abuse and on into recognition of himself as erring man. Shakespeare never lets Timon grow in this way. Timon's prolonged denunciations register not only disgust with evil but—I suggest—self-protection. As long as he can go on madly cataloging human shortcomings, he can feel superior to other men. As long as he can think the world only a cesspool of ingratitude, he need ask himself no hard questions about his extraordinary benefactional sprees. As long as he can lash evil, he need take no look at his earlier philanthropic operation, at its quality, and at his own motives. To say this is not to ignore or deny the satirical cast of the play, especially the second half; it is rather to say that our attention is deflected from the satire by the problem of the satirical voice. Timon does not gain magnitude by becoming a madder Apeimantus, the professional misanthrope whose self-worshiping attacks on others are so histrionic that to their victims they seem hardly more than an annoying but endurable case of un-Athenian conduct (hence he does not come across as Fool to Timon's Lear). The Thersites-Bosola vein, with the mechanized hyperbole of vilification, ceases to hold; one's interest shifts from the mouthings to the mouth, and the mind and motives that govern it.

What could Timon, consciously or unconsciously, be protecting himself from? With only a little bit of self-awareness Timon might discover and acknowledge several truths about his give-away program. The first is that the exhaustion of resources has its penalties. Surely we are to sympathize with the efforts of the loyal steward Flavius to persuade "noble Timon" to take a sensible look at his shrinking capital. To give away everything has at least the disadvantage of making one unable to give help when other suppliants appear, as they are sure to do; but then, too, it renders one materially defenseless in a world that is less likely to assist than shun or take advantage of defenselessness. Total divestment of holdings is rational only if one intends to leave the world and become hermit or monk, a role that Timon in no way seeks.

Second, Timon might realize that his manic largesse is not so much a blessing to others as it is a way of leading them into temptation. Indiscriminate, mechanical handouts bring out the worst in people; it is not so much that they are irremediably corrupt in nature, or suffer from Calvinistic total depravity, as that the latent corruptibility of the human race is activated by opportunities thrust recklessly upon average human beings. (As Congreve's Lady Wishfort said, in a different context, "What's Integrity to an Opportunity?") Great laxness or great rigidity in the practice of a virtue renders one predictable; predictability leads to vulnerability, and vulnerability is tempting (both Coriolanus and Timon so manage their quite different virtues as to present an inviting vulnerability). Timon brings out the darker side of man by making robbery too easy. In modern idiom, he invites rape, which is never tolerable, but which in certain circumstances is close to inevitable.

Finally, Timon misconstrues prodigality with cash as generosity of spirit. This is to say, not that he is not generous, but that his giving does not quite manage to be an end in itself. Or for him the permissible pleasure of enjoying the pleasure of the recipients is not enough. Without knowing it, Timon banks on a quid pro quo; he acts the part of a charitable institution, but he has some acquisitive tendencies of his own. If he loves men, he is also in effect procuring goodwill and gratitude. He is practicing what we might call timony—that is secular simony, a buying of good offices. Only an expectation that other men have made a compact with him—have obligated themselves to him—can explain the rancorous violence and indefatigability of his rants against Athenians and mankind.

It is such matters that Timon, were he capable of self-knowledge, might reflect upon. That he does not do so may mean that Shakespeare had worn out his earlier interest in self-awareness, or that for a time he was luxuriating in the simpler rhetoric of disillusionment—that disillusionment about the world that feeds on unpunctured illusion about oneself. Or perhaps he was temporarily fascinated by the energy that men put into self-justification, direct or indirect, and into apparently self-justifying lines of action—the abandonment to a virtue that seems absolute—even as these lines take them steadily toward destruction. We have to feel the energy; and the irony of outcomes that contradict expectations is effective. Still, it is difficult not to find in the protagonists' self-ignorance a limitation that accounts for the lesser status of some plays, most notably *Timon*. Few critics have tried to rescue it from a disesteem usually based more on structural or other technical defects than on a major constriction of character, of adult humanity.

V

The final context for an estimate of *Timon* is that of several later plays, ironically enough all comedies, which deal independently with the Timon theme. They all tend to confirm the reading of *Timon* presented here. In Goldsmith's *The Good Natured Man* (1768) Honeywood believes that "universal benevolence is the first law of nature"; hence, just like Timon, he falls into a help-everyone habit that would leave him, like Timon, financially ruined did not a wise uncle administer a shock that makes him, unlike Timon, see what he has been up to: "How have I sunk by too great an assiduity to please! . . . [I] perceive my . . . vanity, in attempting to please all by fearing to offend any." Surely his words identify a Timon motive. The uncle debunks universal-benevolence people as "men who desire to cover their private ill-nature by a pretended regard for all" (later a theme in Dickens). Although this is probably not applicable to Timon, still it would help explain the quickness of his complete about-face to total misanthropy. In Brecht's *The Good Woman of Setzuan* (ca. 1940) the issue is not the motive of the benefactor but the effect of benefactions upon beneficiaries: Shen Te, a female Timon and Honeywood, is called "good" by everyone; that is, she is susceptible to appeals for material help. Unlike Timon, she quickly sees what is happening: her gifts turn the recipients of them into rapacious spongers. To save herself from ruin by these leeches she must partly become a stern disciplinarian, that is, discriminate among petitioners, reject freeloaders, and make people earn what they get. (This tack leads to other complications not germane to the issue of timony.) Finally, the title character in Christopher Hampton's *The Philanthropist* (1970), Philip, is madly generous in another way: in his anxiety to "please"—the same word literally used of Honeywood and Shen

Te, and applicable to Timon—he simply approves of, likes, agrees with, or praises everybody. What overtakes him is not financial, but spiritual, bankruptcy: others pity, ignore, scoff at, or desert him. (Compare Camus's description of a character: "C., who plays at seducing people, who gives too much to everybody, but whose feelings never last, who needs to seduce, to win love and friendship, and who is incapable of both. A fine character to have in a novel, but lamentable as a friend.")[2] What is fascinating about Philip is his origin: Hampton created him by literally transforming Alceste, the title character of Molière's *Misanthrope,* into his opposite. Thus Hampton has perceived the subtle link between unlimited misanthropy and philanthropy, the convertibility of one into the other that Shakespeare had traced in the opposite direction.

Despite the validity of this central perception, *Timon* does not achieve what it might. The unrelentingness of Timon's practice, first in one mode and then in the other, makes his transformation, though plausible, emblematic, and this quality rules out the qualifications, the complications, and above all the human self-understanding that seem probable and that later dramatists such as Goldsmith would find in the Timon type. The content of the later plays enables us to see that the materials are more effective in the comic treatment than in the style of unrelieved satirical melodrama. At the time he did *Timon,* however, Shakespeare was in his period of the single-valued protagonist, who either was inflexible from the start or gradually excluded alternatives. Now, suppose Shakespeare had come to *Timon* a little later when, in the period of the romances, he characteristically saw beneficent action or circumstance forestalling disaster until the erring agent could come into improved vision. One could imagine him altering sources and making Timon less univocal and more aware of his actions and himself. In *The Winter's Tale* Leontes, as stiff-necked as Coriolanus and Timon, is shocked into self-understanding, and in *Cymbeline* Posthumus and Iachimo are volubly self-condemnatory. Iachimo is Shakespeare's final variation on the theme of self-knowledge: he relishes thinking, or seeming to think, evil of himself. He makes a good thing of pointing the finger of blame at himself. He explores the posture, prolongs it, seizes stage with it (V.v.153–209): self-knowledge is theatricalized as public self-accusation. Maybe this is easier when one has done a bad thing that has not prevented a good end than when one believes one has done only good things that have not prevented a bad end. But, as later dramatists show, even Timon types could see the light.

----

2. Albert Camus, *Notebooks 1935–1942,* trans. Philip Thody (New York: Knopf, 1963), 87.

vi

A final word on the Shakespeare trio of late tragedies. The heroes, if we take them at their simplest, exemplify three essential human virtues: devotion to a loved one, integrity in the world, and charity toward all. A great achievement of Shakespeare, in dealing with this group, is to avoid a simplistic attitude to the virtues. Instead he shows how the possessor of the virtue may hold to it questionably, and even suggests that the virtues themselves are contingent rather than absolute. But it is the spectators rather than the characters who gain this perception. For more perceptive men of virtue we have to go to earlier Shakespeare or later literature. As for the generous man: we have seen later Timons who could learn how charitableness becomes tainted. As for the man of integrity: Molière's Alceste could partly grasp his errors; true, he did not clearly see that his integrity was badly infected by love of power, but he did know that there was some failure in himself. As for the lover, Antony—it is a hard case. But one thinks of the speaker in Richard Lovelace's lyric "To Lucasta, On Going to the Wars": "I could not love thee, dear, so much, / Loved I not honor more."

IV

literary
types and
problems
inspected

Later Writers

Here we proceed with discussions of various literary problems as they are exemplified in writers who came long after Shakespeare—Hardy and others, conspicuously such recent fiction writers as William Corrington and Eudora Welty.

12

Good Guys and Bad Guys and What the Stage Does with Them

Dramatic Types

I used once to think that any play that dealt with good guys and bad guys was a pretty sad affair. In time I gave up this comfortable position. But another prejudice has grown stronger with the years. It is a prejudice against the popular, the widespread, the positively endemic use of the word *tragedy*—its dreadful hourly use in broadcasts, and its dreadful daily use in headlines and news stories. I have been airing this prejudice for twenty years, but I confess with tears in my eyes that media usage has been getting more addictive all the time. Daily the media announce tragedies by the gross. To them, a tragedy is anything that goes wrong, any kind of misfortune or accident, and most of all any death that occurs ahead of what seems sound scheduling. All right, why be prejudiced against the use of *tragedy* to describe any accident, any random act of violence, any unpleasant terminal experience? Surely it is hideously undiscriminating to use the same term for miscellaneous unhappy misadventures and for such magnificent dramas as Aeschylus's *Oresteia* trilogy, Sophocles' *Oedipus* and *Antigone,* Marlowe's *Dr. Faustus,* Shakespeare's *King Lear* and *Hamlet,* and Racine's *Phèdre.* These dramas are light-years away from the medley of commonplace misfortunes that are day-in-and-day-out occurrences on highways and byways, country lanes and air lanes, barrooms and bedrooms, inns and homes. In the dramas we have great characters whose actions reveal profound and critical problems of mankind. In the media events we have nothing but accidents that either have no meaning at all, or meanings too simple to have any value—namely, that not everyone drives as well as he should, that machinery is not always reliable, and that weather can be unfriendly. Or we see the truism that not everyone behaves as well as he should. But the media turn a world of

179

casualty and foul deeds into a cosmic McDonald's farm—here a tragedy, there a tragedy, and everywhere a tragic, tragic event.

Now why this national mania for applying the once noble word *tragedy* to all the ignoble mischances that afflict us? The answer: it is a kind of moral social climbing. It is an unconscious effort to steal the depth, dignity, and grandeur of traditional tragedy, and by this stolen glory elevate mundane accidents into solemn and splendid experience. No one has ever put this moral social climbing better than Thomas Mann when he was writing about the development of the Nazi movement in Germany. Mann said, "It is a melancholy affair—I call it that, instead of 'tragic,' because misfortune should not boast." Isn't that excellent? "Misfortune" should not "boast." How does misfortune "boast" when it snatches the name "tragedy"? It boasts by seeming to be more than it is, by claiming promotion into a higher category of catastrophic experience. "Higher" in what way?

To see what is higher, we need a clear picture of the classes into which catastrophes fall. (*Catastrophe* is a good neutral term for all kinds of bad events.) There are three types of catastrophe. They range from very simple to very complex. In the simplest form, man is done in by a nonhuman force, that is, a natural or mechanical cause—an avalanche, a hurricane, a gas leak, a brake failure, a broken bolt in a plane, a virus. The second kind of catastrophe is due to human action—to careless or reckless driving, to individual hostility (as in crimes of passion and revenge), to group hatred as in anti-Semitism, or to political tyranny or fanatical revolutionary spirit. The third and most complex kind of catastrophe is also due to human action, but in this type, man brings it on himself. In the first two kinds, man is a victim of some thing or someone outside himself; in the third, he is the victim of himself. So we have two kinds of bad trips—the one that comes from without, and the one that comes from within. If we call them the same thing, we are cheating ourselves by failing to make an essential distinction. We are confusing bad luck and bad choices; we are refusing a wholesome discrimination such as is natural to adult intelligence and vital to human understanding.

My distinction has been expressed independently by a member of the very media that have been the chief sinners in calling the untragic tragic. In a brilliant editorial of April 1981, the *Washington Star* said that *tragedy,* "a gem of a word, is being steadily reduced to a dull and lumpish pebble of cliché. . . . You hear or read it almost every day. . . . A small child falls from a ladder. It is tragic. A tornado strikes a town unexpectedly. It is tragic. A car hits a telephone pole, killing three. It is tragic. 'Tragedy' has become our portmanteau word for almost any misfortune, accident, calamity, outrage, or disaster—almost any event that touches us with sadness or regret. But of course a word that means almost anything soon begins to mean almost nothing. A word so rich and fine in deep shadings as 'tragedy' should not suffer that fate."

For nontragedies the *Star* uses one word of especial significance. That is the word *disaster*. *Disaster* is exactly the right term for nontragic catastrophes—for those that come upon us from without, whether from destructive people or destructive things. Think of the etymology: *disaster* means literally that the stars are against you. What a fitting image for injury generated elsewhere and not by oneself. What is more, *disaster* is a strong word such as we need: it does ample justice to the unhappiness, misery, or grief caused by catastrophes that come from without. If only the media would take it up and let it replace the *tragedy* which they are reducing to meaninglessness. By the way, the distinction between *disaster* and *tragedy* was first made in 1872 by the great novelist George Eliot. In *Middlemarch* she says of a character that he was "ill acquainted with disaster," that is, "a lot where everything is below the level of tragedy except the passionate egoism of the sufferer."

My prejudice against the use of the word *tragedy* for all catastrophes has, then, two grounds. First, it is logically wrong, for we can objectively distinguish the catastrophe from without—that is, disaster—from the catastrophe from within—that is, tragedy. Second, to call disaster "tragedy" is morally pretentious: we try to make the lower into the higher. So we come back to an earlier question: in what way "higher"? Tragedy is the higher because it involves a wider and deeper range of human nature; it simultaneously puts a finger on man's capacity for good and his capacity for evil. The tragic hero is not a simple villain whom we draw away from; rather he is an everyman in whom we must see ourselves. And by now you can see me coming back to the words of my title: tragedy gets the good guy and the bad guy together in the same character. And this slangy statement happens to coincide exactly with Aristotle's more formal description of the tragic hero: he is a man like ourselves, an ordinarily good man, who however has a fatal weakness or makes a fatal mistake. We usually call it the "tragic flaw." The tragic hero often suffers from ambition or pride or arrogance, for which the technical term is *hubris;* he thinks he can beat the rules. Or he is driven by some passion that he cannot control, even when he knows his action is wrong. Or in a very subtle case, he is caught between two conflicting obligations; whichever one he heeds, he will violate the other.

A few examples of this great range of true tragic character. Dr. Faustus, a fine Christian scholar, has a lust for power that drives him into a pact with the devil. King Lear, good and venerable, thinks he can order his daughters to declare in public their love for him, and then can reward or punish them by the way he divides up his kingdom. Phaedra, an otherwise unblemished queen, has an incestuous passion that she knows is wrong, but she cannot control it. Othello, a fine warrior, loves his wife, but believes that he must execute her for what he is sure is her adultery. Antigone is caught between the common tradition that she must have her dead brothers buried, and the civil decree that they cannot be buried because they were traitors to the state. Most striking of all is Oedipus, who tries to circumvent a prophecy that he will kill his father and marry his mother; yet when an obviously older man abuses him in a traffic squabble, Oedipus feels perfectly free to kill the older man, and indeed to marry an older woman when he goes on into the next town. Compare the vast depth and range of human meaning in these stories to the absence of depth and meaning in any highway, airstrip, or domestic accident.

We see how all these cases are versions of Aristotle's definition of the tragic hero as the good man with the flaw. Since he is the good man, the hero feels the force of all the rules as to what man cannot do; his flaw is the intense pressure of the individual drives that make him want to ignore the rules. Thus the very center of the tragic experience is the inner conflict. The personality is "divided"—the good guy versus the inner bad guy in one character. Inner conflict means a personality spacious enough to be divided, to feel the power on both sides of the fence. What is the difference between Macbeth and Richard III, who as plotters and rulers are alike in their ruthless cruelties? The difference is that from the start Macbeth knows that what he is doing is wrong, while Richard has no such problem and only faces practical issues. Macbeth has to spend the rest of his life fighting his knowledge of what he is and does; Richard is little bothered by the issue of good and evil. So Richard, as undivided, is a lesser personality than Macbeth; he does not have the tragic magnitude.

Now to say that Richard is a lesser character than Macbeth does not mean that we should ignore Richard, not make a play about him, or not read it if someone makes it. The bad guy is a reality of life, and so he is going to be a reality of drama. Here you can see me rejecting a prejudice. I once thought any drama of good guys versus bad guys had to be stereotyped and therefore false. I was wrong, for the simple reason that life does sometimes take the form of good guys versus bad guys, and the theater is bound to make use of this human conflict. There are evil people in the world, for example, Stalin and Hitler. When such a person seeks or gains power, others must and do fight against him. These opponents, if not always good or wholly good, are at least good during the fight: they are in fact the good guys against the bad guys.

So then we have a struggle *between* characters instead of a conflict *within* a character. What do we call it? I think the term *melodrama* does best. It is familiar, and that may be an advantage, though it would be easy to invent a new term. Second, *melodrama* implies something different from *tragedy*, as the term should. Now there is of course a risk in the use of the term *melodrama*, and we can all see what it is: the term has always seemed to be a disparaging one, whereas here we are not disparaging that kind of plot. But I overcame my prejudice against the term when I realized that we have never used it altogether disparagingly. For we do have a truly and wholly disparaging term: "popular melodrama." This implies, rightly, that there are better and worse forms of this kind of drama. It implies that melodrama can be good enough; it is only when it gets "popular" that it is regrettable. By "popular" we mean that it is hackneyed, superficial, going by formulas and standardized expectations, with heroes who never fail in the end and villains who are bound to be done in, and no sense of the cost of the struggle. But in true melodramas the heroes may fail, and the cost is always made clear.

So a case can be made for the term *melodrama*. No case really needs to be made for the form itself. Granted, it has technically a narrower range than tragedy, since it does not utilize the inner conflict that makes for an ultimate magnitude of character, but it may achieve its own kind of greatness. There are great melodramatic portraits of evil people—of Richard III, of Iago in *Othello,* of the revengers in half a dozen works contemporary with Shakespeare, of the modern revenger in Dürrenmatt's *The Visit* and Frisch's *The Firebugs.* The clashes between the evil people and their opponents can take many forms. War is the greatest of melodramas; each side is the good guys against the bad guys. Political fights often imitate it. The dramatist can turn popular melodrama upside down by positioning us with the losers rather than with the winners. He may pity those who are getting it in the neck; he may see them as victims of nature (everything from floods to disease), of society, of jobs, of crime, of political ruthlessness. His subject will then be the great world of *disasters,* of nontragic catastrophes. But the dramatist may picture triumphs—in the medical realm, or the social, or the political. For instance, in Shakespeare's "dark comedies" and in the late "dramatic romances" there is a great deal of evil loose in the world, but the final, shaping power lies with the benevolent people.

ii

If in tragedy the struggle is for the control of the individual by an internal good guy and bad guy, and if in melodrama the struggle is for the control of an outer world by competing good guys and bad guys, what other uses, if any, may we make of these two types? How do they figure, if they do, in that other traditional form, comedy? I'll get back to this question later.

It is impossible to think about tragedy and melodrama without thinking about comedy. These forms may contrast or overlap. For instance, there is one clear overlap: both tragic and comic characters may make judgments about themselves. But what they have to say about themselves is different. The tragic character says, "I have done wrong," but the comic character says, "I have been foolish." In tragedy: I have violated a moral principle, that is, an absolute which lies beyond changes in taste and opinion. But "I have been foolish" means "I have not shown good sense" or "common sense." Common sense is the sum total of the social concerns of the community, of our ordinary getting on with each other. The issue is less one of good and evil than of what is prudent and imprudent, workable and unworkable, pleasing and unpleasing, gratifying and vexatious, charming and off-putting. For instance, there is a consensus of feeling against the person who is too clever, the person who feels he's getting the better of everybody, the person who is stuck on himself. Now this consensus is remarkably similar to an idea of Plato's. Plato defined "the ridiculous" as a situation in which a man thinks he is wiser, or richer, or handsomer than he is, and then is exposed—but when exposed, adds Plato, cannot take revenge. This addition is very shrewd. For if the exposed person can take revenge, destructive emotions get into the act, and the ridiculous gives way to the more combative realm that I call melodrama. Now the ridiculous is certainly a good word for the comic. If it can by a simple gear-shift— by the addition of a destructive emotion—move over into melodrama, it seems clear that there is some sort of relationship between melodrama and comedy. It has to do with different attitudes to the world. Note that word—the *world*. A little later we'll get a clearer idea of it. It is an idea that often appears in comedies. Characters talk about "the world" and take it seriously. Some may be angry at it, but the majority of characters talk about "the world" as a desirable place and indeed as the possessor of a certain authority that they respect. In *Lady Windermere's Fan* Lord Darlington argues that "the world" and "the world's voice . . . matter a great deal . . . matter far too much." Mrs. Erlynne, who has been socially blackballed for an adulterous elopement, wants to get back into "the world," which she declares "is an intensely amusing place." Even the priggish Lady Windermere finally learns that "there is the same world for all of us," with its mixture of "good and evil, sin and innocence." In Boucicault's *London Assurance* (1841), Sir Harcourt Courtly admires himself as the successful seducer-to-be of another man's wife. But then he finds that she has just been kidding him and that "the world [has] been laughing at me." This is the thought that brings him back to earth and makes him resolve to act more sensibly. Likewise Honeywood, the hero of Goldsmith's *The Good-Natured Man* (1768); he has been so good-natured that he has given away all his money, and it is only when he learns that he is "contemptible to the world" that he resolves to be more sensible. Then there is Congreve's *The Way of the World* (1700). The phrase "the way of the world" is used frequently throughout the play. People who are in trouble dislike the world; others desire its approval. A wife is unfaithful; her husband comments ironically, "all in the way of the world." When he and his girlfriend are about to be exposed in their plotting, he observes in a what-will-be-will-be tone, "let 'em know it, 'tis all in the way of the world." His wife is preserved against his effort to grab her money by a wise protective step, and an observer calls this "the way of the world." That is, the way of the world includes irregular conduct and getting exposed, but it also includes practical prudence, self-protection against dirty tricks.

Such passages fortified my sense that a sense of the world is a strong force in comedy. It is not so in tragedy. True, the world may suffer because of the choices made by the tragic hero—you know the torment that Lear caused Britain, and Macbeth caused Scotland, and the plague that Oedipus's misdeeds brought to Thebes—but the hero does not base his choices on what the world thinks or even on his attitude to the world. What makes him act is emotional pressures and needs in himself. Yet in comedy the world around one—be it the family world, the larger community, society in general, or even the times—in some ways looms large for the characters. Now, if we go back, we remember that likewise in melodrama the world looms large. In melodrama there is a competition, a rivalry, a battle in the world. To repeat, in melodrama a good man wants to triumph over evil, good people resist an evil person or power, an evil person seeks power or revenge, two neutral forces compete for power (as in an election), men compete with or struggle against nature. There are winners and losers in the world.

Thus melodrama involves all-out conflicts. But comedy does not. In comedy you rarely get the total defeat that is frequent in melodrama—that is, the total loss of the world by death. In comedy you may be embarrassed or lose something strongly desired, but you survive. You don't really have incorrigible bad guys that you hate as winners, or crow over as losers. For that matter, you rarely have good guys that are all good; the better the comedy, the less perfect the characters. In comedy it's not all or nothing; instead it's more or less. Few go to jail or down the drain or to the dogs. I had about reached this point in perceiving the differences between comedy and melodrama as dramas of the world when I came across a formulation that shaped up my ideas exactly. It was made by Anthony Burgess, the Irish-English novelist. Comedy, he says, involves "acceptance of the world, of the fundamental disparateness of all the elements in the world." He says it produces "elation"; it "makes one, if not laugh, at least consider laughing. One feels one can push on." I will refer only briefly to these emotional effects. "Elation," I'd say, is the pleasurable sense of having got a sound view of reality, of having come to terms with a reality that is always mixed, of knowing what's what. "If not laugh, at least consider laughing"—how good that is to describe effects that may range from belly laughs to smiles to just a pleasant sense of well-being or being with it. "One feels one can push on"—that is, the world depicted in comedy is not a perfect world; it is simply a possible world. We know its shortcomings, but they do not make us despair.

But now back to the heart of the definition: "acceptance . . . of the fundamental disparateness of all the elements of the world." First, disparateness: the world is an inconsistent place, a mixed place, an illogical place, an uneven place. The word *fundamental* is important: it says that the inconsistency, the mixture of sense and silliness, of good taste and bad taste, of dullness and fancifulness, of reasonableness and neurosis, of stolidity and unreliability (even of professors and civilized people, I might add), is pretty much in the nature of things. We don't think of the world as a lamentable falling-short of a perfection we ought to have; rather we take a mixture of excellences and failures as a reality to be lived with.

Now to move on from "disparateness" to "accept." As I have implied, *accept* really means our understanding that inconsistencies—personal, social, aesthetic, and even moral—are irrevocably present in the nature of things. We are not angry because some people do better and some do worse; it is just that this is the way it is. We do not grieve for those who do less well, or envy those who are more sensible or wiser or better balanced or governed by better values, and who may do better in the world. We do not get rid of the less well behaved ones—exile them, jail them, pauperize them, reform them, or even hate them. They may be embarrassed, humiliated, get less than they want, or even suffer; but they are still there, as they always will be. We live with it. Instead of raging, we smile, or consider laughing.

We can clarify the idea of "accept" a little further by looking at some familiar types of nonacceptance. It is not acceptance to retire from the world, to become a hermit or join a supposedly ideal commune; such moves show that we cannot stand the disparateness of human society. It is not acceptance to write satire, which grows out of disgust for the less amiable parts of the human scene. Now the comic and the satirical may appear in the same play, but the stronger the satirical becomes, the bigger the break with comedy. Satire lashes vice rather than smiles at shortcomings. Ben Jonson's famous *Volpone* (1606) is about greed; it treats greed not as a bad habit, as Molière does, but as a terrible vice that makes people behave wickedly. Thus its tone is less comic than satirical. If the satirist wants to change things, he is a reformer, and as such, a long way from comedy. In fact we could almost say that the opposite of comedy is not tragedy but reform. Why? Because reformism is nonacceptance of the actual. Reformers cannot have a sense of humor; they must be single-minded crusaders. You see why: a sense of humor is the opposite of single-mindedness; it is at bottom a sense of discrepancy or disparateness, and amusement at it, whereas the reformer wants to eliminate discrepancies. Likewise all utopian writing is noncomic, for the utopian mind will not accept anything but what he defines as good conduct. Any work that glorifies triumph or sympathizes with victims is not comic, for the writer is taking sides, and taking sides is not accepting disparateness, but pushing a single value. Finally, there is a very good definition of acceptance in T. S. Eliot's *The Cocktail Party* (1949). Eliot's spokesman in the play gives the rule: "avoid excessive expectation." That is the comic way of the world. For excessive expectation for oneself leads to tragedy, and excessive expectation of the world leads to disillusionment or revenge, or to foredoomed utopian schemes—all forms of melodrama. In these, you do not accept or smile; instead, you battle.

iii

Now let's go on from generalizations to an individual play, so that we can see how principles work out in practice. One play that shows beautifully how comic spirit works is *The Playboy of the Western World* (1907), the masterwork of the Irish playwright John M. Synge. You remember that Christy Mahon, a young outsider, arrives at a County Mayo village and turns it upside down. He says that he has killed his cruel father, and thus he becomes a local hero, especially fascinating to the women, several of whom would like to marry him. A romantic murderer—what a mate to capture. Christy picturesquely describes the blow by which he had split his father's skull and cut him down to the middle. With "such poet's talking and such bravery of heart" he wins the love of the heroine, Pegeen Mike, whose local fiancé, she complains, has "no savagery or fine words in him at all." Then suddenly the supposedly murdered father shows up, with just enough of an injury to need a bandage on his head. Everyone begins to think that as a heroic parricide, Christy is a sorry fraud. He didn't kill his father at all. To regain his local status, Christy grabs a spade and socks his father again. But now, led by Pegeen Mike, the community turns against Christy in a different way: seeing the act before their eyes, they call him a brutal criminal, tie him up, and propose to hang him as a murderer. But in this jam he is rescued by his father, who has come to again, and the pair go off cheerily, sneering at the locals as a sorry set of sad sacks. Still the play closes with the forlorn, almost teary line of Pegeen Mike, the heroine, who has done another turnaround: "I've lost the only playboy of the western world." That little sadness comes briefly into almost every great comedy—a part of that wide range of disparate experiences that comedy accepts, that is, presents as being in the unalterable nature of things.

We should be entirely clear that this play is not satirizing, not deriding, not putting down anything or anybody. Whatever the characters do, however unexpected or apparently inconsistent, is justified, that is, treated as understandable or even as inevitable in individuals or community character. So the play accepts all kinds of disparateness.

1. When Christy says he killed his father and becomes a hero, what is accepted is the fondness for violence in people generally, especially for the revolution of the young against the old, which in some form or other occurs in every generation. There is also a love of the unusual, of the bold stroke, of the turning worm, of the ruthlessness that seems just and heroic because the victim is not seen and is said to deserve what he got.

2. When Christy tries to sustain his role by striking a live and present father and is turned on by his erstwhile hero-worshipers who have now become murder-haters, the play is not satirizing the locals for unreliability and inconsistency: rather it accepts the fact that changed circumstances change the quality of the action. A present and seen murder seems wholly different from a distant and reported one. It is the difference between poetry and life, between art and blunt fact, between myth and history, between symbolic act and literal act. You can do in one what you never can do in the other. If people saw in real life what they see on the stage in the final scene of *Hamlet,* they would be so sickened and traumatized that many would never get over it.

3. When father and son leave together and sneer at the village folk, we are not, I am sure, to read them as authoritative voices damning a miserable village. The community may seem fearful and limited, but it is doing what it has to do. If there is to be stable, ongoing community life, you can't have sons murdering fathers to look brave, however poetically they speak. Ordinary life has its own justifications, though it may often be—as we all often are—unheroic, narrow, overcautious, and so on.

4. Christy and his father get together despite long hostility, and despite the actual violence that inaugurated the action. We accept this apparent inconsistency. While the father presumably doesn't enjoy being knocked cold with a spade any more than any of us would, he is imaginative enough to see that the blow means that his son is growing up at last. Hence they can have a partnership that was impossible before, when daddy scorned a childish, unaccomplishing son. They have in common with each other more than they have with the County Mayo village, and they naturally express this by sneering at the village.

5. What the Mahons, on the one hand, and the community, on the other, represent, is simply two different aspects of life. The play makes a case for each. The Mahons are the special types, the individualists, the artists, the actors, the adventurers, the wandering minstrels, the bohemians; the townspeople are ordinary society, citizens, bourgeois (I borrow the contrasting terms *bohemian* and *bourgeois* from Thomas Mann). There is a sort of love-hate relationship between the two sides; each needs the other, but neither consistently has a high tolerance for the other. In accepting both, the play implies a basic truth: that the community needs art, and art needs a community. The playboy is the person who writes plays; he may charm or shock the public.

6. Pegeen Mike's cry of loss at the end is awfully good. She has to stay in her village world, because that is what she is fitted for. But still she yearns for that other one (as do several other women in the community), and that yearning is a symbolic bridge between them. In time, we suspect, the wandering Mahons will yearn for the stability of the ordinary society which is not their primary dish.

The play asks us to accept both sides—to understand both, and see them as inevitable. Thus comedy invites the highest act of our sense of humor—to appreciate and even to relish such basically disparate elements. We push on; we expect to change neither; we enjoy the ironies of different modes of life that are incompatible and yet necessary to each other. Both sides, so to speak, contain something of the good guy and something of the bad guy.

iv

One real problem remains: sometimes the very idea of "acceptance" raises doubts for people. It may seem to be too uncritical, to imply that anything goes. Haven't you any standards, and principles? There are real problems. There is no completely clear-cut, final answer to this. Occasionally a play may seem to put a seal of approval on a situation that we find it very hard, or perhaps impossible, to go along with. Such a play, we might say, accepts the unacceptable. The author writes comedy when we feel he should be writing melodrama. Now when something like this happens, we call the result "black comedy." It is rather frequent with us because with our loss of traditional values there is great uncertainty about all values, and hence a tendency to act as if anything does go. One fine example of black comedy is *Entertaining Mr. Sloane* by the late Joe Orton. A young man has had a hand in a couple of murders, and thus he can be blackmailed by two people, each of whom knows about one of the murders. The two blackmailers are a middle-aged brother and sister. The sister is alcoholic and sluttish, and she lusts after the young murderer. The brother is homosexual, and he also lusts after the young murderer. Quite a juicy triangle, you see. The brother and sister might easily come to melodramatic violence over the young man who is so sexually appetizing, but they don't. In comic fashion they compromise: they make a deal. Each of them will have sole possession of their joint sex object for six months of the year, and the one who is on sexual sabbatical will have occasional visiting rights to ease the pain of deprivation. With this happy treaty the play ends. It illustrates well the idea of black comedy as accepting the unacceptable—at least in the sense that most of us, I assume, would not gladly belong to such a triangle. But the play invites us to approve it. Somewhat similar strains are imposed on readers by certain plays in most ages—by certain comedies in the Restoration period, and by the Shakespeare plays sometimes called "dark comedies"—*All's Well That Ends Well, Measure for Measure,* and *Troilus and Cressida.* In this matter, we probably have to live with some uncertainty, some differences in taste. For it is a fact that the borderline between acceptable and unacceptable is not always clear, and that any act of acceptance always runs the risk of overacceptance. In black comedy, in short, we are asked to tolerate, or withhold judgment on, characters who have in them more bad guy than good guy.

But such special and difficult cases aside, comedy generally is the good-humored, nonreforming, compromising, realistic observation—and therefore acceptance—of the differences, the contrasts, the inconsistencies, and the inevitable inequities that make up human reality. Comedy is about everything that you can't legislate about. You can't legislate that A shall be as intelligent at B, as handsome as B, or as strong as B, as sensible as B, as tasteful as B, as healthy as B, as lucky as B, as respected as B, or as well rewarded as B (though nowadays we do attempt to legislate equality of rewards). Nor can we legislate that B shall be equally bright, strong, sensible, healthy, lucky, and successful every day of the week or every week of the year. A sense of humor is simply a quiet awareness of, and amusement at, all these disparities between individuals and occasions. A person with no sense of humor cannot stand disparateness, and so he becomes a reformer, an egalitarian, a utopian, an ideologue, or a dictator. We might call him a uniformalist, or an antidisparatist.

V

We have come quite a way with the good guys and the bad guys. To my own surprise, these simple souls that I hit upon for a title have been rather useful. When they are at their purest, with the smallest alloy of human complexities, they make great entertainment for those who love formula action—that is, the thrills of what we call "popular melodrama." But let the bad guy take on the stature of real evil that has real victims: then the victims become good by definition, and we are into the large world of melodrama, be it the melodrama of critical conflicts in the world, or the contemplation of these on the stage. Then let the bad guy become not a unique deviate but a figure of the passions and lusts of all humanity, and let the good guy be not a spotless Galahad but the ordinarily decent person, and we can see the two coming together in that divided figure, complex and often profound, of the tragic hero. Next step: change the scene from the realm of moral good and evil to the practical, workaday region of good sense and folly, and we move over into comedy, where virtually everyone has in him something of the good guy and the bad guy. This mixture of elements may be the best evidence of that connection between tragedy and comedy that is often asserted but rarely demonstrated.

The Czech novelist Milan Kundera, long a political refugee in Paris, has said that the two great threats to the modern world are fanaticism and absolute skepticism. Note what both of these do to the dramatic forms we have been looking at. Fanaticism would simply eliminate tragedy and comedy and turn all life into a melodrama: the self-appointed good guys making everyone good by force, be it the Inquisition, the guillotine, or the secret police. Absolute skepticism would eliminate all three forms, because it would undermine all conceptions of good and evil. No one could be certified as a good guy or a bad guy. Maybe, if we want to hold on to these simple but convenient types, and our basic dramatic forms, we should become fanatics against fanaticism and skeptics of skepticism

13

The Novel

Ideas versus Drama in Hardy

My use of the word *ideas* may suggest a prejudice against ideas in novelistic art. No way. Novelists always embody ideas; novelists are always thinking as well as storytelling. The problem is one of how they "think." Do ideas govern the actions novelists portray? Or are they, as it were, external additions dear to the novelist's heart? In four major novels Hardy illustrates this problem: the ideas he enunciates seem extraneous to the stories told, or actually in conflict with the stories. We need to distinguish the ideas enunciated from the ideas actually implicit in the actions depicted.

Of the nineteenth-century big guns in the novel, Hardy is the one most likely to lace his stories with salvoes of partisan ideas and opinions. He is particularly prone to fire away at traditions, conventions, and institutions. However, his shots do not come from a trained philosophical mind such as George Eliot has. She is a much more disciplined thinker, and more meditative by temperament. No less than Hardy is she aware of the disasters and antagonisms of life, but she is more likely to view these as phenomena to be understood, demanding sympathy of course, but not resentment and anger. She is contemplative, whereas Hardy tends to be polemic. He wants to see failure and unhappiness as due to inimical forces that ought to be blamed. He looks for someone or some thing to castigate. Hardy was somewhat under the influence of the new science and the new philosophy of the day (Darwin's biology and Comte's positivism), and since both of these rejected or modified ancient traditions of truth and value, both doubtless contributed to his oppositionist habit of mind. Society and conventions are at fault, education and marriage are at fault, the gods beat men down for the fun of it, the cosmos is hostile to mankind. If Hardy had heard of what we call "the system," he would have been a major abuser of it. If he had ever heard of the popular adjective *absurd,* he would have made it doubly popular. (As a matter of fact, two of the best criticisms of the absurdist fashion that I know can be applied to Hardy. The playwright Eugene Ionesco rejected the word *absurd;* the proper word, he said, is *paradoxical.* That is, the world is full of apparent contradictions. Henri Peyre has said that calling the world absurd is simply a way of complaining that the world does not suit man's convenience. One at times wants to say that of Hardy's complaints.)

It is likely that Hardy's addiction to side-mouth cracks about the forces that beat men down is simply a phase of his personality. It can hardly be accounted for by ill luck, which for him was less than for most people. True, he was a sickly child, had little schooling, and never made it to a university. But he was a born student, and by sheer steady book-work gave himself a better education than he would have got at prep school and college; at times he even seems a bit pedantic. Apprenticed in architecture, he had various jobs from ages sixteen to about thirty. He married the girl of his dreams, though the dream turned out to be a little uncomfortable at times. He consoled himself with sentimental relationships with several younger women, and when his wife died, he married a faithful secretary who slaved for him the rest of his life. By age forty he had published eight novels and was a recognized literary figure. By age forty-three he built a big house in Dorchester and was a very big frog in that pond, as well as much larger ones, for another forty-five years.

It is hard to find personal reasons for his official moroseness, his charges against the world and cosmos for doing so badly by people. Maybe he was not aware of how much griping and complaining he was doing. He seemed surprised, and was displeased, when he was understandably accused of pessimism. He denied that he was a pessimist and claimed to be a "meliorist," that is, a "betterist," a believer in the possibility of improvement. He also said, and this is very much to the point, that he was not trying to advance a coherent philosophical system but was only stating a set of impressions that he could not guarantee would be consistent with each other. His censoriousness can easily take him in two directions at once. One example only: In *Jude the Obscure* he criticizes Oxford for being set in its ways, for sticking to old traditions and not getting in line with modernity. On the other hand he criticizes equally what he calls "the modern vice of unrest." What is unrest but love of change? So in different moods he is for change and against it. He is inconsistent. But I do not treat this inconsistency as a vice. On the contrary I will propose later that it contributed to his salvation as an artist.

First, however, let us note the impact of his fondness for charging institutions and divinities with causing unhappiness and misery. In his own day it made him look like an unsavory disturber of the peace, and he drew a good deal of flak. For instance, some readers said that the title of his last novel should be *Jude the Obscene,* a crack hard to understand today. On the other hand, Hardy's sniping at habits and attitudes of his own day is likely to make us think him an admirably clearheaded and advanced person. He thinks like us; therefore he is good. But this is all wrong. Hardy is a great novelist not because of opinions that we may find congenial but because of the human reality that he got into his characters. In fact, if his characters existed only as gun barrels ready to discharge his angers and indignations, they would no longer be interesting, or indeed alive. There is nothing so lifeless as an outmoded partisan opinion. Hardy was in part an attacker, but fortunately he was also a writer of fine imagination. In the end it was almost always his imagination that determined how his characters acted, grew, shrank, or changed. They were not mouthpieces for Hardy the challenger of the accepted. True, he tried at times to make them so, but in the end his imagination—his intuition of human reality—won out. The characters were themselves, not propositions or arguments. Even when Hardy thought they were arguments, they were better than that.

That is why I said earlier that Hardy's tendency to voice "impressions" that were inconsistent benefited him as an artist. If he had worked out a wholly consistent system of thought, he would have had a hard time freeing his characters from it, letting them act independently and jump the traces of a system, as full human beings characteristically do. A true ideologist keeps his imagination in bondage to his ideas. Happily Hardy failed to do this, partly, at least, because his ideas never shaped up into an ideology.

I now move on from generalizations to specifics—the evidence in four major novels that report on human failures—*The Return of the Native,* 1878; *The Mayor of Casterbridge,* 1886; *Tess of the d'Urbervilles,* 1891; *Jude the Obscure,* 1895. They take us from Hardy's thirty-eighth to his fifty-fifth birthday.

ii

In *The Return of the Native* the native is Clym Yeobright, who gives up a job in a Paris jewelry store to come back to Egdon Heath, a rather wild area near Dorchester, where Hardy lived and which he has made famous. Clym wants to uplift the culturally underprivileged by teaching school on the Heath. He falls in love with and marries Eustacia Vye, a beautiful and temperamental exile on the Heath who Clym thinks will be a great teacher's assistant. She in her turn thinks of Clym as a ticket to Paris, which stirs her to great fantasies about a glamorous and exotic life. Clym studies so hard that his sight is affected, and he has to settle for manual labor. Eustacia, depressed, resumes an affair she had been having with Damon Wildeve, an innkeeper of romantic inclinations. When Eustacia married Clym, Wildeve rebounded by marrying Clym's cousin Thomasin, a good-natured, sensible girl whom Wildeve makes as unhappy as Clym has made Eustacia. Wildeve and Eustacia elope. A big storm causes floods, and both are drowned. Clym becomes an itinerant preacher. Thomasin marries her faithful follower, the peddler Diggory Venn, and things go well with them.

Hardy keeps pushing a recurrent idea of his that the world is an un-friendly place that will injure or destroy all sentient people. He keeps making cracks about "life as a thing to be put up with," a view "replacing that zest for existence" which he alleges ruled long ago. He speaks of "the grimness of the human situation," which he says often causes youthful suicides in France. Hardy makes Eustacia refer to "the cruel satires that fate loves to indulge in," and Clym at one time say that life is so sad an affair that men, instead of "aiming to advance in [it] with glory . . . calculate how to retreat out of it without shame." Hardy directly blames mankind because they don't see that a "First Cause," that is, divinity, has a "lower moral quality than their own"; hence men "invent excuses for the oppression which prompts their tears." At another time Hardy is upset by the divine mismanagement that accounts for the "inequality of lot" and the "captious alternation of caresses and blows that we endure now." Not only does Hardy in such ways declare the world an unredeemable hoodooed place, but he himself acts like an unkind divinity by surrounding his characters with land mines and booby traps that are bound to wreck them. He of course believed literally in coincidence as a source of disaster, and he worked it relentlessly. Overhearings and meetings, unfortunate or disastrous, abound. Wildeve and Mrs. Yeobright both pick the same day to visit Clym and Eustacia; Clym is asleep, Eustacia sees Wildeve alone, and Mrs. Yeobright is accidentally turned away. For this sad adventure she has not only picked an unbearably hot day, but lest this not finish her, Hardy has her fatally bitten by a poisonous snake. People make preposterous errors of fact and judgment as Hardy suborns disaster by every device that comes to mind.

Despite all this idea-pushing, the novel is very good. It is good because Hardy's imagination takes over from his gloomy doctrines: it gets him into his characters so well that it is their natures, and not external events, that determine what happens to them. What does Clym and Eustacia in is not bad luck or a dismal cosmos, but a central obsessiveness that determines their courses. They are not great human figures as Hardy alleges, but they are very true ones. He puts his finger on the fact that they are irresistibly drawn to each other although they are wholly incompatible. They make use of each other, not as sex objects, to apply our current term, but as ego-maintaining objects, as fantasies made flesh. Before Eustacia meets Clym, we see her passionateness and her power-love in her relations with Wildeve. She feels superior to him, which is probably the reason he gets engaged to Thomasin; so then Eustacia wants to get him back—until her attention is caught by the charms of Clym, fresh in from Paris. Wildeve then marries Thomasin, at least partly to spite Eustacia. All these moves are exactly in character. But the big thing is the attraction between Clym and Eustacia, and Hardy excellently portrays its sources. Eustacia has a sense of status and of being above the Heath; so a Parisian seems exactly her dish. To her, Hardy says, Clym is "like a man coming from heaven" (that is, a manna man), and he stirs up all sorts of dreams in her. She does not see him; she creates him. Clym does the same. She is the single striking local figure who catches his eye; besides, some local peasants think she is a witch, and so she arouses the protective feeling of the do-gooder in Clym. Neither one listens when the other tells the truth. Clym doesn't listen when she says she adores Paris, hates the Heath, and couldn't care less about school teaching; she doesn't listen when he says he's left shallow Paris forever and will make a lifelong career of helping the local populace. Neither listens because neither can. In the egoism of passion each one thinks he can co-opt the other into sharing his own social goals. So they get married, and all goes downhill, as it must when two counter self-delusions are joined. Of course Hardy hits upon some preposterous mechanics in arranging ultimate disaster, but the inner history is absolutely right. Hardy has caught both the inevitable attraction between them and the fact that it can lead only to failure. He has caught, in Eustacia, a great combination of romantic drives, visions of a glamorous life, a power-sense that she hardly understands herself, and a blindness to brute facts; and in Clym, the eternal do-gooder, he sees the theorist of benevolence who pays little attention to human actuality and who hence can turn out to be a fantast, a busybody, or an enforcer (the man of good will who wills to impose his good on others), the dogmatic man who makes up his mind in advance and ignores the views of others. Becoming an itinerant preacher is the right end for him. He can lecture the world and avoid the responsibility for which he is unfitted.

It is fascinating that at one moment Hardy makes a judgment of Eustacia that is in effect a critique of himself. He says: "instead of blaming herself for the issue she laid the fault upon the shoulders of some indistinct, colossal Prince of the World, who had framed her situation and ruled her lot." That is exactly what Hardy does in his comments along the way. Indeed he is very sympathetic with her when she complains, "how destiny has been against me! . . . O, how hard it is of Heaven to devise such tortures for me, who have done no harm to Heaven at all!" Hardy wants to believe this, but at the same time he knows that it is self-pity. We are never sure when his sound imagination or his unsound judgment is going to take over. For instance, he concludes the novel with an account of the charming working marriage of Thomasin and Diggory Venn, two ordinary, faithful, warm human beings who keep their feet on the ground. Now Hardy actually apologizes for this change of gears, this infidelity to his credo of universal failure. But his self-judgment is simply wrong. The chapters on Thomasin and Diggory are spontaneous and wholly plausible, not an artificial sop to a public that wants a happy ending. Again, Hardy's imagination is better than his doctrine. His doctrine is that all goes wrong, but his imagination tells him that decent, sensible people who do not have unrealistic expectations do indeed make out quite well.

iii

Eight years later, in *The Mayor of Casterbridge* (1886), Hardy continues his habit of glum and grim comments on the sad state of mankind. But, very gratifyingly, he makes no gloomy observations on the central character, Michael Henchard. Instead he quotes the German writer Novalis (pseudonym of Friedrich von Hardenberg, 1772–1801), who says "Character is Fate," and lets this rule the career of Henchard. Henchard, an unstable young man given to tantrums and drink, literally sells his wife to a passerby. Shocked by his action into a new stability and application, he becomes in twenty years a successful grain merchant and then mayor of Casterbridge. His discarded wife, with her daughter by the man who had bought her from Henchard, looks up Henchard, and they are reunited. But Henchard's bad guesses about a grain season, technical changes in the business, the greater skill of Donald Farfrae (first Henchard's assistant and then his rival), and Henchard's return to instability and drink bring him down. Farfrae succeeds him as business leader and mayor, and Henchard wanders off to die as the nobody he had been initially. Hardy gives a fine portrait of a man in whom a complex mixture of elements leads now to success, and now to failure. It is truly tragic. Happily Hardy does not garnish it with sour comments about unfriendly destiny and sardonic gods.

But the gloomy editorialist in Hardy is still very much alive, and it really muddles the scene when the chief women characters are on stage.

However, in talking about Henchard's wife, Susan, Hardy makes a different kind of misstatement. Because Susan accepted Henchard's sale of her to Newson, Hardy evidently feels that she has to be very mild and passive and even dim-witted, and he keeps giving us a barrage of such terms as these: "her simplicity," "poor woman," "had no practical hand at anything"; Henchard refers to her "idiotic simplicity," and he and Newson agree that she "was simple-minded" and "warm-hearted, homespun . . . not what they call shrewd or sharp at all." But such statements are totally out of line with the dramatic portrait of her, that is, with what Hardy makes of her in action. Hardy imagines her as energetic and shrewd. When she sees that Henchard really means to sell her, she leaves with a real dash of independence; then when she comes to feel that her relationship with Newson is wrong, she has so much character that Newson stages a fake drowning to release her. To provide for Newson's and her daughter, Elizabeth-Jane, Susan plans, after twenty years, to recapture Henchard. She carries out an incredibly difficult search, and she finds her man. Then, instead of rushing in, she acts very cautiously until she finds out how he is doing and what sort of man he is now. She uses Elizabeth to make a masterly approach to him; she lets him think that Elizabeth is his daughter instead of Newson's, a move that requires some agile footwork and her getting Elizabeth's help in this without Elizabeth's knowing what is up (and Elizabeth, Hardy tells us, is very bright). Finally she so times the revelation of the truth that it does no damage; she has successfully secured Henchard's devotion to Elizabeth. Meanwhile, she has managed to throw Elizabeth into the arms of the most eligible bachelor in town, Farfrae, and after various delays and difficulties— Farfrae marries Lucetta first—Elizabeth is eventually married to the number-one citizen of Casterbridge. Rarely does a wife and mother manage things so beautifully. Instead of calling Susan poor, simple, impractical, dull, and idiotic, Hardy might better have called her spirited, energetic, determined, smart, and even devious. In short, she affords an excellent example of the difference between what Hardy officially *thinks* about a character and how he *imagines* the character in action.

Still, Hardy's inconsistencies with Susan are mild in comparison with those that plague him in his dealing with Elizabeth. I will ignore his plain inconsistencies in dealing with her character—he makes her half a competent peasant and half a dream girl combining beauty, skills, and Latin scholarship—in order to concentrate on his more characteristic inconsistencies in dealing with her history and fate. His mind tells him that she is another of the innocent victims of a wretched world that he sees everywhere. Here are some phrases he uses about her early life: "casual disfigurements . . . from straitened circumstances"; "carking accidents of daily existence"; "strait waistcoat of poverty." Elizabeth felt, he insists, that "life and its surroundings . . . were a tragical rather than a comic thing"; she "had known so little friendship." "Like all people who have known rough times, light-heartedness seemed to her . . . a reckless dram"; she was "early habituated to anxious reasoning"; she had "that fieldmouse fear . . . which is common among the thoughtful who have suffered from poverty and oppression." "Poverty and oppression"? What can he be thinking of? Up until recently she and her mother had been living happily with Newson, a decent, kind, and responsible man, as both women testify; neither says anything about want. After his supposed death they have "a month or so" of hard physical work, but they soon find a new home with the rich Mayor Henchard. We see Elizabeth in pleasant relations inside and outside the family circle, but Hardy insists that she was "a lonely girl." He reports sadly that she knew "the lessons of renunciation" and was "familiar with the wreckage of each day's wishes." "Wreckage of each day's wishes"? We might think she was an orphan in a slum. True, she had a disappointment when Farfrae turned to Lucetta and married her, but Lucetta soon conveniently died, and Elizabeth then did get Farfrae, the economic and political head of the city (the local catch for whom nineteen other girls were competing). It's a Cinderella story. But Hardy goes right on insisting that Elizabeth believes that life is "a brief transit through a sorry world" and that "happiness was but a brief episode in a drama of pain." Hardy could justify such lugubrious observations only by making her a neurotic, but he does no such thing. His own obsessive need to be querulous drives Hardy into foisting his morose contentions upon other characters too. Susan, one of the most successful marrying mothers in fiction, has learned from "Civilization," he assures us, to expect anything "from Time and Chance, except, perhaps, fair play." But Susan got much better than fair play; she planned so well that she eliminated Chance and made Time serve her ends. Finally Hardy insists that Henchard, after his ultimate failure, is kept from a new rise to the top by "the ingenious machinery contrived by the Gods for reducing human possibilities of amelioration to a minimum." One can only say that this is nonsense. What keeps Henchard down is not the Gods but his own nature, which by now has run out of the psychic energy required for going to the top.

In *The Mayor of Casterbridge* we see some of Hardy's most overt and continuous whining (one can only call it that). He had a mysterious compulsion to peddle to others his dismal gospel of a nasty cosmos. But the great thing is that he forgot his gospel when he was imagining his characters. He did *imagine* them; he did not take thought and by act of will construct his characters as illustrations of his ideas and his obsessions. If he had done so, we would now remember neither the characters nor the novels. Hence we can only be thankful for the truly amazing split between what he thought and what he imagined. If Hardy had been able to know a familiar modern command to the public, he could have said, "Do not read what I say, but read what I do."

iv

Five years later, in *Tess of the d'Urbervilles* (1892), Hardy again causes problems by appearing to interpret his materials much more simply than he actually does. Unlike Susan and Elizabeth in *The Mayor,* Tess suffers a series of disasters that are fatal. She is seduced by Alec d'Urberville and has a child by him; she faces derision and hostility from fellow-workers on farm jobs. Things look up when she and Angel Clare, a minister's son who gave up the church for agriculture, fall in love and are married. Then, when she tells Angel about Alec and the child, which died, Angel throws her out and goes abroad. Tess has a very hard time; her family is broke and irresponsible, and she has to take on hard jobs as a farm laborer. Things are so bad that when Alec pursues her again, she goes to live with him. Her husband, Angel, returns, ready to forgive, but is again embittered by finding her as Alec's mistress. She kills Alec, she and Angel have at last a brief honeymoon before she is arrested and executed. Here Hardy has a woman who does seem the victim he is always holding forth about—a victim of a seducer, of conventional ideas, of a feckless family, of at least one brutal employer, and, most notably, of a husband acting from rigid ideas of right and wrong. In his final paragraph Hardy sums up in a sentence that is the most quoted single line in all his work: "the President of the Immortals had ended his sport with Tess." That is, Tess was a mere plaything of the Gods, who got a big sadistic bang out of making people to kick her around. And for a long time the book was read as if it were only a bitter history of dreadful wrongs inflicted on an innocent.

This reading applies a familiar pattern of melodrama—the nice girl, the villainous seducer, and the self-righteous husband. Or, at a nobler level, it sees a combination of the pathetic and the satirical: pathos is the pitiableness of the victim, and satire is scorn of those who abuse the victim. There is of course much pathos, and Hardy, as usual, cooks up mischances and coincidences to magnify Tess's pitiable difficulties. Likewise he offers much satire—of the uncharitable Christianity of Angel's family, of Tess's father's pretentiousness, of various kinds of convention and selfishness. Perhaps Hardy's major intention was to weep for sufferers and to whip bad actors. But that is a rather easy kind of undertaking, and it would hardly account for the vitality of the book through more than a century. Old cruelties and conventions die, and we are no longer moved by editorials against them. For instance, changes in sex mores probably make incomprehensible, in our day, Angel's fierce reactions to finding his wife not a virgin.

But *Tess* is very much alive, and the reason I think is the one I now cite for the third time: whatever ideas Hardy had about his characters, his imagination produced an art more spacious than stereotypes, than contemporary problems, and than the limited styles of the pathetic and the satirical. The three central characters are larger than the evil seducer, the innocent victim, and the stuffy and stupid husband. The Immortals weren't in the act at all, unless we want to blame them for creating characters complex enough to have some virtues and yet act imperfectly, like the rest of us. What readers have slowly been coming to see is that the three central characters are much more than puppets swung through old routines by strings managed from above.

Take Alec the seducer. He is an interesting and often attractive figure. He has a jesting playfulness, an ironic humor; he does not really plot against Tess; rather he thinks that she is as available as other farm girls he has known. He is grieved when Tess leaves him; he wants to help her; he has a kind of misguided imagination that makes him think he is a born-again Christian and evangelist, and he is shrewd enough to understand the loss of his new faith. He bawls out a farmer who mistreats Tess; he appears to her in a comic guise; he wants to marry her—that is, he reverses the old "Make an honest woman of me" by wanting her to make a self-respecting man of him. When at the end he puts indecent pressure on her and makes her again his mistress, it is not that he is a vain scalp-collector but that he is powerfully attracted to her. He mingles crassness and opportunism with charm and a wish to do well. Tess's murdering him comes across as a shock. I am not saying that he is a fine man, but that he is not a stereotype and has enough range to be humanly interesting.

We need to be aware of this to understand Tess's being drawn to him. Hardy never says it overtly, but he gives us a sense of a strong attraction on both sides. Hardy officially makes Tess a victim, but his artistic instinct is to make her more than that. She is a bit flattered by Alec's attention, even "dazzled," she says. She feels "mastered"—not tricked or violated—by him. It was not a one-shot power play; her relations with Alec went on for at least a month. Very ironically, when Alec catches up with her after Angel has evicted her, she spouts Angel's liberal doctrines to Alec and thus ends his evangelical phase and, with it, the very sanctions that would set boundaries to his pursuit of her. To go back, when she realized that Angel was falling in love with her, she knew what was required in such a relationship: she had to tell him about Alec and the child and to hope that Angel's love would surmount these facts. To conceal the facts would inevitably seem deliberate misrepresentation. In brief, she simply could not follow through on this. To say this is not to blame her; on the contrary it is to grant her the status of a truly tragic character and not reduce her to a mere victim: like all tragic figures, she has a profound split between desire and obligation. She has an agonizingly difficult choice to make—like contemporary characters in Ibsen and H. G. Wells—and she makes the choice that turns out badly. Hardy's picture of her inner struggle is one of the best parts of the novel. He makes her a fully representative human being, not a mere volleyball to be batted around by nasty fun-seeking gods.

Careful readers have slowly come around to see that Alec is more than a simple villain, and Tess more than a simple victim. They have been much slower to see that Angel Clare is more than a hard, self-righteous, literal-minded enforcer of an old rule that has come to seem outmoded. It has long been customary to call him a prig, that is, a morally overconfident espouser of dubious proprieties. In my view, this does a great injustice to Hardy's art, for if Angel is a prig, Hardy is just setting up an allegorical figure as an easy target. Hardy is better than that. He is actually creating a full and complex figure—basically a man of charm and of many virtues who, in a totally unforeseen crisis, acts very badly but with an understandable human frailty, not a special nastiness. He is not a villain but, in Conrad's phrase, "one of us." Hardy has shown him to be a better-than-average decent man: he has rebelled against family beliefs but kept peace with the family; he is a modest farmworker; he is scrupulous with the milkmaids who keep falling in love with him, and very responsible with Tess. We forget that he also belongs to imperfect humanity. Hence we get sentimental and seem to think that, when he finds his new bride has been a mistress and mother, he ought to say immediately, "Think nothing of it, darling; come to my arms." Instead he is wounded and punitive, and we cry "prig." We should remember Othello and R. P. Warren's Jerry Beaumont, a great romantic who in comparable circumstances sets out on a great self-destructive binge of avenging the lady's honor. Angel is not a shallow monster but a quite normal human being who is understandably shocked to find that, in a fundamental relationship where the essence is total reciprocal confidence, the other's concealment has denied the essence and scorned the partner. I think that what happens in our reading of this is that we forget the total thing—the concealment plus the fact concealed—and focus on one part: the fact concealed. Since that fact happens to be less important now, we lose sight of the symbolic weight of the act of concealment. Hence, if we are to appreciate the shock to Angel, we probably have to substitute a concealed fact that would have greater weight for us now. What would it be—a history of syphilis, of drug addiction, or a criminal record? The issue is the external one of the extent to which past history helps define the present character and hence may not be held back—a matter about which, in any given case, reasonable men may differ. The point is simply that the issue presented to Angel was a terribly difficult one, and that we underrate Hardy if we think Angel had an easy way out. Angel ought to make us think, not "That prig," but "There go I."

In saying that Alec is more than a villain, I am not exonerating him; in saying that Tess shares responsibility for what happened to her, I am not suggesting that she be blamed; in saying that Angel's rejection of her is not a unique and arbitrary folly but is thoroughly understandable in terms of the humanity that is our common possession, I am not saying that what he does is innocent or commendable. All I am saying is that Hardy's imagination, fortunately, creates full characters who are plausible and complex and hence cannot serve as blind instruments of some antagonistic agency that without cause beats up Tess and sets Hardy roaring about injustice.

V

In his last novel, *Jude the Obscure* (1895), Hardy once again carries on mournfully and often bitterly about external forces that do in innocent human beings. Once again, despite this obstinate set of his mind, his imagination is creating dramatis personae whose fate is in their characters rather than in the impact of faulty institutions. Jude Fawley is a bright and studious boy who has the makings of a scholar, but he is seduced by a scheming country wench, Arabella Donn, and marries her. Hardy's first count is against this convention. Jude attempts suicide and gets drunk. After Arabella runs off to Australia, Jude studies on in private and wants to go to Oxford (Christminster), but he only tries to get in by writing a letter to some professor whose looks he likes. The professor suggests that he stick to his work as a stonemason. Hardy holds forth about the backward, self-satisfied, and unhelpful university. Jude gets drunk, loses his job, and goes back to the country. He falls in love with his vivacious and unstable cousin Sue Bridehead; after a harmless episode that violates appearances, she is thrown out of a teacher-training school she is attending. More counts against convention. For safety she marries Phillotson, a schoolteacher who is twenty years older than she and whom she does not like—another Hardy blow against convention. Jude spends a night with earthy Arabella, just back from Australia. Hardy's point is that the conventions bring into being two badly mixed couples and prevent the right one. Eventually Jude and Sue do live together, but they have very difficult times because they are not married. When divorces make their marriage possible, Sue doesn't want marriage, which she calls that "hopelessly vulgar institution," and Hardy cadges up a couple of episodes to make marriage look as bad as possible. On one occasion the couple can't get rooms in Oxford because Sue is pregnant and Jude spends time haranguing a street crowd on how badly the world has treated him. The eldest child (Jude's and Arabella's), despairing, kills two younger children and commits suicide. The shock drives Sue back to beliefs she thought she had rationally eliminated, and she neurotically sentences herself to a penitential life with Phillotson, whom she cannot stand. Jude goes back to drink and Arabella, and he dies of TB while Arabella and her latest earthy boyfriend survive merrily.

You see Hardy's pitch: while the coarse do well, nice guys, and nice gals as well, finish last, and it is all the fault of conventions, marriage, the university, and the church. But again, what Hardy says is quite different from what he does; what he asserts is quite different from what he imagines. If what he says governed the book, it would be only a pretty simple tale of the pathos of victims. But his imagination is unwilling to settle for that: what it has made him do is create characters of such quirkiness and such limited ability to cope that they would go down in any world less than ideal. They are spontaneous, well-intending, truth-seeking, but they expect the world to conform to their idea of it. They are not strong enough to endure the hard life of an independent do-your-own-thing; they lack balance because their feet are not on the ground. Hardy has the artistic merit of making their histories due to themselves and not to a system that he likes to abuse. He picked the right people for his purpose. He was set on defeat but he did not push his point by defeating the undefeatable. Now suppose his attention had focused on a couple much in the public eye forty years earlier—George Eliot and her lover G. H. Lewes. They too could not get married, and their living together was a scandal; they were long rebuffed and even ostracized, and they underwent all the punishments that could be inflicted by the conventions that Hardy loves to abuse. But Eliot and Lewes had minds rather than dreams, and strength rather than quirks and weakness, and they survived impressively.

One remaining problem with Jude and Sue is whether people of so little stamina are worth so much attention. But the details of their relationship, and of their relationships with others, are so well done that this pair somehow take on an aesthetic vitality that they do not have as individuals facing an ordinary world. Above all, Sue is a marvelously representative figure, and she is brilliantly done. She takes herself to be a liberated intellectual, a rationalist free of all religious and moral traditions, a bold rejector of conventions, taboos, and accepted beliefs about good and evil. Like many professional iconoclasts, she is brutally inconsiderate of others: she contributes to the destruction of Jude by deriding the tradition of Christian humanism that was his intellectual and spiritual center. But Hardy does not say this. From the beginning we see her as wonderfully and provocatively inconsistent, coquettish without at all planning to be, saying yes and acting no (or vice versa), undergoing puzzling changes of mood and attitude, wholly unpredictable and having the full charm of unpredictability. In time we understand why—why all the shifts and about-faces, the welcoming manner and the offishness, the call for paganism and the discomfort with sex. All the uncertainty and indeed instability are due to a hopeless split in her personality. She is never separated, as she thinks she is and as no man can be, from all the nonrational supports of life. She has tried to go it on rationalism alone, but she is not up to it, as even very great minds are not up to it. Given strains and a terrible shock, she loses her precarious grip on an inadequate support; she throws rationality overboard and goes into complete irrationality. Instead of a true religion she takes refuge in a perverse punitive religiosity that makes her life, as she now craves, a living hell. Of all Hardy's characters, she is the most significant, in the sense that she embodies a modern problem that is almost a central one. It is that overburdening of mind which always tends to produce a rebound into total mindlessness. Hence the portrait is a great achievement. Hardy says nary an editorial word about this. Perhaps he did not know what a great act of imagination he was performing.

vi

Now for a brief reminder of what we have seen Hardy strangely doing in his four major novels. In *The Return of the Native* he talks a great deal about the grimness and painfulness of life, and about divine mismanagement, and he invents many mischances to plague people or make things worse for them. But his imagination creates characters who themselves are responsible for their misfortunes, and not victims of some hostile force. Clym and Eustacia, obsessed in their different ways, simply fail to see the facts that are bound to lead to serious trouble. More sensible and earthy characters make out all right. In *The Mayor of Casterbridge,* Hardy fortunately lets the title character succeed and then fail on his own, without any allegations that hostile forces are doing him in. But Hardy makes it up by all sorts of inapplicable statements about the mayor's wife and stepdaughter. In half a dozen different ways he calls Susan a simpleton, but his drama portrays her as almost a genius in practical affairs. In discussing Elizabeth, Hardy is back in his old driver's seat, and he lets his gloom rip at full throttle: he claims that Elizabeth is a depressed observer of sad life, a sufferer, an expecter of the worst, a bare survivor of a faulty universe. But what we actually see is her happy home life, a mother devoted to her and skillfully operating in her behalf, two brief periods of disappointment and a little difficulty—far less than the human average—and then marriage to the rich mayor who is also the chief male sex object in the town. It's really a success story. In *Tess*, Hardy officially thinks that Tess is a plaything of sadistic gods, acting through a nasty seducer and an impossible husband. But his imagination saves him from such stereotypes as this: Tess is actually a great tragic figure, who feels some attraction for her seducer and has much responsibility for her husband's rejection of her. The seducer has a certain charm, and the husband is not a stupid prig but a shocked man who acts disastrously for both of them indeed, but quite understandably. Finally, in *Jude the Obscure*, Hardy again lectures copiously on how badly life is set up, and how institutional indifference and harshness do fine people in. But he makes the fine and deserving people inept and myopic and driven by quite unreasonable expectations of life. Their disasters lie in their characters, not in the fiat of an author set on proving them innocent victims of a world that is out of joint.

Let me conclude by identifying two problems, not discussing them. One problem is with Hardy's personality; the other is with his art. There is room, I think, for a study of the man, primarily of the forces that made him habitually insist that everything is bad and that the worthy and aspiring go down, and at the same time write stories that are not arbitrary and tendentious but are faithful to characters as they are. The problem with the art is that all the talk about hostile events and gods, a faulty system, and unsympathetic human beings may mislead readers as to what is really going on in the novels. Hardy's ideas may actually blind readers to his true art, which in my opinion is very good. He creates characters and then sees how things go with them, rather than making things go as he says they go when he is generalizing about life. I hope that all readers of Hardy will be alert to this problem. And I hope that this problem in Hardy will alert readers to a general problem in literary art—the distinction that has to be made between what the artist thinks when he is simply formulating abstract ideas or letting fly with some uncriticized prejudices, and what the artist does with his proper tools when his imagination is in control. I admit, however, that I know of no other major writer in which the problem is as marked as it is in Hardy.

14

Short Story and Novella
Corrington's Tales

 I first heard of Shreveport, Louisiana, in the 1930s when I taught at Louisiana State University. We teachers, especially those of us who had a hand in teaching Freshman English, would usually gain some awareness of the high schools from which our students came, especially those in the major cities such as New Orleans, Baton Rouge, and Lake Charles. Shreveport's Byrd High was in the group of known origins, and my impression, after all these years, is that we expected Byrd alumni to be at least a bit above average. And of course it was a notable producer of football players who, we feared, since they lived close to foreign parts, might be tempted to schools in Texas and Arkansas instead of coming, as of course honest men would, to LSU.

I did not actually see Shreveport until the early 1940s, when a faculty committee of which I was a member drove there one Sunday to call upon the then president of the ruling board of the university. We hoped to get his support for the man who seemed to us the best successor to James Monroe Smith as president of the university. We failed, of course. In my now dim impressions of the city, the downtown seemed quite bustling, and the residential section had an enduring well-heeled look. One sensed achievement in a provincial rather than a cosmopolitan key, and yet a touch of amplitude, and perhaps grace, beyond that of the capital city, Baton Rouge.

A play for cosmopolitan status of a kind came quite a few decades later when Shreveport invented a postseason football game. Then I came into a renewed awareness of Shreveport, for the football team of the University of Washington, where I then taught, played in the Shreveport bowl in 1987. Although in the large community of bowls the Shreveport affair was a latecomer *pis aller,* as a public-relations venture it strove to reduce the provincial and to beget a larger urban renown. And since I shall be writing

207

about Louisiana, it is fitting to note that the Washington opponent in the Shreveport bowl was Tulane.

A few years later I came across William Corrington (a discovery for whose belatedness I cannot account), read his collected stories, and thought, spontaneously if not elegantly, "Shreveport never had it so good." Nothing for the Chamber of Commerce, of course; nothing for the standard routines of metropolitan promotion. If Corrington were to get into paperback, the book would hardly be peddled at the December football bowl. What he does for Shreveport is not to give praise, or even attention-seizing blame, but to use it in various stories as the scene of significant human actions. It enters the life of imagination and thus takes on a new and hardly erasable reality. The local virtues and vices, actions and passions, reveal humanity in representative ways; they are so conceived that representation of them takes on, as William Mills has noted, the generalized value of myth (and myth in various modes, such as the lyric and the epic). This is not to say that Shreveport is now rivaling Gopher Prairie or Spoon River or Winesburg, not to mention Dublin, but it is to say that the city takes on a dimension beyond that of the facts—economic, demographic, and the like—that define cities in reference books. It becomes, so to speak, a living place, its vitality conferred by the emotional and moral lives of people who reside there but are more than local characters. They are local, of course, but in their vitality they make a history more than local.

I am using Shreveport both literally and as a metaphor for Louisiana generally. Of the twenty tales in the *Collected Stories,* eight are sited in Shreveport, six elsewhere in Louisiana, and two across the river in Mississippi (two in Georgia have Civil War themes, and two deal with Louisianans and Alabamans in California). For many readers, Faulkner's Yoknapatawpha will come to mind. But the use of a fictional name for a geographical area is a mode of imaging reality different from what we might call "atlas realism"; in the former, the strange name, however familiar it becomes, does part of the work, while in the latter the blunt quotidian reality is infused with new life by imaginative penetration. To rename is in some sense to reorder or reidentify (think of the transformations sought by secular rebaptisms in Hollywood); to start literally with Shreveport or Pineville au naturel is to put an additional burden on the imaginative transformer. Another difference: the creation of Yoknapatawpha (or Ruritania or Narnia or the Tolkien lands) requires novel-length tales. As though feeling the imperative toward novelistic re-creation, Corrington's stories repeatedly push toward novella length. His line is the strong infusion of known everyday scenes with imagined human reality shaped by but not limited to the scenes used. To make such distinctions, however, is not to distinguish greater and smaller, but to note the differences that accompany resemblances. The similarity is clear enough: Yoknapatawpha confers mythical status upon Mississippi, as do Corrington's stories, though their geography is traceable on contemporary driving maps, upon Shreveport and Louisiana.

ii

The shorter tales with Shreveport scenes reveal Corrington at ease in several modes best identified by traditional terms—romance, lyric, and a special-effects narrative in which a rite of passage is embedded in a farcical tall tale. "The Retrievers" (1968) belongs to the phase of romance that Poe virtually invented in the "tales of ratiocination," but Corrington invests it with un-Poe-like high spirits. Two bright teenagers, a brother and sister, find an old local map and, working from directions it gives, unearth a buried treasure that alters family fortunes. (There is some incidental mention of the Sentells, an old family with a Civil War background; the family reappears in the Corrington oeuvre, reminding us somewhat of the Sartorises and such tradition-bearing families in Faulkner.) Corrington hints at a symbolic dimension in the story when he introduces Joe Hobbs, a "memory machine" who remembers everything from the past but never knows the "why" of it: a satirical thrust at a certain kind of historian, one who would not sense, for instance, the long-living impact of the Civil War felt by various Corrington characters whom we will come to later. It appears, also, that the "buried treasure" is to symbolize the enrichment of life by possession of the past; the narrator asserts that "all of us are retrievers" who "want to recapture the past." The teenagers, we are told, sought not money but "the past . . . special money from a special place." But this is afterthought-ish; it lacks the built-in quality of conceptual elements in later stories; the narrative energy is all in the tracing of clues, the singular dig, and the literal find that changes family life from stringency to comfort and even style.

In "Old Men Dream Dreams, Young Men See Visions" (1972)—the title is from Joel 2:28—Corrington manages the symbolic dimension much more convincingly; it is not literally urged but dramatically implied. A young couple, on their first date, are told by the girl's father to be back by eleven; sitting by a lake and talking, absorbed in each other, the sexual content of their attraction dominant only in brief embraces, they forget time and do not return until 4 A.M. The father, drunk, rages and threatens, then bursts into tears, turns, and clings to his wife. He sheds the *lacrimae rerum;* his grief is for the passage of things, perhaps with an infusion of unrecognized incestuous feeling. The effect is lyric: the brief brush of transitory innocence and relentless experience. And Corrington adds a small mysterious accent, as he would occasionally do: the presence, during the boy's several visits at the girl's house, of a silent, observant, strange little sister whom the narrator (the boy, looking back from adulthood) calls "Cassandra" and who, reenacting myth, as it were, prophesies the generational transmission of human imperfections and their emotional consequences.

In "The Man Who Slept with Women" (1981), the third of the relatively brief stories that I call "lyric," we see a development toward a climactic moment of recognition: a combination of farce and melodrama eventuates in a rite of passage. A teenage boy, tutored by a roughneck man-about-town uncle, declares independence of a mother who has kept him in bed with her whenever her husband is abroad on one of his many business trips (the second unconsciously incestuous parent in this series). As he is moving toward filial freedom, the boy once exclaims, "Oh Dad, poor Dad," an allusion to Arthur Kopit's fierce satirical "tragifarce" (Kopit's term) of 1960 (a woman keeps the corpse of her symbolically murdered husband in the closet). This is a clue to the dominance of farcical effects over a potential note of adolescent anguish; the uproarious comedy is a little reminiscent of Welty, though Corrington is much more boisterous and bawdy. The mother was a crude country girl who studied French and can affect the lady, somewhat à la Molière, but who can drop down into the tough tongue of early life. A larger figure is her brother Shad, who endeavors to rescue his nephew from his mother by picking him up after school and, "playing Virgil in a jeep," taking him on tours of the local underworld, that is, bars, to see a world of men, hear their talk, watch them drink, and, above all, listen to Uncle Shad, a "Mean Ass," next to "Bad Son of a Bitch" as a local honorific title, engage in artful, picturesque exchanges of jocose insults with friends, barkeeps, and cops. Uncle Shad wrecks his jeep and puts the boy in a hospital. Uncle Shad brings him presents—a large mess of fried chicken, a case of beer, and a puppy who vomits all over the bed—but Shad quickly shifts attention to the nurse and somehow maneuvers her into the bathroom. The mother complains, abuses the hospital staff, including the doctor, and accidentally opens the bathroom door to reveal her brother and the nurse in a standing *flagrante delicto* (while in a delightful genre detail, the dog laps water out of the commode). She exclaims, with excellent "breeding" as her son admiringly says, "Mon dieu"—she who a little earlier had declared, "I'll sue the ass off this place." I risk detailed summary because I want to picture concretely the charming farcical milieu for a subject, teenage growth, that often evokes a note of rather solemn suffering.

In two stories, more ambitious but perhaps a little less successful than others in the Shreveport group, the actions take place alternately in

Shreveport and in Europe—"The Arrangement" and "The Dark Corner" (both 1968). The former title alludes to a practice of a couple named Grosvenor: John has an annual "sabbatical," a week on his own, not subject to questioning by Sara (the Grosvenors have lived in California, in Corrington usually a symbol of the unsound). Sara looks deeply miserable, an authorial comment on modern permissiveness. In London, John takes a "sabbatical" disguised as an unavoidable business trip; it cancels a holiday that the two were to have together in Paris. Sara, desperate, goes to Paris alone and bitterly endeavors to copy her husband's style by enacting the streetwalker: she picks up bums and is treated with contempt by them. By quite extraordinary chance the narrator, Edward, a friend of the Grosvenors, sees some of her awful failures and could himself be a partner in her sought compensatory degradation but is repelled by her cold, effortful, retaliatory eroticism, and his inadvertent "Poor Sara" cuts off her would-be enticement of him. At a later party in Shreveport she looks awful, as if trapped in a prison she cannot break out of, and her husband is jovially planning another "sabbatical." There is something just a little mechanical about this. Of course we grasp the paradox that Sara's not committing murder, and continuing in the relationship, may be the suicide of which she has apparently thought. Perhaps seeking to make her comprehensible, Corrington calls her "sincere" rather than "honest," but this strikingly epigrammatic distinction hardly explains her staying on, especially after she has shown the furious initiative needed for her sad stab at moral recrimination in Paris. The overall portrait does not quite carry conviction, however vital the details and fitting the symbolism.

Although "The Dark Corner" belongs to the half of the stories that are of, or close to, standard short-story length, it is crowded with materials that make it press the novella character of the other half of the stories. It has a congestion of themes and characters, and at the same time it is one of the most broken up of those stories in which Corrington uses numbered subdivisions: there are ten of these in only seventeen pages. There is much diversity of scene and time. One barely gets set in one place or date when one is swept off to another. Two segments of action take place in Paris, three at the Anzio battleground of World War II, three in Shreveport, and two at a rural burying ground in the area; in half the scenes, the time is 1946, in three it is the earlier 1940s, and in two the focus is on background events of the nineteenth century. One is so busy tracing out the maze of ingredients and their relationships that one's imaginative participation in the reality created lags behind. The action begins and ends in Paris, where the narrator, Edward Lee Turner (evidently Corrington's persona for international affairs; he appears as "Edward" in "The Arrangement"), begins and ends a trip to Anzio to choose a final disposition of the body of his younger brother Billy, a decorated hero killed there; Edward constantly ponders the meaning of the past events that are the source of his present actions. In three scenes at Anzio, Edward learns about the battle and the burial site as he listens to the unphilosophical factuality of the officer in charge, and he considers whether to have the body cremated, leave it at Anzio, or return it to Shreveport. Long uncertain, he decides suddenly, "Send him home." Meanwhile another set of issues has been raised at the Shreveport and burial-ground scenes, which occupy about half the story. We plunge back to the burial ground where Uncle Ellender (mentioning a Sentell ancestor), holding forth at length in the colloquial tongue by which Corrington gives immediacy and vitality to many scenes, records for the family a long and almost impenetrably complex history of the spot, a history that, involving eighteenth-century, Civil War, and later nineteenth-century events, exhibits the sense of continuity between past and present that often figures in Corrington stories. Meanwhile, in a Shreveport scene, we backtrack to the death of Edward and Billy's father and focus on an argument in which Billy opposes burying his father in the out-of-the-way burial ground (the "Dark Corner"). Later Billy, joining the service for World War II, says that if he is killed he wants to be buried elsewhere than in the "Dark Corner"; after his death there is some family talk of whether in this matter his word is law. Meanwhile, several characters hold forth on another theme: if one goes to war, does one need to know why? This intensifies our feeling that the story is overloaded.

An epigraph from Sophocles' *Antigone* focuses attention on the human need to be buried in one's own soil. So one wonders why the narrator delays so long in deciding to take Billy's body back to Shreveport. Perhaps it is his awareness of the impingement upon this central action of all the other issues raised in the story: they permit us to see Billy, formally an antitraditionalist, restored to tradition. Such a reading would be a way of seeing unity in a story that feels centrifugal because of Corrington's apparent inability to resist every possible associational tie-in.

The individual scenes have great life, as always—the life of feeling and of thoughtfulness. And here we see, for the first time, a recurrent theme in Corrington, the sense of the past in general and of the Civil War in particular.

iii

(Here I omit the comments on several stories that appeared in my quite long original essay, an omission made in order to leave ample space for the discussion of two long stories that are among Corrington's best and also for some general observations about the Corrington oeuvre.) The two successful stories are late works, and they happen to be the longest of the twenty in *The Collected Stories*. In both stories the central figure, the possessor of the recording consciousness, is a lawyer, and, still more important, both stories turn on the actions of a private sensibility, shaped by a tradition, that is in conflict with a public situation or a kind of community action. The scope is large. And the approach is a central one in Corrington.

The title of "Nothing Succeeds" (1980) derives from an ironic verbal jest in the mind of the central character, René Landry, a senior lawyer settling an estate: "Nothing succeeds but succession" (and some of the events of the story, as we shall see, inevitably bring to mind Oscar Wilde's witticism, "Nothing succeeds like excess"). Mr. Landry's pun is suggestive in several ways. There is the foreground legal application: Landry, attorney for the multi-million-dollar Boudreaux estate (a pepper agribusiness in southern Louisiana), is in California trying to find the heir, Lance (for Lancelot) Boudreaux III. Then we gradually come to see the succession of generations and styles in the Boudreaux family. And over all looms the succession of cultures: the move from the traditional one, implicitly present in Louisiana life as represented by Mr. Landry, to the 1960s modernity as evidenced in Berkeley, California, "Sodom by the sea," the term used by Mr. Landry's co-attorney. Although the picture is vivid enough, it perhaps rings bells especially for anyone who observed that era of anarchism, utopianism, outrageousness, self-indulgence, and downright destructiveness. In drawing this picture Corrington evidently strives for an ultimate portrayal of the California that in his stories always has at least a tinge of corruption. He describes with extraordinary vividness the dress and speech and public style of hippie life, pop-cult, rock-cult, drug-cult, new-freedom youth; of their nonnegotiable causes and demands, of multiple "freaks" in "weirdsville"; of a youth doing fellatio on a young woman in public; of girls reporting on fellatio as the only way to an A in a math course; of a pop-revivalist debating a pop-diabolist. In such a scene a singer announces, "This is for Lance . . . the One Who Stands," a key identifying phrase which, with its double entendre, is used a number of times to identify the epic hero of this disordered world. Mr. Landry gradually learns more about the Boudeaux heir, absent from Louisiana for five years, as yet invisible in Berkeley, but a felt magical presence in the local revolutionary crowd.

Memories, flashbacks fill us in. Lance I, the creator of the pepper empire, has just died. Lance II, an aviator, was killed in a World War II raid on Ploesti in Romania. Lance III's mother was a common woman whom the family had bought off by a grandiose payment. Lance III was almost incredibly precocious: found in his room in the Louisiana home was an amazing collection of books, albums, chemicals, microscopes, archaeological tools, and other evidences of historical, scientific, and speculative interests. In Berkeley, an anti-Semitic professor of Middle Eastern thought and a professor of physics both describe Lance as a student of superlative brilliance and originality. We learn that he has sought, or taken, degrees in medicine, law, and philosophy (a parallel to the postwar career of Captain Pepper in "A Time to Embrace": that tireless polymath had become his town's beloved physician whereas Lance becomes guru to a sick quasi community) while playing in a rock band and sleeping only four hours a night. We learn about his preaching a formal sermon and, as a doctor, saving the life of a wounded policeman. He has become a cult divinity for turned-off youth. A police report indicates his involvement in drug-running, his participation in a group that resembles the "Manson family," and his ruthlessness. When he causes deaths, he leaves behind a symbolic fingerprint, a Tarot card of "The Hanged Man."

Mr. Landry gradually acquires this information. He is worldly enough, but the story essentially contrasts the Berkeley state of affairs with the more traditional Louisiana life that Mr. Landry represents. Corrington makes him periodically remember his dead wife and her playing Mozart or Haydn on the piano, this in a serene setting in New Orleans. Once Mr. Landry thinks, "What was real in the South was fantasy here; what was real in California was a joke down South." There is also some contrast between Mr. Landry and his much younger assistant, Louis Fourier, more knowing, not less appalled by the Berkeley scenes, but perhaps a shade more susceptible to whatever charms it may have, for example, those of "Minerva," a subdivinity under Lance III (born of the Jovian brain, as it were).

I risk detailed summary—and even it is pretty sketchy—to make clear Corrington's extraordinary diversity, fullness, and ingenuity in magnificently portraying a flawed genius with his own scheme of universal conquest, his mad egomaniac talent exactly adapted to the needs of a terribly deformed community which, sick in its denial of all traditional ties and commitments, is ready for any new-style dictator dispensing handouts and drugs and charismatically exacting total devotion. In the long penultimate scene Landry and Fourier, having passed security inspection by Minerva, are picked up by a satanically got-up driver in a van weirdly decorated with exotic symbols of mysterious alien powers and driven up from Berkeley to a mountaintop royal resort, an Olympian fortress or castle where Lance III plays God. He is almost ingratiating to the visitors. He talks a great deal about himself—one of the longest segments of a long story. He records his pain at being separated from or deserted by his parents, especially his mother. Insofar as this is to be taken as a source of his career, it seems rather a drop into pop psychology—his own, one hopes, rather than Corrington's, since satanic divinities are more than unloved children. Lance III is truest when he reveals himself, in his present life, as the king or god of a host of wounded, partial human beings—"my people. They need me." They are dreamers, failures, wrecks, zombies living on drugs he supplies, and utterly dependent on him. It is his "duty" to go out on a high balcony and let the believers, down below, "see their God." He is what they lack. "They worship wholeness." His philosophic omniscience has turned to cynical knowingness. At the same time he tells his Olympian company, ironically, that Mr. Landry, here evidently viewed as a symbol, was always present in his life, "like the goddamned statue of the Confederate dead"—presumably an ideal that he can never quite escape.

A police raid breaks this up—a rush of melodrama that perhaps Corrington found unavoidable. It goes on for some pages, and the carnage is great. Lance III is badly wounded (symbolically in the head), and we last see him, heavily bandaged and virtually a zombie, seated between the two lawyers on the plane back to New Orleans. Genius, so to speak, has overplayed its hand; the megalomaniac native son does come home again, having squandered talent which, under the guidance of sound order, might have been creative. It is not that the old order enjoys a triumph; it is just that we see its relative durability against lunatic innovation.

Corrington has written what is, in some ways, a version of the Faust myth. Early on, Mr. Landry's eye is caught by some words in a old volume in Lance III's extraordinary library and research-equipment storehouse: "O Diabolus, Dominus Mundi, ad Servum Tuum, Veniat"—the invocation to the devil that began the original Faust's career in power ("Dominus Mundi": "The Prince of the World," a theme also hinted in "The Lonesome Traveler"). Then there is the remarkable Faustian development of Lance III: the pursuit of all knowledge as it appears in his taking degrees in many fields. There is even a Gretchen episode, really identified by its reversal of all the terms of the original. The innocent virgin of the old myth is now a whore (who tells the Louisiana lawyers all about Lance); when she gets pregnant, it is a problem, not for her, but for him; he is infuriated and kicks her in the stomach to make her abort; and when he leaves her, he provides a very substantial payoff. At one point the satanist conductor of the lawyers to the Olympus of Lance III says of Minerva, "She is Helena," which makes sense only as a reference to Faust's great love in Goethe's Part II. Given these suggestions and allusions, it is easy to read the Berkeley public goings-on as a sort of nonstop daytime Walpurgisnacht, though here less a flamboyant witches' jollification than what Landry calls "a disease of the soul." And, toward the end, Lance III's sardonic knowingness is reminiscent of Mephistophelian cynicism, the spirit that denies.

To note these suggestive parallels is not to say that Corrington's story *is* a version of the Faust myth. It is rather to say that the echoes of, or similarities to, the Faust story suggest the range and depth of "Nothing Succeeds," the representativeness that makes it more than a horror story of a brilliant but weird megalomaniac exerting power through the manipulation of social illness. It reminds one a little of Mann's "Mario the Magician": a master of magical powers playing upon a community until his play generates homicidal revolt. Even more does the Corrington story remind us of Mann's *Doktor Faustus,* where the neologistic work of a mad musical genius symbolizes the Nazi revolt against an indispensable tradition. To make these comparisons is my final way of suggesting the strength and range of "Nothing Succeeds": it depicts a traditional order threatened by a deformed community accepting as divinity a disordered genius who with bad coin buys absolute rulership rather than leads toward a communion marked by sustaining or creative membership.

To move from "Nothing Succeeds" to "Every Act Whatever of Man" is to stay within the general realm of the lawyer as moral commentator upon a community style, but with a major difference. In "Every Act Whatever of Man" the standard community appears to be acting in a normal way for its own preservation, but it is bitterly opposed by the lawyer who speaks for an imperative that would render community life far more difficult and could even be disruptive. The troublemaker is not a mad Faustian bent on power but a civilized insider who is the voice of an uncomfortable absolute against an expediency that would make everyone's life easier. It is the community's small but audible better self against a coalition of all its self-serving smaller selves. But it is not clear that the story takes sides; the issue may be inherently unresolvable.

The second-longest story in the book (a world inclusive enough to justify a novel is condensed into a novelette) has a complexity of narrative form that matches the complexity of substance. It is divided into twenty-six numbered parts that present diverse actions in the present and a series of actions in the past; it seems to scatter in many directions, and one needs several readings to assemble these into a coherent picture moving through time and bringing multiple lives together into a present crisis that in parts has a savage intensity. We have to infer dates from casual remarks or incidental thoughts of characters. The big event in the present (1976) is a massive stroke that has rendered the much-liked Father O'Malley, the priest in a small Louisiana town since 1927, "brain dead," though kept technically alive by mechanical means (a matter that gets Corrington's attention in several stories; it is again central in his final story, "Heroic Measures / Vital Signs"). Suddenly the brain-dead priest starts talking aloud, and what he does is repeat the contents of various confessional interviews over the years—what he has heard from parishioners and what he has said in his pastoral role. He has become a hopelessly torn laundry bag spreading the community's dirty linen all over his hospital room. Auditors are there, others sneak in, and the word soon gets out and all over town. The reader is now able to fill in the missing elements in various stories that he has heard only in part (Corrington is always skillful in seeming to be telling us all that needs to be known while actually forcing the reader to rely on inference—for instance, by pronouns of unclear reference). We proceed from hints to fuller information about past and present infidelities, an adultery followed by pregnancy and abortion, parental failure, a murder, an "act against nature," guilt neurosis and moral intransigence. The public knowledge of such deeds and experiences creates great anguish in the sinners identified, and the strains lead to several deaths.

Finally all of the private dramas are brought together in a central fore-ground drama, in which a chief figure is Walter Journe, seventy-five, a lawyer and practicing Catholic, from whose point of view the main story is told. His friend Judge Mike Soniat has appointed him "Curator" (that is, "caretaker") of the brain-dead Father O'Malley, and we see him reflecting on the significance and obligations of the role, which had come down from Roman law through the Napoleonic code into continuing Louisiana practice. Enter Father Veulon, a young archdiocesan troubleshooter from New Orleans, who had studied "decision-making at the Harvard Business School." He is front man for a "John Doe" petition to Judge Soniat to end "heroic measures" (a phrase that obviously stuck in Corrington's mind) to prolong the life of Father O'Malley and thus to permit "death with dignity." The central action of the second half of the story is Journe's battle, as Curator, to save Father O'Malley from the anti-life-support forces of Father Veulon (who testifies that the archbishop concurs), the doctor, a Baton Rouge lawyer for "John Doe," and even Judge Soniat (Journe and Soniat have shifted from first-name friendliness to chilly formality). The long court scene before Judge Soniat has wonderful detail and tension; the judge finally rules for "death with dignity," and he foresees and circum-vents Journe's appeal to the state Supreme Court. At the termination-of-life scene the hospital is surrounded by reporters. Journe says, "Vultures follow killers," angering the judge.

This extraordinary story, the best in the 1978 volume, and one of the best in the *Collected Stories,* combines a vast picture of a citizenry, in its mingling of public lives and private lusts, with a tense portrayal of leading decision makers and the differences among them in the crucial trial scene. Corrington even has the Curator debate the central issue with himself. He recalls a passage in the Civil Code from which Corrington takes the title of the story—"Every act whatever of man that causes injury to another obliges him by whose fault it occurs to repair it"—and wonders about the culpability of the priest whom he is trying to keep alive. This is one way of stressing the moral complexity of the issue, its resistance to the simple answers that in a sense both sides before Judge Soniat want. Journe concludes, "Ah, Lord, today we do not send the scapegoat forth. If he names the sins put upon his head, we simply pull him off the machine." Thus he identifies an old mythic pattern which, as more than once in Corrington, inheres in a situation primarily managed in contemporary realistic terms.

Corrington is at his best in this story, in which he finds his most inclusive pattern of action. He presents two aspects of human reality: the vast public scene in which we see all the ranges of conduct possible to a diverse humanity, and the small enclosed scene in which we see the moral conflict between two kinds of felt obligation—that to a principle that tries to ignore the immediate fallout, and, opposite this, a pragmatic sense that would make absolutes subservient to what is publicly expedient at a given moment. Here Corrington is really down to basics. His story, I think, does not so much imply a ruling as dramatize all the issues with remarkable understanding. He even lets the combatants, apparently secure as they are in their positions, register small moments of counterfeeling as their humanity influences their formal legal stances. Journe, as we have seen, wonders whether the priest's unconscious revelations make him in some way culpable. And, at the disconnection of the life support—the final scene in the story—Judge Soniat kneels by the bed of the priest and exclaims, "Oh, my God." Corrington exhibits a marvelously full imagination of human uncertainties in a moral crisis where the leading figures have to have the appearance of certainty.

One might understandably wish that "A Day in Thy Court" ("is better than a thousand"—Psalms 84:10) were Corrington's last published story, since it records the last day in the life of a senior-lawyer figure (like the author, he is also something of a poet) who appears in various stories as W. C. Grierson, René Landry, and Walter Journe. Here he is Bob Sentell, the last bearer of that family name that appears in various Corrington stories involving personal histories during the century after the Civil War. Although the title implies a religious feeling or theme, the quotation from Psalms seems to have mainly a suggestive or metaphorical sense: the story records a dying man's view of life *sub specie aeternitatis*. In part Corrington utilizes the popular myth that a dying person reviews all of his life just before death.

Here this recollection extends into an all-day internal monologue, or rather, the internal monologue that persists throughout a fully described all-day fishing trip on an eastern Louisiana river (apparently the Tchefuncta). But the vital record is also implicitly a trial and judgment: the last sentence of the story is "A court adjourned, another opening." The "another" is no doubt "thy court," where, when Sentell has his ultimate day in court, a last judgment will be made, perhaps different from Sentell's own.

The all-day fishing trip is recounted with a fullness of detail that makes it an immensely concrete physical experience, one vividly recognizable to anyone who has ever fished in Louisiana. But gradually we identify two symbolisms implicit in the physical world and activity. The river is in some sense the river of life, more or less navigable by the boatsman with skill and a program, but also full of dangers that could be fatal. At the same time the process of fishing is a kind of figurative summation of a life history—knowing how to deal with a succession of situations, a series of individual antagonists, using all one's equipment of tools, methods, and experience; making mistakes, winning some small ones, and perhaps triumphing over a major antagonist. Toward the end of the day Sentell, after a long and difficult struggle, lands the biggest fish he has ever caught—a thirty-pound bass—and then throws it back into the river. In the river of life Sentell has twice gone for large prizes, pursuits that recur in his memory throughout the day—one in law, one in love. He has various recollections of experiences at court, including some comic ones, for example the judge and the rival attorneys consuming the booze that was the evidence in the trial of a bootlegger. But his "Great Case had never materialized"— the big fish always dreamed of by the voyager on the river of life. He goes on, at this point in memory, "No, in his life, only the she." His big triumph had been in love. But she had died, it appears, in childbirth: in the controlling figure, the big one had got away. During the day on the river his memories re-create, albeit sketchily, his courtship and marriage. At the very end he sheds tears "mourning not so much the losing as the time wasted in not remembering," in "crushing out the anguish of losing her." (We recall that René Landry, the lawyer in "Nothing Succeeds," also had intermittent memories of the death of a young wife.) Here Corrington turns upside down the usual prescription for dealing with loss: the past is gone, forget about it. Sentell, on the contrary, mourns his failure to feel loss constantly: that would have been better than nothing. What we see is his severely limited success in managing the usual folk wisdom handed out to survivors. All day long "she" keeps coming into his consciousness, resisting his efforts to block her out, and yet not triumphing over the efforts completely. Corrington has hit upon a distinct narrative device for indicating her recurrent presence in Sentell's mind—recurrent, yet often quickly transitory and fragmentary: bursts of incomplete grammatical units thrust without introduction or explanation into the otherwise fluent orderly account of activities on the river. Sometimes the intruding thought is in a short complete sentence, but often it is simply in a phrase or a single word or two, most frequently just a "she" or a "her" without antecedent. One example: "But bass don't reach thirty pounds. He did not remember those last hours. She." He uses this technique some thirty times in the story, a narrative species of imitative form. At first it is bothersome, and I am not sure that the reader is ever entirely comfortable with it. But once one has the key—the intermittent struggles toward self-assertion by memories partly rejected—one sees how the sudden intrusions of isolated or incomplete locutions do symbolize effectively the failures of consciousness to govern its own form by willed exclusion of parts of the past.

This device, as well as the symbolisms of the river and of fishing, helps identify a remarkable tour de force. Then there is another tour de force: the story recounts the last day of a Bob Sentell dying of cancer. But the recognition of this drama sneaks up on the reader, who, as often in Corrington, is not informed directly of a significant fact. At first we see Sentell, aged sixty-nine, trying to deal with what he calls "the Thing"—his metaphor for an active presence that seems to be burrowing about in his chest and abdomen, causing trouble wherever it goes. In time the cancer is identified, and descriptions make the pain almost palpable. But the main thing is the state of mind of the dying man, amid all the anguish of body and mind enjoying a freedom from all the rules of survival. Sentell smokes some cigarettes, identified as the cause of the cancer. He tosses down pain pills in forbidden quantity. He ignores the severest verboten and drinks rye steadily, finishing a bottle (the first he ever took along on a fishing trip) by dusk. Then he goes to "The Grove," a spot he has avoided all day because of its associations with "her," and falls into the water. The rich elements passing through his mind have created a life history, or better a history of the consciousness, of a protagonist who is at once everyman and an unusually perceptive and inquiring individual. I hope that my summation of the parts has indicated the skill of a rich narrative that manages to enclose so extensive a history within the amply recorded minutiae of a single day's fishing trip.

Corrington's basic theme is frequently the interaction between an individual—an individual with an observing, recording, and judging consciousness—and a community of whose standards or of whose conduct in a specific situation he is a critic or opponent. But in "A Day in Thy Court" he works entirely within an individual consciousness, its relations with the larger world illustrative and reflective rather than the source of dramatic conflict. Now it is interesting, and perhaps significant for Corrington's own creative history, that in another late story, in fact in his last published story, "Heroic Measures / Vital Signs" (1986), he undertakes the same kind of project: the elaborate and searching investigation of a private self seen either alone or in relationships that are revelatory rather than antagonists in a defining action. Hence one may wonder whether, in his latter years, Corrington was moving definitely toward a kind of fiction in which the private life or inner life, rather than the individual's engagement in community or political or legal life, would be his central theme.

iv

Corrington's stories as a whole have so much richness and vitality that it seems possible to do justice to the whole only by attention to the parts. Even this may not be adequate, for some stories are complex enough to make the critic feel that he has fallen short, if only because problems of length have made him cut down more than he would like. The better the story, the more it is like an iceberg: the visible part is vast enough, but one knows how much more still lurks beneath the surface. However fully one describes either what is visible or what may be inferred from the rich visibility, one is still plagued by a sense of neglected dimensions. And of course one is never sure that one has seen all that is visible.

The great sense of human mass and spread that one has in reading Corrington does not derive from geographical variety or world-hopping; no jet-setter he. Like various first-rate southern novelists (one thinks especially of Welty), Corrington is a stay-at-home writer. Louisiana is his Wessex. The two stories in which action shifts back and forth between Louisiana and Europe ("The Dark Corner" and "The Arrangement") are not among his strongest; they seem to derive less from a spontaneous envisaging of human reality than from conceptual manipulations of plot elements. But counting these two, Louisiana is the scene of fourteen of the twenty stories; two have Mississippi scenes; two deal with Georgians; and in the two in which California is the scene the actors are displaced southerners (one from Louisiana).

If Corrington's Wessex is Louisiana, his Casterbridge is Shreveport (without fictionalizing by rebaptism): eight of the twenty stories are sited in Shreveport. That city takes on a "mythic" character; it is the site of a wide range of human actions that give it an imaginative existence quite different from the mundane reality presented by atlases. There we see the romantic story of recovered treasure (with hints of a recovered past); the brief lyric confrontation of new young love and the disenchantment of elders; the struggle, wonderfully farcical in detail but serious in meaning, between a vulgar, worldly, and bright brother and sister for the soul of the sister's son; the strange ambiguous history of a visionary who may be triumphing over daily ordinariness or retreating into a fantasy of his own; an all-night storytelling in which popular contemporary gossip is corrected by a meticulous record of a rare extralegal love growing out of Civil War intensities; and the story of a trial in which the criminal escapes formal public justice but meets it at the hand of a private citizen who translates an old sense of freedom into a new sense of obligation. If to present this record is in some sense to praise Shreveport, it is rather to praise Corrington, who did not give Shreveport the "Main Street" treatment frequent in nonmetropolitan American fiction but recognized it as a reliable scene for an extended range of fundamental human activities—young love, growing up, digging up old treasure, midlife sadness, man-about-town-ism (from the farcical to the sinister), modern permissiveness, cultural changes, drugs, and the impact of the Civil War and its felt meanings—through oral tradition, private memories, and public monuments—that stirred him to write, in comic vein, in lyric mode, in epic mode, as a reflective recorder and interpreter of wide and deep human reality.

The myth of Shreveport extends into the myth of Louisiana, and the myth of Louisiana enfolds the myth of the South. A recurrent element in the consciousness of characters is the Civil War. In America the South is unique in having the memory of a war that was lost and cherishing that past (in the Vietnam war, much of the country was so unable to deal with defeat that it took refuge in the moral smugness of reviling American participants); that memory is present in one way or another in many of the Corrington stories. The experience of defeat does not lead to nostalgia or to self-pity; rather it allows a special sense of human vulnerability, vulnerability not only to the persisting accidents that inevitably trouble life, but vulnerability as a built-in element of human experience. It forbids the sense of triumph that leads to hubris or to disabling dismay at misfortune. But it encourages the sense of the human fortitude, endurance, and obligation that human beings may exhibit in the face of unequal combat and of eventual disaster. Memory is an avenue to range of possibility, and to maturity, in human beings who can surmount inexperience, inattentiveness, and the temptations of innocence. It can become the best entry into the realm of moral concern.

Corrington's memory of the war is persistent, and it is worth a summary note. Three stories deal directly with the war. "First Blood" portrays the sense of honor in some combatants even in a desperate situation. "Reunion" contrasts the sharp historical sense of some Southern soldiers at Gettysburg with celebrants who see the fiftieth anniversary of the battle as only an occasion for pageantry. "A Time to Embrace" traces the evolution of very intense wartime feelings, ones that could be endlessly destructive in later years, into the enduring management of a singular triangular love affair that might have been the matrix of inclusive disaster; it is as if the irrationality of war could be translated into a singular rationality in peace. In "The Dark Corner" the history of a family burial ground, a history that had Civil War and even pre–Civil War elements, is a factor in twentieth-century attitudes and decisions. The war is a very important element in "If Time Were Not / A Moving Thing"—a kind of measure or test of the emotions of a convent-bred woman to whom God is a secret lover. This is placed first in the *Collected Stories*. In the next-to-last story in the volume, "The Southern Reporter," the war has a still more important role: the monuments to war heroes inspire a twentieth-century "little man" to fierce acts aimed at a justice which a court trial has failed to achieve. In "The Actes and Monuments" Harry Cohen, newly settled in Vicksburg, thinks of "an old Confederate monument" as an influence on a life; he wonders about the aliveness of the war in the contemporary South, about nonslaveholders dying for slavery, "dying for the rights of states that had no care for their rights"; he angers an old southern lawyer when he declares, "The past is past." Able Gone, the Bible agent in "The Lonesome Traveler," defines his territory as "the Old Confederacy"; he knows a man who knew General Lee and could correct his war history; and, to guarantee Sheriff Wilson's ability to circumvent the would-be lynchers, he tells a tale of the ferocity of the sheriff's uncle, who was a Confederate officer. In "Nothing Succeeds," the tale of California hippie-land in the 1960s, we learn that the Boudreaux land in southern Louisiana was first acquired from a carpetbagger given a bad local reception, and that lawyer Landry's ancestor "had been cast loose from Forrest's cavalry after his nation had died" (in "Reunion" the words were "when their country died"); Lance III, the self-appointed divinity to derelicts in Berkeley, says of Landry that he "was always there. Like the goddamned statue of the Confederate dead"—as if even a mad expatriate genius cannot escape a central symbol of the culture from which he had fled to his own Olympus, and to which he returns as a human wreck. There is a fascinating note on the ecclesiastical history of the town in "Every Act Whatever of Man": the local church had once been in the hands of a German priest who had served in the Union army and who became unpopular by preaching "the evils of rebellion"; but then things had got much better when Father O'Malley took over, alluded to his origins among "rebellious" people, compared the Easter Rising to the Civil War, and thus made it possible to declare, without offense, that "only resurrection, not insurrection, could cure the anguish of a proud people." In the pleasant tale of treasure hunt, "The Retrievers," Corrington insists on the Civil War connections of the treasure found, including "bundles of Confederate money," and on the underlying historical sense of the hunters. And on the last day of his life the lawyer Bob Sentell remembers a trial recess in which Judge Blakely, drinking a bootlegger's confiscated booze with the opposing attorneys, makes a toast, "I give you Robert E. Lee." In various stories children are named for Confederate generals. In that sad tale of southern folk musicians making out as best they may in California, "Keep Them Cards and Letters Comin' In," we note, in the family history of one of them, a brother named "Pickett." And in "Pleadings," the mother of a mongoloid child, as if to save it, had named it after "Albert Sidney Johnson at Shiloh." And an adventurous pilot describes the quick end of a career flying arms for a rebellion in Katanga in southern Zaire (in "The Arrangement") thus: "But that secession went the way of my great-grandfather's."

Thus in fifteen of twenty stories the Civil War is in some way present— as a major theme, as a source of meaning and values a century later, as an object of devotion, as a spur to memories and associations. Of the five stories in which there is no allusion to the war, three are among the shortest in the book; it is as if they were dealing with smaller worlds that could not accommodate an element otherwise present constantly as a force or casually as a point of significant reference. Still, in the shortest story, "Old Men Dream Dreams, Young Men See Visions," when we see two characters named "Helena" and "Cassandra," we wonder whether a different myth of a still older war is being hinted. This is one of three stories that deal with a more limited, nonhistorical past and present, a younger generation against its immediate predecessor, still literally rather than figuratively alive. This first one stresses the contrast of fresh young love with parental loss and disenchantment. The jolly "The Man Who Slept with Women" portrays, on the other hand, youth's necessary revolt against parental sexual possessiveness. In "The Great Pumpkin" the situation is again quite different: evil youths savage an innocuous older pair.

It is as if, in the relatively shorter stories, Corrington could not move into the larger societal scenes in which some sense of the past regularly figures. Besides, there is another issue here: when his satirical sense is dominant, he stays immersed in the present, even in some cases where a sense of the past might have moral relevance. Certainly "The Great Pumpkin" and "Night School" stick to a satirical picture of contemporary evil and failure, an area in which, as I have said, Corrington seems not to be at his fullest and strongest. He is at his best when he is most inclusive, going beyond a rootless world into the larger world that still has a historical sense. Hence "Heroic Measures / Vital Signs" is somewhat puzzling: it is one of the longer stories (ninth longest, in fact), but, aside from some satirical elements that partly ally it with "The Great Pumpkin" and "Night School," it stays within an individual consciousness that is barely in touch with a limited immediate world of job, family, and hospital. It invokes no sense of history at all. In this collection it is unique: a study of a solipsistic figure shut off not only from the past but essentially from a few points of possible contact in the present. It is not clear whether finally he breaks through into a vision of some ultimate truth, or in his imaginings achieves an ultimate form of self-enclosure.

The phrases "when their country died" in "Reunion" and "after his nation had died" in "Nothing Succeeds" remind us of the number of deaths in Corrington's stories and let us ask whether death has a thematic status that helps define the Corrington art. We inevitably see death in the four stories that deal, directly or by extension, with the Civil War: "First Blood," "Reunion," "A Time to Embrace," and "If Time Were Not / A Moving Thing"; there are two murders in "The Lonesome Traveler," three in "The Southern Reporter" (not to mention a suicide in the offing), and six in "The Great Pumpkin"; three people are burnt to death in "Pleadings"; presumably there are multiple deaths in the shootout in "Nothing Succeeds"; we watch the long dying of Father O'Malley in "Every Act Whatever of Man" and of Bob Sentell in "A Day in Thy Court," and we see "brain-dead" characters in "Every Act Whatever of Man" and "Heroic Measures / Vital Signs"; we learn about a criminal's suicide and the long-ago deaths of martyrs in "The Actes and Monuments"; "The Dark Corner" concerns the burial of the dead; and there are symbolic deaths in "The Arrangement" and "Keep Them Cards and Letters Comin' In."

This blunt summation of deaths might suggest, in the Corrington mode, a fixation on human terminality, a conviction of impermanence, a toughening up of Khayyam's gentle mournfulness about transiency. No such thing. The very resonance of the Civil War and of the "dead nation" for a century reveals Corrington's sense of the endurance of vital things. In his fiction physical deaths symbolize not irrational closures, unearned endings, but modes of life. Only in romance do soldiers whom we know survive. The inevitable beast in man leads to murder, but to recognize that beast does not mean that all men are beasts. If he plays god to men but a little above the beasts, man uses methods that will bring on destructive gunfire. A good man may feel, when courts fail, driven to deal death to those who deserve it. A brilliant criminal, shocked by the legal loopholes allowed him, may elect suicide. Or death "from natural causes": how to deal with it? By relying on a divine lover within? Let it take its course, or delay it by prolonging a "brain-dead" state? Let community convenience determine its duration? Use its imminence as an occasion for a meditation on how one has lived? Death is not an irrational, undeserved menace, but a revelation about modes of life.

Put it another way: in Corrington death is a way into a basic theme, the modes of moral or spiritual survival, a key to how man lives. Since Corrington, as William Mills has pointed out, continued, despite various troubles with Catholic authorities, to inscribe "AMDG" in all his books, one might well look for Catholic points of view, and a Catholic critic might come up with readings different from those I have proposed. What a lay reader feels as a constant presence in Corrington is inevitable crises of mind and spirit where men may not do without obligatory codes—designs of order that might come out of religious discipline or philosophical reflection or exist as a residue of secular or regional tradition. The specifically Catholic seems rare. In "If Time Were Not / A Moving Thing," the issue is a contrast between an enveloping love of God that carries with it a separation from the world about one, and a godless love of doing good that misfires in the world supposed to be the beneficiary. In "Every Act Whatever of Man" the church, finding a gifted priest a community and hence an ecclesiastical liability, appears as hardboiled pragmatist, opposed by an individual conscience (the Protestant mode) not defined by origin. And at the end of the book comes Corrington's "Vedic story," essaying perhaps to depict, though at best cloudily, another doctrine, the merging with the All.

The "individual conscience" that opposes cutting off the brain-dead priest from mechanically maintained life is, as we have seen, that of a lawyer, and the legal tradition affords Corrington his most frequent entry into the problems of good and evil. He does not idealize: we see always the difference between what an actual court does and the ideal justice that it is supposed to serve. If that justice fails, it is because human beings are imperfect; yet the struggle to deal with imperfection is always there. Original sin coexists with moves toward salvation—procedures, individual insights, codes that emanate from memories, regional history, felt tradition. We see all of man's naughtiness, but along with it a persistent sense of rule and obligation that enables the race somehow to make out. Everywhere there are random lusts, but codes never wither wholly away; present profits rule many lives, but historical memories provide shapings against disorder; honor as well as opportunism shapes lives. Man oscillates between absolutes and pragmatics, between lust and the letter of the law, or, in a metaphor often implicitly present, between the Californian and the Confederate. At their best, individual histories enclose cultural turmoil. The law and the courts may drift into routines, trivialities, personal gambits, and of course the human weakness of all its practitioners, but still courts symbolize a justice that, despite shortcomings and even perversions, remains alive in the human imagination. It may compel a criminal pervert to scorn its failure and enact it against himself. A court may let beasts off, but still it remains a barrier against the triumph of bestiality. To alter the terms: Corrington has a strong sense of the deformed society but also of the forms that survive critical disorder, and even of the order that may be managed outside the forms (and he no romantic).

This effort to summarize the range and depth of the substance of the Corrington oeuvre would falsify matters if it implied that individual stories make firm decisions in all matters of conduct and value that come up. They do not. They leave much apparently unresolved. They dangle us between possibilities. If we were using certain abstractions to summarize what Corrington does, we would have to speak not only of his variety and range and inclusiveness but also of his ambiguity, indeed of his tincture of mystery. He can use grammatical devices that leave us insecure at some points (just as at others, occasionally, he may impose a design that cuts into imaginative vitality). He can rest in a kind of uncertainty of event. He can resist a full definition of character or experience, as if he were giving the narrative materials their head and letting them take what direction they will. Is a character having a spiritual vision or a mental problem? Is a character who knowingly quotes Satan a diabolical figure, an ironist, or a playful artist? Corrington manages such matters richly enough to forestall self-confident readings. For him, life itself is something of a mystery story. But in no way is his fiction a self-written offspring of prior fictions, an imitation of modal habits. It is a unique imitation of a human reality that is rich enough to impede our pinning it down wholly.

15

Comic Prose Epic

Welty's Losing Battles

On the face of it, reading the long *Losing Battles* is like taking an extended ramble through a lush, variegated natural and human landscape in which there are many paths and so many enticements that one is constantly led off in new and unforeseen directions, always fascinated, often uncertain amid apparent aimlessness, and yet constantly suspecting the unclear presence of a controlling route, however camouflaged by the rich growths, vivid scenes, and surprising roadside attractions.[1] Or it is like traveling in a canoe or boat moved and steered only by the current of a stream that is now an all-but-massive pool allowing plenty of time to look at tropical banks and multicolored bottom, now a languid eddy that turns us about rather than pushes us forward, now a short stretch of whitewater that brings on a tumultuous dash, now a sturdy little creek with a great deal of push, but most often a meandering flow that brings the craft to a succession of little stops and visits at dozens of logs, beaver dams, islets, gravelly promontories, sandbanks, coves, and inlets. No stop may seem to have much to do with where you're going, but then you aren't sure about the where, either; once a where begins to shape up, you may see the relevance of the stops in retrospect, or perhaps decide that some of them are there just for the fun of it. Occasionally what you sense as the prevalent drift may tighten up in a millrace drive taking you to a desperate pitch over a deep waterfall wave. But Welty may somehow slip around a danger spot hastily, or settle for an anticlimactic splash in an unforeseen pond, or just let motion die away strangely. Or

---

1. When I coined, as I thought, the term *Comic Prose Epic* for the title of my essay on Welty's *Losing Battles,* I forgot that it had already been used as a title by Mary Ann Ferguson in the volume *Eudora Welty: Critical Essays,* ed. Peggy Whitman Prenshaw (Jackson: University Press of Mississippi, 1979). I am glad to acknowledge this duplication here.

the voyage through *Losing Battles* may be like listening to a perpetual-motion raconteur—drawling on breathless but always commanding, too full of stories even to stop for applause or a drink, dashing as if driven from one to another, knowing what their connection is but rarely bothering to make the connection explicit, seeming less to manipulate what is told than to be charmed by it as by an independent entity that the narrator barely touches on its way to an audience; getting from one episode to another by such devices (implicit only, never overt) as "You'd never guess what happened next," "I tell you, it was just one crazy thing after another," "Oh, I forgot to tell you what happened before that," "You see, there was this little thing in the past," "And by the way, that reminds me of another story," or "Now is as good a time as any to let Billy have his say," and so on. The surface impression, in other words, is one of haste, casualness, haphazardness, movement rather than direction, scattershot unselectiveness, of rushing ahead rather than rounding out, or of stopping short rather than keeping on, of ringing in the new before the old has been wrung out and hung clearly on the line of the finished and understood, of madcap tumbleweed hop-skip-jumping rather than of steady advance on a marked public route. This impression needs to be mentioned (a) because readers are hardly likely to escape it and (b) because the storytelling surface does not truly reflect the narrative substance. In brief, *Losing Battles* is a highly ordered book, but it does not wear its order on its sleeve. Perhaps Welty did what Sterne did in the parts of *Tristram Shandy* that he had time to polish: strove for an outer air of the accidental, the interrupted, and the inconsecutive (in Sterne, a formal mimesis of psychological disorderliness in humanity; in Welty, a capturing of diversionary tendencies inevitable in a multitude of individuals even when they are seen as a group with a purpose). Perhaps she was simply the compulsive raconteur driven to transmit episode after episode, tale after tale, as they welled up in her imagination, and yet somehow mastering them with an instinctive grasp of their potential coherence. Perhaps she is basically a designer who worked out a governing pattern with great care, instituting a relationship of parts subtle enough, or letting them have enough of an air of spontaneity, to stir up a sense of the chancy, the lively but unselected, or even the willful. Whatever comes first, this is true: Welty digs deep enough to bring in a gusher, but she has an excellent supply of caps, valves, and piping.

The numerous ebullient parts are held together by personal and thematic relationships that I will try to spell out. A more visible kind of form is provided by typographic breaks: Welty divides the book into six uncaptioned parts and establishes most of these as logical divisions by providing them with conspicuous "closers." Jack and Gloria Renfro, the young couple just getting their married life under way, end part 1 by leaving a family reunion to go on a family mission; the mission having taken a wholly ironic turn, they end part 2 by returning to the reunion. Parts 3 and 4 end identifiable phases of the reunion, the latter involving Jack's startling return from another mission. Part 5 ends the reunion day: departures, bedding down, and several private excursions that look ahead to the next day. Part 6 includes the events of the next morning; again Jack and Gloria occupy the closing pages, affectionate but not unanimous about plans for the future. Jack is everybody's hero, and Gloria the hopeful young wife; still they are less a full counterpoint to the older generation than they are an accent. The central business is the revelation of patterns of living (feelings, values, attitudes) that are firmly established in the older reunionists. Jack and Gloria may alter, conform to, or even fall short of the family and village patterns gradually revealed through crowding episodes.

In each part we can discover an ordering of the materials that come at us through apparently rambling, scrambling, scurrying segments of conversational action. We can do this by the rather academic exercise of outlining the contents: thus we can see how Welty, through the surging hullabaloo of reunion talk, gradually introduces and identifies characters and issues, skillfully weaves in past events that generate emotions and speculations in the present, makes random chatter—greetings, cracks, claims or putdowns, in-house allusions, brief flytings—hover about major thematic concerns, and canvasses these concerns in a surrogate, a Chekhovian one carried to ultimate limits, for the linear plot or the special situation evolving toward a terminal point. I will simply assert this congruence instead of making the longish demonstration needed to describe fully the underlying order of any of the six parts.

ii

The "terminal point" is arbitrary: the ending of the reunion, and the picking up of some of the pieces scattered by the windfall events of the occasion. The compacting of various lifetimes into a single day (this one of about thirty hours, from Sunday sunrise to Monday noon, with due time out for sleeping) is less of a tour de force than it was when Frank Swinnerton did it in *Nocturne* (1917) and Joyce in *Ulysses* (1922). The center of the reunion is Granny Vaughn's ninetieth birthday. Since her daughter and son-in-law are dead, the chief reunionists are half a dozen middle-aged grandchildren, the five Beecham men and their sister Beulah Beecham Renfro, plus many spouses and offspring. "Beechams' Day," to borrow a phrase from the Joycean world, is the first Sunday in August some time in the 1930s. Welty gets the essential past into the picture through many flashbacks. These are rarely arbitrary moves of her own: they are rather stories told by reunionists who want, or have some good reason, to tell them (the old epic tradition of the inset story that covers more time without breaking unity of time). Welty manages these stories with great variety and verve: they may be long or short, the speaker may be called on or seize stage or struggle to hold it, he may repeat a twice-told tale ("Oh why does he have to go into that again?"), he will always face interruptions (questions, objections, pure irrelevancies, reactions to the history narrated), and at times a story comes as a group composition. If Welty is calling on a speaker only because the time has come to get some facts before us, she conceals the fact well; the narrated pasts seem to flow easily out of ongoing talk into present time.

What is told, like what goes on in the present, is not always clear; we may have to live with some fuzziness about the edge of motive, intention, relationship, and even historical or physical fact. Ultimately this may be due to Welty's conviction that all mystery and ambiguity cannot be washed out in the water of logical explanation; its immediate source is her basic technique of thrusting us plumb into the life of the reunion, submerging us in the flood of domestic doings and family feelings—partisan, predictive, philosophical, fluctuating between the casual and the intense. This is Joycean of course: the artist as distant divinity, electing an air of Olympian independence from all the scrabble and pother and sound effects he has plunged his readers into. He interprets nothing; readers intuit reality from its direct impact on their senses. They have no help from a Jamesian recording consciousness. But Joyce's management of our total immersion in actuality, his all-around-the-town odyssey, has an air of cool calculation in the library; Welty's is more like a flashing succession of on-the-spot interviews, a village neighborhood odyssey dashed off by a Dickens with Mark Twain as coauthor here and there. But unlike these lively recorders of community doings and spirit—mostly comic, frequently farcical, sometimes edging on the grotesque or the pathetic and, implicitly and in held-down ways, on effects rooted in still deeper feelings—Welty does no emceeing, no open steering of actors or audience; she provides no overt introductions, explanations, or transitions. She is directly present in only one way: she sets up scenes with marvelous fullness and concreteness of detail, naming with utmost ease all kinds of flowers, fruits, vegetables, weeds, trees, animals, soils, terrains, articles of clothing, household objects, dinner dishes, parts and shapes of bodies. At gifts-for-Granny time she lists and gives quick reality to sixteen presents (287).[2] Perhaps no other modern novel would yield so

---

2. Page references are to the first edition (New York: Random House, 1970), but it is helpful that the pagination is identical in the paperback edition (New York: Vintage, 1990).

massive a concordance of nouns and adjectives. Yet there is nothing of the relentlessly encyclopedic; Welty never lingers, caressing a scene or a detail of it (as George Eliot does at times); she seems always in haste, sensory images pouring out as from an overturned cornucopia, yet giving life rather than making a mess. Her pictures flash by with a cinematic fluency that makes them almost elusive.

Dialogue must occupy 90 percent of more than four hundred pages. It looks uncontrolled, uncentered, and often irrelevant. Yet through it we have to learn virtually everything significant—identities, moral and mental natures, the feelings and ideas that inform life in the town of Banner, old events that influence life now. In other words, far more than most novelists Welty is using the techniques of drama. A dialogue that must be plausible in itself must effect an immense exposition of past and present for a reader who has none of the information possessed by the speakers, and must produce and sustain a tension about what is going to happen in two hours or two weeks or two years. The writer of novel-as-drama has one advantage over the writer of drama-as-stage-play: he is not bedeviled by limits of time. Hence Welty can let go on anyone who wants to talk, whether to get attention, to defend or attack or correct, to yield to a compulsion, or just to let us know what we need to know (in a very effective scene Miss Lexie Renfro, kneeling or squatting, repairs damage to Gloria's skirt while telling us about what she did as companion or nurse to a key figure, Miss Julia Mortimer, the schoolteacher who has just died; what with interruptions, Miss Lexie goes on for fifteen pages [271–86]). Welty makes excellent use of the figure convenient to both dramatists and novelists, the newcomer who must learn what others know. This is Uncle Noah Webster's new wife, Cleo, who not only comes from away but, in an endless itch of curiosity, never stops probing with questions that we too need to have answered. Yet Cleo is more than a prop, for Welty colors her questioning with something of a prosecutor's drive; Cleo comes in on a narrow line between an itch to puncture and put down and the candor of a nonpartisan inquisitor whose quest for the complete and probably discreditable record surpasses her tact. Thus she contributes to dramatic tension; there are many little needlings between her and Beulah Beecham Renfro, hostess to the reunion and a lively tongued defender of Beechams. "Well, what's he got to hide?" asks Cleo about a Beecham urged not to "jabber," and Beulah replies, "Sister Cleo, I don't know what in the world ever guides your tongue into asking the questions it does! . . . By now you ought to know this is a strict, law-abiding, God-fearing, close-knit family" (343–44). But a moment's sharpness seems never to generate an hour's antagonism.

While she keeps clashes constantly going in the foreground, Welty is skilled in focusing on events to come and making the most of the characters' and our expectations: notably his mother's faith that Jack Renfro, the young hero of the family, will make it home for the reunion, and at length his striking leap into the scene. Meanwhile we have had to wait to find out where he would make it home from (the state "pen" at Parchman), how he got there in the first place, and how he got out and traveled home. All that done, we look ahead again: Jack's handling of a mission—to embarrass Judge Moody, who had sentenced him to the pen, and who is known to be in the Banner area. Meanwhile various questions needing answers crystallize gradually from misty hints in the family talk: why Uncle Nathan's artificial hand, why his wandering life (Beechams stay put), why the biblical texts he plants about the country? What is Judge Moody's mission, once or twice mentioned quickly by the judge or his wife, in these parts? Who are the parents of Jack's wife, Gloria, an orphan who was the local teacher before her marriage? What, above all, was the community role of Miss Julia, the legendary retired teacher who chooses reunion day to die? So the constant drama of questions awaiting answer joins the dominant dialogue to commit the novel to a theater way of doing things. It is still novel, for it aspires no whit to the stringent selectiveness of drama; instead it clings to all the extrinsic constituents of full daily life that stage life cuts back ruthlessly.

Losing Battles periodically reminds us of several dramas of family life— Eliot's *Family Reunion* and Albee's *The American Dream* and *All Over*. Although the novel, like Eliot's play, explores some unclear but serious history that has an impact on the present, it vastly expands Eliot's farcical elements and cuts back and underplays the notes of pain and grief; and though it in no way minimizes rifts and tensions, the novel perceives reunion as a symbol of residual unity among country kinfolk rather than as an ironic recorder of disunity in a county family. Some resemblances to the Albee plays help set in relief the sharply different Welty mode. In *All Over* a family and various appendages await the imminent death of a father-and-husband, and they reveal themselves through their interchanges; in *Losing Battles* the death of the teacher releases a flux of commentary that is a principal means of characterizing the Beecham way of life. Otherwise all is different, notably the tone. In Albee everybody wields a hatchet of hostility or a stiletto of self-pity; aggression and self-defense or self-serving are everywhere; the scene is harsh, and the tone falls little short of disgust. Welty's people have a comparable candor, and it can be combative; but the various selfhoods are mostly held in check by a sense of the fitting, an unspoken acceptance of limited role, and even a talent for sympathy. Welty feels friendly amusement; Albee sneers bitterly. The contrast is made sharper by *The American Dream,* since major characters match: needle-tongued Grandma is paralleled by tart Granny, domineering Mommy by competently managerial Beulah Renfro, downtrodden Daddy by misadventure-and-miscalculation-prone Mr. Renfro, and "The American Dream" Young Man by Jack Renfro. One brief look at the Albee monsters, their nastiness a filtrate of the author's malice, and we see the relative fullness of Welty's people, neither whittled down to allegories of human unlovableness nor without shortcomings; limited enough, but their limitations set off by saving spurts of energy, goodwill, good nature, devotion, or endurance. Albee is narrow-eyed satirist, Welty broad-gauge humorist.

iii

Banner people are often feckless, foolish, parochial, prejudiced, thoughtless, thick-skinned, and rich in other frailties, and they can be petty, suspicious, tactless, or calculating; but we have little sense that their less glorious moments are seriously hurtful to others. Welty does not focus on the sly, the underhanded, the devious, or the malicious; and there is not a neurotic in the carloads of reunionists that come from away. Welty rarely makes us take sides between virtue and vice. I would almost bet, knowing as I do how such generalizations can ricochet against the maker, that the only truly satirical passages are brief ones near the end. At Miss Julia's funeral several people, who sound exactly like Hardy conventionalists, sneer audibly at Jack and Gloria as a sorry pair, whose failings include not being properly dressed for cemetery rites. Here is the complacent snobbery that is an old target of satire. The pressure on the reader to reject false values is stronger when the sinner is known and acts as well as talks crassly. On each of two days Jack has spent laborious hours at the task of getting Judge Moody's Buick, which had leaped to a precarious perch high above road and river, put back on the road, towed into town, and restored to running condition. It is now funeral time, a long rain keeps up, and the road to the cemetery is all mud. The judge suggests giving Jack and Gloria a ride to the cemetery. Jack demurs; all muddied up, he may soil the Buick velvet. Mrs. Moody settles the matter: "They're young. . . . They can walk" (422). Here the priority of things over people, and people who have our sympathy, makes the passage strongly satirical. The episode lacks the sheer laughableness of a little earlier when, during the risky Buick-rescue process, the car door swings open, something pops out and is gobbled by wild pigs, and Mrs. Moody mourns, "My cake!" (394); when a runaway truck crashes into a ditch and makes Miss Lexie cry out that it "splashed my dress" (395); and when, after drastic steps get the Buick almost miraculously down on the road again, Mrs. Moody complains, "You bring it to me covered with mud!" (396). Here are not the grossnesses that catch the eye of the censor, but the irrelevancies and anticlimaxes that appeal to the humorist. There are dozens of these.

The comic range is very wide: it extends from the ironic to the farcical. In a central irony Jack sets out to discomfit the judge by causing his car to go off the road; instead Judge Moody causes himself much greater trouble by driving his car off the road to avoid running down Jack's wife and baby. Welty often credits people with epigrams that we hardly expect of them, for example, Mrs. Moody's "Your real secrets are the ones you don't know you've got" (306). Numerous comic moments hinge on replies that suddenly veer away from created expectation (a traditional mode), as when Gloria reports that Miss Julia warned her against marrying into the Beecham family, and Beulah exclaims, "For mercy's sakes! Only one of the biggest families there is!" (251). Miss Julia rescues Rachel Sojourner from an apparent suicide attempt; since Rachel is cold and stockingless, Miss Julia strips off her own stockings, puts them on Rachel, and rushes Rachel to a doctor. Rachel takes the stockings off again, telling the doctor, "I don't care if it kills me, I wouldn't be caught dead in Miss Julia's old yarn stockings" (258). Brother Bethune, the aged parson, speaks defensively of his lack of descendants, "I ain't got a one. Now I have killed me a fairly large number of snakes. . . . The grand sum total is four hundred and twenty six" (213). Such incongruities in thought and values pour out from the Welty imagination. Parts of verbal games can be scattered over several pages. Jack fought Curly Stovall because Curly was "aggravating"; Jack then carried off Curly's safe, not to "rob" him but "just to aggravate him." At Jack's trial Judge Moody scorns Jack's plea that Curly was "aggravating" and finds Jack guilty of "aggravated battery."

Welty is brilliant in farce—in scenes where intentions are defeated by accidents, where coincidence and mishap crowd in to upset plans, where helter-skelter events keep up a dizzy pace, where people are prone to collisions and pratfalls but don't really get hurt, where objects themselves seem to conspire against order. She may describe an episode with the hyperbole natural to farce: "a crowd of his sons and their jumping children and their wives . . . poured out of the car," and then comes a "pick-up riding on a flat tire, packed in behind with people too crowded in to wave" (9)—reminiscences of old dizzy movie scenes of dozens of people in a single car. Aunt Nanny seemed to have been "harnessed into her print dress along with six or seven watermelons" (10). In their "aggravated battery" brawl Jack hit

Curly Stovall with a sack of cottonseed meal; it "busted" and "covered that booger from head to foot with enough fertilize to last him the rest of his life" (26). Next thing, Jack ties Curly up in a coffin made for Curly and lying inconveniently on his store floor. Curly later complains that he has been "pulled on by a hundred and seventy-five pound woman [his sister]" and "talked back to by a eight-ounce schoolteacher [Gloria]" (37). Jack lugs off Curly's safe like a farcical Hercules; it comes open and scatters contents all over the road; Curly never locked it because it was too hard to get it open again. When it is brought into court at Jack's trial, it has a nesting bird in it.

When Judge Moody drives his car off the road to avoid hitting Gloria and her baby, Lady May, Welty could play for the melodrama of near-disaster. She does nothing of the kind. Lady May got on the road when Jack slid down a bank and fell into a ditch, and then failed to get to her because he ran into Gloria and fell into the ditch again—the pratfall series of the two-reeler. A moment later Jack whispers to Gloria, "Face 'em, from now on. Your dress is tore behind" (121). The car has stopped at a Chaplinesquely precarious spot on the edge of a small cliff, its motor still running. Its wheels are off the ground, for it is resting on a sign recently planted by evangelical Uncle Nathan, "Destruction Is At Hand," the balance that saves it depending on the weight of Jack's friend Aycock Comfort, who chased the careening car with his banjo and somehow got into it when it stopped, and who now has to stay there for nearly twenty-four hours. For half of a very hot and dusty Sunday, and several hours on a rainy and very muddy Monday, efforts to deal with the car produce round after round of farce, genuine risk though there is: everybody has contradictory ideas, advice and commentary are endless, potential helpers drive away, plans go wrong, towlines break and bodies pop in various directions, tires blow out, a dozen dogs bark assistance, Jack's baby kicks him in the eye, and then he is badly stretched in a tug-of-war with the escaping Buick (it gets away over the cliff and lands on a ledge on its "nose"), Jack's father makes a mess by dynamiting a partially obstructing tree ("with all its yesterdays tangled up in it now" [391]), and an unexpected secondary explosion not only tosses people and things about but brings forth Beulah's ironic observation on her husband's work: "Some folks' dynamite blows up once and gets through with it, but you don't reckon on that little from Mr. Renfro" (392). In this marvelous long-continuing zany struggle it is as if fictional life in the thirties were imitating the great two-reelers of the twenties.

Yet superabundant farce—and one could go on for pages describing it—does not supplant the comedy of events that come out of differences and inconsistencies of personality, or obscure the recurrent flickering presence of noncomic materials. There is much wit, ranging, as we have seen, from jeers to epigrams. The comedy that reflects humanity, in contrast with the farce that runs roughshod over it, usually has some share even in the most boisterous physical scenes. Some matters are wholly comic—for instance, the forgiveness theme. An annual reunion feature is a preacher's discourse, which traditionally combines family history, humor, and homily—a task long carried out by the late Grandpa Vaughn, evidently a Mosaic figure, and this year committed to Brother Bethune, who is, Beulah says, "a comedown after Grandpa" and of whom Granny Vaughn asks, "Who went so far as to let him through the bars?" (175). The reunion alternately ignores him, interrupts him, helps him get things straight, and cheers him on as if he were the day's floor show—a comic medley of attitudes. Various Beechams express the hope that he will officially "forgive" Jack, apparently for doing time in the pen, and discuss styles of forgiving; Jack feels that "Nobody . . . would have forgiven" him for not making it from pen to reunion. As in drama, these quick references build up to a scene in which everything then goes quite unexpectedly. Brother Bethune suddenly directs his discourse to Judge Moody and declares, "We're going to forgive you." The judge is nonplussed; his wife says that they can't be forgiven for coming to the reunion, since Jack invited them. Uncle Noah Webster comments wittily that "hospitality . . . ain't no guarantee you ain't going to be forgiven when you get there," and the judge's growing annoyance catalyzes further forgivings of him "for bringing your wife" (Aunt Nanny), "for livin'" (Aunt Birdie), "for calling me 'old man'" (Brother Bethune). Brother Bethune urges him to "do like the majority begs and *be* forgiven." The comic irony of it is that the Beechams have unconsciously used "forgive" to mean "condemn" and hence have happily had it both ways. Moody is enraged at being "forgiven" for "being a fair judge at a trial." Beulah, politely passing cake to the judge, assails him with a lovely non sequitur, "Don't tell me, sir, you've nothing to be forgiven for, I'm his mother." Three good ironies follow. The first is that Jack, who was sentenced by the judge, strongly opposes all the forgiving; now immensely grateful to the judge for "saving" his wife and baby (by diverting the Buick), he seems to be apologizing for the family's tactlessness in practicing a needless and needling absolution. The second irony is that in thus seeming to draw away from his family, Jack is actually allying himself with them more strongly, but by a novel tactic: he springs a surprise by declaring openly that he will not forgive the judge, because the judge's unforgivable act was depriving the family of Jack's indispensable labors for eighteen months. The third irony is that the judge approves Jack's nonforgiveness, and judge and erstwhile defendant shake hands on it, each cherishing his own interpretation of the rite of concord. Beulah ends things by lamenting "this headlong forgiving" and helpfully suggesting to

Mrs. Moody that she use a spoon to eat the "tender" coconut cake. This substantial scene (208–13) is not only prepared for, as we have seen, but is followed up by a number of brief variations on the forgiveness theme (321, 372, 427), the best of them the judge's witty "Forgiving seems the besetting sin of this house" (319).

Peeping through the regular crevices in the dominant farce and comedy are diverse touches of the somber, the pathetic, the disastrous, and even the tragic. Since she has a many-toned sense of reality, Welty is equally spontaneous in these noncomic notes, but she never, never holds them. Her rich sense of the wry does not diminish her sense of what goes awry, goes wrong, wreaks injury, but she does not linger over these; whether from stoicism or an instinct that does not crystallize as formal choice, she so manages human troubles that the reader may escape a solid sense of the real difficulties faced by the characters. The very energy of the tireless dialogue somehow denies the power of events over the characters, singular in apparent hopefulness or gift for survival. The Renfros say little of their poverty, of their losses during the time when Jack, in jail, could not help them; it is from the cracks of others that we learn that their farm has become almost a wasteland (drought now, against dangerous floods in the past). It is never called so overtly, but the new tin roof is a pathetic disclaimer of defeat, a chin-up welcome to Jack as he returns to serious farm problems. Miss Julia's death makes a picnic excursion for other teachers, but at the news "Gloria stood as if she had been struck in the forehead by a stone out of a slingshot" (157). She had been Miss Julia's successor and special protégée, but then we learn of their troubled split over Gloria's marriage to Jack. Most touches of pathos are lightning quick. Lifted to a table top, Granny does a determined little dance routine: "She danced in their faces"— not only visibility, but a little defiance. She starts absentmindedly to walk off the table, is caught by Jack making a cinematic split-second entry, and in her "eyes gathered the helpless tears of the rescued" (308).

In the past there were destructive fires as well as floods; the Beechams' parents were drowned in strange circumstances; the woman whom the Beechams take to be Gloria's mother attempted suicide and, though prevented, died of the aftereffects; Gloria's years at an orphanage and teacher's college were bleak ones; the most admired of the Beecham boys, Sam Dale, died young; much neighborhood damage, as well as losses for the Renfros, was due to a piratical transient named Dearman (possibly Gloria's father). We see Uncle Nathan's artificial hand, then the stump of his arm, and we assume a self-dismemberment as the center of a lifelong penance (wandering endlessly and putting up religious signs). Suddenly he blurts out the reason: "I killed Mr. Dearman with a stone to his head, and let 'em hang a sawmill nigger for it" (344). The death of Miss Julia on reunion day brings forth many reminiscences of her zealous pedagogical career and quotations from her. The key one is "All my life I've fought a hard war with ignorance. Except in those cases that you can count off on your fingers, I lost every battle" (298)—the source of Welty's title. Her dying words were, "What was the trip for?" (241). The implicit despair, quick hints suggest, also has a place in Judge Moody's inner reflections on her career and last months; dying, she had to make heroic efforts to mail letters through a strange barricade by Miss Lexie Renfro, a nurse-companion who had mysteriously become a kind of jailer. The funeral of Miss Julia is the penultimate episode; it is followed only by a short tender scene between Jack and Gloria.

iv

Yet all such actions and effects are contained within the comic framework: the pattern is survival within a world in which one accepts, makes do with, a prevailing disparateness where much is out of whack with logic or desire. The diversity of narrative materials, however, does not imply a diversity of style. Not that a uniformity of manner disregards heterogeneity of matter: "each face as grief-stricken as the other" and "Ella Fay Renfro in front tossing a sweat-fraught pitcher's glove," which are only two lines apart (288), use different vocabularies, and even so few words reveal difference in tone. But both are brief absolute phrases; they suggest, without proving anything, that Welty likes certain basic syntactic arrangements. Ordinarily she does not write very long sentences or use complex structures; she coordinates a good deal; she has almost none of the involutions (such as parentheses within parentheses) of Faulkner, and she does not draw on different traditions of style as much as K. A. Porter does. To say this is to identify a difference, in no way to assert a shortcoming. Welty does not make much use of the logical, analytic, judicial manner (she uses very few abstract nouns) and the comedy of manners style (wit framed in syntactic formalities) ideally represented in Jane Austen and at times equally available to Charlotte Brontë (who thought Austen trivial) and George Eliot—Brontë with her unique emotional intensity of vocabulary and rhythm, and Eliot with her dual at-home-ness in a concrete natural world and a reflective or philosophical one. Porter likewise can combine sensory concreteness with an Austen wit and a sort of combed-out, almost Jamesian thoughtful hovering. Welty has an enormous idiom of homely actuality, domestic and rural; she is still more earthy than George Eliot, handicapped by neither the Victorian reticences (Eliot could not have an Aunt Nanny say to a spelling-bee victor, "You got it spelled but wet your britches" [289]), nor by the chic vulgarities now often mistaken by the naive for proofs of vitality, liberty, honesty, and so forth. A varied and rampaging actuality of animals, nature (weather, earth, growing things), and even objects is what her bounding style throws us into; though the resulting atmosphere is occasionally sharpened by witty observations, on the whole it is rather suffused by humor, a tireless sense of incongruities, human fallibility, the grotesque, and the jokes of circumstance, even when disaster may be dimly underfoot or just around the corner.

Welty's language falls into two not wholly distinguishable categories— her own words when she acts as scene-shifter, and the speech of her characters. The vast extents of dialogue are never flat; they rush on colloquially like the freshets of spring, splashing with expletives, exclamations, loose connections, pronouns without antecedents, verbs without subjects, and now and then a local vocabulary. Syntax can be enormously compact. Jack: "Here's Papa something to open" (31), and, of the new roof, "I could see it a mile coming" (73). Granny: "I'm in a hurry for him back" (51). Lexie: "I listened hard to be asked for and I wasn't" (337). Uncle Noah Webster of the jail-keeper: "Drunk and two pistols. Makes his wife answer the phone" (50). Verbal or prepositional phrases may hold off stubbornly or hang on loosely. Willy Trimble: "Told him better to stay put with who he's with" (154). Beulah: "Cleo, what in the name of goodness did you think we ever started this in order to tell?" (39) and "Vaughn's got the teacher to tell he's misput the bus" (373). Miss Lexie, of Miss Julia's retirement: "So, where she had left to go, when they put her to pasture, was across the river" (296). The colloquial may substitute for an expected solemnity, as in two comments on Miss Julia's coming funeral. Uncle Homer to Brother Bethune: "And you can have your whack at her. I think you can look for a good crowd" (339), and Brother Bethune, "I'm just good enough to get her into the ground" (351). Scores of such locutions, unhackneyed and unpretentious, make for wonderfully lively speech.

Willy Trimble, who found Miss Julia's body, likes his phrase for her demise and uses it twice: "Down fell she. End of *her*" (162, 230). This is clipped and unsolemn, but instead of tumbling out, it is patterned. Likewise Beulah can put words into more of a pattern than we expect in colloquial style: "Well, you have to trust people of the giving-stripe to give you the thing you want and not something they'd be just as happy to get rid of" (243). Frequently speakers use phrases that have a slightly more formal (or even bookish or archaic) flavor than the context suggests. Some instances: Miss Lexie, "I at present call Alliance my home" (18); Uncle Noah Webster,

"Cleo, I wish it had been your privilege to be with us our day in court" (51); Jack, referring to the late Grandpa Vaughn, "I miss his frowning presence just as I get myself ready to perform something" (102); Jack to his father, "What brought you forth?" (138); uncouth Curly Stovall, "I'll come back and see what story the night has told" (152); Mr. Renfro, a "thing surpassing strange" (294); Uncle Nathan, "I must needs," followed first by "be on my way" and then by "not stop to take comfort" (375); and Jack again, "Mr. Comfort elected to put in his appearance" (418). Some repetitions go beyond the casual: Beulah, "She run-run-run down the hill . . . followed behind 'em trot-a-trot, trot-a-trot, galloping, galloping" (217), and Miss Lexie or Miss Julia, "pencil racing, racing, racing" (283). Beulah can combine singular precision and balance: "I'm ashamed *of* her and *for* her" (296). Often speakers use so organized a locution as the series, from Jack's quick summary for his jailer—"I got my daddy's hay to get in the barn, his syrup to grind, his hog to kill, his cotton to pick and the rest of it" (44–45)—to Beulah's remarkably shaped "But the truth is you don't know, nor I don't, nor anybody else within the reach of my voice, because that ring—it's our own dead mother's, Granny's one child's wedding ring, that was keeping safe in her Bible—it's gone, the same as if we never had it" (40). Beulah uses such series in describing Gloria (69) and her late brother Sam Dale (221), Jack in picturing the beleaguered Buick ("Singing along, good as gold, fighting along against the laws of gravity, and just daring you to come near her" [150]), Gloria of the normal school, "Not enough of anything to go round, not enough room, not enough teachers, not enough money, not enough beds, not enough electric light bulbs, not enough books," setting off the catalog with a quick irony, "It wasn't too different from the orphanage" (245). Mostly the series provide compact and speedy summaries, as in Vaughn's list of the bonds holding together the parts of the tow-train at the end, "Trace chains, well rope, Moody towline, fence wire, and Elvie's swing" (399), but a series can produce a pounding intensity à la Brontë, as in Miss Julia's last letter: "Something walls me in, crowds me around, outwits me, dims my eyesight, loses the pencil I had in my hand. I don't trust this, I have my suspicions of it, I don't know what it is I've come to. I don't know any longer" (299).

Welty can have characters speak in antithetical form, as in Judge Moody's "I'm not asking for a Good Samaritan, I'm asking for a man with some know-how" (125); Gloria's double antithesis that has almost an Austen ring, "Jack, I don't know which is worse. . . . What you thought you were going to do, or what you're ending up doing. For the sake of the reunion you were willing to run Judge Moody in the ditch. Now for his sake you are just as willing to break your neck" (126); and Mrs. Moody's exclamation over their fate, "To be saved from falling to the bottom of nowhere by getting blown sky-high with a stick of dynamite!" (140). Others can generalize with the pith of the epigram—Beulah's "You can die from anything if you try good and hard" (279), and Aunt Beck's "Feelings don't get old! . . . We do, but they don't. They go on" (345). And Miss Lexie can annotate an epigram with a series: "But they die. . . . The ones who think highly of you. Or they change, or leave you behind, get married, flit, go crazy" (272), another quick touch of the occasional pathos. Beulah can manage a paradox: when a night-blooming cereus produces, though "not a drop of precious water" was ever diverted to it, she comments, "I reckon it must have thrived on going famished" (349).

Welty has been praised for her "listening," for her "ear." No need to reaffirm that, or dispute it. Yet the passages that I have just been quoting, with their air of the formal or the formed, have a tone or orderedness that is created by the rhetoric of a self-conscious controlling mind rather than that of lay talkers letting fly with native woodnotes wild. To say that Welty has an ear, then, is not the same thing as to say that she is a human tape recorder whose authenticity in dialogue would be confirmed by a linguistic survey of the region where her characters live. We have rather to say that she composes dialogue that has an impressive air of authenticity. Now it may be that certain locutions and that even certain parallelisms and antitheses do come out of a heard speech, but I suspect that Welty is hearing—what? a probability rather than a going practice of speech. That is, given the feelings they have and a rhetorical impulse (rather than a contentment with an unplanned dribble of words about the things to be expressed), the speakers might speak as she makes them do. The special orderings of words symbolize an element—a mood, an ambition, perhaps even a parodic sense—not lacking or unimaginable in these characters. In making such a surmise I am seeking an approach to the authenticity, as I have called it, of unexpected elements in colloquial style.

A writer with a good ear for regional or dialectal speech has of course other sources of style. Hardy can suddenly shift from a fluid Wessex idiom to a heavy-weather cumbersomeness and even the pedantries of the auto-didact. Welty, however, has not a trace of the academic or the inadvertently pretentious. She does not philosophize, as Hardy does; as I have already said, she is rarely analytical or interpretive. Hence she has little need for the kind of logical language used by virtually all nineteenth-century novelists, who were constantly doing formal commentary. In her nondialogue passages she rarely shapes sentences up by balance, symmetry, counterpoise, and so on. She characteristically uses a series not to control the materials but to hurry over them unsentimentally, as Meredith often did. Jack pursues Gloria, she "rounding the bank its whole way around, swiftly past the piecrust edge, streaking by the peephole, clicking across the limestone, bounding over the hummocks, taking the hollow places skip by skip without a miss, threading serpentine through the plum bushes, softly around the baby, and back to the tree, where he reached with both hands and had her" (111).

Choice and ordering of words both serve an antisentimental effect. Granny "put kisses on top of their heads like a quick way to count them" (10); Jack "bounced kisses . . . on cheeks and . . . chin" (228); Uncle Noah Webster "kissed [Beulah] with such a bang that she nearly dropped" his present (12). There are unexpected combinations: the boy's "stubborn voice still soft as a girl's" (8); the moon "going down on flushed cheek" (3); the honey's "clover smell as strong as hot pepper" (11); a "stinging veil of long-dead grass . . . hid cowpats dry as gunpowder" (98); Brother Bethune's fingers "rainbow-colored with tobacco stain" (106); and the bus-load of funeral-bound schoolteachers "rainbow dressed" (157); and Gloria's phrasing of her devotion to Jack: "I love him worse than any boy I'd ever seen" (320). Visual images abound, fresh in themselves or in combination. A single abstract word adds a note of mystery to an early-morning scene: "Mists, voids, patches of wood and naked clay, flickered like live ashes, pink and blue" (4). Several strong-action verbs and an engineering simile picture the hairdos of Renfro females: they "raked their hair straight back, cleaved it down the middle, pulled it skintight into plaits. Miss Beulah ran hers straight as a railroad track around her head" (7). A special eye appears in many visual images. Once there is a "wall of copper-colored dust" (8); later "bales of dust tumbled behind" a truck (153). Welty distinguishes "solid" mud like "the balled roots of a tree out of the ground" from a "thinner, fresher mud like gingerbread batter" (395). She can do the quick snapshot—"She prisses to meet him" (30)—or the more painstaking camera study, as of the child's eyes "open nearly to squares, almost shadowless, the blue so clear that bright points like cloverheads could be seen in them deep down" (47), or make what sounds commonplace very suggestive, as in hills "near but of faint substance against the August sky" (99). Some effective verbs: "the baby . . . peep-eyed at Judge Moody with the puff of her sleeve" (141); the wagon "tunnelled into the shade" (229); the "cutting smell of coal oil" (347). Auditory images can be very original: "the air shook with birdsong" (46–47); the mockingbird was "singing the two sides of a fight" (22); a man's "thready voice" (22). The numerousness of "loud" words for speaking— "screamed," "shouted," "shrieked"—gives point to the ironic "again quiet threatened" (340). A subtle and often beguiling use of the auditory appears in synesthetic metaphors, which more than once define the seen by the heard, as in "A long thin cloud crossed [the moon] slowly, drawing itself out like a name being called" (3); dresses "rattling clean" (8); a quilt looking "rubbed over every inch with soft-colored chalks that repeated themselves, more softly than the voices sounding off on the porch" (46); a burning caterpillar web made "an oval cottony glow, like utterly soft sound" (348). Once Welty interprets the olfactory by the tactile—"a smell, more of warmth than wet" (3)—and a sound by a striking use of the visual: a "female voice, superfine, carrying, but thin as a moonbeam" (359). Welty then goes on into a rare lyric description of the night as perceived by twelve-year-old Vaughn Renfro, a passage that might have a place in *A Midsummer Night's Dream*. In this, she has a flux of images for the moonlight: it had "the thickness of china" (362); the world "had been dosed with moonlight, it might have been poured from a bottle" (363); Vaughn "waded through the moonlight"; the flowers "looked like big clods of the moonlight freshly turned up from this night" (366). Then, in contrast with this viscous, palpable light: "Lightning branched and ran over the world with an insect lightness" (367). She can get the same kind of speed in the one long sentence in the novel (about 175 words) by a quick succession of relatively short syntactic units joined by ten *and's* (407–8).

Welty has another stylistic device that amplifies the sense of vibrant life: she uses verbs that imply will, intention, and feelings in animals, plants, and even inanimate objects. The dogs "tried to bark [the teetering car] on over as fast as possible" (120), one dog "barked the truck off the road in spite of a dozen hounds" (381–82), and dogs along the road were "barking everything on past" (403). Stovall's pair of oxen would be a dubious rescue team since they are, Mr. Renfro alleges, "as set on mischief as they can be . . . as you'll know if you can read the glints in their eyes" (140). Plant life can be libertine or cooperative. The cactus "grew down in long reaches as if trying to clamber out of the tub," and Buelah is sure "it's making up its mind to bloom tonight" (18); when it does, Aunt Birdie claims, "We scared it into blooming" (349). The Renfro-dynamited tree exposes a mass of roots, "bringing along their bed of clay, as if a piece of Boone County had decided to get up on its side"; Jack says it's "clinging. . . . Waiting to see what's the next thing to come along," and Welty adds a brilliantly imaginative note, "Nothing but memory seemed ever to have propped the tree" (378); when it finally falls over the edge, Gloria interprets, "Mrs. Moody scared it down" (393). A cyclone animated many objects: "our stove, waltzing around with our lunch pails, and the map flapping its wings and flying away, and our coats was galloping over our heads with Miss Julia's cape trying to catch 'em. And the wind shrieking like a bunch of rivals at us children!" (237). The wind ruined the Methodist church but spared the close-by Baptist church;

Mr. Renfro concludes, "I'll tell you something as contrary as people are. Cyclones" (238). When a tire on the stranded Buick blows, Jack has a recipe for saving the others: "let the air out of the others before they start copying" (142). Jack is sure that the car is "Just breaking its heart to go over" (148); Beulah says that someone is "going to have to coax that car *down*" (199), and Gloria's analysis of the situation is, "I scared it up. . . . I only wish it was in my power this morning to scare it down again" (with that elegant moving forward of "this morning" from the final spot where it would normally clomp down: one of these occasional modifications of ordinary run-on speech by a special control over some part, 377).

In trying to describe Welty's style—with its speed, bounce, freshness, and frequent unexpectedness, and with its creation of a sense of movement and life in all the elements of the world—I have saved last place for her most frequent rhetorical device: her comparisons. She uses "like," "as," "as if," "as though," and "as-adjective-as" almost 700 times (a casual count induced by my own curiosity and claiming only approximate accuracy); of these, almost 400 are similes with "like." Welty instinctively—perhaps obsessively, provided the word is not used pejoratively—presents people and things by means of resemblances. She may portray one element more sharply, bring quite different things together into one existence, or heighten attention by surprise or shock. She wars against clichés and the hackneyed; she makes familiar life take on newness from striking or even thrilling comparisons. To show the range, here are three different sensory effects on succeeding pages: visual—"her vaccination scar shone at them like a tricky little mirror" (13); olfactory—"white organdy, smelling like hot bread from the near-scorch of her perfect ironing" (14); auditory—"four yards of organdy that with scratching sounds, like frolicking mice, covered all three steps" (15). She can make an old taste new—"fall plums . . . whose sucked skins tasted like pennies" (101)—and give unusual reality to an embrace by means of a surprising tactile effect: "Their hearts shook them, like two people pounding at the same time on both sides of a very thin door" (99). A machine may be pictured through the animal—"The truck sprang up like some whole flock of chickens alarmed to the pitch of lunacy" (392); the animal through the human—hounds "loudly sniffing, like ladies being unjustly accused" (142); and nature through the human—"whirly-winds of dust marched, like scatterbrained people" (21).

Visual surprises are constant: "The distant point of the ridge, like the tongue of a calf, put its red lick on the sky" (3–4); "trees . . . lit up, like roosters astrut with golden tails" (4); "butterflies . . . whirling around each other as though lifted through the air by an invisible eggbeater" (30); "hair . . . red as a cat's ear against the sun" (47); dust "climbed . . . in clouds like boxcars" (105), "went up like a big revival tent with the flaps popping" (153); "There stood the moon, like somebody at the door" (286); "The moon, like an eye turned up in a trance, filmed over" (367); a part of the truck "motor . . . glistening like a chocolate cake" (402); a "horse ran lightly as a blown thistledown" (434). Auditory images have the same novelty. Watermelons, "spanked" by Mr. Renfro, "resounded like horses ready to go" (63); the tin roof made a "sound like all the family spoons set to jingling in their glass" (71); the "song of the locusts" was "a long sound like a stream of dry seed being poured into an empty bucket" (271). Welty can impute a palpable body to sound—"a sound . . . thin as that of a veil being parted" (118); a mockingbird "threw down two or three hard notes on him like a blacksmith driving in nails" (119); to light—the "substance fine as dust that began to sift down . . . was moonlight" (311); "lights hard as pickaxe blows drove down from every ceiling" (312); as Jack and Gloria came into a shady spot, "The final glare dropped from them like a set of clothes" (99); to smell—"The smell of the cloth flooded over them, like a bottle of school ink spilled" (78); to atmosphere—a "shaft of heat, solid as a hickory stick" (4). Welty can be ironic—insect bites make the baby look "like she's been embroidered in French knots" (358)—or playful and fantastic: a cake of ice is "Dense with ammonia, like fifty cents' worth of the moon" (184). The similes that increase the liveliness of an already pulsating and bounding prose by declaring or hinting the likeness of unlikes (numerous metaphors do this too) may also hint at thematic elements that are not much articulated openly. "'I bet you Banner School had a library as long as your arm,' cried Aunt Birdie as though she saw a snake" (274). The "as though" clause tells us something about the local state of mind that makes the scene a trying one for teachers. The high heels of Gloria "tilted her nearly to tiptoe, like a bird ready to fly" (19); later we learn that Gloria would take Jack and fly away if she could. But we already have got, and continue to get, figurative hints about such aspirations: "flickered the yellow butterflies of August like dreams" (20). The same image and idea soon surface again: "Out there with her [Gloria] flew the yellow butterflies of August—as wild and bright as people's notions and dreams, but filled with a dream of their own; in one bright body, as though against a headwind, they were flying toward the east" (39). Again, "The old man came . . . climbing the path like a rickety ladder of his dreams" (103–4). If Welty does not openly interpret man's fate, such figures give a furtive imaginative clue to her sense of how things go.

The encyclopedic quotation in this section is risky. I can only protest that I have been highly selective, so much so as constantly to feel that I am not adequately communicating Welty's rich campaigns that win stylistic wars. But quoting and quoting and quoting, be it too much viewed one way or too little viewed another, can alone give a sense of a literary reality. The other alternative is the critic's abstract words of identification and praise, words that cannot absent themselves for a long while but that at their best remain a large distance from the objects they strive to account for.

V

Welty's natural tendency to juxtapose, and often unite, diverse matters— many local stories of past and present, farcical and disastrous events, dramatic dialogue and novelistic description of scene and tone, and above all the sharply contrasting materials brought together in the comparisons that gush forth inexhaustibly—appears more in her themes than in her characters. There is a very large cast of characters, too many to distinguish fully: we tend to be more aware of their common elements as members of a community than of their individualizing traits of personality. They all adhere to the same basic ideas, customs, rites; they have the same general emotional contours. The four married Beecham brothers and their wives can hardly be separated without special effort. Yet no characters are ciphers; virtually all of them have great general vitality; the Dickensian humor that I mentioned earlier appears in the characterization. We see types, key motives, psychological colorations providing the felt life of reunionists and others. Granny is frail, forgetful, and free to mow down anybody at any time. Mr. Renfro is the born loser—his mishaps with the dynamite to which he is addicted symbolize the way things go with him—who still manages a singular equanimity. His wife, Beulah, the reunion hostess, is an energetic manager, immensely talkative, sharp on occasions, ironic, an immense admirer of her son Jack, but able to say of him, since he wrote no letters during his eighteen months in the pen, that he "never did unduly care for pencil and paper" (16) and to "hope" that his Grandpa's death will "help him grow up a little" (69). Aunt Beck is regularly identified as "gentle," Aunt Nanny as ballooning and hearty. Aunt Cleo is blunt and disparaging: of the home-towns of reunionists, "Never heard of any of it" (18); of Gloria's wedding ring, "What'd you have to do? Steal it?" (48); of Jack's having a truck, "You-all [the Renfros] don't look like you was ever that well-fixed" (67). Vaughn Renfro, age twelve, is a bit jealous of the heroic stature that all attribute to Jack and can show considerable competence in the tasks he takes on. Gloria, the teacher who married into the Beechams, passionately longs not to be a Beecham; in marrying Jack, she chose "feeling" over a teaching career and over Miss Julia's opposition; she is aloof but not rude and can be strong at key moments. Hero Jack is strong, lively, helpful, fond of the hill country, devoted to the family, tender and affectionate to his wife and daughter; he takes charge of the Buick rescue but is not very effective except for one astonishing strong-man feat; normally considerate, he surpasses himself in thinking of his imprisonment as a kind of penance for the murder committed by Uncle Nathan: "maybe it's evened up, and now the poor old man can rest" (431). Judge Moody and his wife have tasted a thin slice of a larger world, and their occasional ironic remarks have a shade more of self-consciousness and knowingness; the judge goes beyond the others in a mildly sad reflectiveness upon the human state as reflected in Miss Julia's career and demise. Mrs. Moody fluctuates between a narrow-gauge ordinariness and occasional sharp insight, as when she says of Miss Julia, "A tyrant, if there ever was one. Oh, for others' own good, of course!" (325).

But even with certain identifying marks that help us keep Jack and Jill, or Tom and Dick, apart, the individual psyche is not quite the business of the novel; individuals may have idiosyncrasies, but basically they participate in the group consciousness—the style, the attitudes, the mores, the traditions of their time and place. The men and women enact parts in the myth that orders their lives. We are not centrally held by the problem of how individual experiences are going to turn out; for the most part we know, or at least are allowed to think we do. There are no demanding plot lines to make us focus on the development of relationships or the resolution of conflicts. But in the medley of passing actions and endless talk that embrace an annual ritual, a social day's trivialities and serious moments, and a few hours' recollections of past crises that helped shape present life—in these there is a kind of plot of meanings that, though we may be incompletely conscious of it, is what holds us. These people's assumptions and values appear, sometimes explicitly but often only implicitly, in thematic strands woven into a quite variegated texture.

Of the themes that operate through gossip, jest, remembered events, and domestic and roadside small movements, the chief one is that of community. To take a fairly obvious phase of this first: Banner is a "Christian community." No one is antichurch, church talk is frequent, a reunion needs a preacher-orator, and nobody works on the Sabbath, especially if work means helpfulness. But what Welty finds underneath this is a kind of secular ecclesiasticism: denominational allusions make us picture the rivalry of clubs or lodges. The Methodist and Baptist churches are across the street from each other, and it is doubtless equally symbolic when they are brought closer together by a cyclone that "picked the Methodist Church all up in one piece and carried it through the air and set it down right next to the Baptist Church!" (238). When Brother Bethune rambles on in his reunion discourse, Aunt Beck demands, "Can't you make that church rivalry sound a little stronger?" (193). Mrs. Moody is sure that Curly Stovall, who has a phone in his store, can be got to open up even on the Sabbath; she argues, "I'm sure he's no more than a Baptist" (128). On the other hand, when Grandpa Vaughn, a "real, real Baptist," went to a Methodist revival and unexpectedly found "infant Baptism" going on, he gave unequaled "heartfelt groans" (182). Rachel Sojourner, Gloria's presumptive mother, may have got into trouble, it is proposed, when she "took to going Sunday-riding with call-him-a-Methodist." Aunt Beck annotates, "Well, you know how Baptists stick together. . . . They like to look far afield to find any sort of transgressor" (265). The style of both Baptists and Methodists leads Mrs. Moody to declare, with the candor that nearly all practice, "I'm neither one, and gladder of it every minute" (406). When a churchful of Methodists, homeward bound after service, indifferently drive by the stranded Buick, Mrs. Moody comments, "I'd just like to see a bunch of Presbyterians try to get by me that fast!" (134). She is a Presbyterian, and she wishes that the graveside service for Miss Julia were in the charge of a "down-to-earth Presbyterian" instead of a Catholic priest, once a student of Miss Julia's who, observers declare, "Worshipped himself, didn't he?" (430). Several years before, Uncle Noah Webster had identified Judge Moody as a Presbyterian because "The whole way through that trial, his mouth was one straight line" (61). Aunt Beck approaches closest to tolerance of Presbyterians. Miss Julia, she says, "was a Presbyterian, and no hiding that. But was she deep-dyed? . . . There's a whole lot of different grades of 'em, some of 'em aren't too far off from Baptists" (277). "Deep-dyed" beautifully conveys the sense of an alien other which, however, may not descend as far into gross error as it might.

Although ecclesiastical affiliation is an important bond, the Bible behind the churches enters the story in only a few casual allusions. (There are, I think, no allusions to classical myth.) Of these, three are used to illustrate Brother Bethune's fuzziness: he calls Jack, just home from prison, "The Prodigal Son" (105, 107); he calls the reunion dinner "Belshazzar's Feast," remembering only belatedly to add, "without no Handwriting on the Wall to mar it" (177); and he alludes to Granny Vaughn and her late husband as "David and Jonathan" (184). One biblical allusion, rather funny at the moment of utterance, may have some value as a pointer. When Jack resolves to use main strength to bounce the Buick off its nose into a more functional position, his mother, Beulah, "cried frantically," that is, with ebullient pride, "Now watch! Reminds me of Samson exactly! . . . Only watch my boy show the judgment Samson's lacking, and move out of the way when it starts coming!" (394). Jack does—double success. We recall this passage in the final scene when Jack and Gloria look at all the problems that still do not cancel hope. Jack says, "And I've got my strength" (434) and again, "But I still got my strength" (435). Gloria is no Delilah to his Samson; indeed, rather than enslave him to another people, she would save him from what she takes to be bondage to his own.

If churches provide some of the ritual forms of local life, place and family appear to be more fundamental sources of community. All the Vaughns and Beechams are, or once were, Bannerites; Aunt Cleo's rude inquisitiveness seems to be that of an alien; and the condescension of the Moodys from Ludlow is less a valid judgment than outsiders' instinct for shortcomings. Jack's love for this hill country, drought stricken though it now is, is the aesthetic affirmation of local loyalty. What an unsympathetic outsider might call provincialism also comes through as a unifying sense of place. Yet this is several times managed humorously rather than solemnly. When a "boy cousin" thinks that Jack, not yet arrived, may be in Arkansas, Beulah exclaims, "Arkansas would be the crowning blow! . . . No, my boy may be in Parchman, but he still hasn't been dragged across the state line" (70). The sentiment arises even more emphatically when all learn that Jack and Gloria may be first cousins, who according to a recent Mississippi law may not marry, and when Judge Moody suggests that they could avoid legal trouble by heading out to Alabama, "not over a few dozen miles" away. "'Alabama!' cried Jack, a chorus of horrified cries behind him. 'Cross the state line? That's what Uncle Nathan's done! . . . leave all we hold dear and all that holds us dear? . . . Why, it would put an end to the reunion'" (321).

The reunion is the preeminent symbol of family feeling. In fact, to lack the symbol is to lack right feeling, the substance that earns respect. Uncle Curtis finishes off the Comfort family: "The Comforts don't know what the word reunion means" (60). The Beechams won family honor because Jack's trial "drew" large crowds from all the villages that Beechams live in. Uncle Curtis provides consolation for the family's temporary loss of Jack to Parchman: of his nine sons, he says, "maybe not a one of 'em had to go to Parchman, but they left home just the same. Married. . . . All nine! And they're never coming home" (66–67). Beulah sums up the Beechams as a "strict, law-abiding, God-fearing, close-knit family, and everybody in it has always struggled the best he knew how and we've all just tried to last as long as we can by sticking together" (344). The day ends with "the joining-of-hands" as they form a circle, sing "Blest Be the Tie," and hear Brother Bethune's benediction (348–49). The reunion even provides a metaphor for the feelings of Vaughn Renfro on a moonlight mission: "the world around him was still one huge, soul-defying reunion" (363).

Behind the esprit de corps, which of course does not eliminate sarcasms and clashes, lie certain patterns of thought and feeling that govern family style and actions. Before Jack arrives on stage, all the talk about him builds him up as a heroic figure—a man of charisma and with the talents of the culture hero: he can right wrongs and solve problems such as those of the drought-ridden farm. When he crashes in, there are epic signs and portents—dogs barking, people screaming, the new roof "seemed to quiver," "the floor drummed and swayed, a pan dropped from its nail in the kitchen wall" (71): half great hurrah and half parody. With little delay a new large task is imposed on the hero. In thumbing his way back from Parchman, he had got one ride by clinging to the spare tire on the rear of a car. When the car went into a ditch, Jack was there to play Hercules as Good Samaritan: "Put shoulder to wheel and upped him out" (79). Now he learns that the driver was the very Judge Moody who had sentenced him to jail, and everyone censures Jack for rescuing an enemy (81 ff.); the consensus is that he must retaliate. As Aunt Birdie puts it, "Now you can make a monkey out of him. . . . That's all the reunion is asking of you" (86). Family feeling develops the spirit of the feud; it gets to Jack, and all the men (with dogs) happily prepare to set off on an anti-Moody skirmish without any clear plans. Jack insists on his "family duty . . . to get Judge Moody tucked away in a ditch like he was in" (103) and "announce myself to him" (117). But the feudist spirit of getting even is not unanimous; Beulah sees only trouble in the plan, Gloria votes her "common sense" (112) against it (we remember the women in *Coriolanus*), Aunt Beck is "always in danger of getting sorry for the other side" (293), and Jack's father a little later takes "a shine" to the judge (359). What finally aborts the feudist foray, however, is wonderfully ironic, as we have seen: not a change of heart, but a combination of farce and melodrama in which the judge is a victim, not of a Beecham plot, but of his own humanity, running his car not down into a ditch but up on to an impossible perch. Jack promptly turns retaliation into gratitude because the judge "saved my wife and baby" (198), and shifts his role from wrecker to rescuer of the car.

The theme of the feud is thus metamorphosed into two other themes. The first is the most amply developed of the biblical materials—the story of the Good Samaritan. There are several roadside scenes in which helpfulness is possible, and Welty's pictures of human responses are always partly ironic. Hitching rides home from jail, Jack was helped by several Good Samaritans but wearied of the pious discourses to which they treated him. Then he hopped onto the rear of the Moody Buick, reporting that "Judge Moody was one and didn't know it" (196). The judge's unconsciousness of role is contrasted with Jack's great consciousness of his; referring to his various roadside efforts, he quite likes to call himself a "Good Samaritan" (125, 149, 163). He in turn is contrasted with other passersby who are indifferent, unhelpful, or profit-seeking, and then his goodwill with his overall competence, so that the judge can wish for expertise instead of Good Samaritanism (125). Thus Welty provides several perspectives on the myth.

While the ethic of the feud is reversed in the Good Samaritan theme, it is continued in another theme implicitly present—that of chivalry: in both, life focuses on recurrent combat. Welty introduces substantial, if subtle, suggestions of the chivalric, this in a village scene where subsistence problems are onerous: another mark of her originality. The relations between the Beechams and Curly Stovall are basically feudist, clearly. But then when Curly and Jack meet, they fall into each other's arms, pound happily on each other, and trade amiable insults; Jack calls Curly "skunk" (146), "rascal," and "greedy hog" (148)—all this in the tradition of frontier humor. But they have been opponents in a way that keeps reminding us of tournament competition; the initiating action of the novel was a duel of theirs in the past, and near the end there is another. In each of these the take-off point is a little interchange between Jack's sister Ella Fay, sixteen, and Curly; thus Jack is not too distant from the traditional defender of womanhood. Further, in a flashback narrative in midnovel we learn that a duel broke out when Curly aspired to the favors of Gloria—a battle that came "close to taking the cake," even though Jack "got beat" (205). A truck has the status of a tournament prize, so that uncertainties over its ownership lead the uncles to happy anticipation: "*Now* we've got a war on that's like old times! Jack and Curly buttin' head-on again!" (206). The final duel has interesting ramifications. After Jack knocks Curly down, Ella Fay hints that she may be engaged to Curly, and this leads to some delicate considerations of decorum. At first Jack sees a political marriage that will bring the opponents into "one happy family"; then on second thought he backs off and advances a substitute motion: he will make Curly a "present" of the truck "not to marry into us" (412). Curly is offended by the thought of receiving a present from Jack (as by an antagonist's boast), and Jack by the refusal; Curly swings, Jack is the loser again, and Curly cuts off his shirttail (413)—a trophy of his victory in the lists. Although the word is never used, what is at stake is "honor."

There are other intimations of an underlying chivalric code. Jack constantly uses a formal "sir" in addressing men; he tells some yokels to mind their language, since "There's ladies present" (132); he imagines himself disciplining an unwilling helper of the judge by "sitting on his chest where I could pound some willingness in him" (143). Curly doesn't want to play second fiddle while Jack "save[s] one more lady" but insists, "*I'm* going to go ahead and save her while you watch" (151). Shortly after Jack's returning home, he and his brother Vaughn got hold of a "pair of dried cornstalks" and "jousted with them" (72); "every day" in the pen Jack and his friend Aycock Comfort called Judge Moody "Sir Pizen Ivy" (83), a soubriquet repeated several times later (116, 117, 130). Jack has a chivalric sense of obligation; first he is "beholden to the reunion . . . to meet that Judge . . . [and] sing him my name out loud and clear" (112)—a symbolic throwing down of the gauntlet; and then he is totally committed to saving the Buick of the driver who saved his family (130). He craves the glory of single combat: when Judge Moody wants to call in his garageman to help with the Buick, Jack responds with "a stricken look" (128; cf. 134). Perhaps his nicest touch of honor appears in his escape from jail one day before the end of his sentence. "Today was my last chance of making my escape. . . . One more day and I'd had to let 'em discharge me" (360). Discharge on schedule: the commonplace routine of the law rather than the heroic romance of escape.

vi

These low-key hints of the chivalric add charm to the character who is primarily the strong man, the culture hero, and the affectionate family member. Yet there is no case-making for Jack: he is not a magically successful competitor, the legal or political or actual may supersede the chivalric at any time, and both his mother and his wife think Jack not altogether grown up. Telling him about the lost shirttail, Gloria positively forbids a resumption of jousting with Curly. Against Jack as agent of Beecham feudist feeling, Gloria sets out to "pit her common sense" (112); she demands that he modify his Good Samaritanism by using "some of my common sense" (126); opposing Mr. Renfro's application of dynamite to the Buick problem, Gloria insists that all the help Jack needs "is a wife's common sense" (140); and if she does not name her common sense, it is implicitly present in her urging him to give up tilting with Curly (153) and to forget about his pet truck—"a play-pretty. . . . A man's something-to-play with" (425). But there is no case-making for Gloria either; of the competing values, none is espoused as an absolute. Jack is ironically ambivalent about Gloria's common sense. When Gloria tells him about her split with Miss Julia over her marriage to him, Jack asks, "wouldn't she pay regard to your common sense?" (171). On the other hand, Jack can allege that his first Buick-rescue scheme failed because "Gloria run in too quick with her common sense" (140), and on another occasion Welty makes a deadpan comment that Jack "gave a nod, as when she mentioned her common sense to him" (172).

If Gloria wants to detach Jack from the youthful heroic games that add zest to community life, she wants even more to detach him from the

Beechams. "When will we move to ourselves?" (111) she asks him soon after they are alone for the first time, and her last words are "And some day . . . some day yet, we'll move to ourselves" (435). In part this is the conventional desire for a private "little two-room house" (431). But it is also Gloria's revolt against the old community, the pressuring Beecham way of life. Symbolically, she sits outside the family group at the reunion. She presents herself—an illusion? a part truth?—as trying to "*save Jack . . . save him! From everybody I see this minute! . . . I'll save him yet! . . . I don't give up easy!*" (198). Again, "I was trying to save him! . . . [From] this mighty family!" (320). She never articulates the Beecham shortcoming; she perhaps believes that they take rather than give. She tells Jack, "The most they ever do for you is brag on you." But Jack insists that, despite her book learning, "about what's at home, there's still a little bit left for you to find out" (137). Near the end they have an argument, both of them affectionate and tender, but both holding to their positions; the summary lines are "Honey, won't you change your mind about my family?" and "Not for all the tea in China." She adds, "You're so believing and blind" (360).

Miss Lexie declares at one point, "The world isn't going to let you have a thing both ways" (280). But the author says, in effect, that you can't help living with it both ways: in this central action we see Jack clinging to two loyalties—to old family and new—and feeling them as equally valid. The two communities are mutually jealous. Gloria's worst moment comes when an old postcard message indicates that her father may have been the late Sam Dale Beecham. Being a Beecham is "ten times worse" than anything else. "Welcome into the family!" cries Aunt Nanny, and they force Gloria through an initiation rite that is a mixture of farce and humiliation. It is a baptism by total immersion—in the watermelon hyperbolically provided for the reunion. They rub her face in it and order her to say "Beecham," but she keeps on denying the identity (268–70). Later Jack says it was just a family welcome, but Gloria bitterly harps on one detail that may be symbolic: "They pulled me down on dusty ground . . . to wash my face in their sticky watermelon juice" (313). "Pulled me down": the rite was various things, and leveling was clearly one of them. The outsider, the teacher, the individual who felt apart, must be cut down to community size. Community survival would demand that.

The matter of Gloria's identity—her actual parenthood remains at least partially speculative, as if facts themselves partook of the "ambiguity" that Welty has recently said is the nature of life—is thematically relevant to her would-be secession from the Beechams. Jack wants her to have only a present, not a past, identity: "She's Mrs. J. J. Renfro, that's who she is" (346). Gloria spells this out more fully: "I'm here to be nobody but myself, Mrs. Gloria Renfro, and have nothing to do with the old dead past" (361)—her version of a recurrent human dream. She is not merely bucking Beechamhood; in general she treats the present not as a residue of the past but as the genesis of a future. Her "common sense" is mingled with a visionary tendency: she constantly looks ahead expectantly, just as she did in settling on a teaching career (47). "All that counts in life is up ahead," she says (315). "That's for the future to say," she says on two occasions (65, 320), on the second of which she falls into romantic prophecy, "We'll live to ourselves one day yet, and do wonders." Another time she humorously modifies her teacher's aspirations: she would no longer "change the world" but "just my husband. I still believe I can do it, if I live long enough" (356). One episode is funny and painful and symbolic. Jack is in his tug-of-war with the Buick and there is this exchange between Gloria and him:

> "I don't see our future, Jack" she gasped.
> "Keep looking, sweetheart."
> "If we can't do any better than we're doing now, what will Lady May think of us when we're old and gray?"
> "Just hang onto my heels, honey," he cried out.
> "We're still where we were yesterday. In the balance," Gloria said. (390)

The moment of doubt enriches a picture that is mostly in another color. Once Gloria says that Lady May is "our future" (358); throughout the Buick ordeal she "tried to keep my mind on the future" (421), and at the end she promises, "I'll just keep right on thinking about the future, Jack" (434).

So there is thematic significance in the clashes between the hereditary community—the embracing Banner-Beecham world summed up in the reunion and its rituals—and the small new community that lives only in the imprecise visions of the orphan-teacher-young wife. But the *only* is inaccurate. For Gloria is carrying on, in her own way, the tradition first voiced by Miss Julia Mortimer, the by now mythical figure whose career was an espousal of values different from those that rule the local scene. She dies on reunion day, the very day when her protégée Gloria starts her life with Jack, just home from prison; Julia was "in love with Banner School" (294), Aunt Beck says (we also learn that Julia was attractive enough to have suitors), while Gloria, over Julia's protests, has married a Beecham. Different arena, but same battle, as key words show. While Gloria eyes the future but no longer seeks to "change the world," Miss Julia writes, just a little before her death, "I always thought . . . I could change the future" (298). Or, as Gloria puts it, Julia "didn't want anybody left in the dark, not about anything. She wanted everything brought out in the wide open, to see and be known" (432). Gloria still hopes for some success; Julia reports that she herself has failed. But through Judge Moody we also learn that she has had some spectacular successes: she coached good pupils and pushed some of them into careers of note, and, early mindful of what we now call the "delivery" of professional services, persuaded the young lawyer Moody to stay in his home county—for which he "never fully forgave her" (305)—instead of following her other protégées into a larger world.

Although we learn much about Miss Julia from her deathbed letter to the judge and from his account of her, the heroic antagonist of the local status quo is presented mainly by a technical tour de force: the memories and commentary of ex-pupils who thus portray both themselves and their relentless quixotic challenger. At times they praise her for having taught them all they know, for having made them what they are; more often they portray her as a tormentor, a dragon, a fiend to be escaped. Julia and later Gloria put teaching above everything; it had to go on, come cyclone, flood, fight, angry parents, or local spectacles. But Miss Beulah says that no children of hers can be kept "shut up in school, if they can figure there's something going on somewhere! . . . They're not exactly idiots" (27), and she promises a chastised child, "And for the rest of your punishment, you're to come straight home from school today and tell me something you've learned" (374). Many such remarks give body to Gloria's assessment of Julia: "All she wanted was a teacher's life. . . . But it looked like past a certain point nobody was willing to let her have it" (294). Having heard some of the facts of "that teacher's life," Jack is sure it sounds like "getting put in the Hole [at the pen]! Kept in the dark, on bread and water, and nobody coming to get you out!" (312). Miss Julia, reports Gloria, "saved me from the orphanage—even if it was just to enter me up at Normal" (316)—an inadvertent picture of the education of an educator. Jack nicely sums up the local view of education when he says he's "thankful I come along in time to save my wife from a life like hers" (313).

This world is not an easy one in which to spread light. Miss Julia was independent, solitary, single-minded, respected, feared, a thorn in the flesh of the community, a Quixote with longer career, more bite, less laughableness. Perhaps in retirement she was a little mad; perhaps it served the ends of Miss Lexie, her attendant, to think her so; or more likely Miss Lexie did think her so. Miss Lexie imprisoned her, "tied her. . . . Tied her in bed" (278), and Miss Julia had to be desperately heroic to get letters out to Judge Moody. At the funeral her former student Dr. Carruthers says briefly, "Neglect, neglect! *Of course* you can die of it! Cheeks were a skeleton's! I call it starvation, pure and simple" (430). It is entirely possible that, through a nurse unimaginative enough to treat illness with tyrannous severity, Welty is satirizing a community for callousness amounting to cruelty. And yet the main drift of her art is not in that direction; the fate of Miss Julia, important as it is, is not made a predominant issue but is one of many matters presented in many tones. Welty does not tend to discover goodies and baddies. She is not bitterly condemning viciousness but rather symbolizing a neglectfulness that may, alas, crop up in any human community.

Miss Julia is the spokesman for one value, not an allegory of an ideal. Nor, on the other hand, do the three B's of folk life—Banner, Baptist, Beecham— simply define a culpable crassness. If this life is limited, it still has its own virtues of clan solidarity, humor, hopefulness; it has been molded by a succession of disasters that in the chatter and clatter of a busy day's doings we may almost lose sight of but that surface now and then in flickers of distressed awareness. As Mr. Renfro says on one occasion, "It's all part of the reunion. We got to live it out, son" (211)—the reunion as not only jolly get-together but also a shared reexperiencing of many troubles. His wife, Beulah, puts this still more strongly after they have gone to bed: "I've got it to stand and I've got to stand it. And you've got to stand it. . . . After they've all gone home, Ralph, and the children's in bed, that's what's left. Standing it" (360). We can't help thinking of Faulkner's "They endured."

If Welty is not a satirist, she is even less a regional historian. A regional idiom she does use—the idiom of spoken style and social style. Yet it is a medium, not of local reportage, but finally of a wide and deep picture of American life. The dualism of this life—or better, one of its dualisms— is the larger reality implicit in the confrontation between Miss Julia and Gloria on the one hand, and Banner and Beechams on the other. On the one hand there is the family, the historical community, with its sustaining and unifying legacy of habits, customs, rites, and loyalties; its sense of actuality, its tendency to see the way things were as the way things are, its embodiment of "the system." On the other hand are the teachers— outsiders in Banner (the Ludlow belle and the orphan) and hence natural voices for alteration of the status quo. In them we see the side of the national personality that turns away from the past and toward the future, places a high value on change, has unlimited faith in education, believes in "enlightenment," is full of aspiration, longs for a "better life," can become visionary and utopian and may bring forth, to borrow from Mrs. Moody's description of Miss Julia, "tyrants . . . for others' own good." Still there are no allegorical rigidities; Miss Julia remains the lifelong prod from without, Gloria marries and hopes to bore from within. Her "future" may turn out to be no more than her small private acreage within the system; feeling superior to the Beechams, she must tearfully acknowledge, "One way or the other, I'm kin to everybody in Banner" (313). If the teachers are in one sense quixotic visionaries, still Gloria believes in her own "common sense," and she turns it against that other chivalry that Jack has imbibed from local tradition. "Family" and "future" both want to possess hero Jack; drawn both ways, he may embody an unresolvable division or foreshadow such reconciliations as now and then we come to for a time. He may refertilize the drought-plagued wasteland or simply duplicate the Beechams in a new Renfro family. Talk of the future though she does, Gloria can still sadly ask at the very end, "Oh, Jack, does this mean it'll all happen over again?" (435)

On all this Welty looks with a vast, but never bitter, irony.

vii

In sketching the ways in which a Mississippi story plays variations on a central American myth—"variations" of course means hitting on innovations, altering patterns, mixing perspectives rather than taking sides—I am trying to communicate the sense of magnitude that this novel creates (as satire, which mostly gratifies prejudices, rarely does). The sense of magnitude is also served by the undercover wispy reminiscences of European myths and specifically of two wholly dissimilar works, a Greek tragedy and an English comic novel—Sophocles' *Oedipus* and Fielding's *Joseph Andrews*. To propose such analogies may seem pretty portentous, a laborious artifice of magnification, but since the resemblances came to me as a spontaneous overflow of powerful impressions on first reading, and since, recollected in tranquillity, they do not die away, I will take the risk.

During the reunion-day conversation, the talk occasionally takes a turn that Beulah tries to head off. In doing this, she somehow reminded me of Jocasta, who catches on to the truth before Oedipus does and urges him not to go further. Neither Jocasta nor Beulah succeeds. Just as Jocasta's son-husband had committed a murder in the past, so, we learn, had Beulah's brother Nathan; both men suffer self-mutilation and exile. Oedipus, coming to Thebes, returns unknowingly to his native city; so does Gloria when she comes to Banner (as Aunt Birdie says, in folk Sophoclean, "you was coming right back to where you started from. . . . Just as dangerous as a little walking stick of dynamite" [319]). Both are "orphans." Oedipus marries a woman who turns out to be his mother; Gloria marries a man who, it turns out, may be her first cousin, which would mean, at that time and place, statutory incest. Oedipus's mother-wife and Gloria's unwed mother are both suicides. Oedipus's horror at discovering his relationship to Jocasta and Laius is paralleled by Gloria's sense of disaster in the discovery that she may be a Beecham. The banishment undergone by Oedipus and Nathan is a possibility for Gloria and Jack.

The identity myth that starts with unknown parenthood and proceeds to a crisis of possible incest is an old romantic device that appears in Roman comedy and then resurfaces in moralistic melodrama in the eighteenth century and in comic form in Fielding's *Joseph Andrews* (which happens also to have a very fine roadside Good Samaritan episode). In the world there depicted, people have a habit of mislaying children, and the last of the vicissitudes that afflict the love of Joseph Andrews and Fanny (the Jack Renfro and Gloria of the story) is that they may be brother and sister. Before bringing in the prestidigitation of parenthood that removes the difficulty, Fielding, who is not given to the ambiguity that Welty elects even here, notes different responses to the possibility. Everybody believed it "except Pamela, who imagined, as she had heard neither of her parents mention such an accident, that it must certainly be false; and except the Lady Booby, who suspected the falsehood of the story from her ardent desire that it should be true; and Joseph, who feared its truth, from his earnest wishes that it might prove false" (IV.xiii). Aunt Beck says simply, of Beulah's response to the story that Gloria may be a Beecham, "if the right story comes along at the right time, she'll be like the rest of us and believe what she wants to believe" (267). The psychological comedy is the same as Fielding's.

Fielding, who revels in allusions, makes another joke about Joseph and Fanny: "They felt perhaps little less anxiety in this interval than Oedipus himself, whilst his fate was revealing" (IX.xv). Welty abstains from such allusions, but her plot does have its sketchy analogies to those of Sophocles and Fielding. Likely she never thought of either. The primary critical point is that in imagining human probabilities she fashioned experience in ways that bring to mind the situations developed by such predecessors. That is, she instinctively moved toward fundamental patterns of action that get at basic springs of human experience. Her materials are central rather than eccentric; or, to risk a rather overused word, they are archetypal. But I want especially to stress the fact that her management of materials clustering about the possible incest is reminiscent of *both* Sophocles and Fielding: that the tragic possibility is often just around the corner, or just under the surface, when the main lines of action in the foreground are comic and often, indeed, farcical. We are plunged into tall tales, folk humor, slapstick episodes of unruly persons and objects, all these mediating a life in which wit, non sequiturs, flashes of pathos and anguish, natural disasters, old patterns of feeling (feudist, chivalric, familial, partisan), and a dominantly good-humored, if not successfully channeled, energizing are kaleidoscopically reflected in indefatigable dialogue. Many tones, often side by side unexpectedly, emerge in this presentation of community: community with a time-created coherence that satisfies but constrains, that is filtered through moment-by-moment diversities of manner and positive inconsistencies of attitude, and that is always troubled by the periodic educational evangels with excelsiors that flicker for a while and then give off a dim persistent light. The characters enact the old modes of existence and the change-bound disturbances of them; the author says little. If she spoke from the shadows in which she remains, she might, we surmise, allude to the *comédie humaine,* pointing out that a wide spectrum of the laughable contains bits of the pitiable and the admirable; that *plus ça change, plus c'est la même chose,* that everyman comes to discover, like Gloria, that he is kin to everybody. But she makes no such observations; she simply sets the scene and makes the actors talk their lives. She does both tasks with immense variety and vitality of style; most characteristically she brings apparent unlikes together. This central habit of style is a symptom of her overall method, which in *Losing Battles* conspicuously wins the artist's war against the chaos of tumbling history and sprawling experience—wins it even while camouflaging the victorious form in the multiplicity and miscellaneousness of the defeated antagonist.

16

Three Generations of English Studies
Impressions

Some three decades ago Douglas Knight, then a young Ph.D. in English (and later a university president), toyed with a theory of literary generations. The idea, as far as I grasped it, was that the birth of literary eminences got bunched in some way, and that the bunching was meaningful. There would be fertile and infertile decades, and the patterning of these would have some significance in literary history.

Whatever the merits of this theory, it suggests a pattern for the professional lives of professors of English born, say, between 1900 and 1920—a pattern that certainly differentiates them from their predecessors, and may differentiate them from their successors. If we of that generation lived long enough, we experienced three generations of English studies (roughly everything from classroom style to practices of learned journals). We grew up, so to speak, during the reign of old literary history; we spent our middle years coming to terms with (resisting, compromising with, being converted to, whatever) the loosely named "new criticism"; and the natural discomforts of later years were not eased by the insurgency of a new force sometimes called the "new new criticism."

I have used, without planning to, political metaphors—"reign," for example. One might speak, alternatively, of successive emphases, approaches, modes, or even fashions. One's metaphor depends upon whether one thinks of a procedure in terms of its legitimacy, its power, or its transitoriness. One may sense in any mode an enduring convincingness, or a forceful but impermanent impact of novelty, surprise, and shock. I mean, however, to stick mainly to the biological metaphor, which works doubly. It applies both to the succession of practices as each goes through the cycle of growth, full season, and decline, and to the successive responses of the generation-by-years-of-birth to the three generations of dominant or at least most publicized practices: feeling ahead of it, feeling with it, and feeling left behind by it—perhaps inevitably the three ages of academic man.

If one is not with it, he may be so through weakness or weariness, through skepticism of novelty, through faith in an apparently superseded validity, through annoyance or amusement at the confident tongues of the new-age types, or simply through his own version of the odium philologicum that is rarely in remission.

ii

The dominant world of literary history into which the 1900–1920 generation was born had existed for nearly a century: the ways of classical scholarship applied to "modern"—that is, medieval—materials as a sort of by-product of German romanticism, specifically its entrancement with German medievalry. The story of this new mode and of its trickling, and then flooding, into American graduate schools is very familiar. The German connection had a long life. As late as World War I the *Who's Who* entries of academic eminentoes were likely to list German degrees or periods of study at German universities. As late as the 1920s Kemp Malone and Raymond Dexter Havens were telling Hopkins graduate students to go to Germany and find out how it was done. Perhaps the last pilgrim to the German mecca did it about 1930. We would define ourselves as observers by saying either "One of their best men did it" or "One of them actually did it."

The assumption that English scholarship meant medieval studies had a long life; the inclusion of later centuries in "literary history" came slowly. To use the "as late as" formula again: as late as the early 1930s (the years of my own graduate study) the chief courses that Ph.D. candidates at Harvard were required or expected to take were Old and Middle English, Gothic, and Old French—all tools, obviously, for dipping about in the Middle Ages. The Renaissance had already become a respectable field, however, originally, one suspects, as a kind of extension, with variations, of medievalry into later centuries; in Kittredge's hands, Shakespeare seemed pretty much a descendant of medieval forebears (no worse a fate, for that matter, than the later one of being made a predictor of things to come, or an example of limitations happily to be overcome, in our wiser times). But the sense of a past worthy of scholarly pursuit ("research" or the more modest "investigation") was also being extended to several post-Renaissance centuries, even though these had to live with a subtle imputation of triviality. The Widener-carrel scuttlebutt was that if a doctor's oral went so far as the nineteenth century, it was only with a lighthearted air of a game or two after the serious business of the day. We were still at some distance from the state of affairs in which a Ph.D. dissertation can be a coded essay entitled, say, "Three Minimalist Fictioneers of the 1980s" or an extended editorial shaped by one or another current cause.

Whatever the ways in which the old history, seen in retrospect, looks narrow, dated, insufficient, it produced much that we take for granted—glossaries, translations, philological knowledge (phonology, semantics, and so on), studies of literary dependencies (sources, influences, family trees of narrative patterns), and of course editions, biographies, and systematic histories. Naturally such labors never end. Insofar as there was antihistoricism in the "new criticism," it never halted or curbed historical study. This study survives both in its original form and in the "new history," which sometimes implies a more complex sense of the forces that impinge upon or constitute developments viewed, as we now say, "diachronically," and sometimes means an extraordinary simplification of them: literature as a mere instrument of "power."

What kind of instruction was received by us who went to school, undergraduate and graduate, in the days of the old literary history? I do not have a clear picture of what went on in undergraduate classes in the 1920s, though, under our vivacious and witty professor (in colleges there was usually only one, with a bevy of new ABs acting as instructors and doing the latrine work in composition), the proceedings seemed to me significant and even exciting. My impression is of lectures on the historical and biographical backgrounds and on the gist of each work, with some explication de texte, some bright observations, and occasional remarks on the quality of the work that had got it into the anthology or the course. The professor must have used one term of praise with some regularity, for I remember it clearly: "sheer lyric beauty." Doubtless it seemed an ultimate statement of aesthetic virtue that it was my obligation to acknowledge and respond to. A man who had a Ph.D. from Hopkins could not be wrong. (An English major no doubt fell into the conviction that the possession of a couple of advanced degrees licensed one to speak with authority about all aesthetic matters. So later one announced truths oneself and hence in adult years was not well prepared to face the kind of student who, initiating the bearded age, would announce, with counterauthority, "I could not disagree with you more.") Anyway "sheer lyric beauty" was evidence that, beyond all matters of provenience and influence, the academic air entertained an unarticulated sense of a nonhistorical literary dimension, of some enduring quality that enabled us to touch a vague but stable shore bordering the flux of time.

Even graduate school could let slip some slender intimations, if not plainly of immortality in literary works, at least of something not quite amenable to final placement under the rubrics of time. In a famous course on Elizabethan drama we had been doing Ben Jonson in the then professional way—classical models, rules, and sources; later sources, influences, editions, theaters; and acting companies and their sponsors, locations, travels, rivalries, changing personnel, and influence on dramatists. All of this required hour upon hour of relentlessly thorough lecturing. When the lecturer, a distinguished man in his day, finished transmitting to us these storehouses of data, he found himself a little short of the bell that would end the hour and the course. Historical science behind him, all packaged for reshipment, he could relax into a genial, nonprofessional burst of feeling to the class: "I like Ben Jonson. Don't you?" Ah, an ever so sketchy reference to some quality beyond the massive historical facts, to an evocativeness of a response beyond recognition of multiple conditioning data. If nothing else, the audience could feel relieved that liking was permissible, and not an amateurish betrayal of the rigor of scientific history.

"Sheer lyric beauty" and "I like Ben Jonson"—faint hints of qualitative differences among all the works that felt the same determinations from outer forces. These personal glimpses of an imagined something beyond history may have been idiosyncratic, but I like to suppose that among my contemporaries there were others who, while hardly revolting against history, still felt that it was not everything. One's own experiences are significant only insofar as they are representative.

Still, when I began to have faint doubts about history, I feared that this might simply prove some severe professional shortcoming, or actual eccentricity, in myself. My problem sprang from my prior idea of graduate study. I had expected that it would provide, not a more ample measure of what went on in undergraduate classes, but new keys, better keys to literary understanding; would supply what, had I been looking for a term, I might have called a "higher criticism"; would provide authentic methods for distinguishing better and worse; would take qualitative assessments out of the realm of opinion. Then a few glimpses of seminars revealed that my expectations were a little inaccurate, and doubtless I made some unkind and unfair judgments. But I hoped I was not alone when I found myself thinking—no, feeling—that it was difficult for grown men, presumably intellectuals, to take seriously the topics announced for various seminars. One professor, whom I was in time to like and admire for his excellent lectures to very large classes (mixed graduate and undergraduate), announced to his seminar, and actually yawned as he announced it, that he was "terribly excited" about the progress of poetic diction, our assigned subject. The prospect of pursuing "finny tribe" from one minor poet to another seemed like fishing in too untroubled waters. Hardly more charming was the prospect of reconsidering the sources of some Canterbury tales in a Chaucer seminar. Well, I forget the rest. I cannot recall communicating with other souls plagued by doubt. Certainly there was a good deal of jesting, sardonic observation, and lighthearted byplay. One fellow student assured me that, criticized for "inadequate scholarship" in a paper, he had tripled his footnote space by inventing a mass of titles of works referred to, and was praised for his new diligence. Another said one better play ball with the system since it held all the keys to the club. Still, jokers and cynics seemed rare; obviously many people relished "the system," and a number of my graduate-school contemporaries were to do outstanding historical work. Perhaps, however, my own doubts and mild recusancy were not unique, but represented a more than individual readiness for an alternative to the old history, that is, for the second generation of professional modi operandi experienced by my chronological generation.

iii

The second generation was actually a dual affair, with a first rather brief phase, and a second very durable one; both seemed to occupy the sensed void in the older academic way with literature. The first phase we know as the "new humanism"; the second as the "new criticism." (Surely we reveal something about ourselves by the frequency with which we apply "new" to each of the successive waves of how-to-do-it in literary studies and stick to the "new" even after the thing itself is aged in the stacks.) To give the new humanism a role here may seem perverse; it was generally unloved by the old historians, was scorned by the new critics (Eliot's censure of Irving Babbitt for lacking an adequate sense of the divine is an odd forerunner of more recent and less elegant complaints about "secular humanism"), is periodically censured as little more than an archaic moralism, and has for the most part fallen into an oblivion from which it makes only transitory mini-emergences in footnotes on American cultural history. I am, however, not making claims for an intrinsic worth that the movement is now widely supposed not to have; I am looking at it only in its impact, in its heyday, on us who felt that literary history, whatever its virtues, was not enough. If one happened to be at Harvard, the impact was felt through the immensely erudite, aggressive, and witty lectures of Irving Babbitt (as doubtless through the lectures of Paul Elmer More at Princeton, of Norman Foerster at North Carolina and Iowa, and of Stuart Pratt Sherman at Illinois). Babbitt was equally vigorous as lecturer and as writer. In his works one felt the activity of a strong intellect; the tools were not professional techniques but ideas. Babbitt was extraordinarily learned; he constantly drew upon the major thinkers of classical times and of the post-Renaissance world, rather than on scholarly articles of recent decades. Here literature was not simply a form of entertainment or a rather inert object for quasi-scientific observation, but an invitation to one's mind. Here literary study seemed indeed an affair for grown-ups; ideas about value were at the center of things; one had to wrestle with rival claims to value, and see how individual works made one claim or another. Babbitt's antiromanticism, jesting or caustic, offered many of us our first experience in looking critically at an age or movement that for the most part seemed to be accepted as the best modern embodiment of human capability. It was not then fashionable to see Shelley plain (to misread Browning a little). Aside from providing fresh views on various pasts, Babbitt was a lively combatant in the immediate arena. One year we could listen, in successive hours, to Babbitt and John Dewey, then on a visiting appointment from Columbia; each lecturer's unflattering references to the other created an unusual academic liveliness. And once we heard Babbitt directly on his colleague John Livingston Lowes's *The Road to Xanadu:* "Think of it: a very long book on the genesis of two short poems." Babbitt was serious enough, but in manner he fell far short of a doleful high seriousness of which new humanists were sometimes accused (and to which few critical schools are immune). And no doubt his appeal did not always generate solid practice; other professors were heard complaining of students who bandied about the Babbitt vocabulary without having too much substance to go on. There was also scuttlebutt to the effect that Babbitt dissertations had hard going with reading committees because they were long on opinion and short on knowledge and care.

Whatever merit lay in hostile responses to it, the new humanism was attractive to many students because it appeared to offer them more substance than the old history had in its tired latter days. The humanistic approach proposed a significance beyond provenience; the history of ideas was a larger domain than the history of texts. Thus it helped nourish an awareness of alternatives to the old history, and hence contributed to a readiness, perhaps rather widespread, for the new criticism.

There was another kind of readiness for the new criticism. This I can trace in my own undergraduate experience, which must have been not unique but representative. I have already said that my undergraduate classes would edge beyond history by assuming the presence of aesthetic virtues evidently taken to be self-evident. But a course in modern drama tried to identify these virtues. In the 1920s the big guns in drama were Barrie, Čapek, D'Annunzio, Galsworthy, Granville-Barker, Lady Gregory, Hauptmann, Stanley Houghton, Henry Arthur Jones, Edward Knoblock, Maeterlinck, Maugham, Molnar, early O'Neill, Pinero, Elmer Rice, T. W. Robertson, Rostand, Synge, and of course Ibsen and Shaw. There was not yet a mass of secondary materials to establish, as it were, a canonical body of learning about such writers. The teacher was pretty much on his own. My own professor kept looking for formal properties that identified the play—structural arrangements, the objective definition of character, motivation, the use of "expectation instead of surprise," symbolism, tonal management, all the matters covered by the recent cliché "subtext," and of course the status of the play as reflection of or commentator on human reality ("mimesis" was not yet "out"). Discussions of this kind naturally turned our attention from the external pressures on the work to the internal characteristics of the work. Then one naturally transferred this way of looking at the work to other forms. Such experiences prepared students—I assume a great many of us—for the lessons of *Understanding Poetry,* however surprising its partial antiromanticism (less surprising if one had heard or read Babbitt).

The new criticism, the second generation of literary study that my chronological generation experienced, "succeeded" because of two kinds of readiness for it (one affirmative, one negative) and two qualities in the work of its creators. The affirmative readiness I have just identified: some prior experience in formal analysis. The negative readiness was the widespread sense that the old history was inattentive to aesthetic matters such as the relation of form and content. New critics often played to this negative readiness by strong attacks on literary history, sometimes in a misleadingly carefree way; they seemed to be saying *historia delenda est.* No such thing. The old new critics were trained in a system far more thoroughly historical than is the regimen in today's graduate programs; they assumed the presence and utility of such historical knowledge; and their question was no more than "What else is there besides history?" (Side note: Brooks and Warren accepted, for the *Southern Review,* an article of mine arguing the relevance of historical knowledge to aesthetic judgments.) But in the usual simplifications of intellectual warfare, denigrators keep on charging the new criticism with a reckless denial of all history. It's a characteristic campaign ploy: if the people believe it, either they want to, or they haven't gone into the matter.

But, if the new critics profited from the two kinds of readiness for their work, they made headway primarily by two solid virtues—good writing and persuasive literary thinking. Good writing: it was fortunate for the new criticism that it was born in the classrooms rather than in arcane journals where dark prose is essential to a sense of belonging and of vanguard authenticity. The various early treatises were textbooks; the writers were committed to a disciplined communication in which self-display by exotic vocabulary and style would have been wholly out of place; the result was consistent lucidity and occasional grace. The tone was not that of dogmatic pronouncement but that of invitation to a banquet of sense. This was notably the style of Brooks and Warren; if they did it better than some others, they were still not unique. But of course the ultimate strength of the new criticism lay in the convincingness of its approach (or approaches), its ability to generate in the profession a wide sense that it offered a valid revealing way into individual literary works, an objective method of distinguishing better and worse (matters that had heretofore seemed to lie entirely in the realm of ex cathedra pronouncement). The identification of the parts of the work, the examination of their role in structure, and hence the study of their impact on tone and statement—these critical activities gave readers a sense of making earned judgments.

The new criticism had forebears in the 1920s, became conspicuous in the late 1930s, and was dominant until the 1970s. But this second generation of approaches to literature was by no means a dictatorship. For one thing historical studies continued to be done, as was desirable and indeed essential, and the historical sense was rarely absent from the work of professional critics; literary history, if no longer a monolithic power, was quite alive. (Recently I was pleased when a middle-aged alumna told me of her amazement at charges, by some new theorists, that a whole generation of students had been "brainwashed" by the new criticism, for, in her view, my classes had regularly combined historical and new critical perspectives. This way of doing things must have been widespread.) For another the new criticism did not grow out of a single autocratic doctrine, but embraced a variety of stances that produced considerable internal disagreement. One has only to mention such names as Eliot, Empson, Leavis, and Richards in England and Blackmur, Brooks, Ransom, Tate, Warren, and Winters in America to sense the diversity of ideas and approaches accommodated under the rubric *new criticism;* the common element was critical analysis and evaluation of the literary work. It is likely that many practitioners were less converted by dogmata than drawn by the congeniality and usefulness of the practice.

Not that the school, insofar as it was one, lacked the dogmatisms, automatic exclusions and inclusions, and temperamental put-downs that plague most generations of literary study. Some practices become overfamiliar and evoke parody. The study of iterative imagery, a field in which I did some work, inspired "Thomas Kyd" (Alfred Harbage) to write "Cosmic Card Game," an amusing burlesque account of cardplaying imagery as the sole key to the meaning of *Antony and Cleopatra* (*American Scholar,* summer 1951). Popularity means converts; the more numerous they are, the smaller the immunity to characteristic professional vices. Converts to the new criticism could forget the civilized style of the masters, become self-indulgent, be charmed by the esoteric, and fall into obscurity. Once, when he was editing the *Sewanee Review,* John Palmer editorialized on the production of "hard writing" in contemporary criticism; perhaps his words involved both acceptance and a warning. But in stylistics the danger in new criticism was less an in-house lexical darkness than an argot public enough to be picked up everywhere, to become overly familiar, and thus to inspire parody like Harbage's. Everybody could talk about irony, wit, paradox, ambiguity, symbol, image, image patterns, tone, and structure. Such a terminology overran many a graduate school. This way of doing things was encouraged by the masters' taking history for granted, the general antihistoricism of our culture, and the subjectivity often evident in people who choose English as a field. Hence some large crops of Ph.D. dissertations that exemplified what a history-oriented colleague of mine, and a very good friend, called "This is the way I see it" criticism. He had a point. Indeed *criticism* became such a buzzword in graduate schools that I found myself lobbying for a more thorough historical discipline in our own graduate programs.

iv

Just as the weariness with small-scale historicism and its apparent sidestepping of essences helped pave the way for the new criticism, so the popularization of the new critical vocabulary and its adoption by many practitioners of small learning and less discipline contributed to a weariness that doubtless helped set the stage for the new literary activity summed up in the word *theory.* Theory, we may assume, will be downstage for a while. This third generation of literary procedures comes upon us as my chronological generation fades away, and we will hardly ingest it fully, just as the old historians did not ingest the new criticism that turned up in their latter days.

About two decades ago a first-rate graduate student said to me: "Your generation invented the new criticism. What can my generation invent?" Interesting, this felt need of invention: doubtless the academic version of Ezra Pound's rule for poetry—"Make it new." Actually my student did popularize, if not invent, a critical product, and became known for it. He is "into" theory now, and nonchalantly tosses some of its key terms, along with occasional quick references to Derrida, into his literary discussions, though to me these seem essentially rather shrewd analyses in a new-critical manner (less the clichés). Thus transition. Parallels: my generation reared on history, and in midlife practicing the new criticism; the next generation reared on criticism, and in midlife venturing into theory. There is some nice irony in varying interpretations of the second and third generations; literary readings by the light of theory have been called the "new new criticism," while theory-borne combatants put down the new criticism (and perhaps also the old history) as "old-fashioned humanistic practice." One has to wonder what the third generation, reared partially on theory if not always dominated by it, will be doing in midlife when its members feel that an academic vita nuova is about due and puzzle over what they can "invent." Two things are sure: there will be a sense of displacement in the ancien regime, and the new order will sparkle with triumph and condescension.

How far on we are toward the next revolution is not clear. One eminento is reported to have said that theory has "succeeded." It has certainly been bruited in the press a good deal, and professional youngsters spread the lingo through the journals. A knowing department chairman, alert to the ways of the world, tells me that his personnel problem is easier now because he feels less pressure to stock theorists than he did several years ago. One recent observer gave theory fifteen more years, another only ten. The repellent vocabulary and style of theorists, who produce quotable passages of marvelous opaqueness and apparent untranslatability, may limit "success"; the insiders' apparent fear of exoteric luminousness may restrict the boundaries of empire. One doesn't know, of course; our profession lusts, at least part of the time, after hard vocabularies that suggest profundities like those of the physics laboratory. But oddly enough the mystery terms become clichés, which may indicate conversion, discreet fellow-traveling, or a noncommittal adjustment to fashion: such verbs as *demystify, foreground, privilege, valorize;* such verbals as *coded, encoded,* and *inscribed;* such adjectives as *diachronic, synchronic,* and *self-referential;* such nouns as *closure, hermeneutics, presence, problematics, textuality, intertextuality, topos, trope, aporia* and of course *langue* and *parole* and *différance.* Glossolalia, when the sounds are infinitely repeated, may pall. The style of the third generation has produced some excellent parodies, and the school is brilliantly portrayed in Malcolm Bradbury's "novel" *My Strange Quest for Mensonge: Structuralism's Hidden Hero* (1988).

"Theory," of course, embraces a congeries of dogmatic identifications and skepticisms of identity. The Marxist (with its strong impact on the "new history"), Freudian, and feminist ways of doing things seem to derive literary works from causes that are absolute; you identify the psychosocial or socio-politico-economical forces that generated the work, and you know what the work has to be, however different from this it looked to other generations. Another form of dictation is the linguistic; according to semiotics, the conventions of language govern its users, whatever the writers' sense of freedom or creativity (hence the "disappearance of the author," a basic theme of Bradbury's *Strange Quest*). These modes of "deconstructive" activity, servants to various causes or credos, look a little different from that fundamentalist deconstruction that takes its stand on radical indeterminacy: whatever the work appears to say, it can also be found to say the opposite. This skepticism of identity goes a step further in the reception theory that appears to make the work the plaything of readers who confer upon it a series of momentary identities. Hence one theorist can declare the critic the equal of the writer of the work, and thus dismiss a long-held supposition that the critic is the servant of the work. It is a singular version of anti-elitism and egalitarianism. Although I have used the words *dogmatism* and *skepticism* for different modes of deconstructive activity, we can perhaps find a link between them: there is a spectrum of placement that ranges from skepticism of the work's independence to skepticism of the work's existence. While skepticism about texts is dogmatic, it rarely includes skepticism about the text that asserts dogmatic skepticism. Skepticism is evidently a faith that deconstructs other faiths. It escapes the self-referentiality that is the fate of all other works.

V

Not all novelty is new, of course. The often weird terminology of the third generation of English studies diverts our attention from the fact that some of its positions have predecessors. Awareness of these might relieve the usual anxiety of innovation.

For instance, decades ago E. E. Stoll was arguing for the force of "theatrical conventions" in determining what characters did and were. Iago was jealous not for reasons that are psychologically identifiable but because jealousy was theatrically expectable or called for. That is, a theatrical mode, not characterological probability, determined Iago's actions. Stoll's views on the compulsions of generic practice did not catch on, but they surely anticipated the theoretical view that the work is constrained by the habits of genre, language, and so forth. "The novel is about itself." (A very innocent outsider might suppose this dogma to oversimplify a complex situation in which what the individual novel "is" is a variable fusion of modal forces and of the independent interpretation of human reality.)

"Radical indeterminacy" is a dogmatic ultimate of a view that has been circulating for some time. Half a century has passed since Kenneth Burke pondered the conflict between the formal, public cast and direction of a literary work and those apparently contradictory elements in it representing some submerged activity of the author's imagination (as in Milton's characterization of Satan)—his conscious and unconscious intentions, so to speak. A similar conception appears in the "ambiguity" that was a frequent presence in textual analyses by the new critics. A decade or so ago the Shakespeare scholar Norman Rabkin, borrowing from theoretical physics, applied the concept of "complementarity" to Shakespeare plays; that is, the plays embody meanings, and can sustain readings, that are inconsistent or even contradictory. And preceding all of these was a fascinating essay of about 1930 that defined a "classic" as a work that could sustain simultaneously five different interpretations (despite considerable research I have been unable to identify this essay, which probably appeared in *Harper's* or the *Atlantic* and was reprinted in a collection of essays we used in Freshman English classes). When Hillis Miller explains defensively that deconstruction means only that there is not one definitive reading of any work, he would hardly seem to be peddling a harsh novelty. But perhaps he is instead declaring the work immune to all definiteness of reading.

The problem of the long line of thought that eventuates in "radical indeterminacy" is whether we have openness to divergent readings or are denied all possibility of convergent readings (convergence is implied, of course, by the theory of "communities of interpretation"). Do we have self-contradictions that cannot be ignored, or self-contradictions that are irresolvable and hence render all coherence illusory? Our age is one of sects and sectaries; it is rigorously anticatholic; it may instinctively press for irreducibly schismatic inner conditions that render the work congenial to a dissonant readership prone to revel in disunity and fractious uniqueness, and hence inhospitable to the concept of oneness as a goal of critical effort. The work must be as schizophrenic as we are. One thinks of Santayana's "skepticism and animal faith." We may practice skepticism of, or have animal faith in, the work as having a pursuable being, as more than an irrational congeries of disparatenesses; we may think of it as a challenging labyrinth or as an inviting trampoline. If the former, we accept its complexities, false leads, and culs de sac, but count upon ultimate order and design; if the latter, the work invites us to leap, bounce, and spring in critical virtuosity. Or try another metaphor: the work can have innumerable valid readings (egalitarianism in criticism) or it can have an ideal reading—the reading, one might say, by the mind of God. Hazard Adams phrases it differently—"the ideal reading demanded by the work." Such a goal imposes a discipline upon the critic; it does not leave him free to cry "indeterminacy" and fly off into wild self-indulgence. The critical act may never reach the goal, but striving for it is the thing. It should be a bar against critical wildcatting.

vi

I have been noting critical ideas that anticipate a prominent deconstructionist view—slender ties among several generations. Other patterns of relationship, by similarity or contrast, exist among the three generations of literary study.

For instance in the old history (first generation), literary works were generally treated as molded by external forces ("sources," "influences"; the determinants were, as we say now, "out there"). In the new criticism (second generation) the determinant forces were internal: the nature and quality of the work could be discovered in identifiable structural relationships. In the third generation (theory) there is a medley of the preceding ways of doing things. Insofar as this is the "new new criticism," it burrows within even more tirelessly, discovering, however, not a direction or a terminus or a oneness but an incurably schizoid condition. But the third generation also uses much old history, albeit in modern dress: the "new history" proposes either more sophisticated versions of the old molding and determining externalities, or else much simpler ones, making literature an unhappy creature, or weapon, of forces not admired by the historian (the power holders at any time, the bourgeoisie, the patriarchal society). Or literature is an unwitting creature of a controlling language or a controlling mode or a controlling reader. In sum the first generation sought the historical context, the second sought the extrahistorical, and the third a new set of historical controls and power plays. Or one can describe the three generations in terms of their relation to mimesis, though this norm is not fashionable now. For the first generation, literature involves a mimesis of external realities past and present; for the second generation a mimesis of human realities beyond the fashioning by time; for the third, a mimesis of past and present power-wielding elements in societies, of linguistic and modal habits (for example, "of itself"), and finally, of a succession of readers (neo-mimesis). One could almost trace another pattern: from an original concept of influence (the old history) through a deviant idea, "the anxiety" of influence, to intertextuality, the influential omnipresence of predecessors in a given text; and, concomitantly, to that strangely simplistic reading of influence, the work as only sociopolitical power play. (This seems one-dimensional—and hence hardly attractive to adult minds. I once heard an esteemed practitioner of the mode discuss a text at some length and then climactically declare that nothing was behind or in the text but a power play. An observer said: "That's how all his articles and lectures end." One can understand the appeal of this kind of thing to the young.) The old historians accused the new critics of subjectivity; one brand of new theorist says that the critic can never get beyond subjectivity. The old historian told how the work came into being (gestation, parturition, lactation, the roles of heredity and environment); the new critics tried to define the being it came into; the new historians attributed the whole history to rape; and the new theorist saw the productive forces as linguistic and modal, and the product a mestizo without rights since it was born to serve the critic.

Oddly enough, the old historians, while always acting as if the literary work were time-bound, that is, conditioned by prior and contemporary circumstance, did not hesitate to call major works "timeless." Although the new critics were intent on discovering the qualities that accounted for timelessness, they rarely used the word. Doubtless it already had an air of outmoded grandeur (our rhetoric has continued its slippage from veneration to domination). The embodiment of timelessness is of course the canon, of which the only begetter is time, but which is now subject to manipulation every month. Once an edict of durability, the canon is now an object of factional outcry. Committees assemble to vote the timely timeless, and to canvass for its canonical status. Organized causes caucus against decisions made by time, proposing to deconstruct the decisions and make political action supersede time. (The concept of timelessness seems to have slid down through various cultural layers to the sports page, which almost daily declares some athlete or team the best "of all time.")

Further synoptic tracings. In old literary history the model was science (research, hard evidence, sources, causes, genesis); in the new criticism the model was aesthetics (the relation of structure to meaning, status, quality) and in some cases psychology (I. A. Richards began as a psychologist and introduced "practical criticism"); theory is a voice of philosophy, especially logic and epistemology, with a skeptical bias. Finally the historical school was of German manufacture; the new criticism was an English and American product; and theory has been mainly a French export (with some parts subcontracted out to German designers).

vii

Predictions about future turns in the profession are very risky. But it seems certain that history will continue to be done, whether from dogmatic postures consciously used, or from observation posts valiantly struggling to be unaligned. Criticism, new or other (explication de texte, exegesis, interpretation, formal analysis, placement, evaluation), will also continue to be done; it is a spontaneous exercise. Traditional practices, in other words, will survive epistemological skepticism, however much it flourishes in the journals and in some graduate schools; ultimate skepticism would terminate the study of literature. The more lasting impact of deconstructive theory, one may guess, would be not the widespread practice of epistemological discourse but instead a reduction of the certainties to which all critical activities are inclined.

At present one hears a great deal about "demystification," but it does often seem that old mysteries are being attacked by obscure new ones. Fortunately the mystery of skepticism seems hardly a faith to attract multitudes, and thus to master great space and time. It is, of course, faith that underlies what we do, however it is rationalized by logical devices. Several years ago a new convert to theory, naturally assuming the superiority of his new faith to its predecessors, lamented that many of us are, more than we suppose alas, still under the influence of British empiricism. If he was correct, the situation is encouraging, for it indicates that certain faiths persist. The old generating faith of literary study was in "books," that is, in *biblia;* if they were less than sacred, they achieved, as secular works, something of the biblical. We may expect a persistence of the faith that literary texts are there, are something rather than everything, are special texts rather than simply neutral members of a textual tribe in which equal membership is held by comics, advertisements, commercial fiction, and the like (a view useful, of course, to sociologists). We may anticipate a residual faith in the "ideal reading," a goal that may never be attained but that has to be the goal of all critical quests, since without it the "critical" exercise becomes calisthenics and aerobics before a mirror. We may expect a continuing faith, at least an underground faith, that the work is more than an unstable compound, a muddle of indeterminacies; one of these days there will emerge critics who will demonstrate what was once taken for granted, that is, the persistent stabilities in works recently said to be all elusiveness and flux. We may suppose, also, a persistent faith in the mimetic element in literary works, a faith flexible enough not to exclude the symbolic, the imaginative, the absurd, and so on. After all, every good faith generates its own escape mechanisms.

All these faiths are of course still very lively, even in the face of considerable intellectual terrorism, whether by direct abuse or by punitively bizarre terminological weapons (perhaps by now partly defanged by familiarity). These faiths are probably held by a majority, though mainly silent or sotto voce, but relishing the witty obiter dicta and charming parodies that occasionally emerge as if from an underground—our own samizdat, as it were.

They will likely endure into, and help form, that post-theoreticism which will be, according to my present way of counting, the fourth generation of English studies—one that may be emerging in the twentieth century and will flourish in the twenty-first. Sheer weariness of the current fashion, especially among the flock of quick converts, may catalyze the emergence of the next mode.

17

Post-Tomorrow and Tomorrow and Tomorrow

An Aspect of the Humanistic Tongue

"Postmodernism"? Not really? It drives one to tautology: incredible beyond belief. But before plunging into that singularity, let me warm up by glancing at some other oddities, lesser and yet similar, of the humanistic tongue.

In his book on D. H. Lawrence published in 1959 Eliseo Vivas actually uses the word *referend* to refer to the thing referred to by a word—in recent academic argot, the "signified." Perhaps this was the last time in the history of modern humanistic writing that the word so used, given its etymology, structure, and history, was the fitting word for the intended sense. *Referend* embodies the gerundive form, with its meaning of necessity, duty, or fitness—"[that which is] to be referred to." Compare, of course, *dividend* (to be divided), *corrigenda* ([things] to be corrected), *agenda* ([things] to be done), *Delenda est Carthago, Amanda, pudendum, multiplicand, analysand*. But before adopting the "signifier-signified" option, and for that matter even while using it, humanistic writers have shown a singular fondness for the unfitting word. When they wish to refer to that-which-is-referred-to by some word, they with near unanimity use the word that means "referring," that is, *referent*. They use a participial form instead of a gerundive, a form that means "do-ing" instead of "to be done." Compare, of course, *sentient* (feeling), *continent* (containing), *pertinent* (pertaining), *nutrient* (nourishing), *revenant* (returning, as of a ghost). Best of all, compare *reverent* (revering) and *reverend* (to be revered). Humanists who speak of the "referent" of a word ought also to speak of "Reverent Smith" (I beg the question of whether the gentleman is capable of either feeling or eliciting reverence, especially when he is routinely deprived of the Mr. and the article *the* which might help). But it is dangerous to suggest this. It might catch on. Maybe it has caught on.

Since *referent* has long been an in-word, there must be few members of the Modern Language Association who have not found occasion to use it, for the MLA runs more to fashion than to taste. Some years back an eminent Americanist, writing in *PMLA,* used "mitigate against" for "militate against" (as did the Jersey judge in the 1986 rented-womb case, unless, as is imaginable, he was untimely delivered of an error by the attendant journalist). Humanists almost universally say "methodology" when all they mean is "method." It may be that "methodology" makes the user of it feel as significant as a physicist in a superconductivity lab.

While we humanists berate the world for its amorous carryings-on with the glamour-girl Science, we do seem inclined to borrow some makeup techniques from her. If we garnish the plain surface with mystery, we too may excite the multitudes; added syllables may disguise our plain mien and dull skin. They tinkle on the tongue too. "Method"—flat plain-Jane stuff; "methodology" is all Hollywood—never mind that its meaning is something different from what we intend. "Theorist" is pretty ordinary, but "theoretician" may suggest a seductive laboratory of arcane equipment. Likewise "linguistician" doubles the syllables, and presumably the allure, of "linguist." We pinch glamour from mathematics too, for example, "parameter"—literally "side measure," and hence "yardstick" or standard or index. But we often seem to take it as a vitamin-enriched or high-tech version of "perimeter," and propose fetching movements "within" such and such parameters. Again, it's rather like using falsies when we enlarge "sketch" or "hint" into "adumbrate," one of the oldest academic cases of cosmetic additives. Same thing, more or less: "problems" into "problematics," "tone" into "tonality," "personal" into "interpersonal," and perhaps, though with a great look of innocent helpfulness, the appending of "back" to "return," "report," and "revert." (Here, as it were, we add bustles to amend the backside, making assurance doubly sure.) "Intertextuality"? As aesthetic amplification, it is a sort of full-length fur coat: underneath may be concealed "allusion," "parody," "imitation," "influence," "resemblance," "family likeness," and so on. Maybe its promotional mode is to keep the man in the street guessing what is to be revealed. And "sex" is far less impressive than "gender" to denote the sex you belong to, despite the cost of "gender": it turns people into pronouns. I have almost given up hope for a campaign against "genderism" or "pronominalism"; after all, the MLA has added "gender" to its display shelves of new goods. Of course you can have the mystery of the alien without adding syllables. Take that favorite of humanists whose intimacy with Latin and Greek is rather on the Shakespearean model—*topos*. Who would say "topic," "theme," or "subject" when he can say *topos*? Who would say "practice" when he can say "praxis"? By all such devices we may achieve the happy condition visualized decades ago by Lionel Trilling: that we become "unable to say 'They fell in love and married,' let alone understand the language of *Romeo and Juliet*, but will as a matter of course say, 'Their libidinal impulses being reciprocal, they activated their erotic drives within the same frame of reference'" (today it would surely be "the same parameters").

Whether such cosmetic enlargements will make us rival Dame Science in the love-life of the public we do not know. But at least we can look in the mirror and feel a rare, quiet happiness. We see the mastery of sexy syllables, the glow of insidership, the erotic satisfaction of achieved academic deke-hood.

ii

Too much love of makeup, and you can go wrong. But even when we are just being ordinary, and not glamour-driven, we do some odd things. We don't have to be fancy to be faulty. Take, for instance, that old term *Renaissance,* which is now likely to be drafted for any state of affairs in which things seem to be a little better than they were before (just as *tragedy* is the handiest term for any state of affairs a little worse than we would like). Although one might expect this use in journalism, it is rampant in scholarship. We keep hearing about the New England Renaissance, the Harlem Renaissance, the Chicago Renaissance, and the Southern Renaissance. But none of these was a "rebirth"; nothing was reborn, nor was there anything in the respective pasts to be reborn. What happened was not a renascence but a florescence. Van Wyck Brooks, hardly a hero of American studies, was more accurate than most of academe in the second word of his title, *The Flowering of New England.*

(Historical note. I first raised this issue in a letter to the editor published in the *Sewanee Review* for summer 1978. René Wellek similarly criticizes the "untenable" claim made in F. O. Matthiessen's title *American Renaissance,* where the word is "used vaguely as the equivalent of flowering, climax, peak, or something similar." This is in volume 6 of his *History of Modern Criticism* [1986]. Dates are not the point here; Wellek may have had the idea years ago. I am pleased by the correspondence of the independent opinions, and by finding myself at one with Wellek. Later I shall note an at-one-ness with him in a larger issue.)

We have returned from the issue of self-enhancement by syllabic addition and verbal gesticulation to the original issue of self-revelation by semantic carefreeness. Professional humanists are much like the general public in forgetting the French connection of *chauvinism,* a connection enduring for a century and a half, and using it, without a qualifying adjective, in the special sense dear to sex politics exactly as if they were using "super patriotism" to mean "male sexism." In a learned article by an Americanist the word *apocalypse* is used in the following senses: revelation, doomsday, second coming, disaster, crisis, turning point, and disturbance. This usage appears to confirm a historical observation on American studies made by an Americanist a few years ago, "Existentialism is out, and apocalypse is in." "In"—precisely. We get with the times instead of presenting what we used to call "the timeless." So we lament the occasional persistence of "old-fashioned humanistic scholarship." Of the up-to-date fashions the oddest has produced a new humanist industry—the industry of manufacturing and marketing "the modern" and "modernism." Its extraordinary, indeed magical, achievement is to transmute the eternally fluid contemporary into a congealed past, the most unstable of relativities into a dated absolute.

We can fittingly approach this extraordinary transformation through a brief prelude on the varieties of "the new criticism," which has also undergone certain metamorphoses. In recent times, criticism has been "new" more than once. The first newness was, as far as I know, the offspring of Joel Elias Spingarn: his "The New Criticism" appeared in 1910. Spingarn was, as Wellek points out, a wholesale importer of Croceanism. "We have done," says Spingarn, "with all the old rules . . . with the *genres,* or literary kinds . . . with the comic, the tragic, the sublime . . . with the theory of style, with metaphor, simile . . . with all moral judgment of art as art . . . with the confusion between the drama and the theatre . . . with technique as separate from art . . . with the history and criticism of poetic themes . . . with the race, the time, the environment of a poet's work." Some of this may seem to anticipate directions of recent theory, but Spingarn is more clearly predictive in other passages. A good critic, he says, will act thus: "Each of us, if we are sensitive to impressions and express ourselves well, will produce a new work of art to replace the one which gave us our sensations"—the neo-Wildean claim that the critic is an artist. Croce, says Spingarn, "has led aesthetic thought inevitably from the concept that art is expression to that conclusion that all expression is art."[1] That is, whatever is written is a text. Interesting, to find in this apparently original new criticism

---

1. See James Cloyd Bowman, ed., *Contemporary American Criticism* (New York: Henry Holt, 1926).

some hints of a later school that has made some hay attacking another post-Spingarn new criticism.

In 1930 E. B. Burgum edited a collection of essays under the title *The New Criticism*. There is no problem about his newness: his first three essays are the one by Spingarn and two by Croce. Then follows an unusual cast of characters, including Santayana, J. B. S. Haldane (science), J. W. N. Sullivan (music), Roger Fry (art), and Oswald Spengler (cyclical history). But Burgum also includes I. A. Richards and T. S. Eliot, invariably named among the begetters of the third "new criticism" in three decades: Ransom's *The New Criticism* appeared in 1941. The Ransom variety, in time to become a vast conglomerate through modifications and accretions, has now lasted over four decades as "the" new criticism. Its hold is so great that recent theory has been called "the new new criticism." What next, when theory yields to a predictable swing of fashion? Since we usually act posthaste in our grabs for nomenclature, perhaps "post new new"? Or just another "new"? Back to this problem later.

As for the 1910–1941 "news," one might find certain thin trails of continuity amid all the forests of apparent novelty, but that is not my present dish. Alternatively one might hiss out a volley of tsk-tsks against later users of "new" for their ignorance of predecessors in the new. But this protest would ignore the nature of things. Whatever happens at any time, insofar as it seems differentiable from what happened before, is "new": the new is always with us, and one may as well call it that, however often the term is used. What is questionable is freezing the term *new* for what is in fact old: for practices whose innovations have become custom and have long persisted as principle (and hence as target). One could wish for a better term for "the" new criticism. "Formal analysis," perhaps? "Structural analysis" would do, but unhappily "structural" appears to have been copyrighted by the school that treats all literary matters as predetermined by the binding habits of language in general.

iii

Now each of the successive "news" might appropriately, accurately have been called "modern," for both terms reflect the current condition that, in its inalienable mobility, is felt to alter what went before. The new and the modern go on, like Tennyson's brook, forever. How singular, then, the practice, which has spread through the humanities like other floodings of fashion, of using *modernism*—that is, the ever changing character of an always temporary present—to denote a single limited present as if it had somehow terminated historical flux, life into mummy. One might think that the inevitable instability of the modern and of modernism was simply not known. But that instability has indeed been well known. In 1979 Peter Allen wrote that the Cambridge Apostles were "persistently modernist," that is, "since the content of modernism alters from one decade to another . . . Coleridgean in the eighteen-thirties [and] Marxist in the nineteen-thirties." In 1980 George Becker noted the difficulty in his own title *Realism in Modern Literature: modern,* he said, is "most unsatisfactory" because of its "extreme relativism: every age must perforce think of itself as modern," and he makes some amusing points about the condescensions of various modernisms to their predecessors. Reviewing Michael Levenson's *A Genealogy of Modernism* in the May 1985 issue of the *New Criterion,* René Wellek cites many meanings of "modernism," argues that it is not a useful term, and suggests that "a modernism" would be a fitting designation for those early-twentieth-century doings now called "modernism." Exactly. For history is an endless sequence of transitory modernisms, and only a genuine provincialism of mind (in our day temporal provincialism is more widespread than spatial provincialism) could elevate the one-before-the-present-one into, as it were, a first one, and only one, final and total. Whoever started this weird operation ignored the implications of the word *modernism* and the long history of its usage since the Renaissance. The Latin *modus,* the ultimate source of *modern,* had a family of meanings (measure, manner, limit, method), none of which is related to the *modernism* of which we speak. But *modus* is best reflected in the word *mode,* and there is the key. What is *modern* is, in effect, "à la mode," in the present style; obviously it's akin to *modish.* The "mode," the "style"—these are always what's current, what's present, what's contemporary, what's now (and "now" is a central meaning of the adverb *modo,* the ablative of *modus*). Modernism is presentism or nowism; every present or now is fleeting; it can never become a nonrelative, supratemporal reality—a contemporary no longer temporary but elevated to timeless singularity among the essences impervious to the history. Every now is soon a then; every mode is outmoded, and every modernism a has-been, recognizable only as "a modernism," once doubtless proud in its innovation or rebellion, but before long only a relic.

And until the strange speech of humanist professors of our time, *modern* has always been used precisely to denote the state of affairs as perceived at the time in which the perceiving person wrote—the current world as varying from or opposed to some past or other. There has been a flux of modernisms, as is inevitable, a stream of nows, none felt to be more than the current condition. The Latin adjective *modernus* was late in appearance; the first recorded usage appears to be that of Cassiodorus in the sixth century. It meant "things or institutions of the present." The moderns in the famous Quarrel of the Ancients and Moderns, exported from France to England in the seventeenth century, were of course all the people writing at the time, as opposed to the classical writers of Greece and Rome. Hence, of course, the term *modern languages,* first used by Bacon in 1620 and still alive in college catalogs, though perhaps doomed to mean varieties of computerese. "Modern" as "not ancient" had a very long run; in 1856 J. Grote alluded to the "attack" on classical study by "Modernists." In a parallel usage "modern" meant, as it still does in professional historical scholarship, non- or post- or antimedieval; in that sense we are still, so to speak, "in" the Renaissance, as the third major era of traditional western history (but compare Beatrice Gottlieb's introduction to her translation of Lucien Lefebvre's *The Problem of Unbelief in the Sixteenth Century* [1982]: "Modern, as the French use the word, means up to the end of the eighteenth century." In 1864 the *Daily Telegraph* referred to "those Guelphs and Ghibellines of art, the modernists and the medievalists"; in 1887 the *Westminster Review* found the Roman Church "typifying medievalism" and the American Republic "illustrating with tolerable fidelity the spirit of modernism"; and the same opposition is implied when W. Cory, in 1888, refers to "the old moderns, say Chaucer, Spenser, and Le Sage."

Whether it implies either not-classical (either falling below or equal to the classical) or not-medieval (generally, improving on the medieval), "modern" obviously means our times, a long-term now, an era. When it does not have either of those two broad-scale denotations, "modern" implies a present which (1) implicitly exhibits some sort of decline from either an ideal or an undefined preceding state of affairs, or (2) is unencumbered by judgment of the current condition alluded to. The writer critical of his present usually has a special spark.

> 1676. Etherege, *The Man of Mode* (a good title for our purposes here):
> Bellinda: He thinks himself the pattern of modern Gallantry.
> Dorimant: He is indeed the pattern of modern Foppery.

> 1701. Defoe, *The True-Born Englishman:*
> But England, modern to the last degree,
> Borrows or makes her own Nobility.

> 1737. Swift, in a letter to Pope, decries writers who corrupt the language with "quaint modernisms."

> 1743. *London Magazine:* "To be modernly polite, introduce Extravagance."

> 1830. H. N. Coleridge: "The women of the Odyssey discover occasionally a modernism and a want of heroic simplicity."

> 1848. Kingsley: "vile modernist naturalism."

1853. Arnold, *The Scholar Gypsy:*
... this strange disease of modern life,
With its sick hurry, its divided aims.

1863. Hawthorne, *Our Old Home:* "Caskets! a vile modern phrase."

1863. Twain, *Life on the Mississippi:* "all the modern inconveniences."

The neutral use of "modern," simply meaning "present," "of our time," "of this period," appears in every century:

1590. Sir J. Smyth: "according to the modern use."

1605. Ben Jonson, *Volpone,* of a popular Italian writer: "He has so moderne, and so facile a veine."

1656. Earl of Monmouth: "the women of this modern age."

1713. Pope: "the authoress of a famous modern romance."

1774. William Mitford: "the most admired modern masters."

1810. E. D. Clarke: "modern Greeks."

1825. William Cobbett, of the Bridewell: "the modernness of its structure."

1843 ff. Ruskin's *Modern Painters* meant mainly J. W. M. Turner, and then early Renaissance artists.

1845. Charles E. Francatelli, *The Modern Cook.*

1848. Marx: "modern industry."

1871. Meredith, concerning Ossian: "The modern tone (under the guise of a weird, primeval, mystical melody and system of verse) is what catches you." "The modern" here means romantic medievalism.

1898. G. Lowes Dickinson, *The Greek View of Life:* "the modern spirit."

1907. Henry Adams, *The Education:* "modern politics."

Two other quotations point up the historical issue very nicely. In *Their Wedding Journey* (1871) Howells identifies "flavours of Tennyson and Browning in his verse, with a moderner tint from Morris." Here Howells is speaking of three contemporaries of his, the third only twenty years younger than the other two, and finding the third "moderner"—nice evidence of the quick succession of one modernism by another. And in *Representative Men,* 1850, Emerson declares, "Perpetual modernness is the measure of merit in every work of art." "Perpetual modernness"—precisely: the modernisms that change from decade to decade or generation to generation.

iv

Contemporary humanists are apparently the first users of such words to speak of their "modernism" as if it were a unique, once-in-a-millennium, terminal phenomenon rather than one small event in a fluid, endless sequence of presentisms. While much humanistic scholarship is ephemeral, still one would not expect humanists to betray the historical sense of ephemerids. The word *modernism* is beguiling; apparently, like drugs, it gives an unwonted sense of power. Well, if it is indispensable as denotator of an age or movement or impulse, we could save it by using it to denote not absolute but relative reality, that is, designating successive new looks by numbers or letters or signs. Let's try numbers:

Modernism 1. Postmedieval: the Renaissance in general, still in progress.

Modernism 2. The activities of contemporaries competing with the classics. The "Quarrel."

Modernism 3. The success of these contemporaries: neoclassicism.

Modernism 4. Postneoclassical. "Nature" represented by "feeling" rather than "reason." (This accepts traditional terms rather than entering the debate on their applicability.)

Modernism 5. Romanticism: individualism and medievalism.

Modernism 6. Victorianism: industrialism, reformism, scientism, democratism, good form-ism, decline of creeds, etc.

Modernism 7. Here is where the fun starts. Fin-de-siècle-ism? Impressionism or postimpressionism? Or both? Aestheticism? Edwardianism? Or how about "the intra-Victorianism which is the matrix of post-Victorianism"?

Modernism 8. Is this last leaf on the tree the one taken to be our ultimate, final "Modernism"?

There could be great debates as to which number should be assigned to each modernism and especially the recent one described as if it were a once-only, first-time, last-in-line affair. We might find we'd need twenty or more numbers—especially if we got Europe into the act, as decent modern history would have to do.

Of course there are defenses "modernly" available for any usage, however absurd. Yes, I know the "communications" argument: if the word works, what matter what kind of word it is. Yes, I know the Humpty-Dumpty argument: "When *I* use a word . . . it means just what I choose it to mean—neither more nor less." (For our purposes, Alice's rejoinder—"The question is . . . whether you *can* make words mean so many different things"—would need to be recast: "The question is whether you can make a word that means so many things mean only *one* thing.") Yes, I know, I know, the relation between signifier and signified is fluid and contingent. Yes, I know, I know, every sign is arbitrary.

Those arguments, it happens, describe man-in-the-street operations, or gross language. We can act like the man in the street if we want to; there is no academy to declare our usage null and void. Unfortunately the theory of arbitrariness in language would have unpleasant effects in medicine and in science generally. Too bad we do not think of ourselves as also engaged in science—in *scientia*—and hence obligated to speech a little more rigorous than that of random fashion. Instead we reveal our kinship with journalists (though I don't suppose we'd like "literature" to be called "journalism"). In speaking as if there was a one-and-only "modernism" we reveal our indifference to the core of a word that for centuries has governed the use of the word. We reveal our indifference to a history of which we are supposed to be spokesmen. We reveal a special sort of parochialism—a parochialism in time which believes that a continuous and timeless process is a separate event that happened for the first and last time in the recent past. We ignore the relevance of illuminating statements made a century apart by an English and an American writer:

> 1820–1823. Lamb, *Essays of Elia,* in an apostrophe to "antiquity": "Thou hadst a remote *antiquity* . . . thou thyself being to thyself flat, jejune, *modern.*"
>
> 1936. Ellen Glasgow, addressing—fittingly enough—the Modern Language Association of America: "No idea is so antiquated that it was not once modern. No idea is so modern that it will not some day be antiquated."

Precisely. Every modernism passes, every one yields to another, and no one of the endless chain of cultural passersby can be accorded a nominal claim to uniqueness. One may wonder how late-twentieth-century practice will look a hundred or five hundred years from now when scholars glance back over the heads of numerous intervening modernisms and contemplate this minor predecessor that appeared to think itself unique, "the" modernism. Well, how would we feel about cultural historians of the 1650s if they had interpreted the death of Charles I and the arrival of the Commonwealth as the end of "modernism"?

V

And where do we go from here? Since in the delivery of nomenclatures we have practically automatic post-all service, we can anticipate that poststructuralism will be followed by postdeconstructionism, and the whole works by post-theoreticism (or post-theory, probably, alas, too plain and simple) and maybe even postskepticism. Within recent weeks I have seen, for the first time, "postphilosophical" and "superstructuralism." In some quarters we are believed to be in postmimeticism, though mimeticism does not yield easily to academic death sentences. But of course: since we have put "modernism" behind us we are happily into "postmodernism." It is a rare journal article that does not refer to "modernism" as an event of some recent past, one that is never defined, but that we all know to have been terminated in some way. Hence we are into "postmodernism." There is a wonderful charm in this word, more delightfully fantastic than all others invented by humanists in their taxonomic zeal and uncontrolled lust for the outrageous. By it we manage, while living as most men must in the contemporary, also to live in the next contemporary, a wonderful duality of life. We are up to the minute by being ahead of it. Our happiest avant-garde ploy is to place ourselves in the postpresent, to have an upcoming then now, the subtlest of the time warps beloved in pop-art midnight cinema. We have become après avant-garde; we have next week this week.

We are the first to achieve post-today-ism. But, alas for these good tidings, what happens when tomorrow, or next week, turns out to have its day too, or when, tired of futurity ahead of schedule, we hurry it to death (even before it is untimely ripped from its mother's womb)? Shall we settle for "post-post-modern"? Maybe. There is, however, a more magnetic possibility, if we will but be open to it. Since in postmodernism we have tomorrow today, let us in time replace post-today-ism with post-tomorrow-ism. "Post-tomorrow." Compact and elegant, surely. But another and deeper utilitarian merit: think of the all-but-infinitely extensible applicability as new modernisms, ruthlessly defying our current terminology, creep in their petty pace from day to day. First we move into "post tomorrow and tomorrow," and then, when forced, into "post tomorrow and tomorrow and tomorrow." That will hold us for a while, if not to the last syllable of recorded time. And it will leave all our yesterdays intact—all the yesterdays now done to dusty death by "a" modernism swelling into all modernism.

Meredith has been of use several times, and I want to quote him again—this time in an 1875 letter to John Morley, who was thinking of changing the name of the *Fortnightly Review* to the *Modern Review:*

> My objection to "modern" is that in English, and to English minds, the slightest stress on the word, if it is not intended for ironic, has the effect of inviting irony.
> "La Revue Moderne" is very well, but with us "modern" has not strength enough for a title.
> "The Review of the Time." This rather takes me. (*Letters,* 1.504)

Yes, it does. And one rather sympathizes with "men" who, Goldsmith wrote in 1774, "glorified in the title of Modernicides." But what we need even more is a few "postmodernicides." "Postmodern" has become a cliché of many journals, especially the *New York Times Book Review*, where the word appears virtually every week. But there is never a hint of definition, notably of the "modern" which the writer now thinks we are "post." Someone should point out that all the fashionable word means is "post-now-ism," which names an impossibility. If it persists because it sounds "with it," one would prefer to see the nonidea reflected in such a term as *post-tomorrow-and-tomorrow-and-tomorrow-ism*. That would have Shakespearean class, which might defy all evident verbal nonsense.

V

education
examined

18

Semicentennial Retrospections

The Past as Perspective

"Well, all right," the young man said, "what can you say for the schooling of your day?" My challenger works in college admissions. "How can you convince anybody that you haven't only got the good-old-days disease? Your generation is prone to it, you know. It's your form of cultural arteriosclerosis. Besides, I'll bet that when you got into college there was no rhyme or reason to it. They didn't have a democracy principle or a selection principle. You just drifted in."

Even without his saying any of this, I would know the risks of a semi-centennial retrospection. Nevertheless, I will risk those risks. My basic assumptions: (1) no one is actually going back to a past; (2) mourning for it is mistaken filial piety; but (3) looking at it may provide a way of looking at the present in which, for better or worse, we are stuck.

In my Pennsylvania high school in the 1920s there were three curricular choices. If you were going right to work, you took what was called the "commercial course." If you were going to college, you took either the "classical" course or the "scientific" course. Each college-prep course was a package deal, with only an elective or two about the edges. In the classical option I took, willy-nilly, four years of Latin, four of English, three of French, two of math, and one of science. The science option also included four years each of Latin and English, but substituted math and science for the second language, thus having a total of three math courses and three laboratory-science courses. This setup meant small need of advising. (About the only counseling I can remember was a warning against the evils of masturbation, which in those pre-Portnoy days was still causing blindness, muscular dystrophy, and premature senility. Things are better since Portnoy. In a Christopher Hampton comedy of the 1970s a character says, "Don't knock masturbation. It is the thinking man's television.")

College courses were mostly required too. When I arrived on the Lafayette College campus, my first-year schedule (six three-hour courses) was simply handed to me. In the second year it was much the same. I majored in English, and that meant taking everything the department offered—a total of six one-year courses, which combined to give a coherent and almost complete picture of English literature. If there was course-advising or career-counseling, I don't remember it.

Today all that may seem pure dark ages. Rarely was I asked what I liked; others mastered my fate and captained my soul; I was given no hot keys to the then contemporary world. Yet I would not trade those eight years for any other educational track that I have seen in fifty years of college teaching. If I had been a term-by-term libertine elector of courses, I probably would not have done nearly so well. I was very lucky. I was lucky in three other ways too. One was that my family, though poor, considered college not a socioeconomic conveyor belt but a provider of learning that in some undefined way was good for one. I was a senior before my father asked me what I was thinking of doing after graduation next spring. I was lucky in that, in our family, reading was a spontaneous, unself-conscious practice; in fact, we read a good deal of Mark Twain aloud. Hence reading seemed a natural activity, not a hideous torture that one had to undergo to meet assignments. (My advice to complaining parents is simple: "Go home and read two hours a day, and let your children see you doing it. The kids just might get the habit. If they did, half the problems you complain of would be solved.") My third bit of luck: Sunday school and church were automatic for us, and my college required three courses in the Bible for all degrees. As it happens, I neither clung to certain literal beliefs nor had the recent faddish illusion of being born again. But I learned much that had great meaning outside catechism and courses, particularly about the nature of the human psyche and the symbolic styles of meeting its needs.

No one, as I have said, is going to propose reinstating the old 1920s style to save education. But it is legitimate to see whether the kind of training I received has any implications for our time. A past may afford a useful perspective.

ii

What I got in on was a later phase of the Renaissance education which, with variations, had endured for about four hundred years. Its unspoken function was the induction of the individual into a community. This community of language and traditions, of a past known to be inseparable from the present, sought a shared understanding of mankind and its ways. Participation in this community could mitigate the human addiction to the provincial, the myopic, the transitory, the subjective, and the half-baked.

My word *community* should highlight the different values and aims of our day. Surely for many today the idea of an influential community of mind and spirit—of perspectives, understanding, and ends—would be embarrassing. Our stress is all on the individual, on needs of his assumed to be unique, on the desires that come out of a supposed special identity, on finding and nurturing that identity (as we see in such unquestioned popular phrases as "finding myself" and "knowing who I am," which never, never imply the discovery that one is much like other people). We focus on, and perhaps unintentionally cultivate, difference rather than actual or potential likeness; anything else seems a threat to independence. We reject interrelatedness, which once shaped educational style.

Hence within fifty years the expansion of my six correlated English courses into several hundred unrelated ones, and of a few basic curricula into scores of majors. A dominant sense of people's differentnesses, though not a sole cause, is at least a sine qua non of infinite courses in multiple fields. If we don't really believe in a human center, we get a wild curricular centrifugality. Our curricular centrifugality raises hell, incidentally, with a central frugality, but fiscal cost is not my theme. I simply ask one question: what would be the impact on education if we really could and did believe that we are—in that wonderful phrase from a past we suppose we have put behind us—members of one another? Or at least candidates for that membership?

A second problem grows out of another contemporary slogan. If I were pushing my own education as a model for us now, I would surely hear anguished cries of "Elitism! Down with elitism!" This is a painfully familiar form of emotion masquerading as thought, the innocent self-deception of democracy. (All political orders have characteristic forms of self-deception; we spot others more easily than our own.) The only legitimate anti-elitism opposes unearned privilege, that is, unacceptable inequity. What I call innocent self-deception is the mistaking of all inequality for unacceptable inequity. Hence we really want to deny inequality and its consequences. But alas, just as there is physical inequality everywhere (even the noisiest anti-elitist is likely to know that fewer than one-tenth of one percent of all professional athletes can play center in basketball), so inequality is rampant all through humanity—moral, intellectual, and imaginative inequality. For the well-being of us all, the gifted—the elite or "chosen"—have to be nourished. In other words, any education that lacks an elitist component is bad for a democratic society.

Indeed, the older high-school and college education—with its uniformity, its traditionalism, its limited field for individual choice, and its implicit nonutilitarianism—was not a class-oriented affair, as some modernists might like to argue. Rather it was, in the best sense, implicitly democratic: it judged all of us equally capable of induction into a community of knowledge and taste. Today, surely, that assumption is unknown. In part this is due to our having underplayed what we have (or could or should have) in common, and overplayed what we call the individualistic. But anti-elitism works like this. It is essentially egalitarianism; it avoids confronting the fact that not all courses are equal. Either we really think that they are all equal, or we fear that acknowledging their inequality is "undemocratic." If we name one field as inherently more worthwhile than another, we give it an elite status.

All colleges and universities have curriculum committees supposed to evaluate proposed new courses, but one seldom hears of such a committee's rejecting a course because its materials are shallow, thin, makeshift, or peripheral. Begetting new courses is one form of passion that leads to no efforts at contraception or calls for abortion. Indeed the fear of elitism, with its abnegation of judgment, is an open invitation to faculty to keep on turning out new courses, and turn them out they do. To shift the image slightly, it is a curricular dysentery for which the profession has yet to find an antibiotic. In fact, it often takes the dysentery to be a symptom of creative vitality.

Our fear of elitism likewise reduces our willingness to judge students. In high school now, apparently, flunking students is unfashionable. In the university, I fear, only the grades of A and B will survive the next decade, though Mother Nature will go on providing us with C, D, and F students in customary abundance. Such forms of donated equality tend, alas, to give the beneficiaries a somewhat misleading picture of the reality that we all have to live with. Furthermore, overgrading increases the number of students. The more numerous the bodies, the larger the pool of C, D, and F students, and they assist the wild increase of fields and courses. But the more substantial, the more rigorous, and the more integrated the field and the course—the fewer the students enrolled. The more sequential its constituent elements, the more committed to depth perception, the more its basic concepts are not reducible to clichés and truisms handy for the press—the greater the number of students either not up to it or unwilling to try it. So we have to invent fields and courses that they are up to, and, in all fields, we do. It is sometimes known as the explosion of knowledge, even though any merchandiser knows that the larger the pool of shoppers, the greater the market for junk goods.

iii

Students, then, just by being so numerous and allegedly diverse, assist the miscellaneousness and populism of the curriculum. Further, about twenty or so years ago many of them decided that the lives being molded by education were their lives and that therefore they alone should do the molding. The addition of ignorance, willfulness, and prejudgment to numerousness did not exactly help higher education, but even a faculty predilection for caving in had its limits. Hence the student dream of curricular satisfaction of countless private passions, still unappeased, led to the formation of extramural setups variously called free universities, experimental colleges, and so on. A recent bulletin of the Seattle version of this academy says it is the biggest in the country and claims an enrollment of thirty thousand. It lists more than five hundred courses in thirty-seven departments.

A good half of these, extending alphabetically from Astrology to Yoga, reflect various recent fashions in feelings, longings, and searchings—irrational hopes for achievement in beauty, skills, life, and truth by recipes that are either outright magical or at least speedier than the usual ways of rational understanding and imaginative penetration. One course in art will reveal the mysteries of the mandala, one in "Prosperity" explains the advantageous use of "the laws of the universe," and one in cooking will teach "Creative Yeast Dough Baking." (The word *creative* is often used in this catalog; how many mortals aspire to that prerogative of divinity.) There are six courses in Meditation, seven each in Astrology and Yoga, and nine in Martial Arts. But the real biggie departments involve physical and psychological self-improvement. There are about seventy-five courses in athletic or physical how-to's, including "Slimnastics," "Polar Energetics," and several in exercises for couples. The forty-three courses in dancing include ballet, belly, burlesque, disco, folk, jitterbug, morris, square, tap, and many ethnic modes. With only about sixty courses, psychic betterment lags a little behind physical, but it does offer seventeen courses in "Psychic Phenomena" and thirty-seven in "Self-Discovery."

Several conclusions are irresistible. One: this proliferation of fields and multiplication of noncredit courses is simply a natural extension of the university principle of having a credit course in everything for everyone. Two: Americans say not only "There ought to be a law" but also "There ought to be a *course*"—a singular faith in the taming of reality by curriculum. Three: when this curricular explosion takes place off campus, at least we need not worry about the dissipation of public and institutional resources in a prodigal accommodation of a thousand random passions. It is a market economy: you pays your money, and you takes your choice. One may do no more than drop a sigh for what the money buys, and for the fact that the sought happiness will remain elusive.

iv

Do those citizens who cry "back to basics" really want to escape from unlimited electivity and take refuge in a set central curriculum resistant to mad idiosyncratic multiplication? No doubt there is some dim craving for a membership that cannot be achieved by hordes of do-your-own-thing courses. But an entryway even vaguely resembling my 1920s schooling would surely elicit such damning words as "regressive," "reactionary," "repressive." Aside from limiting freedom, it would lack contemporaneity; it would ignore the blind conviction that current events are a field of study, like physics. Just as some students say, "It is my life; only I can decide how it will be educated," so many others say, "I live in these times, and they are what education must be about." We should look at this idea a little. It is easy to imagine what my own 1920s education would have been had it been under the influence of passionate presentism, unfettered electivity, and the illusion that the ever moving hours of a brief lifetime are a separable, stable, and identifiable entity, and hence a self-sufficient educational subject matter.

Well, I majored in English. If we had eliminated European classics and English literature from Chaucer to Hardy, and stuck to the bright, exciting American world around us, we would zealously have studied the fiction of Percy Marks, James Branch Cabell, Floyd Dell, Dorothy Canfield Fisher, Ruth Suckow, and Sinclair Lewis. Maybe we would have had courses in Dos Passos, Dreiser, and Ellen Glasgow, but even that relative altitude would seem a sad comedown from the Fielding-Sterne-Austen-Brontë-Dickens-Thackeray-Eliot-Hardy-Conrad heights. In poetry we would have been "with it" with Stephen Vincent Benét, Witter Bynner, Robinson Jeffers, William Ellery Leonard, Edna St. Vincent Millay, and Elinor Wylie. No Chaucer, Donne, Milton, Pope, Dryden, Wordsworth, Coleridge, Keats, and so on. In drama, Maxwell Anderson and Marc Connelly; maybe even O'Neill. But no Shakespeare, Congreve, Molière, Sheridan, Ibsen, Chekhov. And so on. Only such lists, mirroring a once glittering present that is now dead, can tell us that an exclusive attachment to any present means being trapped in a morgue. From that morgue a ghost or two may rise to a secular eternal life, but at the time we never know which ones, if any, will. Time is the only critic. It has cased all the morgues and identified the living spirits that are the only measure of, and indeed the only key to, any other present. Without them we can't tell jewels from junk. Without them we can't tell the difference between reading literature and reading newspapers.

Likewise I can guess what my nonliterary education, tuned in only to the twenties, would have been like. There would surely have been a course in the Theory and Practice of Prohibition (and the Experimental College would have a dozen offerings in the Manufacture and Merchandising of Bootleg Liquor). Doubtless I would have taken many courses such as the following:

> Transportation: Carriage Aesthetics and the Touring Car Comparative Values of Dirt and Gravel Roads
> Economics: The Speed/Cost Ratio of Local Trains and Express Trains
> Agriculture and Merchandising: Variant Functions of the Horse
> International Relations: The Validity of the Versailles Treaty
> Health Sciences: Problems and Issues of the Influenza Epidemic
> Banking and Investment: The Rising Market, or, Understanding American Prosperity
> Art History: Americans in Paris: Issues of Expatriation Hollywood and a New American Art Form Wallace Reid and the Racing-Car Film
> Sociology: The Social Roles of the Buggy and the Street Car
> Political Science: The Tempest at Teapot Dome
> The Death of the Democratic Party

What a nightmare! Being buried alive in that tomb of once-upon-a-time up-to-dateness, and then being thrown out, without information or ideas, to face five or six more decades. The truth is that an ad hoc curriculum leads to massive ad hokum. We can learn that sad fact only by seeing the actuality of a "relevant" education in a once-live present that is now a dead past.

I have glanced retrospectively at an old educational tradition and then at alternatives cadged up, and justified, by the clichés of a later day. The cliché of the glorified individual, incarnate as it is in multitudinous seas of courses, assumes that uniqueness is a sole truth and neglects a shared humanity. The cliché of anti-elitism ignores inequality of talent, as well as democracy's need of the superior, and leads to the assumption that all students, curricula, and courses are either equal or indistinguishable in value. From this there comes, with ironic inconsistency, the counter cliché that the present time is a more valuable topic of study than any other time.

Another cliché began its long life in the 1960s: that the students of the 1950s were poor stuff—torpid and inelastic. This bad-mouthing is grossly unjust. The truth is that the 1950s generation was the last educable one before the later 1970s. The 1950s people were open to knowledge and ideas and were ready to work and ingest. Their alleged passivity was merely an absence of revolutionary fervor, and this freedom from utopian scheming is precisely what made them educable. The anti-1950s cliché was nothing but a middle-age self-defensive tactic of the old 1930s radicals, who felt an implicit criticism of themselves in the mere existence of students unlike themselves. The anti-1950s cliché was then picked up in self-praise by the 1960s successors to the old 1930s crowd.

The 1960s types added a new cliché, which still has some circulation: namely, that they were the best thing to hit the campus in decades. Actually, the opposite is true. The late 1960s produced the most successful anti-educational putsch that I saw in fifty campus years. In the vanguard of it you had the active ideologues, who were uneducable because they already knew all the answers, which they had learned by rote in various cells, nonmonastic in type; their aim was only to disrupt education and produce a chaos through which they could take over. Their slogans victimized a much larger segment, the innocent idealists, who were seduced into supposing that they could protest, sit, march, burn, or bomb virtue into the world. Between them these two groups—the ideologues and the idealists—made such an uproar that learning became very difficult for the majority who still rightly felt in their bones that the steady intake of knowledge was the best way to be of use to the world. So we really had, almost fifty years after the term was coined, a "lost generation." Many of them have never got unlost.

For variety I pass with pleasure from discounting clichés that have benighted many to recounting a grace that has delighted some, including me. In my latter years as teacher I found myself, in each new class, looking around the room to see if I was lucky enough to have drawn again a recent kind of student who was almost invariably a blessing to a course. I mean the older woman coming back to study again, to carry on what had been interrupted years before by economic pressure, indifference, motherhood, wifehood, or other acts of God. Ah, what a human being to have in class. Her extra years of experience, five or twenty, dull or difficult, meant a clearer insight, a fuller sense of actuality, a greater freedom from illusion—in a word, a vastly superior equipment for understanding and appreciating literature. She could roll with the art and, as for the world it depicted, know that there were no perfect answers. A few such students, and I began to wonder whether anyone should study literature before the age of twenty-five.

V

Should anyone study literature before the age of twenty-five? Perhaps one could turn this question into a rule. This mad thought reminded me of my young friend's insistence that in my day people just drifted into college, that no principle of selection governed the admissions process then as it does in the system over which he now presides. Everything came together for me at once, and, like a medieval poet recording a dream-vision, I drifted off and found myself hosting a comprehensive picture of an ideal admissions process for our day. I hastened to set down the discriminating questions before I forgot them. I did this despite a nagging discomfort: in my nocturnal admissions achievement of ideality, I had somehow lost all my spiritual fig leaves and was exposing myself terribly. But I ignore this, for I want to acquaint the world with my dream college-board exam. These are the questions that came to me from a higher guiding spirit:

1. *What is your age?* (If the answer is less than twenty-five, the wisdom-laden computer pops out an advisory: "Go get a job for a few years, and then try again. Seven years of job bondage may free you for real headwork, or even free you from all pressure to go to college.")

2. *Do you believe that the twentieth century is morally superior to the nineteenth, i.e., more realistic, more honest, less hypocritical, etc.?* (If the answer is "yes," the applicant will be assigned to remedial sections.)

3. *Is the study of foreign languages un-American? Undemocratic? Elitist?* (If the answer is "yes," the examinee is advised not to waste time in college but to go directly into a political career.)

4. *Do you believe that America is a very bad place, and that we must use force to make it like the better countries of the world?* (If the answer is "yes," the applicant is certified for the Jane Fonda Institute of Moral Philosophy.)

5. *Do you believe that you are unique, and that it would be educational iniquity not to cater to your uniquity?* (Here the computer makes a rather puzzling comment: "Iniquity has ubiquity; uniquity doesn't.")

6. *In college, should you be laboring to improve the world or learning to save yourself from making it worse?* (The computer gets coy again. It whispers to the examiner, "If the applicant opts for world-improvement, he will scream at the vices of others; if he takes the second option, he will work on his own. Decide what you want, baby.")

7. *A former president of the University of Chicago is reported to have said: "We have to get football back, or we'll have all the kooks in the country here." Discuss.* (If the applicant attacks the president, he has a premature case of high seriousness and should be rated "Doubtful." He can be admitted later to balance off a flock of low-seriousness types. After all, football is the last instrument of community in a do-your-own-thing world.)

8. Language tests that involve a series of choices.

(a) *Which do you believe is the better word to denote boundaries—"perimeters" or "parameters"?* (If he opts for "parameters," he can be recommended to a school of journalism.)

(b) *If you are talking about the way you do something, should you call it your "method" or your "methodology"? Which is the superior term, "telephone" or "communicational installation"?* (If the applicant opts for "methodology" and "communicational installation," he is beyond education and may be considered for faculty status in the social sciences or a college of education. It is also possible that he may suffer from a pathological enlargement of the A.S.S.—the Added Syllable Syndrome—and should be sent to a shrink.)

(c) *Translate this phrase: "reprioritization of resource-allocation in institutional services-delivery to multiple constituencies."* (The computer answer is "budget revision," but some examiners suspect that the person who gets this right may have a simplicity of mind maladapted to the world in which we live.)

(d) *Do the words "enthusiastic," "caring," and "concerned" mean anything without modifiers?* (If the applicant says they do, he may be recommended to the Experimental College of the Secular Bleeding Heart.)

9. The ninth and final test is physical but symbolic, and it shifts from the literary to the moral. It is a walk. The examinee's tour includes first an up-escalator and then a down-escalator. If he stands still on the up-escalator, a minus will be added to his grade on the mental tests; that is, a *B* goes to a *B-*, and so on. But if he stands still on the down-escalator, he flunks the exam automatically; that is, his action, or nonaction, symbolizes an inner conviction that the world owes him a free ride. This will render him impervious even to the most tempting educators, such as the man in English who offers the best-seller course in "Recent Detective Stories for Children."

When I awoke, I could not resist the profound conviction that here was a purely modern educational idea which was fully self-justifying. By conceiving it and delivering it, I felt as if I had at least partly mitigated the onus necessarily borne by one who could speak well of what went on academically in the olden days of the 1920s.

19

Back to Basics

Issues

The apparent popularity of the call "Back to Basics" is worth a little further inspection. It might seem to indicate a coinciding of certain academic voices and a widespread readiness for an educational task. While certain academics were voicing their discontents with academic methods and performance, many citizens were becoming aware that more than half the holders of bachelor's degrees were verbally and numerically underequipped, that is, semiliterate and seminumerate, and that many high-school graduates could barely read, write, or figure. Various happenings in the schools have made basics look like more than a flurry of noble talk. If newspaper reports are reliable, Marva Collins's West Side Prep School in Chicago has succeeded by a thorough discipline in central subject matter and even traditional processes such as memorizing. There are evidently comparable developments—notably a primary insistence on being able to read—in the Leif Ericson Elementary School under Marjorie Branch. Just at this time a Chicano head of minority programs at my university publicly described our curriculum as a "smorgasbord of uneven quality." Those sharp words are a notable understatement. About the same time I myself was proposing that our era of whirlwind educational experiment was ready for a totally new experiment, namely a college in which all the courses would be required. (Parenthetically, that's easier said than done. Who would do the requiring? I get seasick thinking of a faculty meeting to decide what would be required. We teachers tend to split both on principle and in defense of our own real estate. In curriculum as in public budgets, we are all for cuts, but always, please, in someone else's property and perks.)

Maybe we *are* half-ready for some change in educational direction. But *how* ready? Even a term like my "all-required curriculum" may scare

301

good people half to death, giving them a hideous picture of pedagogical Stalinism. Put this another way: do those who earnestly call "back to basics" really want basics, or do they think of literacy and numeracy simply as mechanical skills, to be acquired without the knowledge and experience of which the skills are manifestations? I doubt that they are teachable as free-floating techniques. I doubt that the decent English now called for can be had without two supports. One is solid foreign-language study, and by that I mean three to five years of another language. But most Americans do not want to learn any language; they are happy to be imprisoned—and imprisoned is what it is—in an American English that for most of them is primitive. Still more important, for a decent English regular reading in good writers—not highbrows and not journalists—is an indispensable support. This means a habit of reading, reading as a natural activity, not as a temporary unpleasantness forced upon one by class assignments. It becomes natural by being learned at home, and mostly this means seeing elders do it spontaneously. But do even the best-intentioned parents who cry "back to basics" really read habitually and thus provide their children with a model that would encourage the *substance* of basics from early on? I only ask.

One historical difficulty is that we have spent a long time rejecting one old system of basics. Our rejection has come out of standard feelings and ideas in America. I want to make this concrete by looking at one specific case, but significant because it is a representative one—namely, my own high-school and college education in the 1920s. In no way do I propose that we *go* back; I am only *looking* back (despite Satchell Paige's warning against it). If I am talking sense, this look-back will seem more than a stereopticon show of quaint old slides found by accident in a mouse-chewed shoe box in the family attic.

As I have noted, my high-school and college education consisted mostly of required courses; there were only a few permissible electives around the edges—nothing like the infinite smorgasbord of possibilities available today—in college and even in high school. Well, that was *one* way of doing basics. It was a late phase of the Renaissance education that, with some variations, had held for about four hundred years. Its unspoken object was to induct the individual into the human community—a community of language, of knowledge, of traditions, and a past felt to be inseparable from a present. Membership in this community might reduce the human addiction to the provincial, the myopic, the transitory, and the half-baked. This concept of basics had eroded very slowly, but the erosion sped up vastly just after my day. Even in my exactly fifty years of college teaching I have seen an enormous decline in the common holdings of students. In my first years in the classroom illustrative uses of words or phrases from other languages—Latin, French, German—would get glances of recognition from up to half the class. Now one cannot count on a single student's knowing a single word in any other language, not to mention English beyond everyday American. When I began, biblical matters—indispensable in all humanities—had a wide range of familiarity; now again one can hardly expect any student to recognize any biblical material at all. Similarly with classical mythology. As for English and European history, it is now a vast mystery, and American history approaches this. We all know the sting of that universal American undergraduate definition of the past, the phrase "in olden days," which means everything from early Egyptian to 1950.

I am not making dirty cracks or even enjoying a binge of therapeutic grousing. I am simply trying to describe where we are. Obviously we cannot simply call for a renewal of that system of basics which persisted from the Renaissance into the twentieth century. But we must be keenly aware of its end—that is, commonly held materials of memory, mind, and imagination, as sources of shared perspective, understanding, and communication. We call for this, but the problem is, as I have already noted, how ready for it we are. I see some less obvious sources of our incomplete readiness for it, and I want to sketch several of them.

To describe the old order of basics I have used the word *community*— of language and intellectual equipment. That word *community* is a key to some of our difficulties in pursuing Basic (suppose I just use that singular from now on). For instance, one of our favorite words is *individualism*. Obviously we must have individualism, but it can get out of hand and become an addiction. We get hooked on the individual as possessor of needs assumed to be unique, of desires that come out of a supposed special identity, and on finding and nurturing that special identity. Look at the continuing popularity of such phrases as "finding myself" and "knowing who I am." These phrases never, but never imply that I will find myself to be much like other people. Being *un*like seems a virtue; resembling others, or belonging to a whole, seems like a threat to independence. We talk a lot about personal relations, we invent ghastly new terms (interpersonal, interface) to describe them, we even, for heaven's sake, give courses in them, but we don't think of interrelatedness as rooted in common possessions of the mind. No, we say, "Invent a new course for me; I'm different." This is at least one reason why within fifty years my six correlated undergraduate English courses have expanded into six score unrelated ones—at least in my university—and several basic curricula into many scores of majors. I know, I know, the explosion of knowledge. But we could channel the explosion into educational patterns that would still reduce the college catalog by one-half or two-thirds. We are hooked on a course in everything for everybody. When we have no sense of a center, we get a wild curricular centrifugality. Two quotations help us see that the concept of individualism, like a red budget, needs some cutbacks. One is ancient, one modern. The ancient quote will need no identification for *this* audience. It is, "We are members of one another." The modern quote is from an essay on Proust, the great French novelist, by C. P. Snow, the English scientist and novelist. Snow wrote: "The realistic and wise, as Proust was to become, emerge with the flat discovery that people anywhere are disconcertingly more alike than different." Membership and likeness—if we felt these two in our bones, and if we could lighten the burden of illusive uniqueness, we would perhaps have a better base for Basic.

Just as we get hooked on the idea of individualism, so we get hooked on the idea of rights. Again, the concept is indispensable, but it gets overworked. Rights are individualism translated into demands. In rights talk, the emphasis is all on what the community owes the individual. He is a recipient rather than a debtor or even a member. I am not saying that the concept of rights has no validity. I am simply saying that when it dominates our consciousness as it seems to do now, without counterbalances, it creates an atmosphere unfavorable to the educational mode I have called "Basic." The big thing becomes what is due me; belonging or membership does not enter the imagination. One expects to be taught what one wants to be taught, and it seems a right. In this sense the idea of rights contributes to a centrifugal scatter-bomb curriculum.

Another influence against Basic is an egalitarianism that indiscriminately totalizes equality. Once again, an indispensable concept is overworked. Our fundamental equality of spirit, opportunity, and political voice fathers a bastard: it is a sense of universal equivalence that ignores differences in talent and potential. It is the old problem of getting equality and quality together in the same household. Grades denoting qualitative differences seem anti-equality, so lower grades disappear. Thus the not-so-good are declared equal to the really good. As long as we have the underqualified with us—because of a mistaken idea of equality or, as often sadly nowadays, for institutional survival—we have to find courses and fields for admittees who are not up to, or are indifferent to, the more significant areas of mind and imagination. They are an unrecognized but real influence on the vast offerings of thin and unrelated courses. But the egalitarian spirit affects us schoolmen too; in practice we regard all courses as equally valid competitors in the marketplace. We vote Democratic but think Republican. Privately we do make distinctions, but publicly—say in curriculum committee decisions—no, never. To judge quality would violate the rule of equality: it would declare some fellow teachers, as Orwell put it, more equal than others. To do that would make one a crank or troublemaker. In sum, one problem for education—notably for that evasive ideal, Basic—is the habit of formally and publicly seeing all individuals (students, courses, or whatever) as equal to each other rather than to the task.

Finally, the sentiment of egalitarianism begets a wide, loose, and unfortunate use of the word *elitism*. This has the effect of attaching all virtue to lowest-common-denominator education. Some anti-elitists use the word to stir up emotional responses that harden into hostility against whatever is superior. But the real damage is done by the numerous people who use the word thoughtlessly, defining it neither in public nor to themselves. As a derogatory term, *elitism* can apply only to one condition—unearned or unmerited privilege. But when *elitism* becomes a popular, undefined, but apparently high-principled word, its effect is to make people back off from earned and merited privilege, or, still worse, from the idea that privilege can be earned and merited. By *privilege* I do not mean material profit or unseemly prerogative. I mean simply whatever may be earned by talent and energy—be it status, respect, special influence, conceded power. *Elite,* as I need hardly say, means chosen, and hence implies excellence. It is harmful to the community if anti-elitism—in popular, and indeed populist, usage—has the side effect of undermining excellence and superiority, of making us dislike them and thus want to hold them in check, and they want to believe that all persons are of equal gifts and that anyway nothing should be done that even implies exceptional talents.

I know how this works in my own field. Loose talk about elitism can even make adequate, controlled, and ordered English seem like highbrow affectation that ought not to taint a democracy. But there is no need to equate democracy with the slipshod, chaotic, and lowest common denominator. Go back to that education of mine and to the Renaissance ideal that lay behind it—classics, language, history, theology, philosophy: it was democratic in the best sense. Why? Because it assumed that every man was capable of being inducted into the community of knowledge and understanding. Even randy lords made it. The Earl of Rochester, best known as a pornographic poet, had mastered Greek and Latin by age fifteen and was always interested in theological problems. His life as combined profligate and philosopher need not be held up as a model, but our anti-elitism would clearly have weakened the philosophical side of it. Nostalgia, however, is not my line. We can never, as I have said, go back. But we can look back to see what we can learn.

ii

In the present, we may alter education a little if our dissatisfactions with it coincide with public dissatisfactions about it. Our own dissatisfactions, of course, are chronic; we do not often slip into the agreeable sloth of public contentment with our common labors. On some dissatisfactions we need not waste energy—those imperfections of students that are due to human nature, fallen as it is, and always producing vexatious types, combative or torpid. But if human nature does not change much, social attitudes and values do. We can work at the slow business of nudging a society, local or larger, in other directions. Some nudging from us may have helped stimulate the familiar cry, "Back to basics." If the feeling behind this is genuine— our passions often turn out to be passing fashions, what with the media's undying lust for novel excitements—then this could be the hour for some redesigning of school and college work. If I were sure of this, I could stop here and announce an educational sunrise—that is, the new bright light of what I have called "Basic."

Instead of hailing the glorious hour, however, I have spent a good deal of time checking out certain kinds of static in the national atmosphere that can work against instant academic glory. Still, I have in no way spoken with a grim and hopeless voice. True, we might have to rein in a little one hereditary American impulse—the what-can-we-do-about-it impulse. Often there is no what, and we can limit unhappiness by accepting insolubility. John Keats's famous phrase "negative capability" is apt: the ability to live with the ambiguous, the uncertain, the unanswered. What Keats called "negative" gives a positive recipe for survival: to be sensible and bypass dragons that might entice one into hopeless battles. Granted, the academic instinct for survival sometimes means marketing educational junk jewelry for a public that wants to shine by such fixings—a rather sorry form of survival. But if the instinct for survival means living with the imperfect, it may qualify us for William Faulkner's encomium on the people, "They endured." At times patience is the only tactic—notably when the problems are those of our post-Edenic human nature. But beyond the instinct for survival there is another preserver that used to be called "vocation." In a more modern idiom, we are instructaholics. We will always find some students that can be teased or driven to respond triumphantly to tough and merciless teaching. We can have the relentlessness of Miss Moffett, the main character in Emlyn Williams's play *The Corn Is Green*. In a situation far more difficult than ours ever is—a remote Welsh mining village—she pounded Latin and Western history and English grammar into a young barely literate miner; he made it to Oxford and became a writer. Untapped geniuses are rare, but we can still spot a potential field and drill it until it perhaps becomes, if not a gusher, at least a steady producer.

As for impact on the outer world? We won't do much by way of Carlyle heroics. We are by nature inch-by-inch workers, and our line is day-by-day pressure, often indirect. If we can keep forever insisting that words be used with precision, we might carry out a worthy enough mission. If society calls for Basic, we can do more than applaud with a "Yum, yum" and a "Me, too." We can try, with quiet persistence, to see that *Basic* is more than a catchword, and to insist that skills without the knowledge on which they rest will remain shaky. We can fight against letting major concepts of our society puff up into fuzzy slogans that turn good intentions into bad ends. I don't mean such old slogans as practicality, relevance, payoff, and training, which have been talked to death and which in the long run may not be as bad as nobler ideas with a hidden kickback. What concerns me much more is the shoddy use of such grander words as *individualism, rights, equality,* and *elitism,* which can all undermine educational ends, especially those of Basic. We can strive against their becoming everyday handyman carriers of vague emotions and confused good intentions.

Clearly the answer to "What can we do?" is not a crashing thunderbolt affair. There are not many white horses around now, and ripsnorting battle cries don't rip very much once the novelty has worn off. Cavalry charges—nowadays tank attacks, no doubt—are for limited concrete issues of the moment. The more lasting and deep-seated the issues, the less the call for the heroic. The line is rather moral attrition through a series of such intellectual pressures as we can mount. It may seem grubby. But education is mostly an unspectacular, unheadlined, day-to-day affair. Trying to alter it isn't much different.

20

Humanistic, Humane, Human

It is quite fashionable, today, to throw around such words as *dehumanizing* and *humanizing* in a variety of contexts. One of these contexts is education. After hearing the term *humanizing education,* and after listening in on some discussion of the theme, I began to feel that it might be worth a little investigation. What sounds like a slogan might have an unforeseen or unintended meaning.

"Humanizing" is like a maternity dress: it only partly conceals an inner burden—in this case, semantic triplets. As adjectives the three are *human, humane,* and *humanistic;* the corresponding nouns are *human nature, humaneness* or *humanity,* and *humanities.* By "humanizing," then, do we mean getting more of human nature into education, making people more humane, or giving them more humanities? To start with the biggest word: the idea of a bigger serving of humanities on the curricular blue-plate does not make my pedagogical saliva flow faster. It is unseemly for anyone to plug for a bigger public intake of the particular entree that he is dishing out from the educational steam table. Some years ago, to describe the barking of their goods by humanists, I put forward the term *humanisticism*—a word sufficiently repellent to betray, amid the warm public air of uplift, the chill downdraft of profit. When the newspapers tell us almost daily of their selfless principled pursuit of everybody's right to know, what reader does not think promptly of the papers' basic quest for circulation and advertising? Desire to survive is understandable, but it should not be disguised as saintly public service.

There are subtler reasons for forgoing humanisticism. For one thing, if the humanistic documents do not seem vital to a society, promotion will not make them so. Public relations will not bring about a change of heart, prone as our age is to quickie rebirths. For another, my half century in universities persuades me that the quantity of humanities in curricular packaging is not likely to fall below a certain minimum. Further, the more humanities courses are multiplied, the greater the danger of sheer inflation, that is, of paper-money offerings quite likely to drive the better coinages out of circulation. The giant bank of a decade's new humanities courses seems full of paper money, little of it convertible into educational gold. Worse, we get used to paper, and gold seems too heavy to handle. Maybe the present decline in humanistic study across America is a kind of normalizing deflation such as often follows an inflationary period. For a decade or two we may have been overregistered through one of those constant flip-flops of campus fashion when tedium or economic visions or utopian fantasies make everyone rush to some new curricular dream-boat for a biennium or two. Ecology seems to be the latest overcrowded academic ferry to salvation. If humanities are undergoing corrective deflation, the sad thing may be where the shrinkage hits: we are too likely to be left with all those foamy, bubbly-gummy curricular hot numbers while the solid center from which they radiated contracts into something like a cosmic black hole whence no light flows.

A final reason for my not pushing the humanities. If I were to cry, "Flood education with the humanities and thus humanize it," some nonhumanist might retort derisively, "Humanist, humanize thyself." That would be the unkindest cut of all, since there can be no anesthetic for truth. Alas, long contact with the humanities does not guarantee anyone automatic possession of humanistic graces. It is not a fail-safe barrier against grace-lessness, pedantry, triviality, self-importance, sentimentality, demagoguery, and more.

ii

Let us then see whether "humanize education" should mean "humane-ize education." "Humane-ize" can apply to either the product or the process. The product, I take it, would be humane people—ones who try to mitigate or avoid what Burns has called man's inhumanity to man. They will not be indifferent, unkind, or cruel; instead they will be benevolent, thoughtful, helpful. These are genuine moral virtues, but unfortunately there is no way to curricularize them. Whatever of humaneness we achieve is, in truth, inculcated by all the influences that impinge upon us from early life on; if these have had no good effect by age eighteen, it is probably too late. Further, humaneness may be achieved without benefit of education; it is a style of spirit to which scholastic routines are hardly relevant.

The other meaning of "humane-ize education" is to tenderize the educational process, lest in its unmarinated state it can be too tough for the consumers. Long ago it was. But we have had a good deal of marination since the reports of Dickens, Charlotte Brontë, and other recorders of school terrors, and the educational meat has become extraordinarily easy to masticate. Letting it hang too long is easily mistaken for humaneness. It is not really a startling paradox that we could humane-ize the educational process by making it more of a privilege to be earned and making it firmer, more demanding to the teeth and muscles of the mind. We could struggle against the present sad inflation in grading, by which the instructor, perhaps meaning well or perhaps coolly self-serving, flatters the student instead of serving him by judging him. We can practice inhumaneness not only by harshness but by the giveaway, by a misplaced Santa Clausery, which is oppression turned upside down. It is a subtle form of man's inhumanity to man not to hold him to what he is up to. By his nature he craves limits, tests, sound judgments, earned possessions. If he doesn't get these, he loses the ability to do what he can do, and he gets a very shallow sense of reality. This encourages a self-centeredness that can make him a permanent nuisance and thus inhumane to others. If he comes to and finds that he has been tricked into a misconception of the world, he may turn revengeful, and this makes him another kind of nuisance—and inhumane.

iii

Our third option as the goal of "humanizing education" is human-ness. We apply the term *human* to many things; to both creditable actions and those which are less admirable, especially those that we are, or may get, caught in. We say "it's only human" about a host of naughtinesses. "Errare humanum est," that is, "to err is human." On this basis, humanizing education might mean cultivating skills in erring. This seems like giving institutional support where there is not much need of it. (I was going to say that erring comes out of an instinct as reliable as sex, but then I remembered that in some quarters it is evidently felt that the race might die out if we did not have courses in sex.) When we applaud "the human," of course, we usually mean only the attitudes and actions that claim our respect. Hence another problem: "human" means only what the user of the word approves of. In a recent volume honoring George Woodcock, one contributor asserts that it is anarchists and pacifists who are truly human. No reason why the writer shouldn't admire them. But pacifism and anarchism are no more human than militancy and strict controls, which may even be necessary in crises. The Dutch science writer Kees Boeke has a quite different view of being human. "If he is to be really human," Boeke says, man "must combine in his being the greatest humility with the most careful and considerate use of the cosmic powers that are at his disposal"—that is, practice technological prudence, and avoid hubris. But once again the opposites are equally human. Imprudence plus hubris leads not to the inhuman or nonhuman but to the tragic, which is a central experience, no less human than survival by safe and modest courses. A sounder definition is given by Judge Moody in Eudora Welty's novel *Losing Battles:* "And of course human nature is dynamite to start with." This prevents the facile use of *human* as a synonym for "admirable." Judge Moody leads us over into André Malraux's perception: "Humanism does not consist in saying, 'No animal could have done what we have done' "—that is, boasting about a kind of unearned superiority—"but in declaring: 'We have refused to do what the beast in us willed to do.' " In this sound view we must accept our kinship with the beasts, and we earn our difference by hard choice.

Now the qualities that we admire and call "human" must indeed be earned. If we think we get them free we suffer from complacency. The complaint about dehumanizing influences—a complaint that has become a terrible cliché—is an indirect self-congratulation: it implies that we are already humanized and in danger of being unjustly deprived of some kind of right or privilege, like voting. Consider the well-paid athlete who turns out a would-be best-seller complaining loudly that his professional sport is dehumanizing. He is in effect boasting publicly about his native spiritual superiority and expecting to make money out of this. But his apparent moral concern would be trustworthy only if he left the profession without fanfare, did not cast himself as an unjust victim of dehumanization, gave away his ill-gotten gains, and only in the privacy of the confessional admitted that as a paid athlete he was giving control to certain traits he would rather not have so well developed.

The ordinary citizen complains that machinery, electronics, computers, and other such are dehumanizing us all. Once again the complainer automatically possesses all the virtues called "human," and they are being ground out of him. By now, however, the steady modern creation of new tools is an old story, and we ought to know that self-pity is not the only option open to us. In fact, there are at least three other wrong options. One is to create a new literal deus ex machina, that is, to deify the machinery. This response is nicely symbolized in O'Neill's *Dynamo,* where the divine dynamo carelessly electrocutes its worshiper. The next option for man is to become a deus ex machina, that is, to deify himself because he has machinery to command. Now self-deification is a voluntary form of dehumanization, and a very dangerous kind too. The third wrong option is to say a kind of "get thee hence" to machinery and computers, as if we could shut them out of our good world. This will not do. It is impossible to return to an earlier machinery, and it would be unprofitable. Feeding a family with bow and arrow will not bring on a great new humanism.

On the other hand, in dealing with technological change, we have several options that may serve us well. If we recognize that new machinery simply changes the style of our continuing relationship with the world around us, we can try to manage the new style in a manner that will keep in play the human traits that we think indispensable. We can identify the needs and values that the machines do not serve and seek out quiet steps to keep some life in them. Finally, if we really want to be superior to machines—if we want to work at it instead of just abusing machines for cutting down on our humanity—there is one sure way to do it: do not talk, think, or act mechanically. This is very hard, like all valid means to good ends.

iv

As a first step in humanizing education, then, we can clear the air by trying to see what we mean by our words, and trying to rule out the easy recipes that in our humanity we love. It might be safest to stop there. But I will risk introducing a view of humanity that may suggest kinds of educational action. Let us go on from the fact that our humanity embraces our flaws and vices as well as our virtues. Along with this moral complexity there is a constitutional complexity in man—his numerous and often contradictory ways of thinking and feeling, attitudes and emphases, ideas of value, self-definitions, longings and rejections. Each such expression represents only a part of humanity; hence they should all be active at the same time to represent the diverse nature of man completely. This ideal fullness is achieved less often than it is defeated in historical actuality. Every age or period tends to pick out some aspect or possibility of human nature, to treat it as basic, and to give it general control. Beginning about mid-seventeenth-century, England and France produced a very fine literature of social observation and satire, for the most part expressions of the then dominant value variously called "reason," "good sense," and "common sense." What was in control was a rational perspective on the human scene. Inevitably it reduced the operating space of the nonrational constituents of the psyche—various emotional and imaginative activities; feeling for mystery, for nature, for fantasy, for the transcendent and the ideal; the highly individual vision that fell outside the going patterns.

So in time there emerged a set of literary and cultural counterforms giving an outlet to the underprivileged human tendencies. They constitute what we now call the Romantic movement. This is, of course, a historical commonplace. I bring it in only to provide one clear concrete example of how an age shortchanges some aspects of human nature when a culture hits on a central blueprint of reality and treats it as an absolute. Such a shortchanging of human nature occurs in some degree in all ages and, needless to say, in our own. If we can detect it, perhaps we can think of the humanizing of education as an effort to bring into play a fuller humanity than contemporary habits and attitudes represent. We could offer reminders of the full range of humanity that gets cut back by current assumptions, complacencies, passions, and obsessions.

This is not an easy business. When we are in an age, it is hard to see it in perspective. We see the unbalance of an age better when the next age has brought in a new unbalance. We see clearly the set ways of the Victorians; it is less easy to see that in reacting against their set ways we have developed a contrasting set of set ways. As Owen Barfield says, in our day it is as difficult to oppose positivism as it was to oppose Aristotelianism in the Middle Ages. He adds, very astutely, "It is a mistake to suppose that we are more open-minded today; we are merely open-minded about different things." Our version of open-mindedness makes it difficult to detect where we are closed. But we can do one thing that does not demand that we be geniuses or look at things from a divine distance: we can try to spot the verbal fashions and automatisms of the day, the key terms, the taken-for-granted words of praise and blame, the slogans, the clichés—all stylistic indicators of our reduction of a whole human nature to some part of it. If we can resist clichés, we may be open to fuller insights. If we can challenge some verbal habits, we may help open the way to a more adequate functioning of the many potentialities of our nature.

V

Style is the man, we know; style may be the age, too. How we say things reveals what we are. As early as the 1940s George Orwell issued the first alert on a modern dreadfulness of style. Orwell quoted Eccles. 9:11: "I returned, and saw under the sun, that the race is not to the swift, nor the battle to the strong, nor yet bread to the wise, nor yet riches to men of understanding, nor yet favor to men of skill; but time and chance happeneth to them all." Then Orwell modernized: "Objective consideration of contemporary phenomena compels the conclusion that success or failure in competitive activities exhibits no tendency to be commensurate with innate capacity, but that a considerable element of the unpredictable must be taken into account." (Today "competitive activities" would be "interpersonal relationships, interface confrontations, and lifestyle adjustments.") Orwell sees that we don't like the directness and concreteness of Ecclesiastes; we find comfort in an idea swathed in the cotton wool of abstractions; we prefer banality to reality. Lionel Trilling, as we have already seen, has dealt with this issue by translating "They fell in love and married" into a mass of the abstractions that today often pass for learned discourse. Allen Tate puts an analogous thought in similar terms: "It is a tragedy of contemporary society that so much of democratic social theory reaches us in the language of *drive, stimulus,* and *response.* This is not the language of free men; it is the language of slaves. The language of free men substitutes for these words, respectively, *end, choice,* and *discrimination*" (1953). When a great English satirist and an American southern conservative point to the same sorriness of language, the issue is real. Such style reduces man to a brute, to a slave, to a mechanical contraption; it eliminates character; what is left is subhuman.

Ironically enough, such language often endeavors to transpose the ordinary into the suprahuman. Once a garbageman said to me, "I've been lifting garbage for ten years." There is directness, there is concreteness, there is live language. Now if that man had had contact with a higher culture, he would doubtless have said, "I have had a decade of executive experience in the container-management division of domestic-premise decontamination." "Executive," yes; these days we say insurance executive when we mean "policy peddler," and "merchandizing-relationship executive" for "floor-walker." Sooner or later English teachers may be known as literacy executives or humanism executives. Recently William Zinsser of Harvard has been struggling against such language among school administrators, who often don't know that they are talking like that. On the other hand, even some scholars and critics write like that; perhaps the stylistic murkiness of some literary criticism is really a writer's snatch at suprahuman status. Since God's words are often obscure, obscure words may hint at divinity in him who uses them.

The relation to our basic theme is clear. If we seek to humanize we can resist a style that, unconsciously degrading or laboriously uplifting, runs away from fullness of humanity: on the one hand, from feeling, will, and thought; on the other hand, from the unexciting realities and the plain down-to-earth ordinariness inseparable from all human life. That is, it subhumanizes or suprahumanizes. The elevator-shoe style clues us in to various forms of the aspiration in which humanity is misconceived, misled, or misused. Uplift plus machinery leads to what we may call bumper-sticker spirituality. In that world of slogans my favorite is, "If you know that Jesus loves you, honk." Athletes honk by crediting Jesus with upping their yardage record, batting average, or whatever. Less knowing upward-bound types fall into the hands of prophets whose divinity is incarnate in

Cadillacs, whose episcopate is composed of bodyguards, whose sanctuary is a Swiss bank, and whose promised land is a stockade where no one can go over the wall. A subtler operator is the professional atheist who seeks to dictate to schools and other institutions. He makes a mere slogan out of an old principle: "the separation of church and state." It is inapplicable, and it conceals an effort to give power to one religion, his own. The center of the atheist religion may be called anthropotheism, or perhaps better, anthropolatry. If, as some observers propose, man was forming God in his own image, then what we are doing is trading in an anthropomorphic deity for theomorphic man. This strange trade is not exactly new. An early apostle of it was Christopher Marlowe's demonic slicker, Mephistopheles, who said to Dr. Faustus, "Thinkest thou heaven is such a glorious thing? / I tell thee, 'tis not half so fair as thou, / Or any man that breathes on earth." This premodern modernist was saying, in effect, "Y'know, man, you're God." The relation of all this to the style problem is clear: when every kind of worker in vineyard, office, or store is known as an "executive," it is man making like God. This is an ultimate, and rather risky, form of dehumanization.

vi

Style gives clues in another direction. The style that we have been describing depersonalizes. Thus it might even be a crazy kind of reaction against an overextended individualism (needed reactions, as we know, can take mad forms). A full humanity needs both the impersonal and the personal, the system and the multiple private variations, and is in trouble if either becomes disproportionate. An overgrown individualism leads to willfulness, self-indulgence, self-centeredness—or narcissism, as it has been called. Narcissism takes several common forms. One appears in that roadblock to action: "I want to know who I am," a detective problem that may use up some years. The seeker is ordinarily someone who is barely beginning to become someone, a process that needs energizing rather than detailed self-scrutiny. Another form of mirror-gazing is "finding myself," which often implies that what is to be found is a uniqueness that can be matched by only one destiny. The discovery that will eventually be made without search is that one is an everyman with general rather than unique needs and possibilities. Then there is the slogan "self-fulfillment," which tends to involve the fear of inadequate intake, of doing without. Now in the complete humanity that I suggest we keep in mind as a goal—that is, a balance of complementary values—there is a need both of self-fulfillment, or getting, if you will, and self-denial, or not getting. Neither is an absolute; both must figure in life. Again, modern fulfillment may mean substituting the result of an action for the quality of an action: not what one becomes, but what one comes by. In a very sharp comedy by Alan Ayckbourn a young wife and husband are having a hostile meal; he is interested only in business, and she is struggling to get herself into his line of vision. She has recently been on a three-week visit to Italy. Finally she snaps at him: "Do you know what I did in Italy? I spent the time with your boss." The husband sinks into a long silent slump, head almost on table, staring at the dark end of the world. At last he struggles up and shoots back accusing words: "You've ruined me. His wife will find out, and I'll never get promoted." Results, clearly. Not that the results of actions are not important; only that, for a full humanity, they are only one criterion of value. Another form of unbalance is self-righteousness, especially the form that makes a speaker, without any effort on his part, superior. In our day the most obvious practitioner of instant moral superiority goes around making contemptuous references to "Vietnam and Watergate." This is a cliché of the facile public assumption of virtue without any of the costs or difficulties of virtue; the speaker admits that he belongs to the good guys. (He always makes the sinner in me want to see what can be said for the bad guys.) The good guy takes half his humanity for the whole.

In a recent book on Sir Philip Sidney, Dorothy Connell finds that the essence of Renaissance thought is the ability to "encompass and balance contradictions." But living with contradictions is difficult, and we tend to absolutize one value and forget its opposite. In this way we fall into dehumanization as I am defining it here: incompleteness. Hence one way of humanizing education is to seek out balancing emphases upon those aspects of human reality that we can see are shortchanged. Often we will have to go against fashions, since every fashion is a form of overemphasis. I have mentioned the fashions of verbal style that do subhumanize or try to suprahumanize us, and the fashions of social style that overemphasize individualism, and lead to exclusive self-concern. What is undervalued here is the need to belong, to be a part, to be formed by a whole, by a community. To repeat John Donne's most famous line, "No man is an island." We need to make a case for the mainland.

All this, as I have said, is not easy. Faculty members who must take a lead against cultural unbalance may share in it and practice unwittingly the age's form of diminished humanity. The old advisory truism, "Take the instructor and not the subject," tells us a lot. The primacy of the teacher rather than the thing taught, the material as an echo of the teacher—this is a familiar form of excessive individualism or islandism. It lives on the illusion that good automatically flows from the antics of the personality on the podium. This leads to what has nicely been called "my-ism" in the professor; it appears in such phrases as "my students" (as though he were the subject of study, as indeed he may be), "my field," and, above all, "my course," as if the material were some sort of preserve, trespassers prohibited, instead of a public domain that he is privileged to help interpret. The tourist guide converts himself into the proprietor. Besides, his private preserve is often a tiny and obscure place. A series of visits to such odd corners does not lead the student toward a full humanity. The faculty form of narcissism appears also in the what-I-want-to-do line. How often I have heard a professor laud his institution because "they let me do what I want to do." This cliché of self-acceptance is rarely balanced by a sense of what ought to be done. Indeed one has the impression that in some faculty circles the only valid ought is that there oughtn't to be any oughts. While the student gloomily seeks to find out who he is, the instructor serenely believes that whoever he is, and whatever he does, is good. We might call him a self-confidence man. Once he simply dictated the truth to his class; now he tells the class, "Call me Charlie," and professes not to have any answers to embarrass the flux of amateur opinion. The claim of ignorance is simply the illusion of omniscience turned upside down: another style of unbalance.

Answerlessness is one answer to trying human complexities. The opposite unbalance is the reductive answer, the single handle, the conversion of what may well be a part-truth into a total reality—by a Freudian handle, or a Marxist handle, or a sexist handle or an absurdist handle or an anarchist handle, or a do-good handle; to use subject matter as a tool of whatever rights movement happens to be in the air at the moment, to interpret man as always a victim or a brute or as material for reform; to hustle for one's own field, that is, to present it, not as having a possibly useful perspective on, but as having a special key to, truth and reality. This Bible-izes the area documents. Finally, our pathetic human longing to have it anti-humanly simple appears in another current cliché—the deploring of an undefined elitism. What looks like a protest against needless inequities may be at heart, and often is, that inherent disability of democratic life: confusing equity and ability, denying special human gifts, disliking to see them encouraged, and resenting the superiorities of achievement, and sometimes of reward, to which they lead. Such egalitarianism tries to ignore human reality.

vii

If these notes on various attitudes and clichés work, they will suggest limitations of understanding that a humanizing of education—that vast project—might try to resist. Education should stimulate the awareness of a full humanity in all its contradictions and paradoxes, its conflicting tendencies and needs, its inconsistencies, its durability and its inevitable vulnerability, its capacity for both good and evil, for both devotion and skepticism, its need of both freedom and order. History is humanity's constant efforts to evade its own ambiguity and doubleness by limited codes and emphases that give a special coloring to each cultural era: the rational, classical, and urban in the eighteenth century; the personal, rural, and exotic in the Romantic period; the pursuit of spiritual triumph in the Victorian. As for us, we are long on permissiveness, privileges, rights, grievances (Kipling says having them is like having leprosy), the democratic that slides into the egalitarian, the human as mechanistic (salvation by techniques), the fantasy of immunity (foods without dangers, drugs without side effects, life without end—what we might call creeping Califanoism), society as infinitely protective but as otherwise powerless, and finally what Angus Wilson calls "ostentatious unfaith." We are constantly utopian; visionary untruths, crushed to earth, always rise again. Utopianism is semihuman because it leaves out so much of human reality. Besides, with us it so often rides on a total faith in tools or instruments that are to be prescribed or proscribed and thus to redeem human nature. We tried prohibition. Today we want to prohibit private weapons and public armaments, and an increasing number of foods, medicines, and other goodies; and we want to require seatbelts, or even hardhats, for everyone on the road. Alas, one does not eliminate slavedriving, flagellation, or fixed horse races by making it illegal to manufacture and market whips. Finally, it is a totally charming fact that the ancient solemn word *tetragrammaton* means "four-letter word." This identity points to another one-sidedness of ours. We are strong on the four-letter-word side, weak on the tetragrammatical; that is, strong on simplistic physiology, and weak on mystery. So we pine for UFOs as a surrogate for the transcendent.

When the problems are of this kind, one cannot propose changes in curriculum, administration, and budget, our magic American ways of achieving instant perfection (by a budget-change, of course, I mean a reprioritization of resource-allocation in institutional services-delivery to multiple parity-based constituencies). No program; not even a new course. No need to get into that game at a time when various departments, we may be sure, are pressure-cooking hot offerings in this style: "The Guyana Syndrome: The Psychic Infra-Structure of Jim Jonesism." I leave programs to others. My basic faith is rather in people's awareness. That awareness, if my examples are persuasive, should stimulate other and better lists than mine of late-twentieth-century angles, foibles, nonseeings, unbalances. Educators might want to move on from there. They could do some slight service to humanity by attempting to revive, at least in consciousness, the alternatives and opposites. They could take apparently perverse attitudes, if need be, to try to balance things out, to alert the understanding to the diverse, and not always reconcilable, possibilities out of which a constant humanity, rarely full-sighted, drifts into its sequence of incomplete cultures.

Many teachers have the right awareness, actually or potentially. At best it is demanding, since it calls for an eye on those restricting habits of the culture, of students, and of ourselves that unfocus, befog, or narrow the view of a full many-natured humanity. It means, to sum up, speaking plainly and not disguising self or ideas in a verbose, pretentious, or quasi-intellectual language; it means not letting the personality of student or teacher take precedence over what is taught and studied; it means trying to spot the limitations in fashions and clichés widely accepted or taken for absolutes—the habits of thought and speech that mechanize man or deify him, that overstress discipline and order or, as is more frequent in our day and in our part of the world, that overstress rights and privileges and my-ism, that encourage hypertrophic self-concern, that let "what I want to do" be a final guide of faculty or student effort.

It means avoiding reductive styles of interpretation that easily divide humanity into good and bad instead of seeing that both are copossessors of everyman. That may be why we shy from tragedy: not that it presents unhappiness, but that people like ourselves bring it on themselves. We are reminded of our vulnerability. At its best comedy also taxes us: its base, as distinct from that of satire, is the acceptance of a humanity that includes the silly, the vain, the grasping, and even the scheming, and above all the sharply diverse, as more or less inevitable and to be lived with. Comedy excludes the obsessive egalitarianism that would try to make both Don Quixote and Sancho Panza more like average men, that is, mediocrities who do not trouble us. Thus both tragedy and comedy help protect us against a simplifying of human reality, against the easy, and easily gratifying, sense of a universe neatly divided between insiders and outsiders.

In alluding to some of our habits—verbal, intellectual, and moral—that in my view need watching because they narrow us down too much, I proceed like any sound moralist: I detect errors primarily by introspection, with just a small supplement of circumspection. My aim is not to abuse but to describe, and to describe in the hope of contributing to the individual awareness in which I trust. With a working view of what *human* means, the teacher may take a small step or two in that immense project of "humanizing education"—a small step by subtle self-modification. He can set an example and hope. Will such quiet, unspectacular efforts have any effect? Perhaps, if there are enough of them. It is a gamble. Two quotations tell what is possible. When a young man asked, "What can I do to save the world?" Thomas Carlyle replied, "Make an honest man of yourself, and then you can be sure there is one less rascal in the world." E. M. Forster puts it differently, "Do good, and possibly good may come from it." He adds, "Beware of the long run"—that is, don't aspire to final solutions. If now and then we can just catch a fad or cliché or tic of the day, and step on its toes, we may also serve.

21

The Great-Teacher Myth

The film *Dead Poets Society* is now well past its once front-page status, and it may be possible to look at some of its implications without having to duck live or postal fisticuffs. Hilary Mantel's review in the *Spectator* (October 7, 1989), charmingly entitled "Alien Corn," ended thus: "[Robin Williams's] dominant, self-conscious presence surely cannot disguise, even from his fans, that the film is platitudinous, overblown and absurd. But enough. Already I hear the postman's tread." Perhaps any anti-Mantel admirer of the film would have been mollified by the *New Yorker*'s "In Brief" encomium, which singularly abjured metropolitan skepticism: "The picture draws out the obvious and turns itself into a classic [which] has a gold ribbon attached to it." These diverse judgments resemble those in the movie house where I saw the film. A fellow academic and I, who at movies are sometimes given to napping or to feeling that the two hours are not well spent, were not only kept awake by *Dead Poets Society* but put into a bit of a snit by it. The audience, however, behaved quite differently: they all but gave it a standing ovation—an amazing response to a film.

Our women companions come in somewhere between asperity and alleluias. They could listen calmly to the opinionated. In saying my piece, I fell into some familiar terms of dramatic criticism. "Well, they take such a stale line. It's old-fashioned melodrama gussied up to look like educational criticism. First you've got this guy on a white horse charging in to save the place. So you need some set-up black hats to make him look like a hero instead of a moral egoist. Look at what a monstrous, trite, overstuffed setup you get—a school principal that looks like a travesty of Thomas Arnold. The type hasn't been seen since Dickens. You get a Hitlerish papa who screams orders about his son's career. These long-dead types in the 1950s! And when the hero sets out to look like an intellectual giant, he takes aim at a textbook passage on poetry that would have seemed dated in

1910. If the guy in the white hat is in the end a rather simple, sentimental self-worshiper, the scriptwriters are unblushingly devious: they not only invent a passage of incredible stupidity, but they attribute it to a volume conspicuously entitled *Understanding Poetry*. This is, of course, the title of an actual textbook, one that was very influential in its day. The authors of it did not say, and would not be caught dead saying, anything faintly resembling the passage that the instructor, John Keating, so spectacularly takes off against. The authors could sue the producers for defamation of character. Well, this falsification of fact goes naturally along with the general falsification of human reality."

When one starts putting into specific words the general annoyance aroused by the film, one warms to the task. "The hero, John Keating, accomplishes nothing. As for the student rebellion against the incredible headmaster, it is only a temporary knee-jerk application of a Keating gesture. Nothing is changed, but we see Keating watching with smirking self-satisfaction, as if he had in fact dethroned a tyrant, instead of choreographing a fake rebellion against a fake villain. The film gets the firing of this rebel all wrong. It says he was fired for fighting injustice. What he should have been fired for was making himself, instead of the works of literature, the object of adulation. The film is immoral: it presents a fraud as a hero."

Oh my, I had slipped into Savonarolese. Or, let's just say I got something off my chest. My male companion was roughly on the same wavelength as I. Then one of our female companions said, "Yes, we never do see Keating *teaching* anything." The matter could not have been better put. What we see is moonlight larks and forest frolics—midsummer nights' dream fantasies taken for actualities, instead of that steady book-work, aided by sensible explication, that might lead to some education. Keating is not a teacher at all but a performer (the boys call him "Captain"). Like Eugene O'Neill's father, he enacts only one lifetime role: he has cast himself as the gutsy, charismatic, infallible, one-in-a-million guide against the system. Any system needs critics, but Keating is only a guy with a mike in a midnight show.

The film, of course, gets only one-half the picture because it gets only one-half the character. The missing element was identified by Bruce Bawer in his excellent review in the *American Spectator* (August 1989). Aside from pointing out such artifices as those described here, Bawer shrewdly noted that *Dead Poets Society* has the same theme as the 1969 film *The Prime of Miss Jean Brodie:* both portray the style and influence of a star teacher in a preparatory school. But in *Miss Jean Brodie* we see the full character: the self-worship and power-love of the spectacular teacher who manages to seem superior to a whole cadre of routine-bound dull souls. When I viewed *Miss Jean Brodie* again on my VCR, I found the older film not only convincing but absorbing, indeed thrilling. In contrast with the myopia of *Dead Poets Society,* it had insight into the singular nexus between certain leadership gifts and the ego that cannot settle for a steady engagement in the common enterprise but must star in public displays of extraordinary powers over the young. I have only one slight reservation about this otherwise excellent film: that Miss Brodie's admiration of Mussolini and Franco should have been hinted at rather than stressed, and her comeuppance less hammered home. Perhaps this overtness seemed necessary in 1961, the date of Muriel Spark's novel on which the film was based. Be that as it may, the film had precisely what *Dead Poets Society,* two decades later, lacked: alertness to the moral reality of the tale—to the cult-Führer implicit in the upset-the-peach-basket lectern star, the eikonoklastes who becomes an eikon.

Some time after seeing *Dead Poets Society* I ran into a friend who was the successful headmaster of a reputable private school. I asked him whether in his professional life he had ever encountered a Keating. Oh yes, he said, you run into them now and then. He identified by name the current Keating at his own school. This man had written a somewhat best-selling book, one that rather questioned the whole educational process. Hence he had become the resident wise man; he was given to acknowledging his own wisdom, running a special classroom show, condescending to his colleagues, and thus creating a followership that did not ease the basic processes of the school.

An older man, he was perhaps on the way to the role depicted in a 1972 drama, Robert Marasco's *Child's Play*—a brilliant portrayal of an increasing but undefined moral epidemic in a boys preparatory school. Marasco successfully dramatizes, by nightmarish situations that cross over into the surrealistic, the growth of an apparently inexplicable evil spirit in the boys. They are cruel to each other; they are insolent and threatening to faculty and officers; and they particularly victimize one instructor who has won the unpopularity prize of the term. We slowly identify the corrupting influence in the school: the faculty member who is the professional student-lover, the grand old man who, adored by the students, calls them "my boys" (exactly the style of Miss Brodie and Keating). In this English teacher—one more of us, alas—Marasco catches the substitution of personality for a decent discipline, of amiability for the instructional integrity that makes demands, of a subtle flattery for the more difficult task of assisting the young to grow up. Behind this style lies the instructor's pure self-love; it appears as an indiscriminate affection for students that nurtures their self-indulgence. This self-indulgence, when students are freed from the authority of learning and of moral direction, helps release the aggressive nastiness that is always present in human nature. Marasco carries out to a logical extreme the "spoiling" of young people by uncritical, apparently affectionate tolerance, and he does it by a brilliant paradox: Mr. Chips as satanic seducer.

It is useful to have a picture of the Brodie-Keating type carried on into advanced years. Brodie and Keating, of course, got fired early, one of them seen through, the other apparently surviving, at least for a moment, in a student style that we are asked to believe is the herald of a new and better world.

The faculty type most recently represented by Keating is, ultimately, less that of a teacher than a performer. He enacts the role of the solitary, anticrowd voice (the "lonely, self-romanticizing egotist," Bruce Bawer calls him). He is not the occasional individual morally committed against a majority, obviously essential to the well-being of a society, but the professional moral soloist who always has it right while the rest of the world drags on routinely and unseeingly. He alerts the young to circumambient evils and neglected truths while colleagues and administrators drudgingly stick to formalistic ruts. He hints that he has to pay a price. The role forced upon him tends to be the central one in the Passion Play. He struggles to push for truth, but it is hard going against centurions, Pharisees, money changers in the temple, and so forth. (The man sometimes said to have been the real-life original of Keating, a university professor for many years, has published several volumes of essays, and several years ago took on the difficult responsibility of membership on a school board. He would have real grounds for complaint about cinematic misrepresentation.)

ii

The Keating types that I have observed directly have performed on the university stage. It is a rare university that does not have its own resident Keating. He tends to become the local Great Teacher, a resonant voice that beguiles its publics (undergraduates and off-campus auditors) while leaving colleagues unmoved, ironic, or simply enduring. As a friend of mine put it, he trades respect from his equals for adulation by a more populous world. I leave unanswered the question of whether the Great Teacher can also be a good teacher. It may be technically possible, if not probable. The Great Teacher is remembered as a hot onstage performer, the good teacher as a cool expositor of a body of knowledge that is the essential survivor in memory. The Great Teacher lives in memory as a striking figure, the good teacher as the voice of a field.

Looking a little further at the Keating roles, one discovers that in one manifestation he is the Great Teacher in only one academic field. There he tends to create a sect by seeming to have provided a basic key to human and societal problems. It is a little difficult, as I know by experience, to have in one's class a delegation of Keatingians, who can hardly put up with textual readings not obviously in accord with their master's finalities. His doctrine gives them a corner on Truth. Eric Voegelin makes this point in *Autobiographical Reflections,* where he has written of students who "will not tolerate information that is not in agreement with their ideological prejudices."

But it is a rare Keating who is content to provide a gospel in only one field of knowledge. He is instinctively a generalist who roams the great wide world of information and ideas and makes authoritative disclosures everywhere. Formally he may be historian, psychologist, sociologist, or master of whatever subject interests him at the moment, but he covers the cosmos, partly as encyclopedist, but more as a celebrator of the unrecognized, and most of all as the revealer of widespread inequities, pretenses, and frauds. One suspects that he has a touch of the Prometheus complex, but he is really less interested in stealing fire from the gods than in lighting fires under them. Hence he may be tempted to join such anti-Olympian activities as student marches, protests, and demos, but these have an inherent shortcoming: they tend to impose anonymity unless the TV cameramen are especially discriminating. Hyde Park is better; it gives full scope to the individual golden tongue. But all lecterns are worthy stages, and they are all essential props.

Keatings will teach summer school, night school, and extension courses, and resist retirement. One woman auditor of a certain Keating (and obviously more an admirer than a detractor) told me, "His life is the podium. He never wants the final bell to ring. When the lecture is over, he is dead." With such a stream of appearances, the performer tends to play familiar roles. More accurately, there is only one role, the White Hat role; it is rather the chosen topics that become familiar. Once my wife and I had to attend an institutional dinner at which the Keating of the time was the featured speaker. We found ourselves coming up with the same question: "What will he do tonight—Vietnam or Watergate?" Our topics were wrong, but our idea was right. The themes were Nagasaki and poverty. Apartheid and Palestine got into the repertory later. And of course all American styles in Central and South America.

Keating's feeling for audiences means that he is a star in the city and the region in which his university is located. He charms listeners as he holds forth on many political, social, and economic topics. His role is instinctively that of the man of insight who, despite institutional indifference or even hostility, is bringing truth home to hearers who would otherwise be deprived of it. What ultimate influence his ideas and attitudes have upon the beliefs and actions of his audiences no one knows. The one unmistakable effect is the admiration for the speaker who enacts, with a great deal of stage presence and skill, this love of truths otherwise neglected, this perception of failure in most of the powers that be, this unique grasp of what are inelegantly phrased as "moral bottom lines."

The listening public attribute to Keating an objective greatness that they are sure is rejoiced in by his professional colleagues. "It must be great to be on the faculty with a man like that." That popular enthusiasm, of course, gets into the press, which regularly refers to Keating as "the university's great political scientist." Public and media simply have no way of knowing that Keating has never, in person or writing, spoken to political scientists, and that political scientists have never heard of him. A faculty friend of mine once said to another colleague, a distinguished scientist, "But these people in the city, the Keating-worshipers—they have no idea at all who our really good professionals are." My friend said that the scientist replied, "But it is better that way." Perhaps he meant that genuine intellectual merit does not lead to popular esteem. Or that the meritorious are saved from the perils of adulation. (Of course, that stance can be dangerous too. One may fall into the Byronic pose, "I have not loved the world, nor the world me," and regard this as proof of unique quality.)

iii

It is one thing to admit one's reservations about the Keating type who evokes worship for his personality and leads innocents to suppose that excited response to charisma improves upon an orderly process of learning, unspectacular and even grinding as this sometimes has to be. One seeks a catharsis for professional dismay. But after acknowledging annoyance, one can look at the scene again and try to understand why it is as it is. One may perceive the falseness of *Dead Poets Society* and yet be aware of, and wonder about, the admiration it excites. To many moviegoers Keating has seemed a true hero. Numerous students, including some of my own grandchildren, are Keating-worshipers. We might simply say that too many people are susceptible to the pied piperism of a charmer who feels undervalued by the system. But it is also possible that Keating-worship has a social use of some kind and hence signifies something less negative than defective taste and uncritical acceptance of cinematic herohood.

In the academic world and in the larger community there are standard ways of feeling about corporate or institutional life. We live, of course, in an indispensable "system" or organizational structure, and no one except anarchists questions its indispensability. Yet a great many people, perhaps even most of the people some of the time, are suspicious of it, complain about it, distrust it. "School spirit"—that is, conformism with enthusiasm—evokes, now and then and here and there, a certain fear that such belonging is simply serving someone else's ends. These doubts come out of the romantic temper, which always goes for private insights seen in conflict with mass myopia (and tends to ignore the extent to which the seer's ego or psychological self-interest may skew his seeing), and which characteristically regards the necessary system as unresponsive or hidebound or downright devious. Keating provides an outlet for these suspicions: in him the public sees an apparently knowledgeable insider publicly voicing complaints that appear to validate the usual suspicions. The point here, of course, is not whether or to what extent the suspicions are justified (the makers of *Dead Poets Society* try to justify them by offering, as the real thing, a dated and incredible headmaster and a ludicrous literary doctrine that the school allegedly takes seriously), but simply that the suspicions exist. They exist because of the romantic cast of mind, or more precisely, a specific mode of the romantic—that is, the melodramatic sense of reality. The melodramatic spirit uses the attack mode: it always sees accepted ends threatened by stupid, ossified, or self-seeking forces that can be identified and hence eliminated.

The actual knowledge generating the attack may be limited or inaccurate; the students who respond to Keatings do not know whether the university, and the world generally, are as marked by ineptitudes, deficiencies, and misdirections as the Keatings declare. But they trust Keating because he voices or embodies their suspicions that all is not well in the management of institutions and societies generally. This is not to say that all *is* well; it is rather to say that the sense that all is not well reflects less an objective institutional situation than the cast of mind that I have called melodramatic.

We are dealing with a kind of social reality: not so much the evil suspected as the act of suspecting it, a psychological impulse in Keating's audience. Keating may tease this audience into some symbolic spectaculars (as he did with the boys in *Dead Poets Society*); but, by and large, he prefers the role of "J'accuse," which thrills both the actor and audience. If he calls for actual revolt, he is pretty likely to pick on a straw man; in the film, for instance, he has the boys tear out of their textbook a passage that was out-of-date, and indeed unimaginable, long before the time depicted. His role is not actual revolt, which may be burdensome and painful, but the much more comfortable and symbolic revolt that validates his audience's prior sense of flaws in the system. They gain a sense of possessing truth, but without serious cost. In fact, Keating may even manage his "J'accuse" rather indirectly: by a style that implies that all other styles are inferior, by a personal touch that devalues all the rest of the institutional procedures. Keating's students revolt only by conversion to the style of the guru, and often by deifying him.

The men and women who really shape and maintain the institution—by professional discourse with colleagues in the larger world and by steady, systematic instruction at home—do not warm up much to the Keatings. But the final picture is a little less simple than it may appear up to this point. It contains an irony that may even be mildly surprising. For the Keatings of the world, one comes to see, are of a certain kind of institutional benefit. Not that they in any way change things, for they do not. Rather, what they accomplish is this: if on the one hand they gratify the students' sense that something is wrong with the situation, on the other hand they convince the students that here is a force for excellence that conterbalances the failures and may even in time triumph over them. One Great Teacher, as it were, redeems the place otherwise thought to be too much in the hands of routinists and dullards often asserted to be indifferent to student interests and needs. The Keating dissonance becomes a symbol that all is, if not well, at least not lost.

Thus, Keating acts as a kind of safety valve for discontents, suspicions, and negative judgments that could be disruptive without being productive. What is more, Keatings may indeed serve to attract subversive emotion that might otherwise be kidnapped by true moral desperadoes with programs. Organized leftists operate wholly within the melodramatic sense of a good-versus-evil world, which I have identified as an element in the American sensibility: the naive leftists believe it, and the activist plotters count upon it and use it. In the 1960s the latter, bent upon disruption as a route to destruction, wanted to close down the universities. This might lead to an anarchy in which force could take over. I have some evidence to go on as I surmise, and would even bet, that the Keatings joined the mainstream in resisting closure. Obviously they were not going to surrender a platform and stage important to their own being, and encourage a dictatorship in which they would not be tolerated. Motive aside, the anticlosure stance was a force for the better against the worse option.

iv

Another irony: the Keating who is hardly a hero to his colleagues, though a shining figure to students and in the nonacademic world, may unconsciously serve the university whose shortcomings, along with those of society, he is always implying or voicing. The outside community has for the most part few means of judging either the university or Keating's status within it. Hence his apparent omniscience and keen judgment of the world seem convincing evidence of his professional distinction and even of the university's quality. Just as a platform man, he is welcome in the city. He is asked often and is always available. He talks easily, as many of his colleagues do not. They rarely make effective public figures, whether from shyness, discomfort with a lay public, immersion in fundamental professional activities, or at times, no doubt, an unfortunate snobbery about a "popular" audience. Hence public gratitude for, and admiration of, one who relishes the public podium; his skill as a speaker creates a pleasurable aesthetic experience for his audiences.

But in addition to this technical skill, he is a natural candidate for herohood in a world glad to have heroes and rarely finding them in academic circles. He always wears the white hat; no doubt at times he seems a solitary voice against the evils of the world. Yet "solitary voice" implies an eye for unacknowledged evils, a willingness to give pain even to an enthusiastic audience, as if he were probing for consciences unknowingly willing to be stirred. Actually Keatings, as I observe them, do not seriously risk arousing major self-awareness, and hence possible resentment, in their audiences. A Keating seems to have an instinct for what one might call acceptable targets. He is far more likely, for instance, to censure South African whites than to point to local shortcomings in the treatment of minorities. He will be harder on national policy than on tough regional cases. Be that as it may, he sounds heroic, and in time he becomes a university star. If he points to shortcomings in the university administration, his very membership in the university makes it seem a better place. It maintains him, the voice of everyman's discontent with institutions. Thus he may help generate, ironically, emotional support for it and also, perhaps, even material support.

"Support." In a day when the standard sources of income—state budgets for public universities, and alumni-provided endowments for private ones—seem increasingly inadequate, an educational institution has to call more and more upon a public with which it may have few obvious connections and upon which it may have fewer incontrovertible claims. Of course the university may argue, and usually does, its concrete benefits to its home area—city, state, region—and indeed to other areas in which a consenting public, according to surveys, may be assumed to exist. The approach is by now familiar: a flock of our MBAs have turned various businesses into multi-million-dollar affairs, and our medical-school inventors have come up with various machines and miracle drugs to make life longer (if not happier).

But few fields of study can make such claims; and the general public is little interested in the intellectual life that is the nominal raison d'etre of the university (unless the intellectual life has striking visible accompaniments, as in space science, seismology, and so forth). Hence the institution is considerably dependent upon irrational goodwill. I suggest that, ironically, some of the goodwill is generated by the Keatings, who manage to voice everyone's vague discontents with life (especially the suspicion that these are owing mainly to institutional imperfections) and at the same time to symbolize the forces that can make things better. The Keatings speak for causes that have appeal, and they put the finger on villains, mostly standard villains rather than figures held high in public esteem.

What I am getting at is a fascinating paradox: the irrational sources of support for institutions nominally devoted to the rational understanding of human experience. There are, of course, rational or apparently rational sources of support—awareness of the need for education, perceived indebtedness for one's own education, and of course Tax Deduction Science—ones that hardly need our attention. But we are quite likely not to notice the irrational sources of support, aspects of institutional life that somehow stir uncritical admiration in the wide outer world. The Keatings of the world apparently have this effect. And then there is a delightful irony: football has the same effect, exciting the emotions that generate support.

Even Keatings sometimes join the public for which football status is a significant indicator of an institutional worthiness that demands support. Only very old universities seem to escape this value judgment; their long life means an adequate mass of big-name alumni to "excite the emotions that generate support." Even in that world, however, too many football defeats may make old boys restive, as if alma mater were slipping in the performance of some significant household rite. But in the great parvenu world of state universities, where I have taught for a lifetime, decent football is, in the public eye, an indispensable symbol of membership in the institutional elect. A winning season is a Nobel or two for hoi polloi, who thus feel stirred to support laboratories and even libraries.

V

This is not the place for a history of irrational motivations that inspire support for institutions formally committed to a rational understanding of life, or for exploring the theoretical issue of whether true good can come out of the constant pointing to naughtiness. I do no more than suggest an ironic reality: the institutional malcontent as somehow guarantor to the public that the forces of truth are strong in the institution, or the maverick as the unintentional assistant in the promotion of the order that makes him a maverick. He satisfies a need for heroes, a role that the true scholar hardly aspires to, and for which the true intellectual would generally be but an ungainly aspirant. The maverick's charisma as dart thrower makes him seem a utopian seer. Fortunately he does not have a program; if he did, he would become a menace, probably Marxist.

As a performer, he prefers role to program, attitude to the complexities of understanding. As Great Teacher, he may crop up even in places able to survive without much football glory. Although attracted, as I have noted, to the Promethean role, he occasionally likes to toss Jovian thunderbolts. He tends to latch on to approved targets: recently he has been tossing harpoons at the Great White Male evil. As a teacher in the humanities, I must acknowledge that he is usually one of us, a teacher of English, or of the softer social sciences; he rarely comes out of mathematics or the sterner sciences, which are less conducive to editorial and theatrical spectaculars by white hats.

But I have been meaning to do him justice, to define his utility. I cannot forget the glowing response of the cinema audience, and subsequently, to descend to the personal, of my grandchildren, two sets of them. When *Dead Poets Society* came up for discussion at family dinners, I plunged in without first testing the waters. I held forth on how it was immoral when the teacher became greater than the thing taught, living in the adulation of innocent youngsters. One set of grandchildren ordered me to leave the table. The other set, more mindful of the infirmities of age, sentenced me only to loss of dessert. When I tried to pull myself together, in later postmortem reflection, I decided that my punishment was a small price to pay for the knowledge that my descendants would all support their various colleges, happy in the certainty that on each campus the local Keating would, by presence and voice, guarantee that truth had a foothold amid institutional apathy and sinuosity.

22

Sabbatical Leaves

Pay for Play, or Pattern for American Life?

A year ago I returned from a year's sabbatical spent in Europe. I am therefore deemed to be full of energy, fruitful experience, and inside knowledge, and hence able to set forth a rationale of the sabbatical system. The assignment makes me pause. On the one hand, I cannot say, "Look what the sabbatical did for me!" If it did something, that something must be judged by others, who, whatever they think, can hardly be quoted here. On the other hand, I can't really say that I blew the year, might just as well have stayed at home, and plan to refund my part-salary to the state. As a firsthand authority I am, it appears, useless, and I shall have to do what the inexperienced writer would do—talk about a Sabbatical in the Abstract, as it may be inferred from the varying practices of those who try this 365-day sabbath (literally, "rest").

A sabbatical may look like different things if you look at different persons. At one extreme is the leave-hound, who can parlay an occasional short leave at his own expense, consultancies, research appointments, foreign lectureships with shadowy duties, and the usual sabbaticals into an in-transit life that keeps him away from the campus from one-third to one-half of the time. The opposite of this absentee landlordism is provided by the man—and he is a much more frequent figure—who is on the campus all the time because he cannot afford to take a sabbatical, at least until relatively late in his professional years. A few weeks ago an old friend, a man of solid repute in the profession, wrote me from Italy, "Here I am on my first sabbatical at the age of 51"; this reminded me that I took my first leave at just that age. But between those of us that the university can never put its finger on and those that are always underfoot is the ordinary middle class of people who manage their first sabbatical before they are antiques, say somewhere in their thirties, and then take leave regularly every seventh year. They are using a system held to by every major college and university in America. Our business is to take a look at that system. Let us approach it indirectly by first noting the relationship of sabbaticals to the securing and holding of faculty.

ii

During the academic year 1965–1966 I spent at least half my administrative time and energy in "recruiting." Faculty recruitment is the fundamental "maintenance" activity of the university. We have to replace staff members who leave or retire; we have to keep expanding the teaching corps as the student body grows ever larger. It makes sense to say that faculty recruitment is like football recruitment. First-rate football players occur in a certain proportion to the total population; the number is not large enough to supply all institutions that want first-rate football teams. First-rate brains, either naturally creative or capable of taking the training that makes scholars and of getting that training, are not numerous enough to supply all the universities that want to be first-rate. So the universities are now competing for intellectual material in much the same way that they compete for athletic material. Although the recruiting of scholars or prospective scholars is relatively recent (from the 1930s to the mid-1950s there were generally more applicants than there were faculty jobs), it is already like football recruiting in intensity, in unremittingness, and in competitiveness that, demanding all the tactics and resources one can muster, may be very fierce indeed.

The recruiter must try to present his own institution as offering substantial advantages for the superior professional life that the new Ph.D. hopes to lead. Some of these advantages are material—salary, fringe benefits, aids to research, and so on. (The inducements are virtually always relevant to professional life: so far I have heard of no offers of new cars.) Our terms have to be "competitive." And here we get back to sabbatical leaves: without a system of such leaves, we could not attract a single first-class young man to the university faculty. Any good young Ph.D. will regard the sabbatical as an indispensable part of academic life. Going to an institution without sabbaticals would be like going to one without libraries and laboratories. Without sabbaticals we could not attract and retain a good faculty, not to mention a distinguished one. So in one sense we could stop talking right here, saying only, "Sabbaticals are essential to a university in its competition for survival."

But we can go further, and we have to go further. Most kinds of competition tend to get highly irrational, but the terms of academic competition for staff are not fundamentally irrational. We are not in the situation—at least not yet!—in which the rules are simply made by what people want, that is, by any kind of irrational desire for profit and pleasure. Prospective faculty rarely want the wrong kind of thing (though they may want pretty much of the right kind of thing). To outside observers of university life, a sabbatical might look suspiciously like the "wrong kind of thing"—that is, a kind of paid or partly paid vacation on top of all other vacations. It might look as if a hard-to-get faculty member were challenging the university frivolously but relentlessly, "Pay me to play, or I won't work."

Now pay-for-play might even make economic sense. It might be cheaper for universities to help subsidize faculty weekend life—the whole realm of recreation, frolic, lark, and leisure—than to support sabbaticals. It might cost less to help a prospect or a restless instructor buy a new car, a motorboat, a sailboat, a golf or tennis club membership, skiing equipment, a piece of a mountain chalet or some other part-time home away from home. But we don't offer sporting goods, or help him get a "small foreign car" or large foreign camera. And now let us make a great leap to the other side of the fence: we don't help a man buy a house, either. A few colleges in communities where housing is in short supply may offer faculty members less costly rentals or temporary quarters for the first year, but in the main, the faculty member has to take care of so fundamentally important a matter as housing himself.

iii

So there is much that we do not do—on the side of serious problems as well as the holiday-vacation-play side. What we do not do should make clear the overriding importance of the things we do do—such as providing sabbatical leaves. Although leaves may look like a large amount of time off with part-pay, they could not have achieved a sense of indispensability if they were only an irrational privilege. The truth of the matter to which we now come—we needed these preliminaries to see the truth in perspective— is that the sabbatical year is primarily a special work period: the one period in which the faculty member gets part-time pay to spend all of his time, or as much of it as he elects, on that half of his compensated work that during the teaching years is likely to get much less than half his time. That other half of his work is "research" (if we stress the fact-finding, or experimental, or investigating phase of the work) or "writing" (if we stress the verbal arranging of results, or theories or ideas, for communicating them to others; or the whole area of creative writing; in the sciences the two phases are probably more distinguishable than in the humanities, where they may be indistinguishable). In our day it is an implicit, and indeed often explicit, part of the contractual understanding between institution and faculty that the latter's obligation includes both teaching and research. The faculty member does less teaching than he would in a college or institution not committed to research; he is given, not time off for good behavior, but time for another kind of intellectual behavior. I do not have space here to justify research. I can only say that if my university did not stress research, it would have to be content to be a minor university. It would appear to have no interest in that advancement of knowledge on which, by a basic creed of our culture, the future depends.

Various kinds of research and writing can be done and are done regularly throughout the school year. This depends in part on whether they can be managed in smaller segments of time and by intermittent application. Some projects, however, can hardly be attacked and carried through without a long period of concentrated thought and work—for instance, the writing of a book. It is amazing that any books get written by people who are not on sabbatical; even an uninterrupted summer, or several such summers, hardly allow the continuity of intellectual work without which the writer is plagued by incompleteness, disconnectedness, inconsistency, and overall lapses of unity. A book is normally conceived and shaped by one large, continuing, inclusive act of mind, and if this is fragmented into a series of lesser acts, the book is likely to seem a loose aggregate of parts rather than an organic whole.

Yet even a year devoted to a book is not unconnected with teaching. Whether he writes or studies, the professor's sabbatical year does bounce back directly into his teaching life. On the one hand, the research and thinking that go into the book make him a different man; he knows more, he has a sharper point of view, and he has probably gained depth as well as variety of thought. He won't be able to fall back into the same old routines in class. Again, a year of study may contribute to both writing and teaching. A man may spend the year in the laboratory of a distinguished scientist, learning new methods and theories that he will use in his own laboratory and classroom. Humanists and social scientists may choose a similar apprenticeship, spending a year at a university where they can have contact with distinguished men. They are bound to bring back something of value both for their own work and for their students. Finally, a professor may devote a sabbatical year simply to reading, reading that will eventually go into both his writing and his teaching. The sheer continuity of what we now call input, and of the thinking inseparable from the input process, may not make a new man of him, but it will do enough renovating to put something different and fresh into all phases of his work.

In other words, whatever the particular style of the sabbatical year, the university is the gainer—in better training for its students or in the increase of professional distinction in its faculty. The latter must not be undervalued, and it can hardly be overvalued. By research and writing the faculty can submit themselves to the judgment of the profession generally, and that judgment, because it is the best informed one, is vital. Distinction can be conferred only by the profession. The greater the distinction of its faculty, the greater the pride the university can have in the fulfillment of its dual mission. Distinction makes for good morale. Aside from that, it has an immense practical advantage: distinction attracts excellence. Here we come back to our starting point, recruiting: the better the university's reputation for harboring and holding on to men of professional eminence, the more attractive it is to those it wants to get, whether neophytes or well-established scholars.

iv

To sum up: the university intent on excellence has a real stake in sabbaticals, for, though they do not guarantee anything, they are highly conducive to the independent self-advancement by which faculty members create distinction for themselves and their institution. At this point, however, some antisabbaticalist—if such there may be—may cry out, "'Not guarantee,' How right you are. You can't even guarantee that a man will do any work on sabbaticals. He may just have a year of fun." I would have to answer, "How right you are. But there are several problems here."

If a man wants to goof off and do nothing during a sabbatical year, there is not much that can be done about him. University people are quite like other human beings; they include the usual small number of irresponsible people and chiselers, who are never happier than when getting something for nothing. If we paid faculty for going to university football games (on the theory that there was some advantage to someone in having them there), a few would want to get credit (and pay) for going to little-league games, for watching a tennis match, or for taking a swim. True, a faculty committee passes on all leave applications, and returnees from sabbatical are supposed to report on the year's good deeds; hence, at both entrance and exit, there is a sort of Checkpoint Charlie. But the truth is that the checkup is nominal, and probably should be, if only because institutional surveillance of private study time is unenforceable. Besides, we don't know in advance who will make good use of the year, and there is little that can be done about it if a man has simply had a jolly good time (except give him black marks that will count against him the next time he applies; but by then we might well think he'd do better on a second try). The principle of freedom works best. Restoration drama, often described as "licentious," was on the whole committed to demonstrating that a decent freedom is the best hedge against licentiousness: wives more readily betray jealous and nastily watchful husbands. The university that partly subsidizes a faculty member for a year of freedom is not often betrayed by misuse of that freedom, and the small number of betrayals is, as always, the price of freedom. What the professor does on sabbatical is in the end a matter of his own pride. If a few have no pride, the majority have much.

But there is another problem: a phrase like *year of fun* implies an absolute distinction between work and fun that may not be tenable. We are addicted to thinking, with some part of our evaluative psyches, that work is good for one, that what is good for one cannot really be pleasant (for example, medicine), that therefore work is naturally disagreeable, and that if we are having a good time at something it naturally cannot be either work or good for us. We manage to forget that a great many people so much enjoy hard work that being away from it is almost a hardship. I have the impression that most of my colleagues in humanities take a positive pleasure in steady library work during sabbaticals; perhaps if they complained more of sabbatical drudgery, the frequenting of libraries might seem less frivolous to the observer with a hangover of Puritan qualms. But there are fewer problems here than on the other side of the fence, where, our hypothetical antisabbatical may protest, there is a lot of good-timing that cannot possibly have professional relevance. Many American professors spend a sabbatical in London, as I did last year, and in London they inevitably go to the theater regularly, as I did. Now this sort of thing is a very great pleasure. Does it make an honest sabbatical? Here, of course, I have picked an easy case, for I happened to be working on a book on drama, and I rarely saw a play on which I did not make notes that I thought might be useful in some part of my manuscript.

But suppose my field had been, not drama, but the novel, or American history, or medieval philosophy, or solid-state physics, or econometrics— what then of theatergoing, concertgoing, gallery visiting, museum "crawl-ing"? Perhaps to some people such activities will seem trivial; to a majority, I hope, they will seem important ones for an educator, whatever his field. For in any field he is more than a technician; willy-nilly, he stands for a broader human world where imagination and interpretation and memory constantly create and revise and maintain man's image of himself. With enough experience in that world to represent it well, the faculty member can hardly help becoming a better teacher in any field. We are of course talking about what is usually called general "culture," though the word has been so debased by overuse that it has become an easy target for critics who need easy targets (those tedious lifelong marksmen, never quite out of their second year in college). Let us say, rather, that the ordinary pleasures of tourism provide, if one is at all alert, a widening and multiplication of perspectives that may, in indirect ways, add something to the quality of even specialized writing, and that will surely add something to the quality of teaching. "Sabatting around Europe," as it has been called—going from one place to another that calls us by charm or history or myth or some other uniqueness or fame—may seem like random vacationing, but it can hardly fail to contribute to the general knowledge and awareness subtly relevant to the art of teaching in many fields. (By "knowledge" I do not mean the rather precious triumphs of touristic one-upmanship, which make it necessary to unearth quaint Italian villages superior in charm to all other places visited by all other tourists, or some out-of-the-way Romanesque church never before seen by camera eye, or in Paris some dimmer *boîte* with a sadder musician than has ever made another tourist feel like a philosophical taster of "life.")

But suppose one had spent his part-paid sabbatical skiing in the Alps, or kayaking the length of the Danube, or cruising in the Mediterranean, or riding Japanese express trains, or visiting Finnish saunas, or climbing the Himalayas, or following the bullfight circuit in Spain, or making an informal comparative study of Parisian restaurants, or sunning himself at Waikiki? I hasten to say that I am not going to ply the reader with paradoxes by insisting that any such sportive doings will in some supersubtle subterranean way make a professor a better trainer of either experts or enlightened citizens. Most of us, surely, would think of the activities I have mentioned as being good examples of the chiseler's delight. But I do want to do this the hard way by suggesting that the boundary line between the frivolous and the professionally useful is not always quite clear. Even activities obviously irrelevant to scholarship and teaching may do one thing for the scholar and teacher: by providing a "complete change" (to use the old medical term) they may bring him back to work fresher, livelier, and more effective. Ordinarily, of course, the sabbatical is intended to provide an invigorating change by permitting a life in which energy goes into a single activity instead of being drained off by multiple demands, or in which productive powers are restored by intellectual retooling and by the gaining of new knowledge. The vast majority use it that way. But I have wanted to say what could be said for the play periods of the sabbatical year, and I am now going so far as to say that, even if the whole year turned into a play period, all might not be lost, either for the university or for the citizenry that pays for it. (In ancient Judaea the "sabbatical year" was a year of rest for the land itself, every seventh year.)

The point is, of course, that for everybody who pursues it seriously, the academic life can be an exhausting one. (A few do not take it seriously; this is a profession that makes possible indifference and laziness, though these happen not to be its besetting sins.) There are of course born showmen— who as teachers may be execrable or superb—for whom a classroom appearance is always pleasurable and perhaps exhilarating. For most of us, I suspect, all classroom appearances are difficult and demanding affairs, which in the aggregate leave us psychologically pretty well worn down. For a few, classroom work is abrasive and punitive; a first-rate man in our department left the profession because of the sheer psychic wear-and-tear of meeting classes day after day. Meeting some classes is like facing a firing squad; meeting others is like being a gardener who suddenly finds his vegetable patch infiltrated by carnivorous plants; meeting still others is like trying to transmute a stone quarry into marble halls, or conduct a revival among a flock well dosed with barbiturates. I quip, of course, for these are special cases; but even when one has alert, uncontentious, well-mannered students who ought to have the best, one can develop a pretty great sense of strain from the obligation to try to produce the best at 10:30 daily for nine months running.

Teaching takes enough out of one to make psychic revitalization desirable: this is the case that might be made for even the sabbatical that takes a wholly playful turn. But still I do not like the line taken by some academics: that the life of teacher-cum-researcher is peculiarly depleting, and that we need quite special mechanics of replenishment. To stay with academe for a moment: the needs of the faculty are no greater than those of administrators, and it is scandalous that institutions generally have no sabbatical provisions for deans, provosts, chancellors, and presidents, most of whom are subject to levels of constant strain that seem to me to be close to destructive. (I do not speak of departmental chairmen such as myself: the chairman is a kind of moral mulatto regarded by the common man as a mere pawn of the Establishment, but still permitted by the archbishops to share the common man's sabbatical privileges.) I have rarely seen faculty members look as tired as administrators—or as much in need of time for reading, for study, for getting new perspectives, for doing something different, or for doing nothing for a time. But whatever we can see within academe, the fact is that most of us are too unfamiliar with other professions and vocations to know their psychic needs, and it is unbecoming to suppose, out of sheer ignorance, that ours are unique. I would far rather argue that what is good for educators is good for everyone else too.

V

In fact, I want now to propose that the sabbatical year should be institutionalized as a part of the general life of the nation, because the principle is relevant to many other modes of life as well as to the academic. We might say that in this matter the university has its usual role as pioneer, as discoverer of a new truth or perspective. Or, to rephrase it, the university has empirically established the advantages of the sabbatical principle. It is only for society to take it over if it will. In an age of "affluence," and particularly in an age of automation and technological unemployment, the "national sabbatical" makes pretty good sense. In the nation generally there would be far less of a problem of getting the work done than in the universities, where for some years to come the labor shortage may continue. In more than one industry we hear that the four-day week is inevitable: well, if one hundred people regularly do a thirty-two-hour week, eighty-six people doing a thirty-eight-hour week (which is still less than the currently accepted norm) will provide approximately the same number of working hours, leaving one-seventh of the population free. To leave one-seventh of the population free for a given working period (obviously it could be a year as well as a week) would mean a rotating system where everyone would come up for a sabbatical every seventh year. (In an age of the "welfare state" and of the "guaranteed national income" the economic problems would not appear to be insuperable.)

I am inclined to think that the "national sabbatical" would be a better institution if it were regarded in one respect as analogous to the academic sabbatical, that is, implying an obligation to do something directly or indirectly profitable to the work of the leave-taker (perhaps this is the vestigial Puritan in me). There are of course limits to this: the research and writing that are the primary reason for academic leave can be done only by people with considerable training or by natively creative people. Too, some kinds of work might not seem capable of much improvement of technical knowledge or methods. But surely there are many fields in which inventive men and women, with a year to work them out, could make a real contribution to the approaches and practices in their fields. Much more numerous than these are the kinds of work in which the workers—lawyers, doctors, bankers, engineers, all kinds of businessmen, architects, mechanics, foresters, restaurateurs, to give just a few examples—can learn more about new practice and theory in their own fields. Above all, there is no end to the study that a man can do in other fields related to his own or even unrelated (there are, for example, the Nieman fellowships for journalists to study what they will). And what is the profit of the latter? Simply the profit of all education—the greater knowledge, the wider perspective, the new point of view that we believe makes the better citizen. Sabbaticals for citizenship might have great social profit. They could include travel—travel to all the places that tourists traditionally visit. Here I'd make one restrictive rule if I could: no travel to beach, gaming, and nightclub spots that many of us pick for short vacations. People would have to manage these in their own time. I would also establish heavy penalties for moonlighting, which would undermine the sabbatical idea.

We could probably enforce a prohibition of sabbatical moonlighting, but we would find it harder to enforce a prohibition of bright-lighting or skylarking. Our general rule would probably have to be, "No formal program, no sabbatical." But we'd have to take the usual risks of freedom. No more can be done about the nonacademic chiseler than about the academic one; as before, we'd have to hope that even an apparently profitless year would have some kind of profit in increased freshness and zest after the sabbatical. Yet I suspect that the very length of the sabbatical might increase the likelihood of its being partly used instead of totally misused. In three idle days out of seven a man can't do much but putter and trifle and take in small-scale transitory entertainment; much the same is true for two or three weeks out of fifty-two. But in one year out of seven? This is too much time for cool breezes or warm sun or hot spots or low-life or high-life gambols. A man might just be forced into studying or learning something he didn't know before.

There would be other promptings toward making the year useful rather than useless. Presumably the individual would foot part of the bill himself, though he would have to have some sort of material incentive for trying the long leave. Normal people need some work to hang life on; only a fool or a sad sack would opt for total play. Most of us fear a life without some sort of pattern; we'd look for a sabbatical schedule, even if a less rigorous one than that of the work years. Other psychological barriers would slow down the hasty leap into sabbatical anarchy. A year of travel, for instance, means much hard work of a trivial sort—an endless day-in-and-day-out laborious working out of arrangements of matters that at home would be taken care of automatically. Then there would be a man's fear of losing touch with the work he must do, with the life he must again return to. An aspect of this would be a fear of the "reentry trauma" (as some academic has called it), which may be a stern fact of life for even the most conscientious faculty member (I know one man who said the trauma was so great he thought he'd never take another sabbatical). Finally, it takes some humility to take a sabbatical: one has to admit that one is completely replaceable.

The "national sabbatical" is a serious proposal. It is not just a gag to make a point. But I do hope the proposal incidentally sheds some light on the not altogether simple business of the academic sabbatical—that nonteaching period which the institution half-pays for in order that the teacher may do research and write under the best conditions, that he may read and study and travel and thus come back a more knowing man and hopefully a better teacher, and that, whether by all these activities or by a certain amount of sheer play if that is what he elects, he may experience enough change to get out of the weariness and doldrums likely to be produced by academic demands, and to return a livelier and sharper and more fertile conductor of the learning process. With these functions, the sabbatical is so highly desirable that it comes close to being a necessity. But it is not a special privilege. We can risk its looking like one because it does serve real ends. Still more important, though it may look like pay for play, it does also provide a pattern for American life that American life may do well to adopt.

23

Citizenship, Imagination, and Novels

I think you all know why we have a commencement speaker.[1] He adds a solemn note to keep the affair from being too frivolous. Without him, the occasion might seem too lighthearted and happy. It would be like Mardi Gras without a Lent to sober up in. That would make us Americans feel self-indulgent and guilty. So you get the sobering speaker, and besides, you get him wholesale—that is, forty days of Lent at a cut rate of twenty minutes.

In picking a commencement speaker, a school has only two basic rules. The speaker must be safe in thought and short of wind. Safe in thought means that he will not pick this occasion to attack post-high-school education. Short of wind means that he can't keep going for longer than twenty minutes. The ideal speaker would have just a touch of emphysema. The Fort Steilacoom officials told me, however, that if I made a mistake and got long-winded, the students might bear up pretty well, but the faculty would be in a snit. I understand this. We faculty are stronger on being listened to than on listening, especially to other professors.

You see I know my place. I have spent two minutes showing this, so now you have only eighteen minutes for the Lenten sobering-up experience. I must get frightfully serious. Still worse, I won't get serious in any standard way. When you know what is coming, you can doze off comfortably. But I am *not* going to tell you graduates that you are now at a turning point, that you must put back into the community piggy bank what it cost to get you here, or that all life lies ahead beckoning you onward like a green

---

1. "Citizenship, Imagination, and Novels" was originally a commencement address at Fort Steilacoom Community College, in Tacoma, Washington, on June 17, 1983. In this case the editors and the speaker, author of this volume, have decided to let the spoken address appear as such rather than to let it appear as a written essay. The reason is that the points made by the speaker-essayist are so often attached to references to the student audience that the elimination of these references would weaken the theoretical points being made.

traffic light. Still worse, I am not going to charge you to go out and remake a world that we old-timers have made a horrible mess of. When speakers take that line, they are just boasting how wonderfully bad they have been. This is a kind of vanity, for no generation is good enough at being bad to make the world much worse than it was before. Anyway, we ought not to stand here recklessly loading on new graduates the burden of making the world better. The world is very stubborn about being made better, and it might drive improvers to despair. You would be better off in joining the man who said, "I hope not to leave the world worse than I found it." Of course this would mean keeping an eye on oneself instead of on others. A century or so ago, an earnest young man asked the philosopher Thomas Carlyle, "What can I do to save the world?" Carlyle gave a delightful answer: "Make an honest man of yourself, and then you can be sure there is one less rascal in the world." It would be hard, but it might work.

I have been sneaking up on my title subject of citizenship. It is a risky old commencement theme. Of course I might try to be original and shocking, and say that citizenship is much overrated. But then your president would probably stop me cold and withhold my honorarium, or six legislators could run for reelection on a platform of getting the Fort Steilacoom administrators fired. But I do want to try a different angle on citizenship. By it I do not mean voting regularly, paying taxes, smiting litterbugs, phoning people at dinnertime, or doing legwork for causes, and thus fingering passive people.

Instead, by citizenship I mean—hold on to your seats—being people of imagination. Imagination? Can the man be mad? Does he mean citizens— or writers or dreamers or wackos? No, we have enough of all those types, especially writers. I am thinking of imaginative people as good citizens. Very few people are born without imagination, but, like muscles or neural connections, imagination needs exercise to make it work well. A man once said to me, "My wife has no imagination." Maybe not, but maybe, also, she never exercised the muscles of her imagination. For instance, the only thing she ever read was ads and recipes. Maybe we could call her imaginative on the bargain and baking fronts, but they are still a small part of the human front. A star in cost-cutting and cookery may be quite limited—unable to enter into or appreciate the minds and personalities of other people. By imagination I mean a developer or filler-out of our humanity, of the qualities that make us more aware of ourselves and others, more agreeable and more interesting companions. Hence by a good citizen I mean, not one who *does* good, but one who *is* good, that is, one who imagines well and is a pleasing associate. He has charm, or good nature, or a relaxed acceptance of differences, both from himself and even from an ideal. It is not that he knows more, but that he understands better. Thus he helps create a comfortable, genial atmosphere. It is not that he is attentive, or courteous, or friendly, though these are all virtues too. Rather he has a good sense of others as human beings, imagines what they are, and is at ease with it. He does not want to argue with it or make it more like what he is, or on the other hand praise it or flatter it. He just gets hold of it and gets along with it. Thus he makes others less taut, less defensive, more likely to be amiable and gracious. They help create a human society that it is good to live in.

Let me sum up. First, to help produce such a world is a first-rate act of good citizenship. Second, such good citizenship is greatly helped by a good imagination. My last point will be that the human imagination is best tuned and brought to its full power by reading. I mean reading all kinds of literature, but with the minutes ticking away, I will stick to fiction. Reading is equally open to everyone—students and jobholders of all kinds. All literature comes in paperback now; you can get twenty or thirty hours of reading for the price of one movie. But reading has to be a choice, not a therapy or a duty. You should never read because it is good for you, or to get what is called culture—that once useful word spoiled by overuse by nice people—or to look educated or to keep up with current chitchat or headlines, that is, best-sellers. Who wants to have his reading list made up by department-store cash registers? Most best-sellers are dead in a decade; if they are alive after a decade, they may be worth a few hours. No, there is only one right reason for reading: it is fun. But it is fun that has good side effects. Reading may be like jogging with the imagination—except that some joggers' faces do not suggest that they are having much fun. Besides, reading does not risk arthritis of the imagination.

For a true exercise of the imagination the best novels are not *best* sellers but those that have long been *steady* sellers. They have lived on because they have continued to exercise people's imaginations in different times with different ideas and concerns. They get at basic things. They best imagine the varieties of human reality. Nineteenth-century novels, winnowed and tested for one hundred to two hundred years, deal with a wider range of human personality than most of our own do. Ours are overfascinated with selfishness and many forms of naughtiness. Older fiction spends less time on erotic wrestling; it does not distract our attention from the centers of personality by those laborious clichés that I call "porn corn" or "sentimentality in blue." Think of every good novel as a detective story—not a whodunit, but a who-is-it; not who is guilty, but who people are, and why. In Victorian fiction both guilty people and others turn out to be people like most of us. Thus they put us through imaginative exercises where we learn more about ourselves and how much of a mixed bag each of us is. This prepares us for greater easiness with other mixed bags.

Now I want to look at some several people and episodes in nineteenth-century novels that live on vigorously in our esteem. I hope they will show how novels do something for the flexibility and fullness of our imaginations as they get us into human personality. In George Meredith's *The Ordeal of Richard Feverel* a devoted, loving father plans an ideal education for his son. He really loves the boy. But also, as we gradually see, the father's love for the boy is infiltrated by his love of his educational plans, and his love of the plans contains a sense of power. The father is unconsciously playing god. So when the boy innocently slips out from under the educational system, the loving father becomes a kind of jealous god, and a punishing god. The point is not that the father is a bad or cruel man, but that he is self-deceptive and cannot see his parental love turning harsh and even revengeful. When we grasp this, surely our imaginations have been deepened a little.

George Eliot's remarkable *Middlemarch* leads our imaginations into some fine exercises. For instance, she portrays various people in a certain walk of life and shows them, not as the type characters we might expect, but as very different individuals. Take her clergymen: one is a dry scholarly man, removed from the world; another a pleasant worldly man fond of fishing; a third, a kind, decent man with a weakness for gambling; a fourth, a harsh and narrow Puritan. A very devout layman is sure that he is on the inside spiritual track and can do no wrong; so he drifts into a wrongdoing that disgraces him. Eliot's leading characters are a young woman and a young man who want to do some good and serve the world—a motive that appears little in the fiction of our day. The young woman, Dorothea, is able on one occasion to restrain a righteous indignation against a crass young woman, Rosamund; her forbearance actually inspires one unusual act of decency in the willful and ruthless Rosamund. When Dorothea gets married, the author says one thing that should really stir our imaginations. "Marriage," she says, "had not yet freed" Dorothea from—from what? From her "oppressive liberty." Think of that shock—of being "freed" from "liberty," and of "liberty" itself called "oppressive." It should be a wonderful imaginative stimulus for our day, with our almost unlimited quest for what we call "freedom." Yet the story is very complex: Dorothea's desire to serve is admirable, but it is not enough. She also needs a sense of reality. Because she lacks it, she marries an older scholar whose research she wants to help—like a student marrying a professor—but finds him a chilly egoist who isn't even a very good scholar. Yet instead of just ducking out, she tries to live with that situation as with others.

Dorothea's opposite number is an idealistic young doctor who we are convinced could improve medical care. But again, good intentions are not enough; he too needs a better sense of reality. He marries a beautiful, selfish, and willful woman, and she turns a scientific innovator into a man who has to do hack medical services for well-to-do patients. Then we get a wonderful new turn in his character: the ruined husband's central emotion—get this—is not hatred of his wife, but fear that he may cease to love her. Again, what a stimulus to imagination in our day, when we are very likely to complain that others do not love us enough.

Two other novels make our imaginations take a lively turn with both characters and ideas. George Eliot's *Silas Marner,* once a high-school staple, and now much underrated, is an excellent portrayal of a miser. Silas becomes a miser when a friend treats him faithlessly. Thus we see why a miser is a miser: when a human being is unreliable, the injured person turns to something that seems wholly reliable—a stable material like gold. We see that any inflated love of material things is a compensation for the instability of a nonmaterial thing like love. The word *miser* means wretched; the same word appears in *misery* and *miserable.* That is, a miser is a miserable person; misery is translated into miserliness. Yet it is not incurable; love of gold can yield to a true human love. These are very fine insights: they come to us not by a classroom demonstration but by imaginative experiences.

Jane Austen's *Pride and Prejudice* says nothing obvious, as the title might lead us to expect. True, at first everyone in the novel thinks that pride is a vice, and they make us think so. But gradually we see that this is only one meaning of pride, and that pride may actually be also an essential human virtue. In its basic sense, we realize, pride is a matter of the way in which we look at ourselves. In looking at ourselves we may say, on one side of the fence, "I'm good; I'm up there," but on the other side of the fence, "I must always try to live up to what I believe is good." On the one hand it is self-admiration; on the other, self-obligation. Now when we see that these two different attitudes—vanity and self-respect—are both denoted by one word, and that the common element is the way a person looks at himself—then we surely have made some progress into a better grasp of the complex human nature that we all share.

I hope that I have picked examples that make fiction look like an exciting and enticing park in which to spend some of our nonworking hours. I am not exhorting you, though at commencement exhortation is a standard indoor sport. I am only trying to tempt or tease you into an old and civilized pleasure. Reading fiction is not a duty, an assignment, a way of improving oneself, moving up in the world, pleasing the English department, getting one-up on nonreaders, or searching for knowledge. Once again, it is simply a pleasure—but not a pleasure that means wear and tear, a hangover, a bad next day. On the contrary, it leaves something good and satisfying behind it. We used to hear of mind-expanding drugs. Long-lasting fiction might be called a mind-expanding drug. But instead of *mind* I have used the word *imagination,* since in fiction we do not *learn* by rule and rote, by organized information and logic, but *grow* by living in other lives, and getting a feel of all their difference and variety. Thus as human beings we become more wide-ranging, perceptive, flexible, and responsive. To be, in this way, more imaginative is a true but little noticed way of being good citizens. For we contribute quietly to the kind of human atmosphere, the kind of understanding society, that it is good to live in. Such citizenship is to be cherished. And it is equally open to all of us, whatever paths—school or work—we follow after Fort Steilacoom College.

Ladies and gentlemen, your brief Lent—I might be fashionable and call it a mini-Lent—is over. Ahead lies only spring and summer—in the rest of these exercises, and in what follows them. Be merry, and when you feel a need of novelties, try novels.

acknowledgments

 The essays in this volume were originally published as indicated and are reprinted here with permission of the copyright holders.

"From Parsonage to Podium" has not been previously published.

"Baseball: Random Connections," *Sewanee Review* 104:4 (fall 1996): 550–67.

"Football: An Addict's Recollections and Observations," *Journal of American Culture* 4:3 (fall 1981): 3–26.

"The Rail Way of the World," *Gettysburg Review* 2:3 (summer 1989). Reprinted here by permission of the editors.

"Eric Voegelin," *Southern Review* n.s. 32:1 (winter 1996): 147–65 (under the title "Eric Voegelin: Reminiscences").

"Robert Penn Warren," *Kentucky Review* 2:3 (1981): 31–46 (under the title "RPW at LSU: Reminiscences").

"Theodore Roethke," *Shenandoah* 16:1 (1964): 55–64 (under the title "Theodore Roethke: Personal Notes"). Reprinted from *Shenandoah,* The Washington and Lee University Review, with the permission of the editor.

"Malcolm Cowley as University Professor," *Horns of Plenty: Malcolm and His Generation* 1:3 (fall 1988): 12–25 (under the title "Malcolm Cowley as University Professor: Episodes in a Societal Neurosis").

"Farce: *The Taming of the Shrew,*" *Modern Language Quarterly* 27:2 (June 1966): 147–61 (under the title "*The Taming* Untamed, or, the Return of the Shrew").

"Romance: *Cymbeline,*" as the Introduction to *Cymbeline,* The Pelican Shakespeare, ed. Alfred Harbage (Penguin Books, 1964). Copyright © 1964 by Penguin Books Inc. on notes and introduction; Renewed Copyright © 1979 by Viking Penguin Inc. Used by permission of Penguin, a division of Penguin Putnam Inc.

"*Timon* in Context," in *Shakespeare: The Tragedies (New Perspectives),* Twentieth Century Views (New York: Prentice Hall, 1984), 218–31.

"Good Guys and Bad Guys and What the Stage Does with Them: Dramatic Types" has not been previously published.

"The Novel: Ideas versus Drama in Hardy" has not been previously published.

"Short Story and Novella: Corrington's Tales," in *John William Corrington: Southern Man of Letters,* ed. William Mills (Conway, Ark.: UCA Press, 1994), 59–105 (in a slightly longer form under the title "Scene, Tradition, and the Unresolved in Corrington's Short Stories").

"Comic Prose Epic: Welty's *Losing Battles,*" in *Eudora Welty: Critical Essays,* ed. Peggy Whitman Prenshaw (Jackson: University Press of Mississippi, 1979), 269–304 (under the title "*Losing Battles* and Winning the War"). Reprinted with the permission of the University Press of Mississippi.

"Three Generations of English Studies: Impressions," *Sewanee Review* 97:4 (fall 1989): 597–611.

"Post-Tomorrow and Tomorrow and Tomorrow: An Aspect of the Humanistic Tongue," *Sewanee Review* 96:4 (fall 1988): 703–13.

"Semicentennial Retrospections: The Past as Perspective," *Georgia Review* 41:2 (summer 1987): 304–14 (in a slightly longer form).

"Back to Basics: Issues" has not been previously published.

"Humanistic, Humane, Human," *University of Portland Review* 31:2 (fall 1979): 3–13.

"The Great-Teacher Myth," *American Scholar* 60:3 (summer 1991): 417–23. Copyright © 1991 by the author.

"Sabbatical Leaves: Pay for Play, or Pattern for American Life?" *Alumnus* (University of Washington) 57 (1966): 28–34.

"Citizenship, Imagination, and Novels" has not been previously published.

index